BLACK HEROES: SEVEN PLAYS

Edited by
Errol Hill

BLACK HEROES: Seven Plays

Library of Congress Cataloging-in-publication data:

Black heroes.

Bibliography: p.
Contents: Emperor of Haiti / by Langston Hughes — Nat Turner / by Randolph Edmonds — Harriet Tubman / by May Miller — [etc.]
1. American drama — Afro-American authors. 2. Heroes Drama. 3. Afro-Americans — Drama. I. Hill, Errol.
PS628.N4B545 1989 812'.5080896073 89-17489
ISBN 1-55783-027-4

APPLAUSE THEATRE BOOK PUBLISHERS, INC.
211 W. 71st Street
New York, NY 10023
212/595-4735

First Applause Printing, 1989

CONTENTS

ACKNOWLEDGEMENTS

I wish first to thank Glenn Young, my publisher, for his prompt and enthusiastic response to my suggestion for a collection of plays on black heroes. With his firm backing, it was then necessary to locate suitable scripts on the heroes I had chosen. Playwrights or their agents of works already published were very cooperative in granting my request for permission to use their plays and I am most grateful to them. In searching for scripts on Marcus Garvey and Martin Luther King Jr., I had the co-operation, first, of the West Indian director Earl Warner, who had premiered the Garvey play in Barbados in 1987 and who kindly supplied me with a copy of the script. Next, the Crossroads Theatre Company of New Brunswick, New Jersey, generously provided a production copy of *Roads of the Mountaintop*. Both authors readily agreed to allow first publication of their plays in this collection. Also helpful in tracking down scripts were Woodie King of the New Federal Theatre, New York, and C. Bernard Jackson of the Inner City Cultural Center, Los Angeles. My thanks go out to them all. As usual the staff of the Reference Department of Dartmouth College Baker Library have been indefatigable in providing source materials and checking references. I continue to be in their debt. Finally, I must record the crucial contribution made by my wife, Grace, in enabling me to complete this manuscript at a time when my health has been anything but stable. Her loving care and concern no less than her willingness to provide logistical support in every way have been phenomenal.

BLACK HEROES

INTRODUCTION

On April 6, 1988, by order of the President of the United States, Matthew Henson was given a hero's burial with military honors at Arlington National Cemetery in Virginia. His remains, previously committed to a simple grave in Woodlawn Cemetery in the Bronx, were reinterred next to the man with whom he had reached the North Pole seventy-nine years earlier, Commander Robert Peary. Henson had been a close companion on Peary's various explorations for over twenty years. Yet while Peary had been hailed for his achievement and was laid to rest in Arlington at his death in 1920, Henson came back to a lowly position as a Customs House messenger and was buried in the Bronx when he died in 1955. His reinterment at the National Cemetery was deemed to be the righting of a wrong he had suffered because of his race. Henson was black.

This extraordinary event, a credit to the ingenuity and persistence of Dr. S. Allen Counter of Harvard University, illumines a hidden corner of black history and poses a challenge for today. In past times social conditions were inimical to the recognition of black heroes whose lives have been largely unheralded and unrecorded. But if such conditions no longer exist, if in fact the leaders of American history and culture are ready to accept Afro-American men and women of renown in the pantheon of American heroes, then efforts like Dr. Counter's should be made to "right the wrongs of history" by identifying black heroes and ensuring that they are appropriately memorialized for present and future generations. The publishing of this play collection is a step in that direction.

Our task seems particularly germane at a time when the civil rights gains of the 1960s and 1970s appear to be in abatement, if not reversal. The nation as a whole needs to recognize that blacks as well as whites have produced their share of heroes who deserve to be honored for their contribution to the nation and to humanity. In the theatrical profession, for instance, there is a statue to George M. Cohan prominently situated on Broadway, and several major playhouses carry names of outstanding white theatre personages. There is, however, no memorial to Bob Cole or Bert Williams, both of whom were, early in the century, acknowledged to be among the finest creators and performers on the musical comedy stage.

It is clearly important that black citizens have around them reminders of those outstanding Afro-Americans who at great personal cost have striven to improve the lot of Americans, whether it be through armed struggle, political action, scientific discovery, the arts and letters, or sports and popular entertainment. These exemplars serve as an inspiration to present and future effort, they instill a sense of pride in one's race, they help instruct the young about their past. Because so much of the history of a nation is perceived through the lives of its great men and women, the absence of recognition seems to imply that black Americans have done little or nothing to move this country along the road to progress, an impression that is demonstrably untrue. One has only to mention names such as Sojourner Truth, abolitionist and first defender of women's rights; George W. Carver, agricultural researcher; Will Marion Cook, the composer who abandoned a classical career to devote himself to the music of his people; Mary McLeod Bethune, women's educator, to begin the roll-call of illustrious Afro-Americans.

While there have been black achievers in quantity, we are inclined to reserve the title of "hero" to a special category that people attain only after meeting specific criteria. It seems necessary first to require of the hero or heroine that he or she should pursue a goal that leads to the betterment of mankind. Next, achievement of this goal should become a passion, indeed almost an obsession, taking priority over all other obligations in the individual's life. Third, the hero should expect to receive no material gain from the achievement. Fourth, the hero should be willing to risk life, if need be, in carrying out this self-imposed mission. Finally, it should appear that the hero is driven by a superior force that sustains him in the quest and allows him to endure whatever hardships are experienced in striving toward his goal.

The principal characters in the plays that comprise this anthology possess most, if not every one, of the credentials cited above. What is most noticeable is that four of the seven plays depict events in the lives of blacks who, born into slavery, devoted their lives to the struggle for emancipation. The other three plays trace the careers of men who were engaged in another kind of struggle—the struggle for social justice, especially as it applied to the broad underclass to which blacks belonged in disproportionate numbers. Plantation slavery, which existed in America for two and a half centuries, denied the humanity of a significant part of the population reduced to the status of "property." Because the slaves were black and the proprietors white, the system created an unnatural chasm between the races—"white" meant power and "black," subservience. The effects of the system are still prevalent today. As a result, Americans have come to view slavery as a most heinous form of human debasement and those who fought for its removal, by whatever means available to them, as heroes. Assaults on the system, whether by black or white, were hailed as significant events in the history of the human race.

But, of course, heroes to one group are villains to another. Heroes are not universally admired because they tend to embody the values and needs of the community that honors them. There will be white Americans who see the black freedom fighters as murderous revolutionaries intent on upsetting the status quo and in the process denying whites the privileges they enjoyed through the vagaries of history. Where a nation is divided, as America is and has been for generations, serious disagreement is likely to occur over granting national recognition to black heroes. (There are still those who refuse to observe Martin Luther King's Day.) A similar situation does not exist in respect to white heroes. Since whites hold power they can name as many national heroes as they like without reference to blacks.

Self-interest will make these opposing views irreconcilable. Taking an ideal position, one might argue that the eradication of slavery followed by the halting steps taken to create a just society in America, should eventually be productive of the common good if they serve to remove bigotry, racial hatred, and inequity in the body politic. Yet it took a Civil War to end slavery and decades of struggle in the courts and on the streets to advance the cause of civil rights.

The period of history covered by the plays in this volume is from 1791 to 1968, beginning with the slave revolt in Haiti up through the apex of the civil rights movement in America. Five of the heroes here represented are American and two are Caribbean. Of the Americans, Nat Turner led an uprising against slavery in Southampton, Virginia, that, although a failure, was not inconsequential. It spread terror in the Southland, exposed the contradictions in the system, inflamed the pro- and anti-slavery debate, and hastened the day of emancipation. Harriet Tubman, on the other hand, after having escaped to freedom, repeatedly risked her life by returning to the South to lead her black sisters and brothers from bondage to freedom in Canada. Frederick Douglass is shown facing a difficult choice — either outwardly supporting the abolitionist John Brown and his doomed raid on Harper's Ferry or withdrawing to continue as leading spokesman for his race. Paul Robeson was an acclaimed concert artist and actor until he began to speak out against oppression; then he was forced into retirement. And Martin Luther King was assassinated for leading non-violent demonstrations in support of racial justice.

Of the two Caribbean heroes, Jean-Jacques Dessalines, one of the leaders of the Haitian revolution, rose from slavery to become emperor of his country. Marcus Garvey was the Jamaican activist who worked ceaselessly to improve the conditions of the black working-class on the world scene. Though not Americans, both of these heroes were strongly influenced by official American policy towards them: the United States refused to recognize the first free and independent nation in the Western World — the black republic of Haiti — because it maintained a slave society itself; and Garvey was imprisoned in Atlanta on a trumped-up charge of mail fraud and subsequently deported back to Jamaica, an action intended to destroy his black mass movement in America.

While these heroes have their place in history, it should be noted that the playwrights who have chosen to write about them are not historians. They do not feel bound to reproduce historical events as they occurred. Rather it is their aim to organize episodes based on the life of their hero so as to create the social atmosphere in which he lived and against which his actions may be judged. The playwright seeks to portray the essence of his hero's character in terms of a dramatic conflict that, when staged, will capture and hold the interest of an audience. Some license for invention is allowed the writer, provided he does not distort what is known and felt about his character's virtues and failings. What most playwrights strive to present is the hero's confrontation with himself in light of his goal so that he may become knowledgeable about the effect of his actions, thus enlightening an audience as to their necessity or inevitability. Because the writer wishes his hero to be a sympathetic figure, this act of self-confrontation is apt to be ennobling to the character.

Preceding each play is a short biographical sketch of the hero and a comment on the way in which the playwright has dealt with his subject. For some writers it was important to place the entire public career of their protagonist before the audience so that the sweep of the hero's triumph and agony could be seen and felt. For others, crucial events have been selected that bring into sharp focus the distinctive character of the hero in responding to these periods of crisis. In either case, the capsule biography will provide a point of reference for the work of the imagination. A note on the playwright will be found at the end of each play.

The plays are worthy of reading and study, but ultimately their full realization is attained in stage production. Because they are chronicles, following the life of the hero in several different locales, it is hardly necessary, in most cases, to mount them in realistic settings. Instead, imaginative use of the available stage area is required, complemented by thoughtful and serviceable lighting. Most important, the individual episodes should flow into each other to create a sense of continuity with blackouts being used sparingly. It is also possible to undertake readings of sections of the plays for discussion before embarking on a full-scale production. However, it should be carefully noted that the plays are covered by copyright and cannot be performed without written permission from the author or his agent and on payment of a royalty fee.

EMPEROR OF HAITI

by
Langston Hughes

JEAN-JACQUES DESSALINES
(1758-1806)

Toward the end of the eighteenth century, the French colony of Haiti, then called St. Domingue (San Domingo), was reputedly the richest colony in the world. Its wealth was created by half a million African slaves who worked the fertile estates and sugar factories. Of the free population, there were 30,000 whites from whom came the estate managers and overseers, traders (including slave traders) and administrators. There were also some 40,000 free mulattoes and blacks who, relegated to the status of second-class citizens, bided their time to claim full citizenship in those tumultuous years of revolutionary fervor.

July 14, 1789, the French masses stormed the Bastille in Paris to begin the French Revolution. In 1791 slaves in the northern part of St. Domingue rose up and struck their first blow for liberty. The insurrection was partly successful; plantations were razed and the blacks took possession of the hills overlooking the town. Within a month Toussaint L'Ouverture, a slave of extraordinary qualities, took command of the rebellion. For the next thirteen years St. Domingue was riven by war as imperialist nations—Britain, Spain, and France—sought to gain control of the colony. By 1802 when Jean-Jacques Dessalines declared the country independent of France and changed its name to the aboriginal Haiti, this once flourishing land was in chaos. Estates had been torched, buildings destroyed, towns razed to the ground. The social divisions between black and white, and between mulatto and black freedmen, had hardened into an irreversible race war. It was a tragedy of colossal proportions.

Dessalines was the second of the triumvirate of great

Haitian leaders. Unlike Toussaint, his predecessor, and Henri Christophe who succeeded him, Dessalines could not read or write. He was, however, a brilliant and fearless general and a fiery speaker who was early picked by Toussaint to be one of his field commanders. Dessalines must have been aware of the treachery and duplicity practiced repeatedly by British and French agents whose aim was to destroy the black revolution. Nearly one-third of the 500,000 slaves had given their lives in the war for freedom, many had been wantonly massacred by imperialist forces.

Throughout the long and debilitating campaigns, Toussaint had always accepted French control of St. Domingue, partly as a form of protection from British designs on the colony but also because he was moving steadily toward a form of home rule under the French. He set himself the idealistic task of maintaining a multi-racial society, requiring that freed slaves return to work on estates in order to restore the economy of the country. His policies failed. Despite his submission to the French, he was seized and taken to France where he ended his life in one of Bonaparte's fortress prisons.

Reversing Toussaint's policy, Dessalines carved up the big estates and parcelled them out to blacks, demanding that work should proceed unremittingly. After twelve years of war and incredible suffering, a time of healing was needed, a time to gather strength, to plan, to build. But no such luxury was allowed the Haitian blacks. The die was cast in 1802 when the French parliament voted to reestablish slavery in the colonies and Bonaparte despatched a contingent of 20,000 men under his brother-in-law General LeClerc to reassert white domination in St. Domingue.

With Toussaint gone, Dessalines not only proclaimed Haiti independent of France but he came to the conclusion that Haiti would only be able to maintain its freedom if it were rid of white people. He symbolized this decision by ripping the white section from the French tricolor and joining together the red and blue to give Haiti its new flag. Bonaparte had made himself emperor of France, and Dessalines took the same title.

He would be of no lesser rank than his enemy.

The purge of whites was carried out systematically by the black army. "There will be no more whites among us," Dessalines told the troops. "What we are doing is most cruel. It must be done, however, to consolidate our independence." Spared in the massacre were British and American whites, priests (one of whom turned out to be a spy for Bonaparte and sent him drawings of Haitian fortifications), skilled workers, and health officers. No one will condone the needless killing, but the historian C.L.R. James has pointed out that the race war was triggered by the fact that LeClerc resolved to exterminate the blacks, that over a thousand blacks were deliberately drowned in the harbor of Le Cap, and that the British promised to trade with Haiti only after the purge had been carried out — a devilish compact intended to drive a lasting wedge between France and Haiti.

Having rid the country of whites, Dessalines then had to contend with the privileged mulattoes—a stronger, more insidious force since they were themselves Haitians. The mulattoes feared that with white power gone, they would be engulfed by a black tide. It was one of his own mulatto generals, Guerin, who arranged to have Dessalines shot as he was crossing the Pont Rouge to enter Port-au-Prince on October 17, 1806. As Father of the Republic, Dessalines is the national hero of Haiti.

Fascinated with the story of the Haitian revolution, Langston Hughes sought to bring it to the stage in drama and song. He first produced *Drums of Haiti* in 1935, revised it in 1936 as *Troubled Island*, turned this version into an opera with music by William Grant Still in 1949, and his final revision which is here published was completed in 1963. Hughes was not the first black American playwright to dramatize Haitian history. In 1893 William Edgar Easton wrote *Dessalines*, which was produced in Chicago by a black company, and in 1912 his *Christophe, a Tragedy in Prose of Imperial Haiti* was staged at Lenox Casino in Harlem. Leslie Pinckney Hill of Cheyney, Pennsylvania, published his dramatic history titled *Toussaint*

L'Ouverture in 1928.

A theme that resonates in these plays and others, even when it is not directly addressed, is why did the most successful slave rebellion in history fail to bring peace and prosperity to the Haitian people? A common assumption has been that the black leaders could fight but they couldn't rule, that they were obsessed with the trappings of power, were corrupted by too much power. Hughes gives us glimpses of the Haiti Dessalines will inherit, one deeply rent with psychological, racial, and social scars. The revolutionary leaders have had their flesh torn by the overseer's whip, they have been branded, some even dismembered. They elected Dessalines as their chief but he is despised by the mulattoes who consider him an ignoramus. Having experienced life under the civilized whites, the blacks were not likely to trust their fate to the "half-civilized" mulattoes.

Of course Dessalines gets carried away by power. But it is the power to make things happen quickly for his people. He will never again trust whites, though he must deal with them in the world marketplace. Of course he models his court ridiculously after those of Europe, assuming that was the accepted way to display one's independence and majesty. The parade of blacks in court dress is the stuff of theatrical burlesque and good for a laugh. But deeper than the posturing, one discerns the passionate desire of a leader to seek for his people on the world scene an equity based on mutual respect, a fierce determination to protect their freedom and independence, and a dream to recreate by their own efforts a new and flourishing Haiti as a sacred trust to the hundreds of thousands of lives sacrificed in the fight for liberty.

Source: C.L.R. James, *The Black Jacobins*, 2nd edition, revised. New York: Vintage Books, 1963.

CHARACTERS

[*In order of Appearance*]

Josef, a young slave, later Grand Marshal
Azelia, wife of Dessalines
Martel, an elderly slave, later Chief Councillor
Dessalines, slave leader, later Emperor
Congo, a slave, later a Baron
Xavier, a slave
Antoine, a slave, later a Baron
Mars, a one-armed slave, later a Duke
Popo, a slave, later Chief Attendant
Celeste, a slave, later a Lady
Lulu, a slave, later a Lady
Dembu, a slave, later a Major
Pierre, a child, later Chief Bugler
Papaloi, Voodoo Priest
Mamaloi, Voodoo Priestess
Vuval, **Beyard**, **Stenio** } free mulattos, later Counts
First Old Woman, **Second Old Woman** } servants at the Court
Claire Heureuse, Consort of the Emperor
Lord Bobo, Grand Treasurer
Mango Vendor, **Pepper Vendor**, **Cocoanut Vendor**, **Melon Vendor**, **Thread Vendor**, **Yam Vendor** } market women on the Quay
Tall Fisherman
Short Fisherman
Ragamuffins
Soldiers

Slaves, Dukes, Duchesses, Courtiers, Servants, Butlers, Pages, Ladies-of-the-Presence, Lady-in-Waiting, a Ragged Boy, a Flower Girl, dancing girls, a male dancer, two children.

PLACE

The Island of Haiti.

TIME

The Napoleonic Era.

SCENES

ACT ONE

An Abandoned Sugar Mill. Night.

ACT TWO

SCENE 1: *A Room at* DESSALINES' *Palace.*

SCENE 2: *The Banquet Terrace. Immediately following.*

ACT THREE

A Quay in a Fishing Village. Noon.

ACT ONE

TIME: *The year 1791.*

PLACE: *An abandoned sugar mill in the French colony of Haiti, then officially known as St. Domingue. It is night. Through the broad open door the moon shines. Without, tall cocoanut palms stand against the stars, and hills rise in the distance.*

AT RISE: JOSEF, *a young black man, stands in the doorway, the curve of a cane knife in his hand. Carefully he inspects the knife. At the noise of footsteps and the breaking of underbrush, his body becomes tense. He listens, then cries in a loud whisper.*

JOSEF: [*Softly, but with great sternness.*] Halt! Who's there?

AZELIA: [*A woman's voice in the darkness.*] Once ...

JOSEF: *[To complete a password.]* ... a slave ...

AZELIA: [*Continuing the formula.*] ... but soon no more!

JOSEF: Free?

AZELIA: Free! It's me, Azelia, from the Riviere Plantation.

JOSEF: Come on, then. You gave the password.

AZELIA: [*Entering, a load of bananas in a flat wicker tray on her head.*] Jean Jacques's coming, too, so I run ahead to see if all's safe here.

JOSEF: [*Astonished.*] Did Jean Jacques send you?

AZELIA: Course not! Jean Jacques fears nothing in Haiti, or anywhere. But he stopped to speak with a guard at the bridge, so I come on. [*Putting her burden down on the corner of the cane grinder.*] Look, Josef, under these bananas all the arms I could find. [*Laughing.*] I put this fruit on top to hide what I was carrying, weapons for tonight.

JOSEF: Did you pass any Frenchmen?

AZELIA: Only one old planter on horseback, and he didn't stop us. We kept to the woods mostly. Look! Lift up these bananas.

JOSEF: [*Helping her move the fruit.*] Um-umh!

AZELIA: Three machetes! See! Two pistols, stolen from the overseer, the butt end of an ax. [*They inspect the weapons.*] Jean Jacques brings a Spanish rifle and a dozen flails.

JOSEF: We'll need 'em all, I reckon. Do the whites on your plantation smell a rat yet?

AZELIA: Don't think so. But the air's full of evil. The overseers drove us like dogs today in the fields.

JOSEF: On our place, as well.

AZELIA: And I'm tired, so tired I can't hardly drag. This "fruit" was heavy.

JOSEF: I'm tired as hell, too. But this is one night we've got to stay awake. [*Turning.*] Say, didn't I hear there was a whipping on your place this morning?

AZELIA: Yes.

JOSEF: Who?

AZELIA: Jean Jacques was whipped.

JOSEF: You mean you ...?

AZELIA: My man.

JOSEF: Good Lord! For what?

AZELIA: Being off the place at night without permission. They caught him coming back this morning.

JOSEF: What'd he tell them?

AZELIA: That he'd been to a voodoo meeting.

JOSEF: Then ...?

AZELIA: Then they hit him across the mouth.

JOSEF: And after that?

AZELIA: They called all the slaves together to watch him beaten. The foreman gave him fifty lashes, hard. And master and his sons stood around and laughed to see a slave with such a fine name taking a lashing.

JOSEF: What about his name?

AZELIA: They said Jean Jacques Dessalines was too much name for a slave to have. Let slaves have just one name, that's what they said.

JOSEF: Well, after tonight, nobody'll give orders to a slave. I cut my last acre of cane today—if I live or die.

AZELIA: And Jean Jacques's took his last beating—if we succeed.

JOSEF: We'll succeed, or else stay in the hills like the runaway maroons until we're free.

[*A noise is heard outside.*]

JOSEF: Be quiet! [*They stop to listen,* JOSEF *goes to the door.*] Halt! Who's that?

MARTEL: [*An old man's voice.*] Once ...

JOSEF: ... a slave ...

MARTEL: ... but soon no more.

JOSEF: Free?

MARTEL: Free!

JOSEF: Come in, Martel. We need you wise old men.

MARTEL: [*Entering.*] Good evening, Josef, son! Azelia, good evening! Where's Dessalines?

AZELIA: Jean Jacques's nearby, Father Martel. I'll tell him you're here.

MARTEL: Thank you, daughter. But keep to the shadows, the moon is bright.

[AZELIA *exits.*]

MARTEL: [*To the young man.*] Josef, yon moon in sky, mark you how it stares at us?

JOSEF: Yes, Father Martel.

MARTEL: A long time that moon's looked down upon Haiti. And tears of dew have fallen from its face in pity upon our troubled island where men are slaves.

JOSEF: True, Father Martel.

MARTEL: Even now yon moon looks out across the silver ocean, watching the slave ships sail toward the western world with their woeful burdens. The cries of black men and women, and the clank of chains in the night, rise up against the face of the moon.

JOSEF: My mother came that way, Martel, in a slave ship. She still remembers Africa.

MARTEL: Africa! So long, so far away! But tonight the moon weeps tears of joy, son, for Africa. And when in its next passage across the sea, it shines on our sweet motherland, it'll smile and say, "Thy black children in Haiti have thrown off the yoke of bondage, and are men again!" Josef, my children grew up slaves. My grandchildren, too ... but yours will be free!

JOSEF: I wait for the beat of the drums to tell me when to lift this knife. *[He raises his machete.]*

MARTEL: For seventy years I've waited. Now our time is come. When the slave Boukman lays his fingers on the great drum hidden in the cane brake tonight, he'll beat out a signal that'll roll from hill to hill, slave hut to slave hut, across the cane field, across the mountains, across the bays from island to island, until every drum in Haiti throbs with the call to rise and seek freedom. Then the moon will smile, son.

JOSEF: And I'll smile, too, Martel.

MARTEL: But come! I've orders for you, Josef. Time is passing.

JOSEF: Yes, sir, I'm listening.

MARTEL: [*Motioning to* JOSEF *to make a light.*] Let us light a lantern. It's safe since sentries now are posted around this mill like the spokes of a wheel. I've just helped Yayou place twenty men who accompanied us from Dondon. So we can have a light. And you need no longer call for the password at the door.

JOSEF: Then what, sir?

MARTEL: Go station yourself by the spring and see that no man poisons our water, should there be traitors among us.

JOSEF: Yes, Father Martel.

MARTEL: When the drums sound, then come here for instructions from Dessalines.

JOSEF: From Jean Jacques Dessalines?

MARTEL: Jean Jacques. Tonight in the name of the slaves the council chose him for our leader.

JOSEF: I'm glad, for he's strong.

MARTEL: And to be trusted.

JOSEF: No one hates the French more than he does.

MARTEL: And no one's worked harder preparing for this night. Jean Jacques has not slept for weeks. Twice he's been caught coming in at dawn and beaten for it by the overseers. But be about your business, son.

JOSEF: I'm going now. [*He goes to the door, but pauses there.*] Someone is coming. It's Jean Jacques— [*As he salutes.*] Dessalines!

DESSALINES: [*Entering. A powerful black man in ragged clothing, followed by* AZELIA.] Hello, Josef. You salute me like a French soldier!

JOSEF: You're our leader now, Jean Jacques.

DESSALINES: [*Pleased.*] I'm your leader, Josef. [*He returns the salute.* JOSEF *exits.*]

MARTEL: Good evening, son! I'm glad you're early.

DESSALINES: I'm glad to find you already here.

[*They shake hands and immediately busy themselves with plans.*]

DESSALINES: You can tell me where the rations are hidden in the hills, can't you, Martel? Twenty miles from the foot of Timber Mountain on the road to La Trou our first supplies are buried? And the sign is three curved marks on a tree? Is that right?

MARTEL: Yes, Jean Jacques.

DESSALINES: Then forty paces in from the road we'll find a scattering of seashells? And there, dig?

MARTEL: Yes, that's how 'twas planned. Food's hidden there in the earth, and arms.

DESSALINES: [*To* AZELIA.] Have the women been told to bring cook-pots?

AZELIA: We looked out for that. Those little things...

DESSALINES: Nothing's little thing now, Zelia.

AZELIA: [*Jokingly.*] How about your pipe, Jean Jacques? [*Producing it from her hair.*] It's a little thing you're crazy about, but you forgot to bring it.

DESSALINES: [*Impatiently.*] Don't trifle, Azelia, There's too much to do.

AZELIA: Forgive me. [*She puts her arm about his shoulder and offers him the pipe.*] Go on with your plans.

DESSALINES: [*Loudly.*] Don't touch me! God! My shoulder's raw as meat!

AZELIA: Oh, I'm sorry, Jean Jacques.

DESSALINES: [*Sarcastically.*] We have a kind master, Martel.

MARTEL: He'll be master no more when the sun rises.

DESSALINES: He'll be less than nothing. He'll be dead. Our gentle master will burn in his bed this evening, roasted between his silken sheets.

AZELIA: Poor man!

DESSALINES: [*Turning on her.*] Strange you should say "Poor man," Azelia! What's he to you? [*Fiercely.*] Have you ever been one of his mistresses? Every black woman he's wanted he's had.

AZELIA: Not me! No, no! Not me!

DESSALINES: Then why cry pity on him? I know you must hate him. But when you say, "Poor man," you make me laugh. The whites never have pity on us. We're just slaves, dogs to them.

AZELIA: You're right, Jean Jacques!

DESSALINES: They burned Mackandal for trying to be free, didn't they? They had no mercy on him. We'll show no mercy on them now.

MARTEL: I remember well the burning of Mackandal. Thirty years gone by, 'tis. They made the slaves for miles around witness it, as an example of what happens to any Negro who wants to be free. Burning is a horrible thing, Jean Jacques! I hate to think that we must do it, too.

DESSALINES: You're over-kind, Martel. I do not love my masters.

MARTEL: I'd let them live, if they'd leave us free.

DESSALINES: They won't, so there's no *if* about it. We have no choice but to kill ... wipe out the whites in all this island ... for if the French are left alive to force us back to slavery, we'll never get a chance to rise again. And for us, you and me—Boukman, Christophe, Toussaint, and all our leaders—there'd be only the rack, the wheel, or burning at the stake like Mackandal. Mackandal! [*Turning and appealing to the night.*] Great Mackandal! Dead leader of rebellious slaves, fight with us now.

MARTEL: Mackandal is with us, son. His spirit walks the Haitian hills crying the name of freedom.

DESSALINES: But the only way to be free is to fight! Or else to die.

MARTEL: Tonight we fight to live, Jean Jacques.

DESSALINES: To live! Men free, alive! Alive! Go, Martel, and tell that to the men on guard without, for some are even yet afraid. I saw it in their eyes. Tell them tonight we strike with all our force, and none must be afraid. There are two ways of being free ... alive or dead. We'll live! This time, the French will die.

MARTEL: I'll go, Jean Jacques. [*He exits.*]

AZELIA: [*Drawing near her husband.*] But you and I, Jean Jacques, we must live. [*Fiercely.*] I will not have you dead.

DESSALINES: Why must *we* live any more than the others, Azelia?

AZELIA: Because we have loved so little, Jean Jacques, been happy too little. Never a night is mine alone — never just you and me—

DESSALINES: That's true, Azelia, but—

AZELIA: Every night there's been something to keep you from me. Ever since we've had a hut together, you've been stealing out to crawl through the forest, in the dark, to some secret meeting of the slaves, planning this break for freedom—and I'm left alone. Tonight has taken all our nights, Jean Jacques, the cane field all our days.

DESSALINES: But what I've planned—it is good, Azelia?

AZELIA: Good, Jean Jacques. But for a woman, love, too, is good.

DESSALINES: Yes, yes. I know, but at a time like this, it's foolish. [*He busies himself inspecting a pistol.*]

AZELIA: Foolish, I know, but I love, you Jean. [*Fearfully.*] Listen to me! If we fail, the French will kill you. They'll tear your body on the rack or break you on the wheel.

DESSALINES: We will not fail, Azelia. Don't worry.

AZELIA: But if we did, I'd share death, too. We've shared so much together. When we were children running wild in the slave quarters, we ate from the same trough where our master fed the dogs. Together we learned to pick the cotton clean. Then in the green cane fields, I watched you swing your knife, big and strong in the sunlight. My man! My Jean Jacques! We tied the cane into bundles, and in the long night learned to stir the bubbling syrup in its copper kettles. But there came a dawn when the kettles boiled, forgotten. That night we knew that love was sweeter than the syrup. Then in our little hut together, and I your wife.

DESSALINES: Wife? [*Laughing.*] A word the whites use. We never had a priest, nor papers, either.

AZELIA: We had ourselves. You, me! I, you!

DESSALINES: [*Bitterly.*] And neither of us freedom.

AZELIA: You always talk of freedom, Jean Jacques! I want to be free, too, but—

DESSALINES: But what?

AZELIA: I'm afraid ...

DESSALINES: Afraid? Afraid of what? Don't rile me, Azelia.

AZELIA: [*Slowly.*] Afraid freedom'll take you away from me.

DESSALINES: Don't be a fool! Why, when we're free, we can go anywhere and do anything we want to, you and me together.

AZELIA: I just want to be together, always with you.

DESSALINES: Then don't worry. I'm not going to leave you. I'll even get a paper and marry you like the white folks do, if that's what you want—except that we couldn't read what's on the paper.

AZELIA: Are we too old to learn to read now?

DESSALINES: I expect we are, Azelia. But not too old to be free. [*Rising.*] Come on, Azelia, let's look about the mill and see if there're any spies hiding in the rafters, or in that vat yonder, waiting to run back to the white folks with word of our meeting place. [*As* AZELIA *puts out her hands to detain him, he flinches with pain.*] Take care, woman.

AZELIA: Forgive me, Jean Jacques, and kiss me just once, for all the years that love has been our chain.

DESSALINES: And slavery our master.

AZELIA: And freedom your hope.

DESSALINES: You're fighting with me, Azelia?

AZELIA: Until the end, Jean Jacques.

DESSALINES: [*As he kisses her.*] Azelia! Azelia! [*Turning away.*] The crowd'll be here in no time, now. Let's look in this bin here and see if it's empty. [*He tries to lift the wooden lid.*] By God, it's heavy! Help me, Zelia.

CONGO: [*A deep voice inside the bin.*] Hands off, less'n you want a shot through the belly.

DESSALINES: [*Brandishing his cane knife.*] Who's there?

CONGO: [*Calmly, from within.*] Who's out there?

DESSALINES: Jean Jacques!

CONGO: [*Drawling.*] Jean Jacques who?

DESSALINES: Jean Jacques Dessalines.

CONGO: [*Lifting up lid of box and emerging.*] Well, tell me something, pal! [*With a half-lazy salute.*] Hello, Jean Jacques! Hello, Azelia!

DESSALINES: What're you doing, Congo?

CONGO: I'm on guard.

DESSALINES: On guard?

CONGO: On guard—locked in the box, so nobody can bother me—nor the guns, neither, we got stacked in there.

DESSALINES: What did you open up for, then, you careless fool?

CONGO: Who wouldn't know your voice, boy, as many times I heard you talking to us slaves around the fire at night—when the white folks thought we was just having a little voodoo dance? You gets around a-plenty, Jean Jacques.

DESSALINES: You knowed me by my voice?

CONGO: Every black man in North Haiti knows you. We're waiting for you to lead us, if them old slaves in the council ever make up their minds who they gonna pick out.

DESSALINES: Then close the box and lock it until I give the word, Congo, for *I am* leader now. [*Proudly.*] Tonight the council picked me.

CONGO: That's good, boy! I'm glad!

DESSALINES: Are there two hundred rifles in there, as there should be?

CONGO: Two hundred, Jean Jacques.

DESSALINES: Then remain on guard! But not inside.

CONGO: I got you, chief.

DESSALINES: [*Laughing.*] Chief?

CONGO: Like in Africa, Jean Jacques—Chief.

DESSALINES: Can you remember Africa, Congo?

CONGO: Sure. I was a big boy when that English ship got hold of me. That's why I can do our dances so well. I learnt 'em in Africa.

DESSALINES: Well, tomorrow, boy, we'll dance a-plenty. If I can loosen up my back.

CONGO: Not whipped again?

DESSALINES: Yes, whipped.

CONGO: You sure got a mean old master. What kind of whip he use?

DESSALINES: A cat-o'-nine tail 'cross my shoulders.

CONGO: [*Laughing.*] Huh! That's nothing! My master uses a tree limb on my head.

DESSALINES: [*Angrily.*] And you laugh and like it?

CONGO: [*Suddenly sober.*] I don't like it; that's why I'm guarding these guns.

AZELIA: [*In the doorway.*] Listen! I hear a horse down the road, coming fast.

CONGO: [*Listening.*] I hear it, too. There ain't no slaves got horses.

DESSALINES: Some free mulatto, perhaps. One of our allies! It's time for everybody to be here, and so far they've only come from Dondon. Where's everyone else? Where's the crowd from Milot, and from Limbe? This is no time to be late!

AZELIA: You know how careful everybody's got to be tonight. You warned them yourself not to hurry in case the white folks get to looking out the corners of their eyes.

CONGO: Folks what's been working all day's just naturally slow, anyhow. I know I am.

DESSALINES: Not when their life depends on it. [*As the horse's hoofs approach.*] Let me go see who's coming there. [*He goes to the door.*]

CONGO: It *must* be a mulatto. No Negro's got a horse to ride on. [*Muttering.*] And I don't trust them mulattoes, myself.

AZELIA: Black mother, white father, free.

CONGO: Free or not, their white fathers treat 'em almost as bad as us slaves.

AZELIA: But they sometimes leave them land and money.

CONGO: Then the mulattoes think they're white for sure!

AZELIA: And look down on us for being black.

CONGO: And for being slaves.

DESSALINES: Keep quiet, you. The mulattoes who've joined us hate the whites.

CONGO: A little hate ain't enough. If they'd ever been driven to the fields like us, they'd know how to hate a-plenty; I tell you, I don't trust 'em.

DESSALINES: Well, they're smart. They've been to school and got an education. We need their heads.

CONGO: I'd like to cut their heads off and play ninepins with 'em.

DESSALINES: Not those that are with us, Congo. [*Going outside the door.*] But that's no mulatto on that horse. Even the moon don't brighten up his face. [*Calling.*] Who's there?

XAVIER: [*Voice out of breath.*] Me, Jean Jacques!

AZELIA: It looks like Xavier from Breda Plantation.

DESSALINES: It is Xavier. [*As a man comes running toward him.*] What's up? A message?

XAVIER: [*Entering, panting.*]Yes, Jean Jacques! A message! Bad news! Some of the white folks done found out.

DESSALINES: What? Where?

CONGO: How?

AZELIA: [*In terror.*] Oh!

XAVIER: That mulatto, Gautier, we thought was with us, he got cold feet and sent his family into the Cape for safety. The whites on the next plantation, related to him, asked what's up, and he told them they'd better leave for the Cape, too. The the white man grabbed him by the throat and made him confess there's trouble in the air.

DESSALINES: A yellow dog! What then?

XAVIER: The house slaves knew something must be wrong,

and old Bajean came out and told me. I gave orders to set fire to the house as soon as I got started on this horse I stole from the stables.

DESSALINES: And did they fire the house?

XAVIER: I didn't see it burning as I looked back.

DESSALINES: It's wise they didn't. T'would alarm the plain for miles about. Everyone had orders not to fire until the drums are beaten. Our plans are to let the whites think they've escaped. Then shoot them down on the road. And the false mulattoes, too! Damn their chicken-hearted souls! Are there many people on the way, Xavier?

XAVIER: The roads were empty as I came, but all along in the woods, slaves creep towards here. Soon there'll be a crowd. And all are wondering who is chief?

DESSALINES: I am, Xavier.

XAVIER: [*Stepping forward and shaking hands.*] We trust you, Jean Jacques.

DESSALINES: Thank you, friend. Now back to your plantation and see if your master's escaped. And if the mulatto who squealed is still living, kill him ere the drums beat.

XAVIER: I will, chief. [*He leaves. Horse's hoofs. Sounds of movement and voices without.*]

CONGO: You see, I tell you about mulattoes! They're dangerous.

DESSALINES: They're not all alike, Congo. Some we can trust. Vuval is one. Stenio's another. These mulattoes are with us. [*Looking out.*] But say, here come the men we're waiting for. [*Calling.*] It's time you got here.

[*Several enter including the slaves* ANTOINE, MARS, POPO, *and the women,* CELESTE *and* LULU, *with her child,* PIERRE, *a boy of six or seven. Greetings are exchanged.*]

ANTOINE: Greetings, Jean Jacques! We're glad you're leader. [*They shake hands.*]

LULU: Hello, Azelia! Ain't you proud of your man now?

AZELIA: I am that, Lulu. He's chief.

POPO: Hello, Jean Jacques

DESSALINES: Hello, Popo. Congratulate me, boy!

POPO: I knew they'd pick you, Jean Jacques! It couldn't be nobody else. We're sticking with you, partner

LULU: Well, it looks like Negroes is getting together at last.

CELESTE: It sho do, Lulu!

DESSALINES: [*To* CELESTE.] How about a dance tomorrow night, Celeste, to celebrate our freedom?

CELESTE: [*Laughing.*] Not without Azelia's say-so! I'm scared of you, Jean Jacques. You're a lady-killer.

DESSALINES: Not much! Too busy now. [*Turning to* MARS.] Hello, Mars! Is Dembu, the powder-maker, with you?

MARS: He was right behind us.

DEMBU: [*Entering.*] Here I am, Jean Jacques.

DESSALINES: Come aside a moment. I want to talk with you. [*They withdraw into the shadows.*]

CONGO: [*To the child,* PIERRE, *who has climbed up on the box of guns.*] Boy, you better get down off that box, you'll burn your feet.

PIERRE: Why, what's in here? [*As he hugs* CONGO *around the neck.*]

CONGO: You'll see by and by. Stop hugging me! I ain't your pappy.

LULU: [*To her child.*] Pierre, behave yourself. Get down, now, hear?

[*The child gets down.*]

ANTOINE: [*To* POPO, *who is bare from the waist up.*] Popo, where's your shirt?

CELESTE: Maybe he ain't got none.

POPO: Yes, I got one, but I hid it soaked in oil in my master's storehouse. My girl's to fire it, when the signal's given.

CELESTE: [*Peering at* POPO*'s breast.*] You've sure had a lot of masters, ain't you, Popo? All them brands they done burnt on your breast.

POPO: I been sold four times, but one master was kind, and didn't put his mark on me. Old man Thibault, he said he liked the way I played the drums.

CELESTE: You was lucky. When Thibault owned me, he branded me twice. Sure wished I'd learned to play the drums.

MARS: [*A man with one arm.*] Talk about drums, we got the biggest drum on the North Plain hidden on our place; Old Lucumi's ready waiting down in the banana grove. He's gonna beat out the freedom signal so's the slaves across the mountains can hear it.

LULU: Them big old goat drums sure can rock the stars.

PIERRE: How far can they sound, Mama?

LULU: Forty kilometers, I reckon, son, or more. Can't they, Mars?

MARS: Farther than that on a clear night.

PIERRE: I'd rather have a bugle, that's what I want.

CELESTE: For what?

PIERRE: A bugle blows pretty. All the white children have 'em.

CELESTE: The white children's free.

MARS: Anyhow, a drum can sound twenty times as far as any bugle ever blowed. Bugles don't belong to black folks.

PIERRE: That's how come I want one.

LULU: You can have one, honey, when we's free.

PIERRE: Tomorrow?

LULU: I 'spects tomorrow.

CELESTE: Drums is what our gods like, though. Drums is for Legba and Dambala, Nannan and M'bo.

CONGO: African gods been knowin' drums a long time. Them tinny bugles just cain't reach they ears.

ANTOINE: Goat's blood, cock's blood, and drums.

MARS: The drum's a black man's heart a-beatin'. Tonight that beatin's goin' to set the Frenchmen's hair on end.

CONGO: This is our night tonight.

CELESTE: A mighty night it'll be, too. Bless Legba!

MARS: My one good arm is ready. [*He lifts his single arm.*]

PIERRE: Where's your other arm, Monsieur Mars?

MARS: [*Bitterly.*] The Black Code, son. The French've got it all writ' down that if a slave raise his hand against a white man, they can cut it off. They cut off mine.

CONGO: We'll remember that tonight.

ANTOINE: Let the French dwell a thousand years in hell, they'll never forget this night.

POPO: If there is a hell, I hope I meet no Frenchmen there.

LULU: Hell's a place for Christians, ain't it? Not for us.

ANTOINE: That's all. Our voodoo gods ain't mixin' with the white gods.

CELESTE: Legba's better.

POPO: White folks must have a special hell, anyhow, for themselves, reserved. They wouldn't go where us black folks goes, would they?

CONGO: They'll find out what hell they're headed for mighty soon.

[*Sounds of chanting and rattles without. People clear the doorway as a* PAPALOI, *in anklets of bone and a high feathered headdress, enters followed by a* MAMALOI *of powerful physique, carrying a live cock. The man has a rattle in one hand and an African drum under his arm.*]

LULU: There's the Mamaloi from Limbe.

CELESTE: And she carries a live cock to sacrifice on the

mountain.

PIERRE: The Papaloi's got a drum. Lemme go see!

[*The women and the child join a crowd that now clusters, chanting, about the high priest and priestess of voodoo, who chatter in an African tongue, calling on the gods.*]

PAPALOI: Uglumbagolaiti! Damballa! Solomini! Keetai!

MAMALOI: Legba! Legba! Legba!

[*The women cry and shout.*]

DESSALINES: [*Who is in conference with a group.*] Not so loud, there, women. We've plans to make. Call the gods a little softer. Please!

[*The group about the priests becomes less noisy. Three mulattoes enter,* VUVAL, BEYARD, *and* STENIO. *They are better dressed than the slaves, and much more polished. They seem out of place.*]

ANTOINE: Who're those mulattoes? Why do they come here?

MARS: Vuval and his friends. They're on our side. They're all right.

ANTOINE: The smart half-breeds!

CONGO: Better we didn't have them with us. They've never been slaves.

MARS: But Vuval's a poor mulatto.

POPO: His French father didn't leave him a thing but books.

ANTOINE: And half-freedom.

CONGO: They're half-men, not black, not white either. Bah!

MARS: [*As the mulattoes approach.*] Hello, Stenio. Evening, Vuval.

STENIO: Gentlemen, good evening.

VUVAL: Good evening, comrades [*Indicating* BEYARD.] My cousin, Beyard.

BEYARD: [*Rather pompously.*] Greetings in the name of liberty.

POPO: [*Shortly.*] Howdy!

[*The mill has gradually begun to fill with slaves standing in groups talking in low voices.*]

VUVAL: Is it true, the slave council has chosen Dessalines as leader?

MARS: It's true, and good, aint' it?

BEYARD: I doubt it's being good. He's ignorant and headstrong.

VUVAL: A brave fellow. But he's been nowhere, and he knows nothing.

CONGO: He knows the whip well enough to hate it.

ANTOINE: And he's not afraid.

POPO: He's the finest man in the North Plain. I grew up with him, and worked beside him. He's my friend.

BEYARD: Friendship has no judgment, Popo.

VUVAL: I thought they might have chosen Stenio or some one of us as leader who can read and write as well as speak.

CONGO: Speaking's not what we need now, Vuval.

ANTOINE: We know what the words are—the same as the French use in Paris! Liberty, Equality, Fraternity.

MARS: But Frenchmen keep us slaves in Haiti.

POPO: We want those words in action, here, now, for blacks as well as whites.

VUVAL: There are many ways of recreating words, Popo.

STENIO: Oh, don't be literary, Vuval. Slaves can't appreciate it. This is not the poetry club we once had in Cap Francais, before the French accused us of being Jacobins.

BEYARD: And closed our meetings.

POPO: You mean before you decided to join with us slaves.

VUVAL: Yes, we mulattoes didn't always realize you blacks were our natural allies, by force of circumstance.

POPO: And you didn't always think we needed to be free, did you?

VUVAL: Perhaps not.

CONGO: You were free already, so you didn't give a damn about us, did you, until you needed our help yourselves?

POPO: [*Bitterly.*] White father, yellow skins. You bastards!

VUVAL: I don't like that word, *bastard*.

POPO: I don't like you, Vuval.

VUVAL: [*Stepping forward to strike the Negro.*] You dirty slave!

BEYARD: [*Grabbing* VUVAL's *arm.*] Stop!

POPO: Let me at him! The yellow dog!

[*But* ANTOINE *holds him back.*]

DESSALINES: [*His voice booming out of the darkness.*] Who's starting trouble there? Whoever it is, I'll bust his brains out with my fist!

ANTOINE: A couple of hot-heads, Jean Jacques! Lost their tempers, nothing more.

VUVAL: Somebody lost his tongue.

DESSALINES: What's wrong, Popo?

POPO: I'm all right, but this yellow dog's been turning his tongue against you.

DESSALINES: [*Laughing.*] What did he say that could hurt Jean Jacques?

POPO: He said he's fit to lead himself

DESSALINES: That might be true. I'll let him lead with me—what would you think of that, Vuval? I know our need of you.

VUVAL: But I don't relish being called a bastard, Jean Jacques.

DESSALINES: [*Laughing.*] Is that all? Why let a word upset you? Only the French have priests and wedding rings. [*To* POPO.] Popo, have a little care what names you call our allies.

AZELIA: [*As she approaches.*] Jean Jacques, the councilors have come. They're ready to begin. Martel's waiting for you.

[DESSALINES *and* AZELIA *disappear in the crowd about the sugar grinder. The mulattos withdraw to one side as several old men and women enter. They are the council of slaves.* MARTEL *is among them.*]

MARS: It must be mighty near midnight!

ANTOINE: Soon, brother!

POPO: I'm ready!

CONGO: There's all the elders.

ANTOINE: And the old man from Limbe.

MARS: Wise old Martel!

POPO: Sss, you! They're beginning.

[MARTEL *is standing on a box that lifts him slightly above the throng. Around him are several very old slaves, both men and women. The crowd gradually becomes silent as someone knocks three times.* MARTEL *begins to speak.*]

MARTEL: Children of slavery, the time is come! For months, in secret and in danger, we've laid our plans. Now we gather here for the final hour. You are the tried and faithful. We old men and women, born in slavery and weary with unpaid labor, have chosen a leader for you. Not one of ourselves, for our backs are bending. We have chosen a man who's young and strong, wise and brave, to lead the slaves of the north to victory in union with all the blacks of Haiti who answer the call of the drums tonight. Your leader is Dessalines.

VOICES: [*In cheers.*] Dessalines! Jean Jacques! Dessalines!

[DESSALINES' *face glows in the lantern light as the old man puts his hand on* DESSALINES' *head in a gesture of blessing. Then* MARTEL *steps down and gives him the box.*]

DESSALINES: [*In a hoarse voice, stirred by emotion.*] I don't need to talk, for we're ready.

VOICES: Yes, indeed! Ready! Ready!

DESSALINES: But I must tell you how full my heart is tonight and how I keep remembering back to when I was a little naked slave among the slaves. Everyday an old man came to dump a pot of yams into a trough where we ate, and the pigs and the dogs, they ate, too. And we got down alongside 'em, on all fours, and ate—us and the dogs. I thought I, too, was a beast. I didn't know I'd ever grow to be a man. I thought only white folks grew up to be men. The Frenchman drove his sheep to market—just so they drove our parents to the fields when the sun came up. They owned them, too. Overseers with their dogs, whip in hand, always driving Negroes to the fields. And when the white man saw me growing tall, big enough to work, he drove me, too. Slowly I moved, too slow. The overseer lifted high his whip and cut me 'cross the back. And when I turned, he lashed me in the face. I cried out, he struck again. Then I lifted up my head and looked him in the eyes, and I knew I was a man, not a dog! I wanted to be free!

VOICES: Free! Free! Want to be free! Free!

DESSALINES: Not I alone—thousands of slaves like me wanted to be free! All over Haiti! Now, we're ready. We will not fail! Our time has come!

VOICES: Come! Come! It's come!

[*Cries of "Legba! Legba! Legba!" from the women and the chanting of the* MAMALOI *and* PAPALOI *grow ever louder as* DESSALINES *continues.*]

DESSALINES: Our masters on this island are fifty thousand whites to *five hundred thousand* Negro slaves. Count on your fingers, black to white—ten to one! Ten Negroes to one white, and yet we're slaves! Shall we go on slaves?

VOICES: No! No! No! No!

DESSALINES: In France, white men—free men—have risen against the king and torn the Bastille down. How much more reason have we, we who are slaves, to rise against our masters! How much more reason to strike back at those who buy and sell us, who beat us with their whips and track us down with their dogs! Why, even the mulattoes are turning against their white fathers and are ready to take our side, too. The poem-writer, Vuval, and his cousins are with us tonight.

VOICES: [*Murmuring.*] Don't want 'em. Can't trust 'em. Put 'em out. Don't need 'em.

DESSALINES: We do need them, my friends. We need their help. Make no mistake of that. They can read and write. I've chosen Vuval as my aide [*To the mulatto.*] Come forward, Vuval, show yourself and march with us. [VUVAL *takes his place beside* DESSALINES.] And now for our plans! Soon the drums of freedom will begin to sound. We'll start for the hills, burning and killing on the way, setting fire to all that's French, their mansions, their barns, their storehouses, their cane fields. Everything from here to Gonaives, Le Mole to Acul, will go up in smoke tonight — tomorrow not a Frenchman must live to tell the tale. In the hills, we'll meet our fellow slaves from the coast, the slaves from the west and all the leaders. Boukman will be there, Christophe, and Toussaint. Food and arms are buried. There on the mountain top we'll sacrifice a goat to Legba. We'll dance obeah. We'll make powder and bullets, and gather strength until the time is ripe for us to come down to the coast to seize the ports, and claim all Haiti as our own. Then we'll be free!

VOICES: [*With a great shout.*] Free! Free! Great God-A-Mighty! Free!

DESSALINES: Our hills await us. Our hills—where freedom lives, our hills—where the French, with their cannons, can never climb. The French! Bah! How my tongue burns when I say that word! Masters of all this sun-warmed land! Cruel monsters of terror! The French, who broke the bones of Oge on the rack! The French—who tortured Chevannes until his life blood ran down, drop by drop—dead for freedom! The French, who cut their scars upon my back—too deep to ever fade away! Look! [*He rips his shirt wide open, exposing his back covered with great red welts.*] Look what they've done to me! Look at my scars! For these the whites must pay!

VOICES: The whites must pay! Make 'em pay! Make 'em pay! Oh, make 'em pay!

[*Women begin to sob and moan.*]

DESSALINES: The sacks of sweet white sugar the French ship off to Paris goes stained with our blood!

VOICES: Blood! Blood! Blood!

DESSALINES: The soft white cotton the French weave into garments is red with my blood!

VOICES: Blood! Blood! Blood! Blood!

DESSALINES: The coffee our masters sip in the cool of evening on their wide verandas is thick with blood!

VOICES: Blood! Blood!

DESSALINES: Our masters live on blood!

VOICES: Black blood! Black Blood! Black blood!

DESSALINES: Oh, make them pay! [*Pausing.*]

Make ... them ... pay!

[*Afar off, a drum begins to beat. The voices rise to a frenzy at its sound.*]

VOICES: Pay! Pay! Pay! Make 'em pay!

[*Instantly, the distant drum-beat multiplies and spreads from plantation to plantation, carrying its signal across the night, until the whole island is throbbing with drum-beats. In the crowded sugar mill there are moans and shouts, hysterical sobs, curses, cries, a crush and swirl of movement.* CONGO *opens the box and begins to distribute guns. Above the tumult, the voice of* DESSALINES *rises in command:*]

DESSALINES: Revolt! Arise! For Freedom!

VOICES: [*Echoing his words.*] Freedom! Freedom!

DESSALINES: Revenge! Revenge! To the hills!

VOICES: To the hills!

DESSALINES: Free! Kill to be free!

VOICES: Free! Free! To be free!

DESSALINES: Fire the cane fields! Poison the springs!

VOICES: To be free! Free!

DESSALINES: Choke the rivers! Ambush the roads!

VOICES: Free! Free!

DESSALINES: [*Raising his cane knife like a sword.*] Kill the whites! Kill to be free!

VOICES: [*In a mighty shout.*] Kill! Kill! Kill!

CELESTE: [*A woman's voice, high and clear.*] To be free!

[*With cane knives and rifles held high, the slaves pour forth into the night. Outside, flames are visible as the cane fields burn. The drums beat louder, ever spreading. Shots are heard. In the distance, harrowing cries, the march of feet.* DESSALINES *stands with his arms uplifted, his back bare. In the lantern light, great red scars gleam like welts of terror across his shoulders. The* MAMALOI *whirls through the crowd, lifting high the sacred cock. The* PAPALOI *chants above his drum, his hands flying, his eyes wild, his feathered headdress waving.* VUVAL *stands, deathly pale, with his back to the canegrinder, as if in mortal terror. Above the tumult,* CELESTE'*s voice is heard crying in a high, musical cry.*]

CELESTE: I want to be free! Let me be free! Free!

AZELIA: [*Lifting her rifle in both hands and calling.*] Jean Jacques! Jean Jacques! Jean Jacques!

[*He does not hear her.* AZELIA *disappears in the crowd that pours through the door. Voices and drum-beats fill the night.*]

CURTAIN

ACT TWO

SCENE 1

TIME: *Several years later.*

PLACE: *Dessalines' Palace, near Petite Riviere. The Council Chamber; a table against red velvet curtains. A coat-of-arms. A chair, empire style, of plush and gilt with a high back. Two smaller chairs.*

AT RISE: *The Emperor,* DESSALINES, *is seated behind the table, many papers before him. He is obviously tired and worried.*

VUVAL *sits at one end of the table, reading a letter.*

VUVAL: [*Reading.*] " ... forty acres of sugarcane, two hundred plantain trees, an estimated three thousand coffee bushes, seventy pepper trees. Beyond that, I have nothing more to report to the Emperor. Signed: Beyard, Count of Acul."

DESSALINES: Is that all?

VUVAL: That's all. Every acre of land on his plantation is productive.

DESSALINES: And yet he says he cannot pay his tax, and so demands another tribute from the peasants?

VUVAL: We have very few markets, sire.

DESSALINES: Why doesn't he plant pineapples? There's always a market for them in the States.

VUVAL: It takes time.

DESSALINES: Time? Time! Always excuses on account of time. We've been free long enough to flourish here. And you mulattos were always free! Yet Beyard can't make his own plantation pay its tax.

VUVAL: He knows how well enough. He can get your money

easily by taxation.

DESSALINES: I don't want it by taxation. By work I want it. We must produce.

VUVAL: [*Shrugging.*] Perhaps!

DESSALINES: If I permit this draining of the peasants, they'll turn on me. Yet if the Empire goes without taxes, how shall we build roads, hire teachers, or run this court? [*Commandingly.*] Write the Count of Acul I must have from him at once the twenty thousand francs he owes the Treasury.

VUVAL: But I thought, perhaps, since Beyard is my cousin…

DESSALINES: I have granted you too many favors now, Vuval. I'll give him no reduction, and no further time. [*Leaning back.*] Read the next communication.

VUVAL: It is from General Gedeon's headquarters, signed by Major Longchamps. He wants, post haste, ten burro loads of powder, to be used at the fall maneuvers, and three hundred new winter uniforms for his men, preferably salmon pink with orange trimmings. He writes that he wants his regiment to look as good as Major Loguet's. He also requests a purple plume for his helmet.

DESSALINES: [*Roaring.*] Tell him … tell him! [*Impatiently.*] Damn it, I wish I could write! Tell him to go to hell!

VUVAL: Very well, sir; but …

DESSALINES: But?

VUVAL: He's an important officer

DESSALINES: Well, send the powder. But as for the uniforms, tell him, no! Everybody in Haiti wants to dress like me—and I'm the Emperor.

VUVAL: True!

DESSALINES: We'd need ten thousand spinning mills to turn out cloth enough to clothe them as they wish.

VUVAL: And a million dyers to dye it, if we had sufficient colors.

DESSALINES: What next?

VUVAL: [*With a gesture of fatigue.*] But you haven't forgotten there's a State banquet tonight, have you, Emperor? It's already dusk.

DESSALINES: The next letter, Vuval. We must get done with this. [*He wipes his brow.*]

VUVAL: [*Reading.*] "Most High and Mighty King of Haiti, Emperor Jean Jacques Dessalines, Chief General of the army and leader of the blacks, your humble servant begs of you this favor. The peasants of Gros Morne have made bricks and built themselves a school. We are six hundred grown-ups and sixty-seven children. We want to learn to read and write, so will you please send to us a teacher? We have already wrote three times to the Duke of Marmelade, Chief Grand Commissioner of Education, but we never got no answer. We are anxious to learn from books, and put our school to a good use. Please, Emperor of the blacks, if you have time, answer this letter yourself. We send you our humble regards. The love of the liberated people of Gros Morne goes to you. Respectfully yours, Henri Bajean, Blacksmith."

DESSALINES: [*Sadly, after a painful silence.*] I can't read myself and we have no teachers. [*Louder.*] Vuval, why did so many mulattos run away to Paris? We black people need you—you were educated. Now we have no teachers to send to Gros Morne.

VUVAL: [*Carelessly.*] That little village couldn't afford to pay a teacher, anyhow.

DESSALINES: Pay? Pay! Pay! Always pay! Does no one know that need fulfilled is pay enough? [*Angrily.*] Does no one, loving Haiti, find his pay in doing for her? But it's money we need, is it? Then change that letter I ordered you to write—tell Beyard I ask forty thousand francs instead of twenty.

VUVAL: [*Controlling his anger.*] You have given me too many letters today, sire. I cannot write them all.

DESSALINES: Write that one now to Beyard and bring it here to me.

[VUVAL *begins to gather up his papers, as* POPO *enters.*]

POPO: The Councillor Martel's to see you, sire. And I've done laid out your robes of state for the banquet. I put the ruby crown out, too, and polished up the scepter. It shine like a lightning rod.

DESSALINES: Let Martel in, Popo. I'll come to dress directly.

[POPO *exits.*]

DESSALINES: [*To* VUVAL.] Write that letter now, and bring it back and leave it. It must be signed tonight.

VUVAL: [*With a note of contempt.*] All right, I will.

[MARTEL *enters, very bent and old, but impressive in his simple robes of Court.*]

MARTEL: Jean Jacques, you must be tired. You've been at this all day.

DESSALINES: [*As* VUVAL *exits.*] If only we had people who would help, Martel. It seems nobody cares. Nobody wants to work.

MARTEL: That's our problem, son. [*Gently.*] But do you think it's all the people's fault? When we was slaves, lots of us thought if we was free, we'd never have to work again. And now it seems there's need of harder work than ever. The peasants wonder why.

DESSALINES: You and me work night and day, work hard. But what comes of it? It's every arm in Haiti we need. [*Wistfully.*] I have a dream for Haiti, Martel. I mean to see it through. That's why I made a law that all of us must work all day, and those who own land pay a tax that Haiti may have roads and docks and harbors fine as any country in the world. The peasants do not understand. They think I'd make them slaves again. And those to whom *I* gave the land, they call me tyrant now. [*Puzzled.*] How would they have me build, how dam the rivers, how make factories—

MARTEL: Some have no vision, son.

DESSALINES: No use to talk, I've talked till I'm hoarse, talked everywhere. I've told them of this Haiti I would make—where every black man lifts his head in pride, where there'll be schools and palaces, big armies and a fleet of boats, forts strong enough to keep the French forever from our shores. [*Confidently.*] But I'm their Liberator. The peasants know that. They know 'twas Dessalines alone that drove the whites away.

MARTEL: But there are still whites in the world, Jean Jacques. And we have need of them, as they once needed us. You've often heard me say, it's time to stop turning our guns against them now.

DESSALINES: Why?

MARTEL: We're free. Let's act like free men, ready to meet others as equals—and no longer speak of *all* white men as enemies. [*Sitting down.*] Our ports are open now, to English traders. In time, we'll open to the French. The world will drink our coffee. From them we'll buy things in return. We'll need the French.

DESSALINES: The French? The French! I never want to hear that word again, Martel. [*Slowly.*] Even now, although I'm Emperor, my back still aches from the blows they've laid upon it.

MARTEL: I know. All my years, before our freedom, I, too, never saw the sun rise but to curse it, but now free men can dream a bigger dream than mere revenge.

DESSALINES: What dream, Martel?

MARTEL: A dream of an island where not only blacks are free, but every man who comes to Haitian shores. Jean Jacques, I'm an old man. But in my old age, I dream of a world where no man hurts another. Where *all* know freedom, and black and white alike will share this earth in peace. Of such I dream, Jean Jacques.

DESSALINES: Too big a dream, Martel. If I could make Haiti a land where *black* men live in peace, I'd be content.

MARTEL: Yes, task enough, I know.

[*A light knock at the door and a woman's silvery voice calling.*]

CLAIRE: [*Outside.*] Jean Jacques, may I come in?

[*Without waiting for an answer,* CLAIRE HEUREUSE, *consort of the Emperor, enters, arrayed in white, ready for the banquet. She is a lovely mulatto with long black hair.* DESSALINES *rises smiling.*]

DESSALINES: Claire Heureuse! Come in!

[*She runs to him and kisses him lightly.*]

CLAIRE: Don't you ever get through work, you two? It's time to play. Hurry, Jean Jacques, get dressed to receive your guests. Father Martel, it's a gorgeous evening. You ought to be in the garden. The sunset is like gold. [*Glancing at the table full of papers.*] It's hot and musty in here. I'm going to run out, Jean Jacques, and get a flower for my hair. On the way, I'll stop by the banquet terrace and see if our stupid servants overlooked anything. Hurry, darling, and put on your crown. [*She pats him on the cheek as if he were a child, then turns and exits, laughing.*]

DESSALINES: Claire, my dear, take care you don't catch cold!

CLAIRE: [*Calling back.*] Oh, how funny! As hot as it is tonight.

MARTEL: [*As the door closes.*] The Empress is very beautiful, Jean Jacques.

DESSALINES: Beautiful, yes. More beautiful than any woman I have ever had.

MARTEL: The others were slave women. [*Coughing.*] They told you, I suppose, in the Lord Treasurer's office, that Azelia would not accept the pension you bestowed upon her?

DESSALINES: [*As if remembering.*] Azelia? Oh, yes! My first wife. They told me so, Martel. Poor, stupid woman! She was good ... but ... well, you know! That was before I was an Emperor. [*Defensively.*] How could I have an empress that can't read or write?

MARTEL: The Emperor himself ...

DESSALINES: [*Good humoredly.*] Can at least sign his name! Vuval has taught me that. But where is Azelia? I loved her—once. [*Musingly.*] And I remember how she stood by me in those years of battle—nursed my wounds and washed my clothes! Where is she?

MARTEL: They say she's a vendor of fruit in a village on the coast ...

DESSALINES: She could have had a job here at Court. At least a servant ...

MARTEL: My son!

DESSALINES: Or maybe, Mistress of the Linens. I wonder why she wouldn't take the pension?

MARTEL: They say she makes her own living—although a poor one — and that she looks much older than she really is.

DESSALINES: Well ... [*Then hesitating, as if loath to say more.*] Come, Martel, let's go. The day's been long and hard. I'm tired.

MARTEL: [*Rising.*] Tomorrow, son, you must take up that matter of the officers wanting a raise in pay.

DESSALINES: Yes, yes—

MARTEL: And you know there's been no word from General Gerin of late, nor Yayou, either.

DESSALINES: Angry, perhaps? I refused to grant them money from the government to go upon a journey.

MARTEL: Gerin's a dangerous man, Jean Jacques. He'll bear watching. He's been known to talk against you.

DESSALINES: I have no fear, Martel. I can take my Palace Guard and wipe up the earth with Gerin. More business for tomorrow?

MARTEL: Nothing pressing. [*Smiling.*] Except that Congo has petitioned several times to be raised from the title of Baron to that of Count.

DESSALINES: [*As they walk toward the exit.*] Damn Congo! He's had all the titles in the book already.

MARTEL: Yes, but he's about to marry Lady Celeste, and he wants to make her a Countess.

DESSALINES: Oh, well, let's make them both Princes and be done with it. Titles are easier to get than money, anyhow.

MARTEL: They're easy enough, but taxing on the brain to think them up.

DESSALINES: The French Napoleon gave himself the name of Emperor. I, too, am Emperor by my own hand. [*He snaps his fingers.*] We might as well get a little glory out of life.

MARTEL: It's not wise to want too much.

DESSALINES: Well, I've got what I want. I built this palace and I've bought myself a crown or two. I am the Emperor, and no one can make me a slave again. What was that Toussaint said about *liberty*, before he left us? How was that, now, Martel?

MARTEL: Toussaint said, "You can lay low the tree of liberty, but it'll shoot forth again from the roots."

DESSALINES: And he was right! Napoleon thought if he imprisoned one of our leaders, there'd be no other. But when Toussaint went down as Governor-General of Haiti, I came up. [*Proudly.*] I've created the first black Empire in the world, so why shouldn't I glory in it, Martel? I'm a king! I'm on top! I'm the glory of Haiti!

MARTEL: The glory of Haiti lies in no one man, Jean Jacques.

DESSALINES: Where does it lie?

MARTEL: In the people's love for freedom.

DESSALINES: Too much freedom—if they no longer obey me, their liberator; I'm their freedom—and this Court's their glory.

MARTEL: Glory is a passing thing, Jean Jacques! Take care!

DESSALINES: [*Laughing.*] This sword takes care of me, Martel. I still can use it!

MARTEL: Swords won't solve all problems, my son.

DESSALINES: No, but they solve a-plenty. Come on, let's dress for the banquet. [*He takes the old man's arm and they exit.*]

[VUVAL *enters, followed by* STENIO, *approaching the table with a sheaf of papers.* VUVAL *addresses his friend.*]

VUVAL: If the Emperor could read, he'd never sign most of the letters I write for him.

STENIO: [*Laughing.*] A dumb clown! He thinks by letting Claire Heureuse read them over for him, he's safe, not knowing she was on our side before she ever met "His Majesty."

VUVAL: A true mulatto, Claire.

STENIO: That's why we brought her back from Paris. I knew he'd fall for her. A mulatto Empress in a black Empire! That's enough to make him the laughing stock of the peasantry.

VUVAL: The fool!

STENIO: His Majesty's head is rather thick.

VUVAL: But not too thick to be broken. If he knew six garrisons in the South revolted against him this morning, he wouldn't sit so pompously beneath his crown tonight.

STENIO: You've had word from Gerin.

VUVAL: Yes, and from General Yayou, too. Port-au-Prince has gone over to the rebels. The mulattos are in full charge.

STENIO: An end of this black rule at last! Maybe now I can get off to Paris again.

VUVAL: Paris! *La Ville Lumiere!* Oh, how I long to see that city of lights, Stenio. It's so damn dark here.

STENIO: In more ways than one, Vuval.

VUVAL: But it won't be long now until I'm out of Haiti. Tonight, we'll flee the Court, while His Majesty wears his crown and stuffs himself with food.

STENIO: Good! As for me, that's not soon enough. What are your plans for Claire?

VUVAL: She's coming by carriage tomorrow. Her jewels are packed except for a few cheap baubles she'll wear tonight. But it's a ten-hour ride to the coast after dark. You'd better order your men ready to start at once, Stenio. And you, too, go ahead. I'll catch you. I've a splendid horse.

STENIO: Do you suppose the Black Napoleon will miss me from his banquet table? If not, I'll order the Guard away shortly.

VUVAL: I'll say you're ill of fever, if he asks.

STENIO: Yes, the fever of being bored.

[POPO *enters. The mulattos look startled. The Negro stops near the door on seeing them.*]

POPO: The Emperor sent me for his letters.

VUVAL: [*Pushing them across the table.*] There they are. I wish the Emperor would learn to write.

POPO: [*Seriously.*] He will, some day.

VUVAL: [*Sarcastically.*] Perhaps you, too, "Count" Popo.

STENIO: [*Lightly.*] Don't be absurd, Vuval. Such poetic fancies on your part! My! My! Come, let's drink a bit of champagne in the garden.

[VUVAL *and* STENIO *exit, leaving* POPO *with the letters in his hand. Slowly and bitterly,* POPO *begins to tear the letters into bits as his eyes follow the two mulattos.*]

CURTAIN

SCENE 2

TIME: *Immediately following Scene 1.*

PLACE: *A covered terrace, consisting of two levels, whose arched portals are open to the sky. It is early evening. The air is still rosy with sunset. On the upper level, a raised banquet table stretches across the width of the entire terrace, its white linen cloths falling to the floor. At either side, steps to the table. The terrace is not yet lighted, but on the table in silhouette against the evening sky may be seen tall silver candle sticks and great bowls of fruit, pineapples, mangoes, grapes, coconuts, bananas, pomegranates, plums. There are goblets for wine; and china, crystal, and silver.*

AT RISE: *Servants move about arranging the table, and two old women in front of the table, on the floor level, are preparing flowers, putting the fruit into bowls, polishing silver.*

FIRST OLD WOMAN: It's getting mighty dark here. How come we can't have no light to work by?

SECOND OLD WOMAN: You know the Emperor don't believe in wasting candles. He don't believe in wasting nothing.

FIRST OLD WOMAN: Tight-fisted, if you ask me! If I had all the money he's got, I'd fling gold to winds every time I kicked up my heels.

SECOND OLD WOMAN: At your age, still talking about kicking up your heels!

FIRST OLD WOMAN: Huh! I might be old, but my heart ain't got no wrinkles.

SECOND OLD WOMAN: Well, I hope the day'll come when we all can have a good time, and nothing else. Look like I work as hard now that I'm free as I did before.

FIRST OLD WOMAN: Well, the Emperor says he want to make Haiti rich—and just as grand as when it belonged to the white folks.

SECOND OLD WOMAN: Huh! Only thing grand I see around

here is that hussy of a new wife he's got and all them diamonds she's a-wearing.

FIRST OLD WOMAN: Shsss! You better stop talking that a-way about the Empress. Lady Celeste'll hear you and out you'll go.

SECOND OLD WOMAN: Lady my eye! Housekeeper, that's what Celeste is!

FIRST OLD WOMAN: Anyhow, Baron Congo's crazy about her. They about to get married.

SECOND OLD WOMAN: Congo's a baron, and she's a Lady. If he marry her, what title do that give 'em both?

FIRST OLD WOMAN: What you mean, 'em both? Celeste gonna run him just like she do everything else, and he'll be a Mr. Lady Baron, that's what! [*Getting to work.*] Hush, here she comes!

[*Enter* CELESTE.]

CELESTE: Hurry up, you servants, and put the flowers on the table. We've got to clear things up now. The guests'll soon be arriving.

FIRST OLD WOMAN: We's hurrying

SECOND OLD WOMAN: We sure are.

CELESTE: [*Calling.*] Lady Lulu! Oh, Lady Lulu! [*To the Servants.*] Have any of you-all seen the High Grand Keeper of the Linens? There's no napkins on this table yet.

SERVANT: [*Behind table.*] Here she comes, now.

[Enter LULU, *well gowned, carrying a pile of napkins.*]

LULU: I'll have you know, Lady Celeste, that you don't need to yell for me like as if I were a dog.

CELESTE: Why, Lady Lulu, I weren't yelling, were I?

LULU: [*Still peeved.*] Well, even if you is engaged to a Baron, I don't have to stand it. My son's a Grand Alimony, hisself.

CELESTE: What's that, Lulu? I didn't know Pierre were anything but the Chief Bugle-Blower. I remember, he always wanted a bugle when he were a little slave.

LULU: [*Placing the napkins.*] Don't bring up them distasteful epochs, Celeste.

CELESTE: Well, we was slaves, once, wasn't we, Lulu?

LULU: And still half-is! I'm gonna give that Jean Jacques a piece of my mind soon, tired as I is o' working in this palace. I want to take myself a trip to Port-au-Prince and look up a new husband!

CELESTE: A husband?

LULU: Yes, a new husband. These men around here's too banana-bellied to suit my taste.

CELESTE: I bet you're sorry you ain't got a man like Congo. He's all right.

LULU: Huh! I could've had Congo long ago, if I'd a-wanted him.

CELESTE: [*Angered.*] Lulu, I'll turn that table over getting to you if you don't hush. You know Congo's never even looked at you.

LULU: [*Starting around the table.*] Just hold your horses, *Lady* Celeste, till I get down to your level.

FIRST OLD WOMAN: [*Warningly.*] You better shsss! Here comes the Empress.

CELESTE: [*Flustered.*] Oh! If you're through your work, you-all just gather up your things and get out of the way. The Empress wants to inspect the table. I guess.

[CLAIRE *enters, accompanied by* VUVAL. *The servants exit gradually, scowling.* LULU *follows them.*]

CLAIRE: This really is a charming terrace, isn't it, Vuval? Such a lush background. Those palm trees and the early evening stars? [*Looking around.*] But why must these serving women be forever getting things ready? Lady Celeste, you! [CELESTE *jumps.*] Can't you manage to prepare a banquet table in less than a week?

CELESTE: I-I-I-started this morning, Empress.

CLAIRE: [*Sighing.*] Oh, well. I suppose I must remember I'm not in Paris where service is an art. [*Dismissing her.*] Go on, Celeste, I'll look about alone.

[*Exit* CELESTE.]

VUVAL: I can hardly wait to see Paris with you, Claire. You've been there so often and know it so well. You can show me everything—the Louvre, the Bois, the Odeon—all the places the great writers write about.

CLAIRE: Of course!

VUVAL: Do you suppose I'll ever be a great writer, Claire?

CLAIRE: [*Lightly.*] If you write enough letters for the Emperor, you might perhaps develop.

VUVAL: Don't joke about it, Claire. It's too near my heart. [*Passionately.*] Darling, there're just two things I want—you, and to write poems as beautiful as Andre Chenier's.

CLAIRE: You have me, dear. Only don't put your hands on my white gown. They may have ink on them. And I have to look nice tonight—for this—am I safe in saying—the last supper at this stupid Palace.

VUVAL: No doubt our last, Claire—for the mulattos have taken over Port-au-Prince, and Gerin the forts to the north! And listen! Should a messenger arrive with news of the uprising for the Emperor, I have given orders to intercept it. Let Dessalines eat, drink and be merry once without being bothered. In the meantime, Stenio can reach the coast.

CLAIRE: Has he gone?

VUVAL: Yes, he's well started. And while you entertain your royal husband at the table, I'll slip away from the banquet early and get off, too. On the way, I'll persuade the garrison commanders to side with us. That ought to be easy, for I've been writing the officers vulgar letters lately, calling them all sorts of names, as you know, and the Emperor in his ignorance has signed them—thinking they're what he's dictated.

CLAIRE: Clever, Vuval.

VUVAL: Now the generals think Dessalines has turned against them. No wonder they're revolting.

CLAIRE: No wonder!

VUVAL: Whereas, on the other hand, the peasants are sure they are going to starve if they don't get a change of government. [*Pleased.*] You see, darling, everything's all set. And early tomorrow, you'll come on to the coast with your attendants. We'll have a boat waiting. It's perfectly planned.

CLAIRE: Most cleverly arranged, Vuval. I didn't know you were such a strategist.

VUVAL: Will you be glad to get away from Haiti, darling?

CLAIRE: Will I be glad? I hate these ignorant people and their drums. I can't stand those drums every night, beating, beating, back there in the hills.

VUVAL: And Jean Jacques?

CLAIRE: That fool, my husband? Vuval, darling, often I can't bear to look at him. He's so common and so—so boorish! And his back! [*With a little cry.*] I cannot bear to touch his back! It's all covered with welts! Ugh! Marks of a rebellious slave! And yet he thinks I love him! Bah!

VUVAL: You've played your part well, Claire.

CLAIRE: I had to. My people were ruined, as were yours. We had to get back our land, and our money. Now, my brother's put away a half-million francs in a Bordeaux bank.

VUVAL: As have my cousin, Beyard, and I.

CLAIRE: We'll be safe now, you and I—married in Paris. So you see why I've played my part well! [*Laughing.*] I've always wanted to be an actress, anyway. Perhaps to be Juliet.

VUVAL: And I your Romeo! Sweet Claire! [*Remembering something.*] But, say, darling, look! With all I've had to do today, I still found time to compose a poem for you.

CLAIRE: Oh, read it to me.

VUVAL: *[Taking a manuscript from his pocket.*] Here it is! Listen! [*Reading.*]

TO THE VENUS OF THE ANTILLES
CLAIRE HEUREUSE

Your eyes are twin stars
In a snow-white face,
Your lips are two rubies
Loveliness has traced,
Your body a flower
Of marble grace—
Oh, Venus strayed
Into a savage palace!

Do you like it, Claire?

CLAIRE: [*Laughing.*] I like that part about the "savage palace." But it's so short! Is that all you could think to say about me, Vuval?

VUVAL: Claire, darling! No pen could write all the lovely things I think of you.

CLAIRE: Dear boy! Give me the poem to keep.

VUVAL: Of course! [*Handing her the manuscript.*] And my heart as well!

CLAIRE: Someone's coming.

[*Voices are heard approaching.*]

Let us go into the garden a moment, where we can be alone. I've still to get a flower for my hair, my sweet.

[*Exit* CLAIRE *and* VUVAL, *as* MARTEL *and* POPO *enter from the other side.*]

MARTEL: In times like these, if Toussaint l'Ouverture were only here to guide us, Popo! Napoleon's heart must be like stone to trick so great a leader away from his people.

POPO: I wish Toussaint was here. It looks like Jean Jacques don't know how to run things very well. I wish I could help him.

MARTEL: Jean Jacques is a mighty soldier, Popo, and a brave man. He's not a statesman. But he's our friend, and we love him—so we must help him.

POPO: We must, Father Martel.

MARTEL: As you protect his body, I'll try to guard his mind. [*Despairingly.*] But sometimes I don't know, Popo, I don't know. [*Looking upward through the open portals.*] Haiti, land that should be so happy, grown instead so sad! Land of golden moonlight and silver rain, bright birds, and brighter sun, perfumed breezes and a sea so green, hills of great woods and valleys of sweet earth. Why can't it be a happy land? So many years of struggle, and still vile intrigue binds our wings like spider webs. Oh, most unhappy Haiti! When the drums beat in the hills at night, mournful and heart-breaking, I can feel your sorrow. No wonder the Empress hates your drums! Where is their power now to make the gods smile upon this troubled island?

POPO: Don't you think, Father Martel, Jean Jacques ought to let the Papaloi come back into Court?

MARTEL: Jean Jacques doesn't believe in voodoo, son. You know that.

POPO: I know, but our people do—and we can't change them overnight. Now the voodoo doctors are mumbling against the Emperor and stirring up the peasants.

MARTEL: And the mulattos are angry because he has designated Haiti officially as the *Black* Empire. They don't like the word *Black.*

POPO: Their mothers were black.

MARTEL: Yes, it's true! Still, they stand apart and claim their white blood makes them better. But what troubles me most, Popo, is why there's been no news from the coast of late. Two days ago, I sent Xavier to see what's happening. He's due back, but he hasn't come.

POPO: Do you think something's happened to Xavier?

MARTEL: I don't know. Be alert, son. All's not well, though it would seem so here at the Palace. [*In a lighter tone.*] But come now! Let's look carefully at the table to see if it's properly set. The Emperor is most particular about these occasions of state. And this one must be perfect—for tomorrow I shall warn him that with the treasury in its present state, the Court cannot often afford such lavishness.

POPO: Even if we go back to eating dried fish and yams, I'll stick by him. Jean Jacques has been a friend of mine ever since we were slaves together.

[*Enter* CELESTE *and* CONGO. CONGO *is carrying a huge pot of flowers.*]

CELESTE: Put it down right there in the center, so's the air'll smell sweet.

CONGO: [*Grunting as he stoops.*] Huh!

CELESTE: And stop grunting! What'd you come up here mooning at me for, anyhow, in my busiest hours?

CONGO: [*Standing up, resplendent in a nile-green uniform with golden tassels on the shoulders.*] I come to show you my new suit, Celeste. This here makes twelve brand new uniforms I bought. How do you like it?

CELESTE: [*Critically.*] I'd like it better if it had more gold on it. [*Approaching* MARTEL *and* POPO.] Good evening, Father Martel. How are you tonight?

MARTEL: Only fair, daughter, only fair.

CELESTE: I hope you got over that little spell of indigestion yesterday so's you can eat this evening well. This is gonna *be* a banquet. And no fooling! We got a dozen roast sheep out there in the ovens, sweet as butter. I wish you could smell 'em.

CONGO: [*Loosening a buckle.*] Um-hum! Lemme loosen up this belt.

[MARTEL *and* POPO *laugh as they exit.*]

CELESTE: Lemme go get dressed, as befits a lady. All them Duchesses are gonna be here tonight, so I wants to look grand, too. Come on, Baron.

CONGO: Gimme a little kiss first.

CELESTE: Can't you wait till we get married?

CONGO: Not for just a kiss.

CELESTE: [*Kissing him.*] Here!

CONGO: It tastes sweeter'n a honey bee.

CELESTE: [*As she starts off.*] Wait till you feel the stinger!

CONGO: [*Running after her.*] Um-huh! Gimme another one.

CELESTE: Come on, man! The guests are arriving. And the orchestra's playing in the throne room. I want to see the excitement. Besides, I'm saving up one for you tonight—if you're around to get it.

[CELESTE *exits as the two old women and other servants enter.*]

CONGO: Aw, come back here and gimme a double kiss now.

CELESTE: [*Calling off stage.*] By and by, baby, by and by.

[CONGO *exits.*]

FIRST OLD WOMAN: The Throne Room's just full o' high falutin' hens and prancin' cocks a-cacklin' and crowin' all over the place.

SECOND OLD WOMAN: [*As she lights the candles.*] Some of 'em's gonna crow their last in a little while, too. Folks is gettin' tired o' seeing some people have everything and the rest of us workin' like dogs. I don't know what the Emperor's thinking about. Why ain't he give me no velvet dress? I'm human!

FIRST OLD WOMAN: I reckon we can't all be Duchesses, and such.

SECOND OLD WOMAN: Well, if we can't be Duchesses, we at least ought to be let alone to dance obeah if we wants to, and have our voodoo here in the Court. Legba's gonna curse Dessalines yet, you watch.

FIRST OLD WOMAN: That hussy of a Claire Heureuse went and brought a Catholic priest over from France for herself—and a French one at that.

SECOND OLD WOMAN: Voodoo was good enough for her mammy. It ought to do for her.

[*Softly, in the distance, the music of an orchestra playing European airs is heard.*]

FIRST OLD WOMAN: Lawsy! We better hurry up. They done opened the big doors! I reckon the procession's forming to march to the tables. [*To a ragged boy.*] Boy, scramble up there and light that big oil lamp, over His Majesty's head. He likes plenty light.

[*The boy lights the hanging lantern, and the terrace is flooded with golden light. Noise and music afar—then a bugle call in the distance. The old women leave, as three butlers, in livery, enter and take places, one at each end of the table near the head of the steps, the other behind the tall chair reserved for the Emperor. On the lower terrace, a* FLOWER GIRL *enters scattering rose leaves. There is a roll of drums;* PIERRE, *a big boy now, and Chief Bugler, enters, crosses the stage, turns with military precision and blows a blast on his horn. The orchestra begins a march.* JOSEF, *the Grand Marshal of the Palace, takes his place at the far end of the table. With a long parchment list in hand, he announces, in a loud voice.*]

JOSEF: Hear ye! Hear ye! Hear ye! The Guests of the Emperor bidden to a Banquet of State in honor of His Majesty.

[*The band continues, the* GRAND MARSHAL *reads from his list, and in the order named, the guests enter from the lower terrace, strutting grandly across it to stand in front of the table, waiting there before mounting the steps until the* EMPEROR *himself arrives. Their costumes are gorgeously grotesque copies of various European Court styles and periods, but giving in the ensemble an effect of gay and savage splendor. Some of the guests are enjoying themselves immensely, but others are obviously uncomfortable in their regal clothes, while many are gnarled old peasants, too bent by slavery to even appear at ease in Parisian finery.* JOSEF *reads, and in the order called, marching gaily to the music, the Royalty of Haiti enter.*]

The Duke and Duchess of Dondon.
Count and Countess Claudel de Zouba.
General Abelard and Madame la Pompeuse.
Lord and Lady Tountemonde.
Baron Antoine and the Baroness.
The Duke of Marmelade and Countess Louise Camille Chaucune Nereide.
The Chevalier of Gonaives and the Chevalieress.
The Governor of Milot, Sir Emil Tuce with Madame the Duchess of Limonade.
Major General Joli-Bois and Lady Fifi Beauregard.
The Most High Grand Keeper of Records and Seals, Count Vuval.
Major General Dembu and Lady Lulu Minette.
The Duke de Savanne-a-Roches and Duchess Coloma Lutetia Floreal.
Grand Duke Mars and Princess Dianne.
Baron Congo with Lady Celeste.
The Grand Chief Treasurer of the Realm, His Highness Lord Bobo Levy.
Duchess Suzanne Roseide and her husband.

[*As the last couple enter the terrace and line up before the table, the music ceases. There is a moment of silence, giggling, and whispering. Several late arrivals sneak in, unannounced.*]

LORD BOBO: [*Sneezing.*] A-choo!

LULU: Your Highness, Lord Bobo, why don't you use better snuff?

BOBO: It ain't my snuff, Lady Lulu. It's that loud perfume some of you-all ladies uses, done got in my nostrils.

DUKE MARMELADE: This collar's mighty near choking me to death!

COUNTESS NEREIDE: But it looks gorgeous, Duke.

DUCHESS OF LIMONADE: Lawd! [*Picking up her feet in pain.*] I'm sure gonna take off these shoes soon as I get myself back home. They ain't my size.

COUNT CLAUDEL: I'm tired of this business, coming here all dressed up every time I turn around.

CELESTE: Shsss! Stop all that giggling and talking! You know the Emperor like silence when he enters.

LORD BOBO: [*After a moment of stillness.*] A-choo!

[*Loud giggling from the women.*]

BARON ANTOINE: That were sure good wine they just passed out in the throne room, huh, Baroness?

BARONESS ANTOINE: It were champagne—but I wants to *eat,* now.

GRAND DUKE MARS: That'll be some time off yet, Baroness. The Emperor serves in courses.

PRINCESS DIANNE: A little bit at a time.

CELESTE: First course is always just tidbits to give you an appetite.

DUCHESS SUZANNE: I got a appetite already!

CONGO: I wants to taste that roast goat.

LADY FIFI: Me, too, Baron.

[*The Lady in Waiting to the Empress enters on the upper terrace and proceeds to arrange Her Majesty's seat. The Bugle Boy blows a mighty blast as the drums roll.*]

JOSEF: The Court arrives!

[*Another roll of the drums.*]

His Majesty, the Emperor, First Liberator of the blacks and Chief Ruler of Haiti, Jean Jacques Dessalines.

[*Preceded by two pages,* DESSALINES *enters on the upper terrace and strides to his chair. He is followed by* MARTEL *in his robes of state, and by* POPO *carrying the royal scepter. Immediately behind comes the* EMPRESS CLAIRE HEUREUSE, *accompanied by the* LADIES OF THE PRESENCE. *All the guests turn and bow low as they enter. The* EMPEROR *and* EMPRESS *take their seats. An attendant offers the Emperor his crown on a silken cushion;* POPO *presents the royal scepter. A great cheer arises.*]

VOICES: Hail the Emperor! Hail Dessalines! Hail! Hail! Hail!

[*The cymbals clash and the drums roll. The band strikes up a lively march. The guests file around both ends of the table to their respective seats. At a trumpet blast from* PIERRE, *they sit down simultaneously, a glittering row of velvet busts and dark, genial faces behind the banquet table with its crystal and silver.*]

LULU: [*Proudly to* CONGO.] That's my son blowing that bugle! You hear him?

CELESTE: Honey, your son ought to learn a new tune! That one hurts my ears.

[*As the butlers pass, filling glasses, the orchestra begins to play a syncopated melody, and a dozen dancing girls whirl across the lower terrace into the empty space before the table. They are wearing anklets of beaten gold; their bushy hair is adorned with precious stones. As they dance before the Court, a weird drum beat becomes audible in the music, gradually louder and more insistent, until finally it drowns out all the other instruments. To the African rhythm of drums alone, a male dancer enters, feathered and painted like a voodoo god. The girls sink to the floor as the tall, godlike one does his dance of the jungle, fierce, provocative, and horrible. Suddenly, the* EMPRESS *turns her head, and covers her ears with her hands. She calls to* DESSALINES.]

CLAIRE: [*Appealingly.*] Jean Jacques! Jean Jacques!

[DESSALINES *rises, raising his hand in command.*]

DESSALINES: [*Loudly.*] Stop it! Stop! The Empress don't like drums! Stop it, I say!

[*The music ceases—but no sooner are the drums on the terrace silent than another drum, far off in the hills, carries on their beat.*]

[DESSALINES *cries frantically.*] Stop them drums, I say. Stop them!

POPO: They are stopped, sire. That drum we hear now's away off in the hills someplace.

DESSALINES: I don't care where it is! Order it stopped! My Empress don't like drums! Vuval!

VUVAL: [*Rising.*] I will send someone to see if can it be located.

[*He leaves the table and confers with one of the attendants. The attendant exits. But the drum is never silent during the rest of the scene. It's monotonous beat continues, as if calling for one knows not what.*]

DESSALINES: [*Who has remained standing, begins to berate his guests.*] Drums in the Court! The idea! Suppose we had guests from abroad, what would they think of us? They'd think we were all savages, that's what. Savages! Here I am, trying to build a civilization in Haiti good as any the whites have in their lands. Trying to set up a Court equal to any Court in Europe. And what do I find—voodoo drums in the banquet hall! Who gave orders for that? [*Ominously.*] Whoever did, will suffer. I'll find out tomorrow. We ought to be done with voodoo drums—all of us! But listen! [*He pauses as the distant drum continues its throbbing beat.*] The peasants, up all night playing drums! And the fields only half productive. But not only the peasants are to blame. You. You Lords and Ladies, Dukes and Counts, are to blame, too. I give you land, and you neglect to work it. Then when crops are scanty, you try to bully your taxes out of the people, taking back their hard earned money to pay me what the Treasury demands. But that's not what I want. And you're not helping Haiti. The land must produce its own riches. Our peasants must work the land, and make it fertile. Being free frees no man from working. We do have to work. And I'm tired of telling you! I'm tired of sending out orders! I've made up my mind to tell my soldiers to *make* you work from now on!

VOICES: What? Do you hear that! Huh! I'm no slave!

DESSALINES: [*Thunderously.*] Silence! Listen to me! We've fought to make Haiti free! I'm going to keep you free—the French'll never return. I'm going to make a great country, trading with all the world—wealthy, and full of plenty to eat. You're going to help me. [*Pausing.*] Long ago I dreamed a dream that I want to carry through. If you won't help me willingly—then I'll make you. I'm the Emperor! Your Liberator! Jean Jacques Dessalines, who came up from a slave hut to a palace, to a crown on my head and an ermine cape covering my scars, to this jeweled scepter in my hand. I did it by fighting. The whites called me the Tiger! [*Fiercely.*] If I have to be a tiger to you, too—I will be! [*Pausing—then lifting his glass.*] Drink to your Emperor! [*Bellowing an imperious command.*] Drink!

[*The frightened guests leap to their feet, raising their glasses in trembling hands.*]

VOICES: [*As they drink.*] To the Emperor!

DESSALINES: [*Calmly.*] Now let there be music and dancing—violins, not drums!

[*The orchestra plays a minuet as* DESSALINES *resumes his seat. The guests come down from the table and begin to dance with knees still shaking. They are awkward at the minuet, and some pitifully grotesque in their attempts at European graces. Some few of the older folks remain in their places at the table.* VUVAL *disappears. Gradually the dancers dance offstage out of sight at either end of the terrace as the* EMPEROR *talks with the* EMPRESS.]

Claire, darling, don't you like the wine? And this caviar? I ordered it all the way from Russia especially for you.

CLAIRE: I like you better than wine, Jean Jacques! You're so strong, so wonderful and wise.

DESSALINES: Maybe not so wise. [*Boastfully.*] But nobody'll get the best of me fighting.

CLAIRE: I'm sure they won't, dear.

DESSALINES: Why, Napoleon ordered me shot once—all the way from France—but I'm not dead yet! [*He laughs.*]

CLAIRE: Not at all, darling.

DESSALINES: But plenty of Napoleon's soldiers are buried right here on Haitian soil, defeated by my troops. Bonaparte rules France—but I rule Haiti!

CLAIRE: And nobly!

DESSALINES: Oh, I know I'm nothing much but a fighter, Claire. [*Determinedly.*] But if fighting's the only way to get things done—then I'll get 'em done!

CLAIRE: You've accomplished such a lot already, dear! And with what ignorant people! Every jewel in that crown's a testimony to your greatness. Why, your scepter holds a realm of power. [*She rubs her fingers over the scepter, purposely touching his hand.*] What beautiful rings you have on your fingers tonight, darling. Some of them I've never seen before. That emerald! [*Lifting his hand.*] Oh, how lovely! Why, it's green as the sea at dawn! Please, let me try it on.

DESSALINES: [*Taking off his huge emerald and slipping it on her finger.*] It's too big for you, dear?

CLAIRE: Not much. Let me keep it tonight, darling. I won't let it slip off. It's too lovely!

DESSALINES: Woman always want to play. [*Rising and offering his arm.*] Shall we dance?

CLAIRE: Jean Jacques, you know you haven't learned the minuet. You'll step on my slippers.

DESSALINES: You're right, darling. [*Sitting down again.*] I'm clumsy as an ox. Let's just sit here and drink our wine.

[*A clatter of horses' hoofs is heard outside.*]

What's that? Who could that be riding into the courtyard at this time of night? Popo, go see!

[POPO *exits.* MARTEL *rises and looks over the edge of the terrace. The distant drum is ever louder in the darkness.* CLAIRE *toys nervously with the emerald on her finger.*]

CLAIRE: Perhaps it's some distant guest arriving tardily.

DESSALINES: I hope it's nobody bringing a message. I've ha enough to worry my head today. Now, I just want to enjc you tonight, and this wine, and the cool breeze. I'm tire honey.

CLAIRE: [*As loud voices are heard without.*] Don't worry wi anything more this evening, darling, please. Refuse receive whatever it is.

DESSALINES: I hope I can, but it may be something pressin [*As* POPO *enters hurriedly.*] What is it, Popo?

[POPO, *his eyes bulging, whispers to the* EMPEROR. DESSALIN *leaps up so quickly he overturns his wine, it runs like blo across the banquet cloth.*]

Order my horse! Bring him to the terrace. Tell Stenio report to me at once with my garrison ready to march.

[POPO *exits, as* DESSALINES *addresses the Treasurer,* LOR BOBO, who sits nearby.]

Lord Bobo, are your vaults locked?

LORD BOBO: Of course, Your Majesty!

DESSALINES: Then give me the keys to the gold.

LORD BOBO: [*Rising, trembling.*] Of course, Your Majesty. Bu but, but — [*He gives* DESSALINES *a huge key fastened to his belt.*

DESSALINES: Martel, remain here! Continue the banquet. I' going to the coast.

MARTEL: But what is it, Jean Jacques? What's happened?

DESSALINES: Word from Archaie that the peasants ha revolted. They're burning the crops, and Yayou's soldie have joined them. That mulatto Gerin's at the bottom this. But I'll stop it. Every man will return to his post, I'll wipe them off the face of the earth!

MARTEL: Take care, son, take care!

[*The remaining guests quickly leave the table and exit hurried*

Sounds of departing carriages without. The servants, too, have disappeared. Only PIERRE, *the bugler, remains.*]

POPO: [*Returning.*] Your horse is ready, sire, and mine.

PIERRE: [*Approaching.*] Emperor, I ride with you, too.

DESSALINES: You'll have to ride fast, Pierre. [*To* POPO.] Popo, take the scepter, and my crown. Bring me my sword. Is the guard forming?

POPO: General Stenio is missing, sire! And the guards are gone.

DESSALINES: [*Roaring.*] What?

POPO: Stenio left word that he precedes you to the Port. Vuval's gone, too.

DESSALINES: The insubordinate rascals! Who gave orders for them to leave? I'll bring them back in chains! Quick! My sword!

[POPO *exits.* DESSALINES *hangs his ermine cape on the back of a chair.* CLAIRE *takes it. He addresses* MARTEL.]

Martel, the Tiger rides again.

MARTEL: Would it not be wise, Jean Jacques, to send some trusted friend ahead to see what conditions are? And would it not be best to pick your soldiers carefully for such a trip?

DESSALINES: No soldier can ride as fast as me, Martel. Besides, I'm commander of all the troops in Haiti, and if any have been misled by their rascally commanders, they've but to hear my voice to call me Chief again. I'm going directly to the headquarters of Gerin and take charge. Then I'll subdue the peasants quickly enough. [*To his wife.*] Claire, go to your rooms. I'll be back within a day, no doubt. Or certainly by the second dawn.

CLAIRE: [*With a peculiar intonation.*] Good luck, Your Majesty. And goodbye.

DESSALINES: Not goodbye, darling. Merely goodnight. [*He kisses her. She draws back slightly. As she exits, she wipes his kiss away.* DESSALINES *addresses* MARTEL.] An Emperor has his troubles, too, same as a slave.

MARTEL: It's not wise to ever be a master, Jean Jacques.

DESSALINES: What do you mean, Martel? A master?

MARTEL: It is not wise.

POPO: [*Entering.*] Here, sire, is your hat! Your sword!

DESSALINES: [*Putting on a plumed helmet and fastening his swor at his belt.*] Somebody's got to govern, Martel. The peasant can't rule themselves.

MARTEL: Some day they can, son.

DESSALINES: Until that day comes, then, I'll be their ruler. Th French used a whip! [*Brandishing his sabre.*] I use a sword [*Exit* DESSALINES, POPO, *and* PIERRE.]

MARTEL: [*Looking after them.*] Take care! Take care, Jea Jacques! [*He peers over the terrace as the clatter of horses' hoof dies down the road.*] Oh, son, beware! Beware!

[*The far-off beating of a voodoo drum fills the silence. The ol man stands alone, facing the stars. Behind him is the cluttere banquet table where wine has spilled like blood. Slowly,* MARTE *turns and begins to blow out the tapers.*]

We might as well save candles, I reckon.

CURTAIN

ACT THREE

TIME: *The following day. Early afternoon.*

PLACE: *The quay in a little fishing village on the coast. At left, th side of a gray stucco building with a wign hanging in the corne* HEADQUARTERS, ROYAL HAITIAN ARMY, Division of th South. *On the wall, below, a tattered poster advertising rum Rear, the low stone wall of an embankment with steps, cente leading up to a seawall, and down on the other side to the beach Beyond the wall may be seen the tops of sails belonging t fishing boats in the harbor. Hanging from a palm tree, a larg fishing net is drying in the sun. At the foot of the wall, on the ground, barefoot market women have spread their wares in the shade of the embankment; mangoes, melons, yams, oranges, limes, sugarcane, cocoanuts, little piles of red peppers. One vendor has thread, thimbles, and other trinkets. The women, in bright headcloths, sit with their backs to the wall.*

AT RISE: *The market women are laughing and chattering among themselves. Some dip snuff. One smokes a pipe.*

MANGO VENDOR: It sho' is a fine day.

PEPPER VENDOR: Yes, indeedy!

COCOANUT VENDOR: I likes weather like this myself.

MELON VENDOR: You can smell the sea when the breeze blow. Don't it smell good?

THREAD VENDOR: Sho' do!

[*Two fishermen enter.*]

TALL FISHERMAN: Hello, ladies dressed so fine! Who's got a good man on her mind?

MANGO VENDOR: Where's the good man at?

TALL FISHERMAN: Right here! Ain't you got a mango for me?

SHORT FISHERMAN: [*To the women.*] Ask him what he's got for you?

MANGO VENDOR: [*Laughing.*] My mangoes are too sweet for men I don't love. [*Holding up a pretty one.*] But I'll sell you one for a sou.

TALL FISHERMAN: You'll want one of my fish some of these days. [*Mounting the seawall.*] My brother's boat's on the horizon now, just loaded down with nice sweet fish.

COCOANUT VENDOR: [*Tossing her head.*] You men always think we womens want something you got. We does very well by ourselves.

SHORT FISHERMAN: Until night comes.

THREAD VENDOR: Huh! If it wasn't for us womens, half the time you mens wouldn't eat. Storm comes, you don't catch nary fish, and we have to feed you.

TALL FISHERMAN: We supposed to eat! Ain't we worth our board and keep?

THREAD VENDOR: I gets tired feeding you-all myself. Every time I turn around, looks like my husband's asking me for ten sous. Ten sous for this, or for that — tobacco, rum, snuff, always something he wants.

MANGO VENDOR: Wouldn't be a man if he didn't.

THREAD VENDOR: Yes, but I gets tired. It looks like all an apron does is work for pants.

SHORT FISHERMAN: Suppose you didn't have us men to work for, then what'd you do?

THREAD VENDOR: Do without.

SHORT FISHERMAN: [*Strutting.*] My woman says she can't do without me.

COCOANUT VENDOR: She must be weak.

MANGO VENDOR: Don't pay no attention to them mens. They's always lying. Here, have a fruit. [*She tosses them each a mango.*] And go on, stop pestering us.

TALL FISHERMAN: I'll see you later, sweetheart, when my ship comes in.

MANGO VENDOR: I hope it ain't no row-boat!

SHORT FISHERMAN: If I got any nice sea-crabs clawing around in the bottom of the boat, I'll give 'em to you when I come back.

THREAD VENDOR: I don't like crabs myself. Rather have squids.

MANGO VENDOR: I'll take the crabs and don't pass me by, neither. I'll be sitting here till sundown.

[*The fishermen exit over the seawall toward the water.*]

MELON VENDOR: Sweet mens! I love 'em! Say, who's still got

the same husband they had when they was freed?

YAM VENDOR: Lord, chile, I done had me six husbands since then!

MANGO VENDOR: What's the use of being free if you can't change husbands?

PEPPER VENDOR: [*A very old woman.*] Well, I's still got the man I always had.

THREAD VENDOR: Aw, Mama Sallie, you know you too old to change.

PEPPER VENDOR: [*Snappily.*] I warn't but seventy when the freedom broke out. What's the matter with you?

[*Enter two children who make a purchase of some sticks of sugarcane, then exit, sucking the cane.*]

MANGO VENDOR: A man is like a palm-leaf fan to me. When I feels the need, I picks one up, and when I cools off, I put him down.

YAM VENDOR: And me, too.

COCOANUT VENDOR: Well, it ain't moral, the priest says.

MANGO VENDOR: That's right, Zoune, you belongs to them white folks' church, don't you? How long you been in there?

COCOANUT VENDOR: [*Righteously.*] Since before the freedom. My master made all his slaves join the Catholic Church. He said if we didn't, he'd beat the stuffings out of us. I been going to mass mighty near as long as I been colored.

YAM VENDOR: That's been a long time!

THREAD VENDOR: Then how come I seed you at the last voodoo dance, just a-calling on Legba?

COCOANUT VENDOR: Oh, I believes in voodoo, too. Who says I didn't? Might as well believe in all kinds of gods, then if one fails you, you got another one to kinder help out.

MELON VENDOR: Right!

[*Enter an old woman, bearing a tray of bananas on her head. As she turns around, one recognizes* AZELIA.]

AZELIA: Bananas! Bananas! Who wants to buy bananas?

THREAD VENDOR: [*As* AZELIA *stoops wearily and is about to sit down.*] Here! You don't pay no taxes for a public stall. Move on!

YAM VENDOR: Yes, sister, move on! We pays to have our market by this wall. General Gerin sends an officer out here to collect every morning of the world.

AZELIA: All right, I'll move on. Maybe I can sell something to the soldiers in the barracks yonder.

COCOANUT VENDOR: Ain't no soldiers. They been gone since sunup.

YAM VENDOR: Well, go on, anyhow.

[AZELIA *tries to lift her basket and fails.*]

COCOANUT VENDOR: What's the matter? You weak?

AZELIA: Tired, awful tired! This basket's mighty heavy. [*Brightening.*] You-all know, I got weapons in here. It's full of weapons!

YAM VENDOR: Huh? What you mean?

MANGO VENDOR: Shsss! Don't pay her no mind.

AZELIA: Don't you see? [*Raising up bananas but disclosing nothing beneath.*] See there! [*Her eyes gleaming.*] Machetes! Three machetes, two pistols, the butt end of an axe to fight our way to freedom. And whips! Oh, yes, two whips!

THREAD VENDOR: [*Rising.*] Get on! Get on! That's enough of your chatter.

MELON VENDOR: Do. Jesus! She's mad as a loon!

AZELIA: [*Lifting her basket and going on.*] That's why I'm tired! So tired! [*As she exits.*] This here's a heavy load. Freedom's heavy load.

MANGO VENDOR: Poor thing! She's crazy.

YAM VENDOR: Oh, so that's it?

THREAD VENDOR: Yes, she's been around here a long time. We know her. Cracked in the head. Always talking about when the slaves rose up against the French.

MANGO VENDOR: Yes, and even claiming she used to be Dessalines' wife before he got to where he is.

[*Everybody laughs.*]

YAM VENDOR: What Dessalines? Not the Emperor?

MANGO VENDOR: That's the one.

COCOANUT VENDOR: [*Still giggling.*] Such lies! Such lies!

YAM VENDOR: I know she's crazy. What's her name?

THREAD VENDOR: Azelia, but the soldiers nicknamed her Defilee.

YAM VENDOR: Why?

THREAD VENDOR: I reckon 'cause she runs after them so much. I don't know. She's always following the troops, selling bananas.

MANGO VENDOR: If she was younger, her basket might not be so heavy. Machetes and pistols! Huh! Don't that take the cake? [*She rises and mounts the steps.*] I'm going up on the wall and see what I can see. Whee! That sun is strong.

THREAD VENDOR: You just want to see what that old long tall fisherman's doing, I reckon.

MANGO VENDOR: I ain't studyin' him.

[*A band of ragamuffins enters, three or four, pushing and playing with each other, laughing loudly and jabbering in a strange dialect.*]

PEPPER VENDOR: [*To the Ragamuffins.*] Get away, you-all! Get away!

[*They run to an opposite corner of the stage, laughing.*]

YAM VENDOR: Old bad boys, just running wild. No manners nor nothing.

MELON VENDOR: Ragamuffins right out the back country,

that's what they is! Can't even talk so's you can understand them.

THREAD VENDOR: They got a dialect all they own, them peoples back yonder in the woods.

PEPPER VENDOR: They're hungry back there, that's why they come to town.

COCOANUT VENDOR: They're just too lazy to work the farms, that's all. The Emperor give 'em land, but they don't work it. They're too free now.

THREAD VENDOR: Then if somebody makes 'em work, they yell about, "We ain't slaves no more!" That's the way with men! Men is lazy.

MELON VENDOR: Lazy, lazy, lazy! If it wasn't fun out riding in a boat on the sea, I don't 'spect they'd even fish.

YAM VENDOR: Well, anyhow, to tell the truth, the farmers ain't got no plows to work with. Looks like since we drove the French out, don't no more ships come here bringing tools nor nothing.

THREAD VENDOR: Things is kinder at a standstill. Haiti's even mighty nigh out of thread and thimbles.

MANGO VENDOR: [*On the embankment.*] Say, look, you-all! I see a strange ship coming. A new one. It's got big red sails!

[*The women all rise and peer over the wall, or mount the steps.*]

MELON VENDOR: It ain't no fishing boat, either, is it?

THREAD VENDOR: It's a passenger boat, I believe.

MANGO VENDOR: I seed it once before, at Saint Marc. It belongs to some of the Emperor's officers. Some rich mulatto or 'nother, I reckon.

THREAD VENDOR: It's sure a big one, all right, 'cause it's anchoring way out in deep water.

[*As the women look at the ship, the ragamuffins steal up to the fruit on the ground. One slyly grabs a melon, another a handful of yams, another a mango.*]

MANGO VENDOR: [*Turning and seeing them. Screaming.*] You rascals! Get away from here! Scat!

[*The boys scatter.*]

YAM VENDOR: Curse your rotten hides! Beat it!

MELON VENDOR: [*Pursuing them.*] Put down my melon, you thieves! Gimme back my melon.

[*The ragamuffins exit with their fruit, yelling and laughing.*]

THREAD VENDOR: Can't take your eyes off things these days. Thieves is getting awful. Young thieves, too.

MELON VENDOR: [*Panting.*] I wish I could get my hands on them hooligans.

COCOANUT VENDOR: We ought to have polices, that's what we needs. Soldiers ain't no good. They steals themselves

MANGO VENDOR: They ain't even a soldier around today, nohow.

YAM VENDOR: [*Going back to the steps and looking toward the shore.*] Wonder what that boat's here for?

COCOANUT VENDOR: I reckon they getting ready for one of their yachting parties. The spendthrift devils!

PEPPER VENDOR: And Haiti gone to rack and ruin.

MELON VENDOR: 'Way back there in the country where I goes to fetch my melons, the farmers done refused to pay taxes.

YAM VENDOR: Yes, and General Gerin took his soldiers away from the barracks today. They say he's put 'em all in that fort ten kilometers down the coast.

THREAD VENDOR: I hear General Yayou's marching, too.

MELON VENDOR: Looks like they getting ready for some more fighting. Look like we'll never be done fighting here in Haiti.

PEPPER VENDOR: Something's wrong! Something's wrong! And poor Jean Jacques, he don't know what to do.

THREAD VENDOR: Huh! All the Emperor knows is fight! He's

done killed off all the white folks. Now he's looking for somebody else to chop up.

MANGO VENDOR: He's a brave man, though! You can't say he ain't. And 'cause of him, I'm free.

PEPPER VENDOR: True, thank God!

YAM VENDOR: Well, he ought to chop off some o' these taxes we got to pay every time I turn around. That's why I never has a sou to my name.

MANGO VENDOR: You got more'n you ever had when you was a slave.

PEPPER VENDOR: Right! Some of you-all's even got shoes.

MELON VENDOR: [*Whispering.*] But the Papaloi says there's gonna be a change soon.

COCOANUT VENDOR: That's what the priest said, too.

THREAD VENDOR: Then you-all's Gods all agree. I 'spects the devil's in it, myself.

MELON VENDOR: Somebody's coming! They look like soldiers to me. [*Beginning to cry her wares.*] Melons! Nice, cool melons!

YAM VENDOR: They is soldiers. Yams! Yams! Yams! Mulatto officers, too! Yams! Must be a high class brigade. Yams! Yams!

MANGO VENDOR: There ain't but a handful, though. We won't sell much to them. Melons! Melons!

THREAD VENDOR: Every little bit helps. Needles! Thimbles! Thread!

[*Enter a squad of soldiers, led by* STENIO. VUVAL *follows. The market women hold out their fruits, calling and beckoning.*]

STENIO: Squad halt! [*The soldiers halt.*] Left face! [*The soldiers obey.*] Men, we'll remain here. Clear the square. Get all these old women out. [*Commanding.*] Break ranks and go ahead.

[*Loud chatter and protestation among the women.*]

MELON VENDOR: What's this?

COCONUT VENDOR: You gonna clear us out?

THREAD VENDOR: What officer is he?

MANGO VENDOR: He don't belong around here.

YAM VENDOR: Don't he know we pay for this space?

STENIO: You women'll have to clear out at once! Military orders! So move and move quickly! And shut up! Or else my soldiers will handle you.

[*The women begin to gather up their wares in clothes and baskets. Meanwhile* VUVAL *has mounted the seawall. Hurriedly the women exit, Left and Right, pushed by the soldiers. One soldier grabs a mango and starts to eat it.*]

SOLDIERS: Move on! Get! Step on it!

STENIO: [*To the one who has the mango.*] Put that mango down! This is no time to eat. [*To* VUVAL.] Is the beach clear?

VUVAL: Yes, only a few fisherman, and they're several hundred yards down the shore. Our boat's approaching, Stenio. Just arrived, apparently, and has anchored in the bay. [*He waves.*] They're waving at me now. Yes, look, they're beginning to lower the skiff.

STENIO: Good! Claire won't have to wait when she arrives. She ought to be here before long.

VUVAL: What did the lookout say about Jean Jacques?

STENIO: The lookout that climbed the palm tree? Oh, he said he could see him clearly crossing the valley without field glasses. He'd passed the Red Bridge, so the Emperor ought to be dashing into the village any moment now.

VUVAL: You'd better place the men, then.

STENIO: It's good he can't ride his horse onto the quay here. He'll have to come up those steps on foot. [*To the soldiers.*] Squad, attention! [*As they form before him.*] Listen carefully, men! A great honor's befallen us, and at the same time a grave patriotic duty! We're chosen by destiny to be the liberators of Haiti! We're to free our country from a power-loving, tax-hungry tyrant. It's our privilege and our honor, men, to put an end to the career of a black monster who cares not at all for us, or for Haiti, or for our people, but only for himself. Now his day of reckoning has come. I did not tell you last night why I picked you out so carefully. But I chose you as men loyal to myself and to freedom. Now, we are to strike the blow that will break the shackles of submission forever. We are to put an end to the presumptious Negro who dares call himself "His Majesty."

A SOLDIER: What?

SECOND SOLDIER: You don't mean ...?

THIRD SOLDIER: Not the Emperor?

STENIO: I mean Dessalines!

SOLDIER: But what'll happen to us?

SECOND SOLDIER: Why, that's treason!

THIRD SOLDIER: I don't want to do that.

FOURTH SOLDIER: We'll be done for!

STENIO: You'll be promoted in rank and made commanders. You need have no fear, men. There'll be a Republic and a President. Perhaps myself as President, General Gerin and General Yayou have already begun to take over the forts for the new government. There'll be an end of Emperors, and of tyranny! And we'll be heroes in the eyes of the people! Heroes, men! Heroes!

SOLDIER: But bullets can't kill Jean Jacques!

SECOND SOLDIER: He's got some kind o' magic about him, I heard.

THIRD SOLDIER: Yes, he has.

STENIO: Aw, don't be foolish. He's got nothing but arrogance!

VUVAL: He's only a man, just like the rest of you.

STENIO: Of course! But he's kept you bluffed too long. We

should have done this years ago. But enough talk. That nearby dust cloud makes me think he must be almost here. Men, take the places I'll assign you. At my command, come forth and take them prisoners. [*Pointing out hiding places.*] You two, there in the doorway of the Army Headquarters. One man behind the embankment wall, near the steps. And the rest of you take the other side.

[*The soldiers hide as ordered.*]

Vuval, you and I will take our hiding places here where we can see when he dismounts, and be ready to give the command as he approaches. This is a moment I've long awaited, friend.

VUVAL: I shall write a poem about this, Stenio. How two young men, believers in liberty, brought down the voracious Tiger, whose jaws devoured the people of Haiti.

STENIO: Write it tomorrow, Vuval. Let's hide now. His horses approach.

[*Noise of horses' hoofs, then pawing and champing as they are tied nearby. A trumpet blast.* DESSALINES enters, *striding like an angry giant, followed by* POPO *and* PIERRE.]

DESSALINES: [*Looking around.*] It's mighty quiet here, and no one comes to greet me. Can't they hear your bugle, Pierre? That villain Gerin must've gone to the hills and taken the whole garrison with him! But where're all the fishermen and the market women?

POPO: Sire, I don't like the feel of things here.

PIERRE: Nor do I, my Emperor

DESSALINES: Let's go further.

[*As the men advance toward Army Headquarters,* STENIO *emerges from his hiding place and gives the traitorous orders.*]

STENIO: Seize the prisoners!

[*The soldiers leap up and seize* POPO *and* PIERRE, *who struggle with them—but no one dares touch* DESSALINES. *Two soldiers approach him, but back away in awe and terror.*]

DESSALINES: Who dares put their hand upon a King? [*The soldiers quail. He turns toward those holding his companions.*] Release those men! [*He draws his sword.*]

STENIO: [*Also drawing a sword.*] You'll give no orders to Stenio's troops, Jean Jacques.

DESSALINES: [*Turning and seeing* STENIO *for the first time.*] You traitorous dog! Your head'll roll at my feet for this! And now!

[*He starts toward him with his sword.* STENIO *backs away, but* VUVAL *lifts his pistol and fires like a coward from behind. The royal sword clatters to earth. The* EMPEROR *staggers, turns, looks at* VUVAL, *and tumbles to the ground, dead.*]

STENIO: [*Laughing.*] Dog! Ha! Ha! Dog, am I? [*He kicks the body of the* EMPEROR.] Well, you're less than a dog, now. Food for worms, you! [*He turns and barks at the men holding* POPO *and* PIERRE.] Take those prisoners to the barracks. Lock them up without water. We'll court-martial them shortly. [*They exit.*] [*To* VUVAL, *who stands now as if in a daze.*] What's the matter with you, man? You've done well. Don't look so woebegone, Vuval. Laugh, poet, laugh! It' not *your* heart that's punctured. You're more than a poet now! Why, you're the new Liberator of Haiti. Your name will go down in history, boy. Put your gun away and come, let's see if we can find a glass of wine. Then you'd better go meet the skiff and prepare for Claire's arrival. Meanwhile, I'll ride south to seek Gerin. Tomorrow we'll set up a Provisional Government at Port-au-Prince in which, no doubt, we'll both have important posts. [*Glancing at the body as they move toward the barracks.*] Come on! Leave that mess for the scavengers to pick up.

[VUVAL, *still silent, accompanies his friend toward the Headquarters. In passing,* STENIO *picks up the* EMPEROR'S *sword.*]

I might keep this trinket as a souvenir. [*They exit.*]

[*The fallen ruler lies alone, in the dust, on his back. From either side of the square come the same ragamuffins who earlier plagued the market women. They steal in awe around the body, then silently creep up and touch it. When they see that the corpse does not move, they cry aloud in their unintelligible dialect, jabbering in wonder at the tassels of gold on his shoulders, the heavy golden cords at his cuffs, his shiny boots. One of the ragamuffins picks up the* EMPEROR'S *hat with the purple plume and puts it on his head.*]

RAGAMUFFIN: [*With the hat.*] Ha! Ha! Ha! Ha!

[*Two of the boys begin to turn the body over as they unbutton his coat and take it off. While they squabble over the coat, a third removes his silken shirt, the color of wine, and rubs it against his face, groaning voluptuously at the sleekness of the cloth.*]

RAGAMUFFIN: [*With the shirt.*] Oh! Ah! Th-sssss!

[*The body of the* EMPEROR *now lies on its face, back bare to the sun. The old welts of his slave days stand out like cords across his shoulders.*]

[AZELIA *enters with the tray of bananas on her head. Fiercely, she turns on the ragamuffins, chasing them away.*]

AZELIA: Get away! Get away! That man's sick! Or dead, maybe! And you young fools dancing and laughing and robbing him out of his clothes. Get away!

[*The three ragamuffins exit, running.*]

[AZELIA *puts away her tray on the wall and goes toward the body, unaware of its identity. She kneels to lift his dusty head in her hands. Suddenly her face is frozen with horror and pain of recognition. Sobbing, she falls across the body.*]

Jean Jacques! Jean Jacques!

[*For a moment her arms cover the heavy scars on his back. Then she rises slowly to her knees and looks down at the man who was once her husband.*]

Oh, my Jean! My dear! [*Remembering.*] So long together! So much we shared! The cane fields, the slave hut! Freedom! [*Bitterly.*] Our freedom, Jean Jacques! That took you away from me—to a palace with a throne of gold, and silken pillows for your head, and women fairer than flowers who made you forget how much we'd shared together. Once we slept in a slave corral, together, you and I. But when you slept in a palace, you didn't need Azelia. [*Tenderly.*] My sweetheart! Oh, my dear! You offered me money, then, too much money for one who loved you. [*Caressingly, she rubs her hands across his body.*] But I still love you, Jean Jacques! I still love you!

[*The sound of voices approaching. Two servants cross the steps, carrying a heavy chest, as* VUVAL *appears on the seawall, pale as a ghost.*]

VUVAL: [*Directing the men.*] Down the beach, to the skiff.

[*The servants exit toward the beach. The others enter with a similar chest and follow the first pair. Then* CLAIRE HEUREUSE *comes swiftly across the square, accompanied by her maid. As she passes, in spite of herself, she pauses to glance at the body of the fallen man. Quickly she puts her hands across her eyes and shudders with a memory she can never lose.*]

CLAIRE: [*In a whisper.*] Those scars! [*As she mounts the steps,* VUVAL *takes her in his arms and they disappear toward the beach. Moaning in crazy monotones,* AZELIA *rocks above her dead. Two fishermen appear on the seawall, carrying strings of silver fish. They pause to look at the strange pair.*]

TALL FISHERMAN: Who's that laying over there with that crazy old woman?

SHORT FISHERMAN: [*Coming closer to the body.*] He musta been a slave once—from the looks of his back.

AZELIA: [*Without turning her head.*] He was a slave, once ... [*She gently spreads her shawl over his shoulders.*] ... then a King!

[*The fishermen remove their hats, as*

CURTAIN

THE END

LANGSTON HUGHES
(1902-1967)

Langston Hughes is the dominant black writer of the mid-twentieth century, his poems, novels, short stories, essays, and dramas covering the period from the Harlem Renaissance of the 1920s to the black arts movement of the 1960s. Hughes was born in Joplin, Missouri, and grew up mainly with his maternal grandmother, Mary Leary Langston, in Lawrence, Kansas. His father had moved to Mexico for business reasons while his mother elected to remain in the United States, though she travelled frequently in search of employment. His grandmother was a widow of one of the black men who fought with John Brown in his 1859 raid to free the slaves. She had a profound influence on the young Hughes until her death in 1915.

Hughes joined his mother and step-father in Cleveland, Ohio, where he entered high school from which he graduated in 1920. At school he wrote and published poems in the student magazine, made the honor roll, and edited the school yearbook. In Cleveland, too, Hughes became acquainted with the inter-racial Karamu House, a newly established arts center under the direction of Russell and Rowena Jelliffe from Oberlin College, Ohio. This relationship would later prove of value when Karamu gave premier productions of several of Hughes' plays from 1936 to 1938.

Hughes had visited his father in Mexico in the summers of 1919-1921 but had become increasingly disaffected with the latter's materialistic outlook. His father wished to send him to college in Europe and only grudgingly agreed to Hughes enrolling at Columbia University in New York City. However, Hughes could not settle into university life and left after one year. He was much more interested in the people and milieu of Harlem that he had begun to write about, as well as in the theatre for which he had already written a one-act play, *The Gold Piece* (1921).

Hughes embarked on a period of sea travel, signing on as a cabin boy on a freighter to Africa. He also visited Paris and Venice in 1924 and returned home with poems and stories of his experiences. Although best known as a poet and short story writer, Hughes continued to write for the stage throughout his long career. His first New York production was *Mulatto* (1935), a melodrama of racial conflict that established a record run for a play by a black American on Broadway. Other New York productions include *Simply Heavenly* (1957), *Tambourines to Glory* (1963), and *The Prodigal Son* (1965). Hughes was also interested in the musical theatre and he collaborated with a number of musicians on the production of operettas such as *Street Scene* (1947), *The Barrier* (1950), and *Esther* (1957).

During the 1930s and 1940s, Hughes established three black theatre groups: the Suitcase Theatre in Harlem, the Negro Art Theatre in Los Angeles, and the Skyloft Players in Chicago. Hughes' most political play is probably *Don't You Want To Be Free?* which he staged at his pocket-sized Suitcase Theatre for 135 performances. A pageant of black struggle and protest, the play employs music, song, and dance to portray the historical oppression of black people and the need for working class blacks and whites to come together and fight for their civil rights. *Emperor of Haiti* was first produced in 1935 under the title *Drums of Haiti* and frequently revised by Hughes to its present version.

Source: *Dictionary of Literary Biography, Vol. 7: Twentieth Century American Dramatists*, and *Vol. 51: Afro-American Writers from the Harlem Renaissance to 1940.* Trudier Harris, ed. Chapel Hill, NC: University of North Carolina, 1981 and 1987.

NAT TURNER

by
Randolph Edmonds

NAT TURNER
(1800-1831)

Nat Turner's slave rebellion has not perhaps received the attention it should and is often dismissed as the ill-conceived attempt of a fanatic who, with a parcel of willing but cowardly conspirators, carried out a number of atrocities against whites before being captured and executed. If one were to read Turner's "Confessions" today as they were written down in prison by a white man, Thomas Gray, it would seem difficult to feel sympathy for Turner who, with a band of slaves varying in number from 15 to 80, set out at night to liberate the slaves by the simple expedient of killing in their beds all white people, including women and children. Difficult, that is, unless we are prepared to see plantation slavery, by definition, as a most violent condition in which blacks were whipped, starved, tortured, torn from their families, forced to labor, to marry and to breed, all without any recourse whatsoever. In short, their humanity was denied them. How else would it be possible to overthrow this system, supported as it was by law and armed power, than by murder under cover of night of the slaveholders and their families?

Turner, however, was no mere rebellious hothead. All his life, it seemed to him and to others, he was destined for some great self-sacrificial act. When he was born a slave in Southampton, Virginia, he had on his head and breast certain marks that were thought to be signs of a high calling. As a child he was able to recount incidents that had occurred prior to his birth, which made others believe he was fated to be a prophet. Turner learned to read and write and knew the Bible well. He was very religious, prayed even when he was at work over the plough, and felt he was in communication with a Spirit that "confirmed me in the impression that I was ordained for some great purpose in the hands of the Almighty." On one occasion he ran away from his overseer but returned voluntarily after thirty days in obedience to his Spirit so that he might carry out his great mission.

After some period had elapsed, Turner began to see signs and symbols that led him to conclude that the time for action was approaching. He gathered about him some trusted aides, discussed various plans and waited for the moment to strike. It came in the form of a solar eclipse in August 1831. As Turner confessed, it was agreed by all that until they had armed and equipped themselves and gathered sufficient force, neither age nor sex would be spared. After six weeks and fifty-five murders, Turner was caught, tried and executed along with sixteen of his followers. But whites also sought their own vigilante justice, slaughtering many innocent blacks "without trial and under circumstances of great barbarity."

Thomas Gray, who had no reason to be partial to the captive, has left us this pen portait of Turner as part of the "Confessions:"

> It has been said he was ignorant and cowardly, and that his object was to murder and rob for the purpose of obtaining money to make his escape. It is notorious, that he was never known to have a dollar in his life; to swear an oath, or drink a drop of spirits. As to his ignorance, he certainly never had the advantages of education, but he can read and write . . . and for natural intelligence and quickness of apprehension, is surpassed by few men I have ever seen. As to his being a coward, his reason as given for not resisting Mr. Phipps shews the decision of his character. When he saw Mr. Phipps present his gun, he said he knew it was impossible for him to escape as the woods were full of men; he therefore thought it was better to surrender, and trust to fortune for his escape. He is a complete fanatic, or plays his part most admirably.

It is in keeping with Professor Edmonds' role as educator and race-man that he should compose a play on Nat Turner. Edmonds is writing for production in black colleges and high schools where production resources are limited. He therefore chooses the tight one-act play form with a simple outdoor wooded setting and decides to concentrate on the moment preceding the uprising and the time immediately following its failure. Edmonds strives to be objective; he does not exonerate Turner's actions though he is no doubt in sympathy with his motive of freeing the slaves.

Edmonds focuses on Turner as a mystic who believes strongly that he is acting at the behest of his Guiding Spirit, which will protect him and his men and crown their rebellion with success. When this doesn't happen, Turner is left questioning his fate, wondering if he had been deceived all his life. In point of fact, although it is unlikely that the insurrection would ever have succeeded, it has been argued that had Turner reached Jeresulem, the county capital, and captured the arsenal as he intended, the rebellion might well have been prolonged with far-reaching effects.

Source: Herbert Aptheker, *Nat Turner's Slave Rebellion*. New York: Grove Press, 1966; and Aptheker, *American Negro Slave Revolts*. New York: International Publishers, 1983.

CHARACTERS

Henry Porter
Hark Travis
Nelson Williams
Samuel Francis
Jack Reese
Will Francis
Jessee Harris
Bob Porters
Job Westbrook
Lucinda Moore
Nat Turner

SCENE 1

A small clearing in the midst of leafy trees on the plantation of JOSEPH TRAVIS *at Cross Keys, Virginia, in Southampton County, on August 21, 1831. Here is gathered that small band of slaves which started the famous Nat Turner Insurrection.*

It is about ten o'clock. The low full moon coming up over the horizon casts orange shadows through the trees down on the group. They are winding up a barbecue feast which has lasted from three o'clock in the afternoon. The small fire on which they roasted a pig has died down to embers; and there is just light enough to see the slaves as they eat their barbecue and drink cider.

HENRY, *who has been walking around, suddenly exclaims:*

HENRY: [*Pointing to the right.*] Look!

[*All spring up.*]

HARK: Whut is hit, Henry?

HENRY: Look at dat moon over dere through de trees.

SAM: Hit sho' is gut a 'culiar color tuh hit.

JACK: Hit's a blood moon, dat's whut.

HARK: Hit means red blood is gwine be spilled.

HENRY: So many things been happenin' round heah lately, judgment day mus' be coming soon.

HARK: Hit is coming soon fuh a whole lot o' white folks in dis county.

WILL: [*Sitting down.*] Les' stop talkin' 'bout de moon and finish up dis barbecue.

[*They all sit down and start eating and drinking again.*]

HENRY: [*Apparently not finished with the conversation.*] Dis August is a funny month. Las' Sattiday on de thirteenth hit was de sun dat was funny, and now hit's de moon.

NELSON: Ah never will fugit dat day ez long ez Ah lives.

HARK: [*After draining a glass of cider.*] Ah won't neither, Nelson. When de sun riz hit was a light green, 'bout nine o'clock hit had turned tuh blue, and at twelve o'clock hit had turned tuh grey wid a black spot on hit.

SAM: "Prophet Nat" said hit was de last sign, and tuh git ready tuh strike fuh freedom.

HENRY: And we is heah ready tuh strike.

JOB: Whut is all dis feast 'bout? Henry told me 'bout organizin' and fightin', but he didn't make hit clear. Ah been settin' heah eatin' and drinkin' since 'bout de middle o' de evenin' and nobody ain't said no mo'. Ah want tuh know why all us was tole tuh bring hoes, pitchforks, and clubs; and whut's all dis feast 'bout?

HENRY: Yuh tell him, Hark.

HARK: When Christ was gittin' ready tuh save de worl' by givin' His life, He had His las' supper, didn't He?

JOB: [*Insisting.*] Yeah, but Ah ain't gittin' ready tuh giv' ma life fuh nothin'.

BOB: Ah'm lak yuh, Job. Ah wants tuh know dese things, too.

HARK: [*To* JOB.] Ef yuh'll jes hab de patience ob de Bible man dat yuh was named arter, Job, Prophet Nat will 'splain things when he gits heah.

BOB: But hit's gittin' late. Ah don't b'lieve Ole Nat is coming.

HARK: He'll be heah all right. Ah's sure he jes' wanted de eatin' and drinkin' tuh git over. Yuh knows he never drank lak de res' ob us.

NELSON: [*Biting on a sandwich.*] He ain't never touched a drap o' likker in his life. When everybody is drinkin' and habin' a good time, Prophet Nat is off prayin'. Ah bet he is somewhar prayin' now.

JOB: Dat part's all right; but ain't nobody yit told me jes' whut we is tuh do.

NELSON: We is gwine tuh organize a army and kill all de white folks and set all de black slaves free.

WILL: [*Getting up and stretching. He is a big, muscular, and athletic looking Negro.*] Ah sho will be glad when hit's time tuh start, too.

HENRY: Ah knows yuh will be glad, Will. Yuh always did lak tuh fight.

HARK: Wait a minute! Ef yuh is gwine tuh talk 'bout fightin' and everythin' we'd better hab a guard. De bushes might have eahs. [*Looking around.*] Jessee, yuh seems tuh be 'bout de only one not eatin', s'pose yuh act as guard and see dat no white folks sneak up on us.

[JESSEE *gets up. He is very young.*]

JACK: How did yuh ever leave yo' gal, Lucinda, Jessee? Wunder she ain't come tuh look fuh yuh by now.

JESSEE: [*Good-naturedly.*] Ah jes' told huh Ah was gwine away. Dat's all Ah ever tells wimmin.

BOB: Yuh must 'a' told huh more'n dat 'cause she is wust dan de Moster on yuh.

NELSON: She'll hardly let him out huh sight. Hit is a wunder she ain't been heah.

JESSEE: Ah's been heah ez long ez anybody else, ain't Ah?

HARK: [*In a positive manner.*] Aw, go on guard, and stop doin' so much talkin'.

JESSEE: Ah's gwine, Hark. [*He goes on guard.*]

JOB: [*Rising.*] Ah's gwine on back tuh de house, Hark. All de rest can stay ez long ez yuh wants tuh.

BOB: [*Rising.*] Ah's gwine wid yuh, Job.

SAM: Ah jes' b'lieve dey want tuh do dat so dey can tell de white folks everything.

JOB: [*Towering over* SAM *and threatening him.*] Yuh watch out how yo' mouf talks, Sam. Hit must not want no mo' teef in hit.

SAM: [*Rising.*] Ain't no man gwine keep me frum talkin' when Ah wants tuh.

HARK: Aw, cut out dat talk. We don't want no fightin' heah.

WILL: Dere ain't gwine be no fightin' 'less Ah do some; and Ah don't be ready jes' yit.

HARK: Aw, go on now. Le's everybody wait fuh Nat.

BOB: Why should everybody wait fuh Old Nat all dis time? Ah ain't never laked him nohow. He is a 'culiar slave.

NELSON: [*Sharply.*] He's gut mo' sense dan any slave in de county. Even de white folks says dat.

JOB: Ah ain't been in dis county long nuff tuh know much 'bout him; but he don't act lak he's gut much sense tuh me. He stay by hisse'f all de time, and walks 'round lak he's gut his haid in de sky.

SAM: Don't yuh fool yo'se'f. Old Nat, ez yuh calls him, gut plenty o' sense laid up in dat head o' hisen. Lemme tell yuh one thing. One day when he was jes' a little boy he was tellin' a story 'bout sompen dat happened on de farm heah befo' he was bawn. Nobody never told him nothin' 'bout hit. De Lawd shows him, dat's whut. De Lawd shows him many things. Dat's why we call him a prophet.

HENRY: And he can read and write jes' lak de white folks.

JACK: And he can make paper and gunpowder, too. And nobody ain't never teached him nothin'.

JOB: Old Nat's gut yuh fooled, dat's all. He is jes' an old conjurer, dat's all.

WILL: Yuh don't know whut yuh is talkin' 'bout, Job. Me and Nat ain't never been good frens; but he ain't no conjure man. He is jes' a smart black slave, dat's all. Yuh can giv' him any old pieces o' iron lak ole plow points and buggy tires, and he'll make yuh a good lookin' bell, or a sword. Ah knows dat 'cause he made some fuh ma Moster.

NELSON: Ah tells yuh sompen else dat yuh don't know neither. He can spit blood whenever he wants tuh, and he can prophesy when strange things gwine tuh happen. He show'd us some plain leaves on de trees and told us dat some strange writin' would be on dem de next day. We went dere de next mawning, and sho nuff, dere 'twas. Nat ain't no conjurer. He's gut de sperit o' God in him, dat's all. He is a prophet.

HARK: Yuh ain't been 'round heah long, Job; but we who has, knows Nat Turner. We knows dat he was 'pinted by Gawd tuh lead de black slaves from dere bondage. Folks thinks he is crazy, 'cause he stays by hisse'f. He's been talkin' tuh de Lawd all day while we's been heah eatin' barbecue and drinkin' cider. When he fust told his plans tuh Henry, Nelson and me, we thought he was crazy. We don't think so now. We know de black slaves ain't never gwine tuh be free 'til dey raise a army and fight fuh demselves. De Lawd told Nat Turner dat.

JOB: Ole Nat jes' outer his head, dat's all. Ef yuh keep listenin' tuh him de white folks is gwine tuh hang yuh all.

BOB: He ain't gwine git me in no trouble.

HARK: Wal, yuh can wait a few minutes tull he gits heah, can't yuh? He ought tuh be heah any minute now.

BOB: Ah done waited long nuff. Come on, Job.

JOB: Yeah, let's go. Nat Turner mout be a prophet tuh yuh;

but he is jes' a crazy buck tuh me. Ah ain't gwine let him make de white folks stretch ma nake on no limb.

SAM: Wal, ef he is scared tuh stay heah and fight, let him go on home and hide behind his old lady's coat tails. Ah's gwine stick wid Prophet Nat.

NELSON: Ah'm stickin', too.

BOB: [*Angry*.] Ah told yuh don't let yo' mouf talk so much, but yuh won't listen; ef yuh don't take back whut yuh said, Ah's gwine separate yo' teef and gums.

WILL: [*Rising*.] Ah said nobody was gwine fight 'less Ah git in hit, too. Ah says anybody dat leaves dis place befo' Nat Turner gits heah, gut tuh beat Will Francis. Is yuh and Bob leavin', Job?

HARK: Be quiet, all ob yuh. Ah told yuh we don't want no fightin'.

JESSEE: [*Before they can get things straight* JESSEE *yells out*.] Be quiet, everybody! Ah heah somebody comin'.

HARK: Hit mus' be Prophet Nat.

JESSEE: Halt! Who's dere! Speak!

NAT: [*In a strong voice*.] Dis is Nat Turner coming! [*He comes in with a firm step. There is a mystical appearance about him. All of his movements and words give the impression that he is a strange man, that he is a part of this world with a strong suggestion of the other. He stops abruptly when he sees* WILL.] How come yuh heah, Will?

WILL: [*Submissively*.] Hark told me 'bout yo' plans tuh git free; and Ah thought ma life is no mo' dan de others, and liberty tuh me is jes' ez dear.

NAT: Do yuh think yuh can obtain liberty?

WILL: [*Proudly*.] Ah can, or lose ma life in de attempt.

NAT: How 'bout dese others, Hark, Job and Bob and Jessee?

HARK: Jessee is all right. Ah thought Job and Bob was, too; but dey was gittin' ready tuh leave jes' befo' yuh come.

NAT: Don't yuh and Bob want tuh be free, Job?

JOB: Cose we does; but we don't know nothin' 'bout whut yuh is gwine tuh do. Ef dere is a good chance, we wants tuh be free lak anybody else.

BOB: Le's heah yo' plans, Nat.

JOB: [*Eagerly.*] Yeah, and ef we sees dere is a chance, we'll be wid yuh.

NAT: [*Apparently satisfied.*] Dat's fair enuff; but Ah never starts tuh do anythin' 'til Ah acknowledge Him who guides us all, Him who made de worl', and Him who told me tuh carry out His plans. Le's bow our heads in prayer. [*They all get down on their knees.* NAT *stands above them. He prays fervently.*] Oh, Lawd Gawd ob Hosts, we is met heah tu-night tuh do Thy will as revealed tuh Thy servant. Come down frum Yo' throne on high, and be wid us tu-night. Open Yo' pearly gates and let Yo' sperit flow down and warm our hearts tuh do Yo' task. Oh, Lawd, Yuh who stood by Jacob and Isaac, be wid us tu-night. Oh Lawd, Yuh who delivered Jonah frum de belly o' de whale, and Daniel frum de lion's den, and walked in de fire wid de three Hebrew chilluns, come down and be wid us heah tu-night. [*In a less rhythmical voice.*] Be wid us, Lawd. Help us do de right thing. Show us de right path and guide our feet in de way ob righteousness fuh Jesus sake, Ahmen!

ALL: Ahmen! Ahmen!

[*They all get up from their knees and sit around for further orders.* NAT *seats himself in the middle on an old stump with an equal number on each side.*]

NAT: Is everybody finished wid de feast, Hark?

HARK: Yeah, dey is jes' 'bout.

NAT: Wal, we is ready tuh start our plans den.

HARK: Yeah, we was waitin' fuh yuh.

NAT: Ah been communicating wid de Holy Sperit all day. Ah wanted tuh be sho we was right. Dis idea ob fightin' fuh our freedom ain't jes' come tuh me. Hit is been in ma head a long time. De Lawd put hit in ma mind yeahs ago.

BOB: Whut is yuh planning tuh do?

JACK: Be quiet, Bob.

NAT: De sperit revealed dis tuh me: dat tu-night is de best possible time tuh start dis insurrection. Most ob de white folks is gone over in North Ca'lina, tuh Winton and Murfreesboro, tuh tend de big meetings. Dat only leaves a few around; and dey won't bother us 'cause dey is so far apart. Even now dey thinks we is away having a meeting ob our own. We can kill dese few white folks, organize all de slaves in a large army and take Jeresulem, de county seat, git all de guns and ammunitions. We can den conquer de whole county, march tuh de Dismal Swamp and work frum dere. Soon we can overcome de whole state, den de whole country lak George Washington did from de British.

WILL: Dat sounds good. Let's start now.

JOB: [*Not convinced.*] Whut yuh want tuh do all dat fuh?

NAT: [*Fiercely.*] Because we wants tuh be free men. Because we wants tuh call de 'tention ob de whole worl' tuh de condition ob slavery. We can strike de blow dat will make de whole worl' tremble at our might. Dere ain't no better way ob declarin' tuh de worl' dat black men is gwine be free dan tuh rise up and fight. With de help ob Gawd we is gwine tuh do hit, too.

JOB: Ah hates tuh see de white folks all killed up lak dat. Our Mosters is treating us all right. We's gut plenty tuh eat, and dey don't whup us lak dey do way down south on de Mississippi.

NAT: [*A little intolerant at his lack of understanding.*] Ah hates tuh kill folks, too; but war ain't no barbecue feast. Yuh thinks 'cause yuh is gut a belly full and a place tuh lay yo' head dat dat is nuff; but hit ain't nuff fuh men made in de image ob Gawd. No real man ain't willing tuh be wurked lak a mule in de fields, whupped lak a dog, and tied tuh one farm and one Moster. [*Eloquently.*] Is yuh willing tuh continue dis servitude, dis slavery? Is yuh willing fuh yo' chilluns tuh look back tuh de time we live, and say dat dey is slaves 'cause we ain't gut guts nuff tuh fight? Is yuh willing tuh be beaten, enslaved, debased? Is yuh willing, everybody?

VOICES: No!! No!!

NAT: Den we mus' fight fuh our freedom. We mus' let dem know we's gut a backbone. We mus' let dem know dat jes' because our skins is black we is not afraid tuh die. Even ef death overtake us in dis struggle, we mus' say lak de 'posle Paul "Ah's fought a good fight, Ah's runned de course; and dere is a crown waiting up in glory fuh me."

JOB: How come yuh git all dis in yo' head? Yuh knows yuh can't do nothin' 'gainst de white folks. Look whut dey done tuh Gabriel Prosser and Denmark Vesey.

HARK: [*Restless.*] Don't answer him. Le's git gwine.

WILL: No matter whut yuh say he ain't gwine b'lieve yuh. Dere ain't but one way tuh make him see. Lemme hammer hit in his thick haid.

NAT: [*Rising and restraining him.*] Don't do dat, Will. Dat ain't de way. Ef he wants tuh know how Gawd works, let him larn; 'cause we ain't doin' dis fuh ourselves, we's doin' hit fuh Him. But Gawd's ways are mysterious. Every man can't understand dem; but He speaks tuh me lak He did tuh de prophets ob old—lak He did tuh Isaiah, Jeremiah, Amos, and Hosea. Gawd talks tuh me lak he did tuh dem. Ah's gwine tuh tell yuh whut He said.

JACK: Tell dem whut He said, Brother Nat!

VOICES: Ahmen! Ahmen!

NAT: Set down and listen! Set down 'round de embers ob de dying fire whar yuh part took ob earthly things and listen tuh whut de Lawd revealed unto me.

[*They all sit down but* BOB *and* JOB.]

HARK: [*Sharply.*] He means yuh, too. Set down!

[*They obey.* NAT *remains standing. He goes into a kind of trance.*]

NAT: 'Bout six yeahs ago Ah was thinkin' 'bout de Bible text "Seek ye fust de kingdom ob heaven, and all dese things will be added unto yuh." I thought and thought 'bout dat text. Ah wundered ef de Lawd meant black slaves. Ah said tuh mase'f, "Surely dis can't be true 'cause black slaves wants tuh be free." Dis wurried me a whole lot, but one day while Ah was walkin' in de field behind de plow, all ob a sudden de sperit said, "Seek ye fust de kingdom ob heaven, and all dese things will be added unto yuh." Ah said, "Lawd, dat can't be Yuh talkin' 'cause Ah want de things ob dis worl'." So Ah ran away frum ma Moster. Ah wanted tuh make ma way tuh freedom lak ma father befo' me. Ah tried tuh dodge de Moster's will; but one day de sperit came tuh me agen, and said in a loud voice, "For he who knoweth de Moster's will and doeth hit not shall be beaten wid many strikes." So Ah came back heah tuh ma Moster. Ah came back tuh yuh. Ah came back tuh do ma Father's will.

HENRY: Yuh came back tuh lead us tuh freedom.

NAT: [*Not noticing the interruption.*] Ah wasn't heah long befo' one day de Lawd showed me a vision. Ah saw white sperits and black sperits engaged in battle, and de sun was darkened, de thunder rolled in heaven, and blood flowed in streams. Den de sperit spoke agen and said, "Such is yo' luck. Such yuh is called tuh see, and let hit come rough or smooth, yuh mus' surely bar hit."

HARK: We'll he'p yuh bar hit! We'll he'p yuh!

VOICES: Ahmen! Ahmen!

NAT: After dis revelation ob de sperit, Ah sought more dan ever true holiness befo' de great day ob judgment should appear. And den Ah began tuh receive de true knowledge ob de faith. And frum de first steps ob righteousness tuh de las' was Ah made perfect, and de Holy Ghost was in me, and said, "Behold me as Ah stand in heaven!" And Ah looked up and saw men in different attitudes. And dere was lights in de sky tuh which de chilluns ob darkness gave other names dan whut dey really was—fuh dey was lights ob de Savior's hands stretched forth frum de east tuh de west, even as dey were extended tuh Calvary fuh de redemption ob sinners.

VOICES: Ahmen! Ahmen!

NAT: And Ah wundered greatly at dese miracles, and prayed tuh be informed ob a certainty ob de meaning therob—and shortly afterwards while laboring in de fields Ah discovered drops ob blood on de corn as dough hit was dew frum heaven, and Ah found on de leaves hieroglyphic characters and numbers wid de forms ob men in different attitudes portrayed in blood, and representing de figgers Ah had seen befo' in de heavens. And so de Holy Ghost revealed hisse'f tuh me and made plain de miracles Ah had seen. For de blood ob Christ had been shed on dis earth and had ascended tuh heaven fuh de salvation ob sinners and was now returning tuh earth in de form ob dew. Den Ah was baptised in de Holy Sperit.

VOICES: Speak de truth! Tell de worl' 'bout hit!

NAT: Ah still wasn't satisfied. Ah couldn't b'lieve Gawd had chosen me fuh His instrument. So Ah axed de sperit fuh a futher sign; and Gawd answered ez He always answers de prayers ob de faithful. Las' February He blotted out de sun, and turned day into night. When dis happened Ah began tuh b'lieve at last. Den Ah had another vision. Ah heard a loud noise in de heaven and de sperit instantly appeared tuh me and said, "De serpent is loosed, and Christ is laid down de yoke dat He bore fuh de sins ob men." De sperit said Ah should take hit up and fight de serpent, fuh de time is at hand when de las' shall be fust and de fust shall be las'. And de sperit said Ah should arise and prepare mase'f, and slay ma enemies wid dere own weapon. [*Pauses dramatically and sits upon stump.*]

WILL: Le's start now! Le's git gwine!

NAT: So Ah's heah not fuh mase'f, fuh Ah could 'a' staye free when Ah run away; but Ah's heah as an instrument o Gawd. He sent me heah tuh lead yuh forth in dis battle. H told me tuh do lak He told Saul 'gainst de Hittites, tuh le not one escape. We is tuh slay every man, woman, an child ob dose who held us in bondage. Thus saith de Lawc "Ah shall deliver dem tuh yuh dis day." Is yuh ready? I yuh willing tuh join de army ob de Lawd? Is yuh ready tu slay yo' enemies? Is yuh ready tuh fight dat yo' blac chilluns mout be free?

VOICES: Yeah! We is ready! Lead us! Lead us into battle!

NAT: [*Reaching down and picking up a bundle of red bands mad out of cloth that he has brought.*] Who will wear one ob des bands tuh show dat yuh is ready tuh fight?

VOICES: Ah will! Gimme one!

[*He rises and distributes them.*]

NAT: Is yuh convinced now, Job? Will yuh wear one ob des bands?

JOB: Yeah, yuh'd better gimme one, too.

BOB: Ah'll take one.

NAT: Everybody gut one?

[*They all drape these bands over their left shoulder and tie ther on their right side.*]

HARK: We's ready! Le's move!

NAT: Git whut weapons yuh gut and fall in line. [*They ge their axes, grubbing hoes, rusty swords, clubs and fall in tu lines.*] Listen! Ah is no longer "Prophet Nat." From now o Ah is General Nat. Hark Travis heah is yo' second i command. Yuh understand?

ALL: We understand.

[*Hark falls out of line and stands before the two columns.*]

NAT: We's gut tuh do a little drillin' befo' we march tuh d fust house. Remember yuh is gut tuh obey orders. We'll g guns ez we go along. Ah'll set de example by strikin' de fust blow.

ALL: We is ready!

NAT: Salute!

[*They salute awkwardly.*]

HARK: Git yo' hand up.

NAT: Le's drill now. Squad right! March! Squad right! March! Squad right! March! Squad left! March! Squad left! March! Squad Front! March! Halt! [*They march around in obedience to these orders. They hold their weapons like guns.*] Ah didn't giv yuh de command tuh retreat, 'cause dere ain't gwine be no retreat. We is gwine now and fight; and we is gwine keep on fightin' and dyin' tull all slaves everywhar is free.

VOICES: We heah yuh, General Nat!

NAT: Squad right! Forward! Forward tuh de line o' battle! March!

ALL: [*While marching.*] Tuh de line o' battle!

NAT: Tuh Jeresulem de County seat!

ALL: Tuh Jeresulem de County seat!

NAT: March, soldiers ob freedom, March!

[*The curtain goes down to indicate the passing of three days. During that time the many assassinations take place. From behind the curtain come the sounds of marching feet, the hoofbeats of horses and the thud of blows. There come, also, sharp commands, the sound of guns, the glee of the army and the moans of the dying. These sounds coalesce into an impression of the fearful days of Nat Turner's Rebellion. Finally there is silence. Then the curtain rises again on Scene 2. During this time no lights have been turned on in the audience. They sit through the above interval in absolute darkness.*]

SCENE 2

WEDNESDAY NIGHT

The same scene as Scene 1. It is darker, however, for no moon rays filter down through the leafy branches. Shadows seem to press in with their ominous silence. Everything seems still and menacing. Suddenly NAT'S *voice rings out in the black night anxiously as if he knows it is in vain to call.*

NAT: Hark! Henry! Nelson! [*There is silence.*] Speak, Hark! Dis is General Nat comin'! [*There is no answer.* NAT *runs in panting with exhaustion. Instead of the God-inspired person who knows no failure, there is a hunted look about him as though he half suspects the white troops to be there ready to capture him and swing him from one of the limbs. He looks around.*] Ah thought Ah heard voices; but dey ain't heah. Dere ain't nobody heah. Dere ain't no sound 'cept ma own talk dyin' away in de dark shadows ob de woods. [*Looking over where the moon was.*] On Sunday night when we started we had de light ob de full moon, even ef hit seem tuh drip blood down on dis wicked world. But now on Wednesday everythin' is dark. Dere ain't no light nowhar in dis wide world. Even de light ob God done faded into de awful blackness which surrounds dis place. [*Reminiscently.*] When de white soldiers fired on ma army up dere near Jeresulem, dey all deserted and run lak cowards. Dey didn't hab guts enuff tuh fight; tuh stand up and be men. At de fust sign ob real battle dey tucked dere tails lak scared dogs and run away wid dere tails between dere legs. Dey ought tuh knowed dey couldn't lose. Nobody can lose when dey fight de battle ob de one true Gawd ob Hosts. [*Walking around.*] We ain't licked yet. We is still gwine fight. Ah sent Jessee and Jack tuh tell Henry and Hark, Nelson and Sam tuh meet me heah last night, and we would raise another army and carry out our plans. But dey didn't come. Ah stayed heah tull nearly daybreak waiting fuh dem. [*Half fearfully, then crying out.*] Ah wunder ef anything happened tuh dem. Naw!

Naw! Dat couldn't be. De Lawd Gawd wouldn't let dat happen! Would yuh, Lawd! Dere ain't no answer; but Ah know dey'll be heah in a few minutes. Dey couldn't git heah last night; but dey'll sho be heah tu-night. [*Pacing around like a lion in a cage.*] Hark! Dere ain't no answer. Ah can't do nothin' but wait! Wait! Dey gut tuh come soon. Dey can't stay way forever.

VOICE: [*Far off and faint.*] General Nat!

NAT: [*Full of life.*] What's dat? Somebody callin'!! Dat's Hark! He's comin'! Ah knowed he would come! Good old Hark! Now we'll git dis army together. We'll fight! We'll kill everybody in de worl' dat own slaves. We'll set all de black folks free! Ah feel lak Ah could kill a hundred white folks wid one blow!

VOICE: [*Closer and in pain.*] General Nat!

NAT: Heah Ah is, Hark. Come right on. Bring de whole army heah. We'll drill dem 'til dey learn tuh obey. We ain't gwine let dem drink cider dis time and git drunk. Dey is gut tuh fight and tend tuh business.

[JESSEE *drags in with great difficulty. He has been wounded and his whole body seems twisted with pain.*]

JESSEE: He'p me, General Nat! Dis is Jessee!

NAT: Jessee! Ah'll he'p yuh! Come on, whut's de matter?

JESSEE: [*In a halting manner.*] Dey gut me! De white folks shoot me down lak a dawg when Ah tries tuh git heah and tell yuh. Ah fell down lak Ah was daid, den Ah gits up somehow and comes heah tuh let yuh know.

NAT: Whut happened? Whar is Hark?

JESSEE: [*In pain.*] Ah's gwine in a few minutes. Ah can't las' much longer.

NAT: Whar is Hark? Did he git de army? [JESSEE *moans and drops to the ground.*] Don't go yit, Jessee! Tell me, whar is Hark! Is everthin' all ready tuh keep on?

JESSEE: [*Rambling.*] Dis pain in ma belly is killin' me.

LUCINDA: [*Calling.*] Jessee!! Jessee!! Whar is yuh?

NAT: Who is dat?

JESSEE: Hit's Lucinda.

LUCINDA: Jessee! Jessee!

NAT: Heah he is, poor boy!

[LUCINDA *comes in. She is a young slave girl dressed in dar[k] clothes. She sees* JESSEE *on the ground moaning.*]

LUCINDA: What's de matter, Jessee?

JESSEE: De white folks gut me. Dey shoot me right in de belly

LUCINDA: [*Getting down and holding his head in her lap.*] Doe[s] hit hurt much, honey?

JESSEE: Yeah, hit hurts turrible. Ah's sinkin'.

NAT: Don't go befo' yuh tells me, Jessee. Tell me 'bout d[e] army. Tell—

LUCINDA: [*Cutting him off.*] Ah thought sompen woul[d] happen tuh yuh. Dat's why Ah followed yuh.

JESSEE: Ah had tuh carry out General Nat's orders.

NAT: Whut did yuh find out, Jesse?

JESSEE: [*Ignoring him.*] Hold me in yo' arms, Lucinda. Ah ain' heah fuh long.

LUCINDA: Is dat better, Jessee?

NAT: Is dere anythin' somebody can do tuh ease yo' misery Jessee?

JESSEE: [*Coughing.*] Naw, dere ain't nothin'. Ah's gwine tu[h] another worl'.

LUCINDA: [*Crying out.*] Yuh can't go. Yuh can't go. Yuh is gu tuh stay heah wid me.

JESSEE: Ah can't stay. [*He raises up out of* LUCINDA*'s arms straightens up and salutes.*] General Nat, dere ain't no mo army. De white folks done captured Hark and all de res' Yuh'd better hide yo'se'f in a safe place. Dey is lookin' fu[h] yuh.

NAT: [*Bursting out.*] No army! Everybody captured! Dis is sho sad news yuh brings tuh me, Jessee.

[JESSEE *crumples up and falls to the ground. He is seized with violent coughing. He shudders violently and lies still.*]

LUCINDA: [*Shaking him.*] Jessee! Jessee! Yuh can't go! Come back, Jessee! [*She bursts into tears.*]

NAT: Poor boy! He's gone!

LUCINDA: [*Springing up, shrieking.*] Yeah he is gone! And yuh killed him! Yuh did hit! Yuh killed him, Ah said. Yuh wid yo' fine notions 'bout slaves should be free. Yuh fooled dem all into jining an army tuh fight 'gainst de white folks. Yuh knowed yuh wa'n't gwine do nothin'! And yuh made dem shoot Jessee. [*Getting more vehement.*] But yuh'll git yours. See ef yuh don't! De white folks is all 'round in dese woods. Dey is gwine ketch yuh and stretch yo' nake on de gallows. Dey is gwine cut yo' body up lak hawgs. Yuh ain't fittin' tuh live, dat's whut. Yuh said Gawd tole yuh tuh git an army. Well, see whut Gawd tells yuh when dey start stretchin' yo' nake. Ah'm gwine tuh tell de white folks whar yuh is. Ah'm gwine tuh tell dem, Ah say! Yuh ain't nothin' but a beast, dat's whut, a beast. [*She rushes off.*]

NAT: [*Bursting out.*] A beast! She called me a beast! Ef Ah's a beast, who made me one? Ef dey buy and sell me, whip me lak dawgs, and feed me dere leavin's, how can Ah be nothin' else but a beast? How can dey blame me ef Ah turns on dem and rend dem? [*Looking down at* JESSEE.] Jessee's daid. A few minutes ago he was heah in dis worl' groaning in misery. Hark is captured, and dere ain't no army. Whut is Ah gwine tuh do now, Lawd? Whut is Ah gwine tuh do? Whut can Ah do? Ah knows whut Ah'll do. Ah'll go hide under dat pile ob fence rails 'til Ah can git another army. Ah done put ma hands tuh de plow and Ah can't turn back. [*The yellow light of the moon filters down through the trees.*] Look at dat moon comin' back tuh light up de worl'. Hit is big and round and yellow. Hit done dripped out all hit's blood. Ma hands is full o' blood, too.

Will dey ever be clean? Was Ah wrong, Lawd, tuh fight dat black men mout be free? Whut is Ah gwine tuh do now? Show me a vision, Lawd, lak yuh did when de sperits was fightin' in de air. Talk tuh me, Holy Ghost, lak yuh did when yuh told me tuh seek de kingdom ob heaven. Didn't yuh say yuh was gwine reveal de secret ob de planets? Speak tuh me and show me, Lawd. [*He stops suddenly.*] Whut's dat noise? Hit mus' be de soldiers lookin' 'bout in de woods fuh me. Ah can't let dem catch me. Ah is gut tuh git me a army and fight some mo' fuh freedom. Ah wants freedom! Ah mus' hab freedom fuh all de black slaves. Show me how tuh git hit, Lawd! [*Shouting wildly as he goes out.*] Sperit ob Gawd! Show me de way! Guide me! Lead me! Lead me!

[*He rushes off the stage. Everything is quiet. The yellow rays of the moonlight filter down through the trees.*]

CURTAIN

THE END

SHEPPARD RANDOLPH EDMONDS
(1900-1983)

During his lifetime "Shep" Edmonds was considered the dean of black theatre educators, one who did more than any other single academic to spread a knowledge and love of theatre to students in traditional black colleges, universities, and high schools. Edmonds was well prepared for the career he had carved out for himself. A graduate of Oberlin College, Columbia University, and the Yale School of Drama, which he attended on a Rockefeller Foundation Fellowship, he next won a Rosenwald Fellowship, which enabled him to attend drama festivals in Britain and to visit British universities.

Returning home, Edmonds embarked on a career of prodigious achievement and invention. He served on the faculties of Morgan State College, Dillard University, and Florida A&M University where for 23 years he was chairman of the Theatre Arts Department. In 1930 he organized the Negro Inter-Collegiate Drama Association and six years later the Southern Association of Drama and Speech Arts, which still exists as a National Association that conducts an annual drama festival.

As a playwright and play director, Edmonds also excelled. He wrote some 46 plays, the most prominent of which have been published in three collections: *Shades and Shadows* (1930), *Six Plays for a Negro Theatre* (1934), and *The Land of Cotton and Other Plays* (1943). Edmonds took his Florida A&M University Players on a State Department tour to ten African countries, and as a Captain during World War II he staged a number of pageants for black troops. For these and other accomplishments he received many awards and citations.

Source: Vicki Ezeokoli, "Sheppard Randolph Edmonds" in *Bulletin of Black Theatre, No. 6, Fall 1975.* The Newsletter of the American Theatre Association Black Theatre Program.

HARRIET TUBMAN

by
May Miller

HARRIET TUBMAN
(1820?-1913)

Among the freedom fighters against the American slave system, there is no nobler figure than Harriet Tubman, the slave who, having escaped to the free north, repeatedly returned to the southland to lead hundreds of other slaves to liberty. Born to a large family on a plantation in Dorchester County, Maryland, Tubman was put to work at various jobs such as field hand, cook, maid, and child-nurse, all of which she performed indifferently. It is reported that at about age 13 she was struck in the head by an overseer and suffered a fractured skull which caused spells of drowsiness the rest of her life.

In 1849, fearing that the slaves on her estate were to be sold on the death of the master, Tubman made a break for freedom and finally reached Ontario, Canada. A year later she had conceived a plan to aid other runaways, including several members of her family. She returned to Baltimore and guided her sister and two children to freedom. In the decade that followed, and despite a reward for her capture that at one time reached the sum of $40,000, Tubman made nineteen trips into Maryland to spirit out some three hundred slaves through what became known as the Underground Railroad. This was an informal network of slaves, free blacks, and whites (people like those of the Quaker faith who believed slavery was evil) who gave assistance to the runaways and provided "stations" where they could rest in hiding until it was safe to continue the journey northward.

Tubman, a deeply religious woman, was convinced that her mission had divine guidance. She believed in dreams and omens, foresaw the Civil War in a vision, and at its outbreak she offered her services to the Union Army in which she served for three years as a spy, scout, nurse, and cook. After the war, she continued to serve others by caring for orphans and the helpless elderly of her race at her home in Auburn, New York. She was also active in the establishment of Freedmen's Schools in the South and in the growth of the African Methodist Episcopal Church in upstate New York.

Writing a short play of this remarkable woman, playwright May Miller focuses on a single incident in one of Tubman's forays into Maryland to collect runaways. Although the Tubman character appears but briefly in the play, her presence is felt throughout and the dangers she faced from both white slave holders and black bounty hunters are clearly portrayed. Also evident is the loyalty Tubman was able to generate even among slaves who were unable to join her trek northward. In its brief time-span, the play reveals some of the personal and emotional issues at stake in becoming a runaway, thus stressing the humanity of the slaves—a factor important to recognize both in the context of the history of those times and for dramatic characters to achieve credibility on stage.

Source: *Notable American Women, 1607-1950: A Biographical Dictionary*. Vol. III. Edward T. James, ed. Cambridge, MA: Belknap Press, 1971.

CHARACTERS

Harriet Tubman
Henry Ross, her brother
Catherine, his sweetheart
Sandy
Sabena
Thomas, a white overseer
Edward, another white overseer
Fugitive Slaves

TIME: *About the Middle of the Nineteenth Century.*

PLACE: *Eastern Shore, Maryland.*

SCENE: *A neck of marsh land on Eastern Shore, Maryland.*

When the curtain rises, the gray mask of twilight hangs over the swamp. Dark shadows play among the tall, straggly trees and touch threateningly the young NEGRO GIRL *and* FELLOW *seated on a fallen log. Only the disconsolate sobbing of the girl breaks the awful stillness. The* FELLOW *puts his arm about the* GIRL*'s shaking shoulders. She clings to him hysterically.*

HENRY: Come on, Cath'rine, thar ain't no use n' yo' breakin' yo'self up lak that. Ain't Ah tole you Ah'm comin' back to git you?

CATHERINE: [*In a tear-choked voice.*] You can't git back.

HENRY: Ain't Harriet comin' back, wid ev'ry slave town 'twixt heah an' Canada off'ring forty thousand dollars foh huh?

CATHERINE: But the Lord leads Harriet. She says she talks wid God.

HENRY: An' why can't the Lord lead me? Ah'm Harriet's brother, an' besides Ah love you. Ah won't neber close mah eyes in peace, Ah won't neber dream no sweet dreams, even in Canada, 'till Ah gits you 'way from heah. Freedom won't be nothin' widout you.

CATHERINE: Ah knows, but Ah'm scared. Mas'r Charles am so mean!

HENRY: Well, it ain't too late. You can still make up yo' mind to go wid us. Harriet'll take you.

CATHERINE: Ah gis Harriet wouldn't mind. She's jes lak a angel. Ah don' know no other slave what's got free an' come back all the way from Canada nine or ten times to git others free—an' wid 'em watchin' foh huh, too.

HENRY: Harriet say when she first crossed the line an' knowed she was free, she made up huh mind that, God helpin' huh, she'd come back to Maryland an' make huh folks free, too.

CATHERINE: She really ought'n be a-comin' at this time though—wid Mas'r Charles so mad at huh. He jes' put up a new reward for huh yistiddy.

HENRY: She had to come now, if she was a-comin' a-tall. She send word through that this was the bes' time foh huh an' the friends what helps huh 'lon' the way. 'Sides that, if we starts foh freedom tonight, being'st it's Saturday, no advertisements kin be sent on Sunday. That'll put us one day 'head o' 'em. That's the way Harriet figgers.

CATHERINE: Ah jes' pray no trouble come up.

HENRY: Ain't no trouble Harriet can't beat. You needn't be scared to come wid us.

CATHERINE: No, you'd neber git 'way wid me in the band. The other Mas'rs on the Eastern Sho' is kinda lazy, but Mas'r Charles's still mad 'bout Joe runnin' 'way wid Harriet the las' time she came down. Thar ain't no way in the worl' he'd let another slave o' his'n git to Canada no time soon. If Ah went now, he'd git out the bloodhounds, cover the roads, an' drag the Ches'peake, too; then he'd catch all o' you.

HENRY: But he didn' catch Joe.

CATHERINE: But look at them advertisements he's put up all ovah the county—fifteen hundred dollars, they say he's off'red, an all 'spenses clar an' clean, foh his body in Eastern Jail.

HENRY: An' Joe safe in Canada, laffin' at him. An' we'll laff, too, when we git thar.

CATHERINE: No, Henry, Ah ain't goin' this time, 'cause Ah knows you'll be safer widout me. Ah didn' mean to cry that-a-way. Mah head sees clar; it's jes' mah heart that hates to hab you lebe me behin'.

HENRY: An' what 'bout Sandy?

CATHERINE: Don' you worry none 'bout him. Ah kin manage him.

HENRY: But 'spose Mistah Charles beat you, an' make you marry him?

CATHERINE: They kin marry me to him, but ain't no way in the worl' they kin make me hab him. Ah'm gonna watch an' wait ev'ry day, 'til the time Harriet send you back foh me.

HENRY: An' Ah'll come. You know Ah'll come; don' you?

[CATHERINE *nods her head vigorously, as if keeping back the tears.* HENRY *draws her in his arms, kisses her fiercely, and rushes off the stage without looking back.* CATHERINE *stares after him as if stunned; then covering her face with her hands, gives vent to her grief. Upon hearing footsteps, she jumps up guiltily and wipes her eyes. She looks around fearfully.* SANDY, *a mulatto youth, has entered. He is carrying a swinging lantern, from which a dim light flickers.*]

SANDY: Hello, Cath'rine.

CATHERINE: Oh, it's you, Sandy. Mah heart was in mah mouth, Ah was that scared when you come tippin' up.

SANDY: What was you doin' down heah, all by yo'self?

CATHERINE: Nothin' much. Ah jes' sat down a-thinkin', an' fust thing Ah knowed, it was late.

SANDY: What was you thinkin' 'bout to make you so sad? You looks lak you bin cryin'.

CATHERINE: Ev'rythin' looks so sad an' dreary-lak, it make me wanta cry.

SANDY: It is kinda lonesome-lak. This ain't no place foh you, no way. Sho you ain't seen no one?

CATHERINE: No. Why?

SANDY: Thar ain't no tellin' who's 'bout. Them scalawags, lak Mistah John's niggers, might be galavantin'.

CATHERINE: Sandy, you do talk so foolish.

SANDY: That ain't so foolish neither. Up in the kitchen, they talk 'bout how one o' Mistah John's bucks lak you. Who is he?

CATHERINE: They's jes' talkin'. They don' know nothin'.

SANDY: Well, all Ah got to say is: You bettah git some good sense in yo' head, 'cause Mas'r Charles ain't neber gonna let you marry none o' Mistah John's niggers. He hates 'em all, 'cause Harriet come o' that pascel.

CATHERINE: What's the mattah wid Harriet? You talk lak you don' think she's a good woman.

SANDY: Ah ain't got nothin' to say foh nor 'gin huh, but Mas'r Charles has. An' he say he ain't gonna let no black wench steal his niggers an' git 'way wid it.

CATHERINE: What's he gonna do 'bout that, wid huh 'way up in Canada?

SANDY: She ain't in no Canada. She's—

[*He pauses, as if regretting his revelation.*]

CATHERINE: What you say 'bout Harriet?

SANDY: [*Guardedly.*] Oh, don' let's talk 'bout huh. [*He sits beside* CATHERINE *on the log.*] Let's talk 'bout you an' me.

CATHERINE: What 'bout you an' me?

SANDY: Mas'r Charles say he's gonna give you to me.

CATHERINE: He ain't said that foh really?

SANDY: Sho, and what you got agin' it?

CATHERINE: But Ah don' love you.

SANDY: Why don' you? Ah love you. What's the mattah wid me?

CATHERINE: Nothin', only you don' dream the dreams Ah dream. You's jes' as happy bein' a slave as Ah'd be bein' free. You don' neber hab no thought of freedom.

SANDY: Ah don', don' Ah! Ah gis' you won't min' marryin' me when you finds Ah'm rich.

CATHERINE: [*Throwing back her head in laughter.*] You rich, Sandy! That's funny.

SANDY: It ain't so funny as you think.

[CATHERINE *continues laughing.*]

You laff if you wants to, but Ah'll show you. This time, tomorrow, I'll hab 'nough money to buy bofe o' us free.

CATHERINE: You mus' be a-thinkin' the angel Gabriel's gonna drap a bag o' gold at yo' feet.

SANDY: Gabriel ain't got nothin' to do wid this. But money's money, an' what Ah'm tellin' you is that you kin be free widout bloodhounds on yo' tracks, if you marries me.

CATHERINE: Jes' the same, Ah do want to know who's givin' 'way that much money foh nothin'.

SANDY: It ain't foh nothin'. Mas'r Charles ain't partin' wid his money foh nothin'. Ah has to do somethin' foh it.

CATHERINE: What?

SANDY: You ain't gonna lak it, Ah gis; but we don' owe nothin' to Mistah John's niggers, an' if we kin git free, we oughtta; ought'n we?

CATHERINE: [*Her voice definitely becomes conciliatory.*] Sho. What you gonna do foh it?

SANDY: Ain't you seen the notices? Mas'r Charles, hisself's gonna give me 'nough money foh bofe you an' me to go 'way from heah an' be free.

CATHERINE: You mean them notices 'bout Harriet? How kin

you catch huh? The bloodhounds ain't been quick 'nough foh huh. She's slippery lak oil.

SANDY: Yeah, but she ain't planned good, this time; she's trapped huhself. She come ovah the road this evenin'. They didn' see huh then, but they knows she come. An' they ain't worried none, 'cause they knows she can't git out. Ev'ry road is watched an' them men ain't gonna see dollars slip through their han's that easy—an' she can't go t'other way.

CATHERINE: Which other way?

SANDY: By the Eastern Branch. She can't make it; the tide's high an' she couldn't git 'way from this end, wid all the boats locked up.

CATHERINE: But the boats rides free, an' thar ain't no one heah to roun' 'em up. Mas'r Charles an' them others is down the road.

SANDY: Thar's me. Ah got to do somethin' foh mah money. You see, if them runaways finds the roads is watched, an' goes foh the boats, they'll be locked tight in the boat-house, wid the key in mah pocket.

CATHERINE: An' standin' on the sho' waitin' to start foh freedom, Mas'r Charles an' t'others'll catch 'em—huh?

SANDY: No. Mas'r Charles say they ain't really a-thinkin' 'bout the watah way. He jes' hab me tie up the boats so as to make sho. What they's really gonna do is go by the back road. Mas'r Charles know; the folks in the kitchen done tole him. Already, he's done sent Mistah Eddie an' Mistah Thomas an' the res' o' the bosses down the road.

CATHERINE: Has they guns?

SANDY: Yeah.

CATHERINE: An' do you think they'd really shoot them folks?

SANDY: Sho. Lawd! Heah Ah'm talkin' to you, an' it mos' dark. You go on back to the house. It ain't safe foh you heah. Ah'll see you when Ah comes back.

CATHERINE: Awright.

[*She rises and starts off the other way, as* SANDY *goes off the stage to the left. Cautiously, she returns. It is growing darker and darker.* SABENA, *an old woman, approaches. She is singing softly, as if to herself.*]

SABENA: [*Singing.*]
Moses, go down in Egypt,
'Til ole Pharaoh let me go;
Hadn't been foh Adam's fall,
Shouldn't hab to die at all.
Moses, go down in Egypt,
'Til old Pharaoh let me go.

CATHERINE: [*Calling gently.*] Sabena, Sabena!

SABENA: Huh?

CATHERINE: Whar's Harriet?

SABENA: Canada, ain't she?

CATHERINE: No, Sabena. You knows bettah'n that. You got to tell me.

SABENA: Tell you what?

CATHERINE: Whar Harriet is.

SABENA: You's one o' Mistah Charley's niggers, an' Ah ain't trustin' none o' 'em. They ain't no good. [*She starts singing again.*]

CATHERINE: [*Grasping her arm.*] Lissen, Sabena, you gotta lissen to me.

SABENA: Gotta?

CATHERINE: You love Harriet, don'cha?

SABENA: What you got to do wid that?

CATHERINE: Ah love Henry. You knows that. Ah don' want him nar Harriet, neither, to git caught, an' they's trappin' 'em.

SABENA: But you ain't trappin' me.

CATHERINE: Ah ain't tryin' to trap you. Ah want to save Harriet—an' Henry.

SABENA: Sho, you do.

CATHERINE: Then, you ain't gonna tell me?

SABENA: You foun' out that much; now fin' out the res'. [*She shakes* CATHERINE'*s hand from her arm.*]

CATHERINE: Neber min'. Ah'll fin' huh, mahself. She musta stop past to see huh mammy an' pappy. Ah'll go thar. Thar ain't no time to waste; but if Henry comes this way, you'd bettah tell him to wait for me.

[CATHERINE *runs rapidly off the stage to the left. One by one, the* SLAVES, *some men, some women, enter. They are carrying lanterns; and as they steal in to join the assembled band, they are crooning softly*]:

"Oh, Freedom! Oh, Freedom!
Oh, Freedom, ovah me, ovah me.
Rather than to be a slave,
Ah'd be burried in mah grave,
An' go on to mah Lawd an' be free."

[HARRIET TUBMAN *comes cautiously in.* HENRY *is at her side. The men and women fall on their knees and kiss her dress.*]

HARRIET: Git up off o' yo' knees; we's got to be startin', an' the way is long, Ah tell you. Once started, you gotta go on or die—thar ain't gonna be no turnin' back.

[*The* SLAVES *groan softly.*]

HENRY: How far we goin'?

HARRIET: Ah takes mah people clar off to Canada. Ah can't trus' Uncle Sam wid 'em.

HENRY: Even if they's trailin' us?

HARRIET: Always they's trailin' you—clar to the line an' back. They was watchin' foh me today, but they ain't caught me. We's the fools an' they's the wise men; but Ah warnt fool 'nough to go down the high road in the broad daylight.

HENRY: Was they watchin' the road?

HARRIET: Sho, but Ah always knows when thar is danger near me. 'Pears lak mah heart go flutter, flutter, an' they may say, "Peace! Peace!" as much as they lak; Ah knows it's gwine to be war.

HENRY: If they was watchin' the road, they's on to us.

HARRIET: Ah ain't scared one jot. Ah always trust the Lawd. Ah says to him, "Ah don' know whar to go, or what to do, but Ah 'spects you to lead me." An' he always do. Now, them what trusts wid me, kin follow; the res' kin stay heah. We takes the back road.

[*The* SLAVES *say "Amen!" in chorus. Some groan softly.* HARRIET *starts off stage.* SABENA *comes forward and grasps* HARRIET*'s arm.*]

SABENA: Harriet, you got to be careful down heah, an' go kinda slow.

HARRIET: John saw the city, didn' he? Well, what did he see? Twelve gates—three o' them gates was on the North, three o' 'em was on the East, three o' 'em was on the West; but thar was three o' 'em on the South, too. An' Ah reckon if they kill me down heah, Ah'll git into one o' them gates, don'cha?

SABENA: But we don' want you to walk right into them rascals' hands.

HARRIET: Ain't we takin' the back road? Why you so het up?

SABENA: A gal was heah a-talkin'.

HARRIET: What gal?

SABENA: One o' Mistah Charley's gals.

HENRY: [*Eagerly.*] Which one, Sabena? Not Cath'rine?

SABENA: Yeah, the one that say she loves you.

HENRY: What'd she say?

SABENA: Somethin' 'bout you waitin' heah foh huh. She only went as far as Ben's an' Ritty's, a-lookin' foh Harriet. She say thar's trouble foh Harriet.

HARRIET: Trouble or no trouble—thar's two things Ah got a right to, an' they is death an' liberty. One or t'other Ah mean to have. No one will take me back into slavery alive. Ah'll fight foh mah liberty, an' when the time come foh me to go, the Lawd'll let 'em kill me.

HENRY: But Harriet, if Cath'rine say that Ah'm waitin', she'll be back 'mos' anytime now.

HARRIET: Well, Ah can't wait on no scattah-brain gal.

HENRY: But she ain't scattah-brain; she loves me.

HARRIET: [*Pausing.*] She loves you, huh? Does you love huh?

HENRY: So much, Harriet, that Ah'd come back from Canada ten times, lak yu done, jes' to git huh free.

HARRIET: Then we's waitin'. Ah trusts the sense o' a man in love, 'cause God speaks in him then.

[*The* SLAVES *say, "Amen" softly. They sing softly*]:

"Aroun' him are ten thousan' angels,
Always ready to 'bey comman';
They is always hov'rin' 'roun' you,
'Till you reach the hebbenly lan'.
Dark an' thorny is the desert
Through the pilgrim makes his ways;
Yet beyon' this field o' sorrow,
Lies the fields of endless days."

HARRIET: Hush! Ah hear someone!

[*The* SLAVES *disappear into the shadows.* CATHERINE *rushes on the stage exhausted. She looks madly around.* HENRY *calls to her softly.*]

HENRY: Cath'rine, Cath'rine, what's the mattah?

CATHERINE: [*Panting.*] Henry, tell Harriet she can't take none o' the roads.

HARRIET: [*Stepping forth.*] What's that?

CATHERINE: [*Clutching* HARRIET'*s arm.*] Harriet, they's

watchin' ev'ry road an' path. You can't git out. You'd bettah hide.

HARRIET: Me stay heah! Ah'll git out. We'll take the rivah.

CATHERINE: They's locked up the boats.

HARRIET: Jesus walked the watah, an' Ah've waded many a stream.

HENRY: You can't wade this one; the tide's high. We'd be washed down lak Pharaoh's army. Cath'rine, how you know the boats is locked up?

CATHERINE: Sandy's lockin' 'em up. But you all's got to git 'way from heah. He'll be 'long in a minute. Ah come that-a-way, an' he was 'mos' nigh finished.

HENRY: Ornry nigger! We'll knock down the do' an' take them boats.

HARRIET: An' hab ev'ryone heah the noise, an' come down on our heads at once, huh?

CATHERINE: But you can't git 'em no other way. Sandy's got the key.

HARRIET: He ain't got to keep it. Didn' you say he was a-comin' this way?

CATHERINE: He's jes' down to the boathouse. He'll be heah any minute.

HARRIET: Well, we'll git that key, if Ah hab to take it.

HENRY: No. If Cath'rine call him, he'd come to huh. He laks huh.

HARRIET: That's good. Now, Cath'rine, if you would kinda git him to stop a minute when he come alon' ...

CATHERINE: Ah could. Ah know Ah could. But you bettah hurry an' don' let him see you. Ah'll call to him an' see if he's started back.

HARRIET: No. We can't take no chances. You walk on down the road an' meet him, while we git things a bit straight. When you come back wid him, sing loud 'nough foh us to heah you comin'.

CATHERINE: Awright, an' we'll stop neah this heah big log.

HENRY: Then we'll 'ten' to the res'.

[CATHERINE *goes off stage to the left.*]

HARRIET: We oughta tie him up so as he can't git to the road; but whar kin we fin' rope this time o' night?

SABENA: To tie one o' Mistah Charley's limbs o' Satan, you kin hab this from 'roun' mah bundle.

ANOTHER SLAVE: An' mine, too. Thar ain't no place in no boat foh all these trappin's, no how.

HARRIET: [*Taking the rope as the* SLAVES *untie their bundles.*] Now, Henry, when they stops heah, you, an' two o' them others, grab him from behin'.

SABENA: Ah jes' hopes that gal o' Mistah Charley's ain't trickin' us.

HENRY: Sabena, you's plumb crazy. Thar ain't no way in the worl' foh Cath'rine to be trickin' me.

SABENA: You know, young gals lak money, an' thar's men when thar ain't money.

HARRIET: An' money an' men ain't nothin' widout freedom. Heah, Henry, take the rope.

SABENA: Ah only hopes you won't hab to wish you could string up the gal, too.

HARRIET: Hush yo' squabblin'; we ain't got no time foh that. Ah think Ah heah some singin' now. Git back in them shadows—out o' the clearin'.

[*The* SLAVES *go to the back of the stage and crouch low. In the distance, growing nearer and nearer, comes* CATHERINE'*s voice. She is singing "Go Down, Moses."* SANDY *and* CATHERINE *enter.*]

SANDY: Why you sing that ole song?

CATHERINE: Ah lak it, don' you? It makes me think o' goin' 'way from heah.

SANDY: This time tomorrow, you kin be goin' if you says so. An' it won't be no foolin', neither, lak them folks tonight.

CATHERINE: Whar you think they is by now?

SANDY: They ain't come this way, so Ah gis' they got stopped on the road.

CATHERINE: An' if they does come heah, they can't git nowhar, huh—[*She stops and speaks distinctly.*]—wid the key safe an' soun' in yo' hip pocket?

SANDY: That they can't!

[*Two* MEN *grab him quickly from behind.* HENRY *goes rapidly through his pockets and finds the key.*]

HENRY: Ah got it—Ah got it!

SANDY: [*Struggling.*] Turn me loose. Mas'r Charles'll kill you, if you take that.

HARRIET: Shet up, shet up, you Judas o' yo' own people. You oughtta burn in torment. Tie him up.

[*The* MEN *begin to tie his hands and feet. He attempts to scream. They clap their hands over his mouth.*]

SANDY: [*Struggling and trying to shout at* CATHERINE.] You two-faced devil! Ah'll tell Mas'r Charles, an' he'll break ev'ry bone in yo' dirty, lyin' body.

HARRIET: Shet up! Ah hates to lebe you livin' anyhow. If you yells out thar once mo', Ah'll choke the breath out o' yo' worthless body wid mah bare han's.

CATHERINE: He's right. Mas'r'll kill me, when he know it. You gott take me wid you.

HARRIET: Sho! An' you ain't thinkin' Ah'd be a-leavin' no smart gal lak you behin'.

HENRY: Cath'rine, you's goin', too! Then, when we git to Canada, we kin git married lak real folks.

HARRIET: Hush yo' nonsense, Henry. Thar ain't no time foh that now—it'll keep 'til we git thar. You stay heah, an' finish tyin' him up, an' keep his mouth shet while we git to the rivah. You kin catch up. Come on, folks, you's boun' foh Canaan.

[HARRIET *leads the little procession off stage to the left.* HENRY *ties* SANDY *and drags him behind the log, stuffing a rag, from* SABENA'*s bundle, into his mouth.*]

HENRY: Wid yo' mouth shet, maybe you kin think a li'l. An' jes' remember when you gits you' reward foh tellin' on you' own folks, that Ah got Cath'rine.

[HENRY *goes off stage.* SANDY *rolls and struggles, groaning. Finally, he gets the gag out of his mouth. He calls weakly, at first, then louder.*]

SANDY: Mas'r Charles! Mas'r Charles! Mas'r Charles!

[EDWARD *enters.*]

EDWARD: Hello! Hello! Did someone call?

SANDY: It's me.

[EDWARD *holds his lantern high.*]

EDWARD: Where? Where the devil are you?

SANDY: [*Weakly.*] Heah. Heah, behin' the log.

EDWARD: Well, I'll be damned. What the devil are you doin' here?

SANDY: They tied me.

EDWARD: Who tied you?

SANDY: Harriet an' them.

EDWARD: They ain't been this way, have they? The men're watchin' for 'em down the road. They plan to come that way.

SANDY: They's gone.

EDWARD: Gone where?

SANDY: To the rivah.

EDWARD: They can't git away. Mistah Charles said the boats was locked up.

SANDY: Ah did lock 'em up, but they taken the key.

EDWARD: I oughtta hang you—lettin' 'em git that key. Mistah Charles is gonna raise the devil.

[*He works roughly at* SANDY'*s bonds.*]

SANDY: [*Half sobbing.*] They beat me—they beat me an' taken the key.

EDWARD: [*Roughly.*] Shut up, an' git out of these ropes. We can beat 'em yet.

[THOMAS *enters from the left.*]

THOMAS: Who's there?

EDWARD: That you, Tom?

THOMAS: Yeah. Who's on the river?

EDWARD: On the river? Have they made the river?

THOMAS: Jes' pushed off. Who was it?

EDWARD: That Harriet, I guess, an' another pascel of niggers gittin' away.

THOMAS: Damn it! A minute sooner, an' I'd had 'em. Did you catch one of 'em?

EDWARD: No. It's only Sandy. They tied him up.

THOMAS: Mistah Charles left him to watch the river-stretch, 'cause he said nobody was comin' that way. I tried to tell him, but no, he believed the niggers, an' they said "the back road."

EDWARD: Didn' you shoot?

THOMAS: Mistah Charles kept my gun for a fellow down the road. He was that certain. 'Sides, I warn't sure 'twas them. I called but they didn' answer.

EDWARD: Can't we follow 'em?

THOMAS: Not a chance. They're 'bout midstream by now. 'Sides, they musta cut ev'ry damned boat, 'cause the rest are ridin'wild on this high tide.

EDWARD: They got the key from this nigger.

THOMAS: Mistah Charles's gonna sell you down the river.

SANDY: They beat me! They beat me an' taken the key!

EDWARD: Shut up, you blubberin' fool, an' git back to the house.

[SANDY *goes off still tugging at the ropes on one arm.*]

THOMAS: That black witch works like magic.

EDWARD: Yeah, damn it—slippin' out like that, with forty thousand dollars on her head.

[*Slowly they start off stage together as the*

CURTAIN FALLS

THE END

MAY MILLER
(1899-)

May Miller was reared in an academic environment, her father being a well-known sociologist who was professor and dean of the College of Liberal Arts, Howard University, from 1907 to 1925. As a child she was privileged to meet outstanding black artists and intellectuals who visited their home in Washington, D.C. Encouraged to participate in the arts, Miller was active in school plays and took to writing at an early age, having her first poem, short story, and play published by age 15.

At Howard University, Miller pursued her interest in theatre, acting with the Howard Dramatic Club under Montgomery Gregory and winning first prize with her play, *Within the Shadow,* which was produced at her graduation in 1920. After college she taught for some twenty years at the Baltimore High School (now called the Frederick Douglass High School) and for two summers she studied drama under Frederick Koch at Columbia University.

Miller belonged to a circle of writers known as the "Saturday Nighters" who met at the home of the poet Georgia Douglas Johnson in Washington, D.C. Among the group were other playwrights such as Marita Bonner, Willis Richardson, and Zora Neale Hurston. Miller was also a member of the Washington branch of the Krigwa Players, a black theatre organization that was started in New York on the initiative of W.E.B. DuBois. She entered the annual playwriting contests conducted by *Opportunity* magazine and gained third prize and a citation for her work. Miller has written some fourteen plays, a number of which were published in two anthologies: *Plays and Pageants on the Life of the Negro* (1930, reprinted 1970) and *Negro History in Thirteen Plays* (1935).

Miller has told this writer that her plays were presented regularly during Negro History Week at high schools and colleges, and they were often directed by Professor Edmonds when he was stationed at Morgan State College in Baltimore. In addition to her plays, she has also published several volumes of poetry.

Source: Addell Austin, "Pioneering Black-Authored Drama, 1924-1927." Unpub. Ph.D. Thesis. State University of New York at Oneonta, New York, 1986.

In Splendid Error

A Play in Three Acts

by
William Branch

FREDERICK DOUGLASS
(1817-1895)

In a career that moved from obscure slave to Minister t Haiti, Frederick Douglass reflected in his life the principles h espoused as leading spokesman for black Americans in th second half of the nineteenth century. Born a slave in Mar land, Douglass hardly knew his mother, who died as a fiel slave while he was still a youth. His father remained anon mous, though Douglass suspected he was white and probab his master.

Sent to work in Baltimore, Douglass learned to read and wri and became an expert caulker in the shipyards. On his second t he succeeded in escaping to freedom, married Anne Murray fro Baltimore who was herself free and had encouraged him to ru away, and set up house in New Bedford, Massachusetts. Howe er, the white shipyard workers refused to work with a black ar Douglass had to find other menial jobs to exist.

After giving an impromptu address at an abolitionist mee ing when he described his experiences as a slave, Douglass w invited to become a regular platform speaker on behalf of th Massachusetts Anti-Slavery Society. Within a short time he w held to be one of their prize speakers, so much so that peop who heard him began to question whether he was ever a slav To allay these doubts, Douglass wrote and published in 18 the first of three autobiographies. It was a bestseller ar promptly exposed Douglass, now a public figure, to the risk recapture by his former master. As a prudent measure, Dou lass left the United States to carry his message of reform to th British Isles. This turned out to be a triumphant tour of tw years. The friends he made raised money to purchase his fre dom; they also gave him financial backing to establish a new paper on his return to America.

Coming home, Douglass moved his family to a new location in Rochester, New York, which became a way station on the Underground Railroad. He published the weekly, *The North Star,* which made him a prominent figure in the free black community by giving them a voice in his paper. In addition to his abolitionist stand, he was now able to speak out against job discrimination and other injustices suffered by blacks in the North. He condemned any form of color prejudice and often made himself a target by going into public places where blacks were denied access.

On the other hand, Douglass constantly advocated vocational training for blacks and urged them to observe the virtues of industry, thrift, honesty, and sobriety as necessary to their development. Though he believed in political action to achieve needed reforms, he was not averse to the need for violence when it was justified. Of the Fugitive Slave Act of 1850 that allowed alleged runaways to be kidnapped and returned to slavery without the right of testimony or trial by jury, he once wrote that the true remedy for the Fugitive Slave Bill was "a good revolver, a steady hand, and a determination to shoot down any man attempting to kidnap."

When the Civil War broke out in 1861, Douglass called on President Lincoln to free the slaves and recruit black freedmen into the Union Army. His advice was ignored until the military situation had so deteriorated that Lincoln proclaimed Emancipation and welcomed blacks into the Armed Forces. After the war, Douglass returned to the lecture platform, speaking out on issues such as voting rights for blacks. A Republican, he was appointed first to the position of Marshall, then Recorder of Deeds for the District of Columbia. Some years later he was named resident Minister and Consul-General to the republic of Haiti. These federal appointments did not, however, constrain this fearless fighter from being the outspoken critic of all practices he saw as prejudicial to his race.

In William Branch's drama, Douglass, who has been tacitly supporting John Brown in his raids against the slave-holding States, is suddenly confronted with a major dilemma. Can he side with Brown in the latter's plan to seize the federal arsenal at

Harper's Ferry, West Virginia? Apart from the possibility th the plan could fail, Douglass realizes that an attack on a feder armory is tantamount to waging war against the United State Government. To associate himself with this daring act would a ienate loyal Americans of every race and class and could jeop ardize the support of northern abolitionists in the fight again slavery. The risk is too great; he must renounce any part in th attack even though he admires Brown's heroism and singular ty of purpose.

John Brown, after all, was white. He and his sons had con mitted their lives to eradicate the pernicious slave systen Their cause transcended race; it was a war against evil. Doug lass was torn by guilt that he had deserted his friend in hi greatest hour of need, but the experience was not without it redeeming aspect. The brilliant platform speaker, writer, an reformer continued to fulfill his destiny even as John Brow fulfilled his. The play presents two kinds of heroes: one wh dares all in a single desperate stroke, and the other, with n less commitment, who is prepared to ride out the treacherou waters until victory is assured.

Decades after the event, Douglass may still have bee haunted by the image of the gallant John Brown at Harper' Ferry. In Washington, D.C., on October 20, 1883, Douglas made the following declaration: "In a composite Nation lik ours, made up of almost every variety of the human famil there should be, as before the Law, no rich, no poor, no hig no low, no black, no white, but one country, one citizenshi equal rights and a common destiny for all. A Government th cannot or does not protect the humblest citizen in his right t life, Liberty and the pursuit of happiness, should be reforme or overthrown, without delay."

Source: *Dictionary of American Negro Biography,* Rayford W. Lo gan and Michael R. Winston, eds. New York: W.W. Norton & Co., 1982.

CHARACTERS

The Reverend Loguen
Joshua, escaped slave
Anna Douglass, Douglass' wife
Lewis Douglass, Douglass' son
George Chatham, white businessman
Theodore Tilton, white newpaper editor
Frederick Douglass
John Brown
Annie Douglass, Douglass' daughter
Sheilds Green, escaped slave
Colonel Hugh Forbes, British mercenary
Frank Sanborn, white Bostonian

SCENES

The entire action takes place in the parlor of Frederick Douglass's residence in Rochester, New York, in 1859-60.

ACT ONE

A late afternoon in the spring of 1859.

ACT TWO

Scene 1. *Several months later. Noon.*
Scene 2. *A few nights later.*
Scene 3. *A few weeks later. Early morning.*

ACT THREE

Six months later. Early evening.

ACT ONE

TIME: *A late afternoon in the spring of 1859, two years before the Civil War.*

SCENE: *The parlor of Frederick Douglass's house in Rochester, New York.*

The parlor is a large, "company" room on the first floor of the Douglasses' modest residence. Furnished in a manner far from lavish—or even necessarily stylish for the period—it nevertheless suffices as a comfortable sitting room for the Douglass family and an orderly, dignified reception room for their guests.

In the center of the left wall is the customary fireplace. Up left, at an angle, are large French doors leading into the dining room, and through the curtained glass may be seen the end of the dining table, a few chairs, sideboard, etc. A low settee squats against the wall up center, to the right of which is a large archway opening onto the front hall. The "front door" of the house is off right of the hallway, while a flight of stairs can be plainly seen rising to the left. There is a window in the hallway wall, and down right is a door opening onto a small library or study.

Left center is a horsehair sofa. To right and left of the sofa are partly upholstered parlor chairs. At far left is another, next to a small table.

At rise, the REVEREND LOGUEN *and* JOSHUA *are discovered. The* REVEREND, *who sits at the table far right, is dressed soberly in a dark suit with clerical collar. He is a Negro, slight of frame and advanced in years. Yet there is perennial youth about him in his sharp, distinct speech and quick, virile mind. His hat is on the table beside him, and with spectacles on he is making entries in a small notebook as he questions* JOSHUA, *who sits to his left.*

JOSHUA *is a young Negro dressed in ill-fitting but clean clothes. He is obviously a little out of place in these surroundings, but endeavors to respond with dignity to* LOGUEN's *queries.*

LOGUEN: [*Writing.*] Haynes ... Point, ... Maryland .... Tell me, where is that near?

JOSHUA: Uh, it's near Washington Town, suh. 'Bout five mile down the 'Tomac River, on the east'n sho'.

LOGUEN: I see. And are all three of you from there?

JOSHUA: Uh, yes suh. We all belongs to d' same massuh.

LOGUEN: [*Chiding gently.*] That's true, very true, Joshua, but a different master than you refer to. Now that you've made your escape you must realize that you never belonged to the man who held you in bondage. Regardless of what they taught you to think, we are all the children of God the father, and equal in His sight. Now ... you and your companions escaped from Haynes Point, and hiding by day, picked your way to New York where you contacted our agents, is that right?

JOSHUA: Uh, yes suh. Ol' Miz Oss'ning, white lady who talk real funny, she giv' us dese clothes and gits us a ride on a big ol' furniture wagon comin' up dis way, an' she tell d' man to put us off in Rochester. Den we s'pose to ax 'round fo' a man name a Douglass. Frederick Douglass.

LOGUEN: I see. And when did you arrive?

JOSHUA: Jus' now, suh. Little befo' you come.

[ANNA DOUGLASS *enters from the dining room. She is a Negro woman of forty, of medium height and build, and though not handsome, she nevertheless radiates the beauty of warmth of heart. Overshadowed outwardly by her husband's fame, she concentrates on being a good wife and mother and manages the household and occasional business with assurance and dispatch.* ANNA *has an apron on over her print dress and holds a cooking spoon in her hand.*]

ANNA: My goodness, Rev'n Loguen, you two still in here talkin'? Let the poor man eat—the other two's nearly finished and the food's gettin' cold!

LOGUEN: Eh? Oh, I've about got it all now, it's all right, Mrs. Douglass. Uh—one thing, Joshua, before you join the others. Joshua, from now on, no matter what happens, you are never to reveal to anyone again the names of the people who helped you get away. I want you to explain that to the others, do you understand?

JOSHUA: Uh, yes suh, I unnerstan's. I tell 'em.

LOGUEN: All right. Now there's a man standing by over at the blacksmith's shop with a rig, ready to take you on to where you'll catch a boat for Canada. You'll be safe there. You'll be among friends, men and women like yourselves who've made their way to freedom, following the northern star. I congratulate you, Joshua, and welcome you to the fraternity of free men.

JOSHUA: [*Nodding.*] Yes suh. Thank you, suh.

LOGUEN: [*Starting again.*] And when you get to the settlement in Canada, Joshua, I want you to —

ANNA: [*Impatiently.*] Rev'n Loguen, if you don't shut your mouth and let this poor man come on in here an' get his supper, you better!

LOGUEN: Oh—I'm sorry, Anna. It was just that—

ANNA: Come on, Joshua. Your plate's all ready for you. If you need anything you jus' call me, now, hear?

JOSHUA: Yes ma'am. Thank you, ma'am. [*He goes out Left.*]

ANNA: [*Turns to* LOGUEN.] I declare, Rev'n Loguen, I don't know what in the world I'm gonna do with you. You know them poor boys is got to get to the boat landin' by six o'clock. Fred's gone down there hisself to make the arrangements and he says have 'em there on time, 'cause the boat don't wait!

LOGUEN: I know, I know, Anna. [*Proudly.*] Do you know how many we've taken care of already this year, Anna? Thirty-three! Thirty-three free souls passing through our little station on the Underground Railroad.

ANNA: Yes, but if you keep on holdin' 'em up to pass the time of day, there's gonna be somebody up here lookin' for 'em 'fore they *gets* their souls free.

[JOSHUA *reappears at the door Up Left*.]

Why Joshua, you want me for something?

JOSHUA: [*Somewhat sheepish.*] Uh, no ma'am. It's jus' dat I—I forgit somethin'.

LOGUEN: Yes? What is it, son?

JOSHUA: Well ... dis Miz Oss—I mean, dis ol' white lady, she ... she gimme what y' call a message. I'se s'pose to tell Mr. Douglass, but I—I forgit.

ANNA: Well, that's not so terrible, Joshua, you can tell us. It'll be all right.

JOSHUA: [*Considers, then.*] Yes, ma'am. Thank you, ma'am. Well, ... dis lady, she say for to tell Mr. Douglass dat dere's a new shipment comin' through mos' any day now. One what's wuth a lots a money. She say for to be on the lookout for it, an' to han'le with care. Dat's it. Dem's d' words she spoke to me, tol' me to use 'em, too. "A new shipment ... handle with care."

LOGUEN: [*Echoes.*] Handle with care ...

JOSHUA: An' now—now kin I go an' eat, ma'am? I feels a whole lots better, now dat I 'members!

ANNA: Yes, Joshua, you go right ahead. You did a fine job.

JOSHUA: [*Grins.*] Thank you, ma'am. Thank you. [*He exits.*]

ANNA: [*Soberly.*] What you make of it, Rev'n?

LOGUEN: I don't know ... I don't know.

ANNA: Sounds to me like somebody awful important. Somebody we have to be extra careful to keep secret about.

LOGUEN: Yes, that's logical. But who?

ANNA: I may be wrong, but seems to me, couldn't be nobody else ... but him! [*Her eyes shine strangely.*]

LOGUEN: Who? [*Looks at her, then comprehends.*] But—it's too dangerous! He'll never make it. Why, they'd pick him off in an instant—you know what a price there is on his head!

ANNA: I know, I know. But he'll get through. Don't know how he does it, but he'll get through.

LOGUEN: God help him ... ! Well, I suppose I'd better go back and get these boys started if they're going to make that boat. [*Starts for the dining room.*]

ANNA: [*Heading him off.*] Hmmph! *Now* you're hurryin', jus' when Joshua's settin' down to eat. I declare, Rev'n, sometimes I think if you wasn't a man of the cloth —

LOGUEN: [*Laughs.*] Now, now, Anna. Give me another sixty years and I promise you, I'll reform! Well, I'll go down to the corner and signal Jim to bring up the rig so we won't lose any time. As soon as Joshua's finished, have them come right out and join me.

ANNA: All right, Rev'n. I'll do that.

[REVEREND LOGUEN *goes up to the hallway as* ANNA *sighs, smoothes her apron and starts for the kitchen. As* LOGUEN *passes the window he halts, glances out and whirls around.*]

LOGUEN: Quick! Anna! Tell them out the back way!

ANNA: What is it, Rev'n?

LOGUEN: Somebody's coming up the walk! Lewis and two white men—quickly, now! We've got to get them out. Here, Joshua—! [*He and* ANNA *hurry Off Left.*]

ANNA: [*Off.*] Wait, I'll get that door for you ...!

[*From Off Left comes the sound of the front door opening and closing. Then* LEWIS *is heard calling.*]

LEWIS: [*Off.*] Mother! Oh, Mother!

[LEWIS *enters, a tall, pleasant-faced Negro youth, ushering in two distinguished-looking white gentlemen:* GEORGE CHATHAM and THEODORE TILTON.]

LEWIS: Come right in, please. Let me take your hats. [*He does so and places them upon the clothes tree as the gentlemen stand poised in the archway, glancing over the room.*]

[CHATHAM *is the larger and older of the two. With balding head and large, graying sideburns, his stout form suggests a successful, comfortable businessman just past middle age.* TILTON *is small, wiry, with sharp quick eyes behind his spectacles, and is perhaps in his middle forties. Both are well dressed and obviously men of importance in their fields.*]

LEWIS: [*Joining them.*] Won't you both be seated? I hope it will not be long before my father arrives.

CHATHAM: Thank you, thank you very much, Lewis. We'll be quite comfortable, I'm sure.

LEWIS: [*Bows and goes out through the dining room, calling.*] Mother! Oh, Mother! I've brought guests ...

CHATHAM: [*Sitting.*] Well-mannered lad, isn't he?

TILTON: [*Has been absorbed in gazing around.*] What? Oh—oh, yes. Very.

CHATHAM: Cigar?

TILTON: Well, if you think it ...

CHATHAM: Of course, of course. I've been here many times before, the lady of the house won't mind in the least. Here, try this if you will. Havana. Deluxe. Imported, mind you, none of these home-grown imitations.

TILTON: Why, thank you.

CHATHAM: [*Smiling.*] Of course, it is still probably not so fancy as those you're accustomed to in your editorial board sessions in New York, but ... [*He breaks off in a little light laughter.*]

TILTON: Oh, come now, come now, Mr. Chatham. Despite the fact that you practically dragged me here by the scruff of my neck, you don't have to flatter me.

CHATHAM: [*Smiling, as he extends a match.*] And if I had to I would have gotten ten strong men to help me, too! Ah—here.

TILTON: Thank you. [*He draws upon the cigar, considering.*] Ah ... excellent. I must be sure to recommend these to my editors.

[CHATHAM *nods in deference.* TILTON *again appraises his surroundings.*]

So this is his house ... I've never been in the home of a ... [*Choosing his words carefully.*] ... of a man of color before. I must say I'm impressed.

CHATHAM: [*Nods.*] And a warmer and more friendly household you'll not find in all of Rochester.

TILTON: Yes, I gather you're all rather proud of him here.

CHATHAM: But of course! Any city would do well to have a man of such prominence as Frederick Douglass choose to live within its bounds. And to think of it, Mr. Tilton. A scant twenty years ago this man was a slave—a chattel, a "thing." A piece of property forced with lash and chain to grovel under the tyranny of his "masters"! Oh, it just goes to show you, sir, that —

TILTON: [*Smiling.*] I take it also, Mr. Chatham, that you are an abolitionist.

CHATHAM: [*Emphatically.*] That I am, sir, and proud of it!

TILTON: [*Calmly.*] Well spoken, sir. I like a man who speaks the courage of his convictions. It makes it so much easier to classify him, then.

CHATHAM: [*Alert.*] Why, sir, what do you mean by that?

TILTON: [*Urbanely.*] Oh, don't misunderstand me, my dear Chatham, I have nothing against the abolitionists. Quite the contrary, I am opposed to slavery, in principle. What I mean is that in New York, a man who declares himself an abolitionist *per se* is sure not to be a very popular figure.

CHATHAM: Popular?

TILTON: Why, yes. There have been cases where men have been stoned in the streets if they so much as spoke a disparaging word over a glass of beer in the corner saloon against the slave system. Why I believe William Lloyd Garrison himself, the "High Priest of Abolition" as it were, has sometimes been forced to close his meetings and flee for his very life before the onslaught of armed ruffians.

CHATHAM: Yes, that is true. I have heard many such accounts, of *New York* and other places.

TILTON: Well, practically each time your own Douglass speaks, outside of a few chosen localities that know him well, he does so at constant risk of personal assault.

CHATHAM: That cannot be denied. It is one of the reasons we admire him so. He has been shot at, stabbed and bludgeoned half to death, but he goes on.

TILTON: Well, you can hardly blame one then, can you, for being rather wary of ...

CHATHAM: [*Frowns.*] Mr. Tilton, since when have we become so debased, so unmanly that we allowed fear of a little retribution to abridge our sacred right of free speech and conviction?

TILTON: Well, now, I —

CHATHAM: And especially, sir, if you will permit me, in terms of the press, with its responsibility for fearless —

TILTON: [*Hastily.*] Yes, yes—let me hasten to apologize, my dear Mr. Chatham, if I have offended through the slightest reflection upon the abolitionists. It merely seems to me at this time rather more *wise* to devote oneself a little less obtrusively to one's ideals. After all, you must admit there are great numbers of good people who intensely hate slavery who are not numbered among the ranks of the abolitionists *per se.*

CHATHAM: True, still —

TILTON: Well, in any event, it should be interesting after all to meet the celebrated Frederick Douglass: escaped slave, abolitionist orator, and self-made genius. [*This last with a trace of amused scorn.*]

CHATHAM: [*Retaliates.*] Yes, it should be. It isn't every day I'd go out of my way to bring even the noted editor of one of New York's most influential newspapers to meet a man like Douglass.

TILTON: [*Smiles icily.*] Again, you do me more than honor.

CHATHAM: It's a pity you must rush on so. On Friday nights, you see, we have a series of public lectures in Corinthian Hall. Douglass is a frequent figure on that rostrum and he is scheduled again for tomorrow. Couldn't you possibly —?

TILTON: You tempt me, my dear Chatham, really you do. But I have pressing appointments in the City, and by the way, what time is it getting to be? [*He reaches for his watch.*]

CHATHAM: Oh, never fear, Mr. Tilton, there is ample time, ample. [*Starts for the window.*] I'm sure if Mr. Douglass knew you were coming he ... [*He breaks off as* ANNA *enters from the dining room.*] Well, Mrs. Douglass!

ANNA: How'd do, Mr. Chatham! It's so nice to see you again. [*She curtsies.*]

CHATHAM: [*With a little bow.*] The pleasure is all mine, Mrs. Douglass. I have the honor to present Mr. Theodore Tilton of New York City, editor and publisher of the *New York Independent*. Mr. Tilton, Mrs. Douglass.

TILTON: It is my very great pleasure. [*He bows stiffly in reply to her curtsey.*]

ANNA: We're happy to have you, Mr. Tilton. Are you enjoyin' our little city?

TILTON: Oh, very much, very much indeed! It's always a pleasure to visit Rochester. And this time I told my friend Mr. Chatham here I should never forgive him if he didn't bring me around to meet your husband.

ANNA: That's very kind of you. Gentlemen ... [*She motions and they sit, after her.*] I understand you went by the office?

CHATHAM: Yes. Young Lewis told us Mr. Douglass had gone

to the Post Office. I should have remembered that Thursday is publication day ...

ANNA: Oh, that's all right. I guess you supply paper to so many big publications you just couldn't expect to remember 'bout all the little ones like us.

CHATHAM: Oh, quite the contrary, Mrs. Douglass. I have no client I think more highly of than *The North Star*.

ANNA: Now, just for that you'll have to stop and have supper with us. Both of you.

[TILTON *looks distressed.*]

CHATHAM: Thank you so much, Mrs. Douglass, but I'm afraid my Ellen has already prepared. Else we surely would take you up on your generosity. [*To* TILTON.] Mrs. Douglass has the reputation of spreading one of the finest tables in Rochester.

TILTON: [*Weakly.*] Yes, I'm sure.

ANNA: [*Flattered.*] Well, at least let me get you a cup of tea while you're waitin'. No, now you just makes yourself 't home.

CHATHAM: All right, Mrs. Douglass. I know there's no use trying to get around you.

[*From off in the hallway a door opens and closes.* ANNA, *who has started for the kitchen, stops and turns.*]

ANNA: Why, I b'lieve that's Mr. Douglass now. [*Calls.*] Fred? That you Fred?

DOUGLASS: [*Off.*] Yes, Anna.

ANNA: [*Coming to the archway.*] You got company ...

DOUGLASS: Well, now.

[FREDERICK DOUGLASS *enters, a bundle of papers under his arms. He is a tall, broad, compelling figure of a man, forty-two years of age. His face, of magnificent bone structure, would be a sculptor's delight with the high cheekbones, the strong broad nose, the proud flare of the nostrils. His eyes, brown, deepset, peer intently from beneath the ridge of his prominent brow, and the straight grim line of the mouth seems on the verge at any moment of an awesome pronouncement. A long mane of crinkly black hair sweeps back from his stern forehead, and, together with heavy moustache and beard, lends a strikingly distinguished, leonine air. His large frame, bolt erect, is dressed conservatively in a suit of black broadcloth, with embroidered waistcoat and gold watch fob. His is an impression of challenge, achievement, dignity, together with strength, quiet but omnipresent.*

DOUGLASS *pauses in the archway, then depositing his bundle on the small table nearby, he strides forward to* CHATHAM, *hand extended.*]

DOUGLASS: George Chatham! Well, this is quite an unexpected pleasure.

CHATHAM: [*Beaming.*] So it is, so it is!

DOUGLASS: [*His voice is sonorous; he speaks with cultured ease.*] And is this a business visit? Am I more than two years behind in my account?

CHATHAM: Well, it that were so, I should hardly have come myself. I should rather have had my creditors, to collect *my* debts from *you!*

[*They both laugh heartily.*]

Frederick—Frederick, I wish to present Mr. Theodore Tilton of New York City. Mr. Tilton is the editor and publisher of the *New York Independent,* and I wanted him to make your acquaintance while he is in the city. Mr. Tilton, Mr. Douglass.

TILTON: [*Again bowing stiffly.*] It is my very great pleasure ...

DOUGLASS: Not at all, the honor is mine, Mr. Tilton. [*He goes to* TILTON *hand extended.*]

[TILTON *shakes hands uncomfortably.*]

Will you be long in Rochester?

TILTON: No, I'm afraid I must return to the City tonight.

DOUGLASS: That's too bad. Anna, have you asked our guests to stay for supper?

CHATHAM: Yes, she has, Frederick, but I'm afraid Mrs. Chatham has already prepared.

ANNA: I was just goin' to make some tea —

TILTON: Pray don't, Mrs. Douglass. You see, we really don't have much more time to stay, I'm afraid.

DOUGLASS: Oh? Well, another time perhaps. Meantime, please be seated again. I refuse to let you leave at once.

ANNA: Oh, uh—Fred ... ? 'Scuse me, but did you get them letters off in the mail while you was out? Three letters, goin' to Canada ... ? [*She looks at him with meaning.*]

DOUGLASS: Oh ... ! Yes, my dear. They're safely in the mail and on the way.

ANNA: [*Smiles.*] I'm glad. 'Scuse me. [*She gives a little curtsey and goes out via the dining room.*]

DOUGLASS: [*Turns back to his guests.*] Now, then ...

CHATHAM: Oh, er—will you have a cigar, Frederick? I have some special —

DOUGLASS: No thank you, George. I've never been able to develop the habit personally, but by all means ... [*Indicates for them to continue. They settle themselves.*]

[*After a pause.*]

Tell me, Mr. Tilton, what is the talk in New York these days?

TILTON: Oh, the same as here, I would suppose. Stocks and bonds ... the railroads ... migration west ... Kansas ... the Indians ...

DOUGLASS: Ah, Kansas! So they speak of Kansas, do they?

TILTON: Oh, yes. It is much in the conversation round about.

DOUGLASS: And what do they say of Kansas, Mr. Tilton?

TILTON: Well, they discuss its impending admission into the

Union. It seems certain by now that it comes as a free State, though there is much bitterness on both sides. And there's a great deal of pro and con about this fellow Brown ...

CHATHAM: You mean Captain John Brown?

TILTON: Yes, yes, I do believe he calls himself by some military title or other. Personally, I will be very happy to see Kansas enter *our* fold, so to speak, instead of the South's. But I can't very well agree with the way in which it was won.

DOUGLASS: Oh? And why?

TILTON: Well, I'm thoroughly against slavery, *per se*, you understand—you'll find our paper has stood out staunchly on that matter. But I think old Brown has done more to hinder the cause of the slaves, with his self-appointed crusade to keep Kansas free, than all the splendid work of the past several decades by persons like yourself to advance things.

DOUGLASS: Has he now?

TILTON: Why, of course! Good God, for him and his lawless band to call men out from their cabins in the dead of night, and without note or warning, judge or jury, run them through with sabres! Why, it's ghastly even to contemplate.

CHATHAM: But, sir, you overlook that it was the partisans of slavery that first made war in Kansas, burning farmhouses and towns, assassinating and driving out those who dared voice opinion that Kansas should be kept free. It was these murderers—known to all—that Captain Brown avenged himself upon.

TILTON: Yes, but—

CHATHAM: And then, when the slave state of Missouri sent an armed militia across the border into Kansas, who but old Ossawatomie Brown, with a comparative handful of men —

TILTON: Oh, there is no doubt as to their bravery—or even

foolhardiness, if you will allow—but to seize the lawful prerogative of the federal government, whose authority it is to protect these territories, is a very dangerous and outlandish course of action!

DOUGLASS: [*Has picked up a copy of his paper, reads.*] " ... still today, and with no help from the federal government, Kansas stands at the gateway to statehood as a free territory. Is there any denying it would not have been so except for old John Brown?"

TILTON: Then you give your endorsement to such guerrilla tactics?

DOUGLASS: I have never particularly enjoyed the prospect of human beings wantonly killing one another. But from what I have gathered, there was left no choice in Kansas. It was either be driven out at gunpoint, or face those guns and fight. And that I think John Brown has done most admirably.

TILTON: [*Frowns—considering.*] Hmm ... well, actually, Mr. Douglass, the conflict in Kansas has proved little point with respect to abolishing slavery. Rather, keeping the system from spreading—Free Soil, as they call it—was the actual issue there. For all his reckless bravado, old Brown liberated not a single slave.

CHATHAM: Ah, but to prevent the spread of the system across a single mile of border is a noble service indeed!

DOUGLASS: Quite so, George, but more than that: Free Soil and freedom for slaves must be regarded as coats of the same cloth. The one will never be secure without the other.

TILTON: Why, how do you mean?

DOUGLASS: [*Smiles—pointedly.*] I mean, sir, that those who seek to exclude slavery from the territories—for their own political or business interests—without concerning themselves about abolishing the system altogether, are merely evading the ultimate issues. Slavery is like a spawning cancer; unless it is cured at its core, then despite all precaution it will eventually infect the whole organism. It must be stamped out entirely, not merely prevented from reaching other parts of the body.

TILTON: Ah—but we are dealing here with semi-sovereign States, not hospital patients. Unlike a physician, we have no license to delve into the internal affairs of the South.

DOUGLASS: Human slavery cannot be considered a purely internal affair of the South, Mr. Tilton. Especially when it seeks with guns and powder to extend the system further.

TILTON: I feel quite confident the federal government is capable of preserving law and order in any such eventuality.

CHATHAM: The government! A government rife from top to bottom with Southerners?

TILTON: [*Protests.*] President Buchanan is not a Southerner —

CHATHAM: Buchanan—hah! A Northern man without Southern principles who bends over backwards to concede every fantastic demand of the hotheads from Dixie! Or take Congress—frightened into hasty compromise every time the "Gentleman" from Carolina or Georgia or Mississippi bellows threats and abuse at his Northern colleagues! Or must I even mention the Supreme Court, it's blasphemous Dred Scott decision still fresh upon the page? And you speak to me of the government, sir! Why, if I had my way, I'd line 'em all up at my sawmill, start up that blade and hold a Bastille Day such as the French never dreamed of … !

DOUGLASS: [*Amused.*] Careful, now, George. You'll have poor Mr. Tilton thinking Rochester's a nest of fiery revolutionists.

TILTON: Well, at least there's an election next year. You may then express your opinions of your government under the protective mantle of party politics—without being liable to arrest for sedition.

CHATHAM: Hah—if I did adequately express my opinions I

should still be arrested. For use in public of profane and obscene language!

TILTON: [*Wryly.*] A great loss to the cause of abolition that would be. [*Turning to* DOUGLASS.] Seriously, though, I do believe the continued existence of slavery is fast becoming the prime political issue of the day.

DOUGLASS: Quite so, quite so! Why, take even last year's Senatorial campaign, the widespread debates out in Illinois between Senator Stephen Douglas and this other fellow, Lincoln —

CHATHAM: [*Interrupts.*] But Lincoln was defeated!—a paltry, small-town, hayseed lawyer with more audacity than ability. Think no more of him. He's politically, uh—*passé.*

DOUGLASS: Nonetheless, George, the issue there was plain: the enslavement of human beings and all the evils it gives rise to must either be sanctioned nationally, or it must be abolished. Try as it may, the nation cannot much longer avoid decision on the matter. I believe the outcome of the election *will* depend upon this one issue.

TILTON: [*Craftily.*] And perhaps the outcome of the nation, too, eh? However, I can only reiterate that drastic measures—such as old Brown's—can at best only aggravate the situation.

CHATHAM: [*Protesting.*] But slavery, sir, is an outrageously drastic condition. And when other measures have failed, drastic conditions call for drastic measures!

TILTON: [*Tolerantly.*] Now, my dear Chatham, I have heard of many instances where masters are voluntarily freeing their Negroes. And of others who provide in their wills for manumission upon their deaths.

CHATHAM: Whose deaths? The master's ?— or the slave's! Ha!

DOUGLASS: [*Calmly.*] May I point out to you, sir, that my own freedom was not given to me: I had to take it. And if you were a slave, Mr. Tilton, knowing full well that you of right ought to be free, would you be content to wait until your master died to walk on your own two feet?

CHATHAM: Ha! I for one would help him along a little.

TILTON: [*Ignoring this—to* DOUGLASS.] But can you not see that to press for all-out abolition at a time like this can but only further alienate the South? Why already they have threatened an ultimatum in the elections next year: unless a man friendly to them and their policies continues to sit in the White House they may bolt the Union! And you know we can never permit such a split.

CHATHAM: Quite so, but —

TILTON: [*Exasperated.*] Well, think of it, man! It would mean war, actual all-out fighting, one section of the citizenry against another, with muskets and sabres and cannon. Why it would be disastrous, catastrophic!

CHATHAM: Certainly—disastrous to the slaveholders, catastrophic to slavery!

TILTON: [*Turning to* DOUGLASS.] Surely, Mr. Douglass—notwithstanding the great multitude of wrongs committed against your enslaved people, the cardinal crime of bondage itself—still, surely you must see that if war comes between the States, not only will your people not benefit, but the nation as a whole stands in imminent peril of perishing!

DOUGLASS: [*Quietly.*] Mr. Tilton, if I spoke to you as a slave, I would say: "No matter, let it perish." As a being denied of all human dignity, reduced to the level of the beasts of the field, it would be of no consequence to me whether this ethereal idea known as a government survived or disintegrated. I would have nothing to lose, quite possibly everything to gain. If I spoke to you as a free man and a citizen, I would say: "War is destructive, cruel, barbaric. It must be avoided—if possible." But wrongs will have their righting, debts will have their due. And if in the last resort it should come to war, then we must make intelligent use of it, once involved, to destroy the malignant growths, to set right the festering wrongs, and to eliminate for all time this present grounds for complaint.

CHATHAM: Hear, hear! [*He thumps the arm of his chair vigorously.*]

TILTON: [*With a smile.*] I see you drive a hard bargain.

DOUGLASS: No more than the slaveholders, sir.

TILTON: [*Slowly.*] Mr. Douglass ... though I cannot say that I altogether agree with you, nonetheless I can recognize a forceful sincerity when I see one. Will you permit me, sir, to make a note or two of this for publication? [*He takes out pad and pencil.*]

DOUGLASS: [*Spreading his hands.*] If my humble words —

TILTON: Oh no, no modesty here. I am sure our readers will be as interested as I in giving your arguments careful thought. [*He busies himself with making notes.*]

[CHATHAM *flashes a congratulatory smile at* DOUGLASS *and is about to speak when from Off in the hallway the front door knocker is heard.*]

DOUGLASS: [*Starting for the door.*] Will you excuse me ...

LEWIS: [*Appears, coming from the rear of the house.*] I'll get it!

DOUGLASS: All right, Lewis.

CHATHAM: I've tried to interest Mr. Tilton in hearing you speak sometime, Frederick. But unfortunately, he's a rather busy man, and —

TILTON: [*Looks up.*] I mean to correct that fault, Mr. Chatham, as soon as possible. When will you be in our city again, Mr. Douglass?

DOUGLASS: New York? Oh, I couldn't say. I've been trying to confine myself as much as possible to the paper lately, and I —

TILTON: [*Reaching inside his coat.*] If you will permit me, here is my card. Please do me the honor of stopping with me when next you're in the City.

DOUGLASS: [*Taking the card.*] Why, that's kind of you, Mr. Tilton.

[LEWIS *appears at the archway.*]

LEWIS: Excuse me, father. There's a Mr. Nelson Hawkins here to see you.

DOUGLASS: [*Puzzled.*] Hawkins? Nelson Hawkins?

LEWIS: Yes sir—he ... well, I mean—[*He seems to be suppressing some excitement.*]—he just got in from out of town, and he—shall I ask him to wait in your study?

CHATHAM: [*Rising.*] Oh, by no means, Frederick, please don't neglect your guest on our account. We have to get going now, anyway. That is, if Mr. Tilton —

TILTON: [*Still writing.*] Yes, yes. I'm nearly ready. Just one minute ...

DOUGLASS: [*To* LEWIS.] Ask him to step into the study for a moment, Lewis. I'll be right with him.

LEWIS: Yes sir! [*He goes off.*]

CHATHAM: Well, Frederick, it's been much too long since I've seen you.

DOUGLASS: Yes, it has. You must have dinner with us again very soon, George. We've missed you.

CHATHAM: I mean to take you up on that. In the meantime, the wife and I will be at the lecture tomorrow night, as usual.

DOUGLASS: Good. I'll be looking for you. [*To* TILTON, *who has put away his notebook and risen.*] And so you're leaving us tonight, Mr. Tilton?

TILTON: Yes, I must. Though I'd very much like to be at the Hall tomorrow. What is your subject?

DOUGLASS: I'm speaking on "The Philosophy of Reforms."

TILTON: Oh, I would mightily like to hear that!

DOUGLASS: Then perhaps you would care to take along a copy of *The North Star* to glance at in your free time. [*He secures a copy.*] My remarks will be merely an expansion of this week's editorial.

TILTON: [*Accepting it.*] Thank you, sir, you are most kind. Our office subscribes to your paper, but it is not every week that I get to read it first hand.

DOUGLASS: Well, I shall have to remedy that by placing you personally on our subscription lists.

TILTON: Excellent! But you must bill me for it.

DOUGLASS: [*Nods in deference.*] You may send us your check if you wish.

CHATHAM: And now, we really must be going, or my Ellen will be furious.

[*They go out via the hallway, ad libbing amenities, the murmur of their voices continuing in the background. After a pause, the door Down Right opens and* LEWIS *appears. Making sure the others are out of sight, he turns smiling and holds open the door.*]

LEWIS: Please step in here now, Mr. Hawkins. Oh, let me get your bag.

[HAWKINS *enters. He is a lean sinewy man of over fifty. His flowing hair and ragged beard are streaked with gray, and his steel-gray eyes bore with deep, lively penetration. Dressed in plain woolen, cowhide boots, and carrying a well-worn leather strap bag, he presents a figure of indomitable energy and determination.*]

HAWKINS: [*Crossing to a chair.*] Oh, no thank you, Lewis. I can manage all right for an old man, don't you think? [*He grins at* LEWIS *with a twinkle in his eye and lays down his bag by the chair.*] Well, Lewis, you've grown—haven't you?—since I was here last. Getting to be quite a young man. How old are you now?

LEWIS: Seventeen, sir.

HAWKINS: Seventeen! Why, that's hard to believe. [*His eyes twinkle.*] And I suppose you cut quite a figure with the young ladies now, do you?

LEWIS: [*Blushes.*] Why, no sir, I —

HAWKINS: Oh, come now! I'll wager you've already pickec out your young lady-fair.

LEWIS: Well, not exactly, sir.

HAWKINS: Not exactly? Ha, then *she* has picked *you* out!

LEWIS: Well—I do like a certain girl, but ... it's just that—well girls can act pretty silly sometimes. You just don't know what they're thinking or what they're going to do next Sometimes they say no when they mean yes and yes when they mean no. I can't understand them at all!

HAWKINS: Well, well. This sounds pretty serious, Lewis. Tel me. Is she pretty?

LEWIS: Oh, yes! She's very pretty, I think. [*Pause.*] She's .. she's the minister's daughter.

HAWKINS: I see. And is she religious?

LEWIS: Well, rather, I suppose. [*An afterthought.*] She's the minister's *daughter*, you understand.

HAWKINS: Ah, yes! That does make a difference.

LEWIS: I walked home with her from church last Sunday. couldn't think of anything much to say, so we started ou talking about the weather. And when we got to her house we were still talking about the weather. Six blocks abou the weather!

HAWKINS: My, that certainly is a lot of weather!

LEWIS: [*Miserably.*] I just don't understand them, that's all.

HAWKINS: Well, Lewis, if you ever arrive at the point where you think you do, come and tell me, will you? I've hac two wives and eleven children, and if God has ever seen fit to distribute understanding of women, then I must hav been behind the barn door when He passed it out!

LEWIS: [*Grins.*] Yes sir.

[DOUGLASS *re-enters from the front, glancing hastily at hi watch.*]

DOUGLASS: And now, Mr. Hawkins ...

[*Pause.* HAWKINS *turns toward him expectantly, but does not speak.*]

Mr. Hawkins? ... [*He stares questioningly at* HAWKINS *while* LEWIS *watches eagerly.*]

HAWKINS: [*An amused twinkle in his eye.*] Hello, Frederick Douglass!

DOUGLASS: [*Slowly recognition—and joy—come into* DOUGLASS*'s face.*] Why ... bless my soul, it's Captain Brown! [*He rushes to him.*] John! John!

[BROWN *laughs and they embrace warmly.* LEWIS *grins in delight and exits toward the kitchen.*]

DOUGLASS: But that beard!—You were always clean-shaven. And these clothes! Why, if it hadn't been for your voice I never would have —!

BROWN: [*Laughs loudly.*] You're looking well, Frederick!

DOUGLASS: Why, so are you, only—well, come and sit down, John. How did you ever manage to get through? Why, there's an alarm out for you in seven States!

BROWN: [*Laughs.*] Oh, I have means, Frederick. I have means.

DOUGLASS: Oh, I must tell Anna. [*Calls.*] Anna! Anna, guess who's here!

[ANNA *rushes in from the kitchen followed by* LEWIS.]

ANNA: Lewis just told me! Welcome, Captain Brown! Welcome!

BROWN: Thank you, thank you, Anna. My, but you're the picture of health and brightness! You've got a wonderful wife here, Frederick. A fine woman!

ANNA: Oh, go on with that kind of foolishness, John Brown!

BROWN: Oh, yes, yes! God has been bountiful to you both. How are all the children?

ANNA: They're all very well, thank you.

BROWN: Good, good.

DOUGLASS: And how's your family, John?

BROWN: [*His smile fading.*] Oh ... well. Well. For the most part, that is. These past few years have been hard on us, Frederick. Kansas ... the price was very dear.

DOUGLASS: [*Concerned.*] Sit down, John. Tell us about it.

BROWN: [*Sitting.*] Thank you. I am a little tired.

ANNA: And you must be hungry too, poor man. Supper's nearly ready, but now that you're here I'll have to get up somethin' special for dessert. A pie, maybe. Sweet potato still your favorite?

BROWN: It certainly is.

ANNA: All right. Now you just make yourself 't home. Lewis! Come on and set the table for me, son.

LEWIS: [*Reluctantly.*] Aw ... [*Glances at his father, then rises quickly and follows* ANNA *out.*]

DOUGLASS: John, we've had no word of you for months. We didn't know if you were alive or dead.

BROWN: [*Smiling.*] Oh, I'm still above ground, Douglass. It will take more than a few cowardly ruffians in the Territories to put John Brown in his grave. And a lot more to keep him there! [*Sobers.*] They did get one of my sons, though. My Frederick.

DOUGLASS: Oh, no ... !

BROWN: Yes. They shot him down one night, not far from Ossawatomie. Owen, too—the big one. But Owen still lives. Back on the farm at North Elba, Mary's nursing him back to health. He's ... paralyzed. The waist down.

DOUGLASS: [*Softly.*] My God! And you, John, are you well?

BROWN: Oh, yes. I've been a little tired, but I'm gathering strength to go on with the work.

DOUGLASS: To go on? But John, Kansas is won! Surely now you can rest. You've done what no other man has been able to do: you've stopped the slave power dead in its tracks!

BROWN: Not quite, Douglass, not quite. Try as we might, the Free Soil constitution adopted in Kansas says nothing about the emancipation of slaves. It offers sanctuary to not a blessed black soul. I must get back to my true work: to free enslaved black folk, and not further waste my energies and resources on political partridges like Kansas. That is why I am here.

DOUGLASS: Yes?

BROWN: I shall want you to put me up for a time, Frederick. Several weeks, a month perhaps.

DOUGLASS: You know, John, that my house is always yours.

BROWN: Good. I knew I could count on you. I will pay for my accommodations. Oh no—no, I insist! I will not stay with you unless I can contribute my share to the household expenses. What shall it be?

DOUGLASS: Now, now, John —

BROWN: Come, come, Douglass! You must be practical.

DOUGLASS: Well, all right. Shall we say—three dollars a week for room and board? No, not a penny more! You are my guest.

BROWN: All right, settled then. [*He withdraws a purse and hands to* DOUGLASS *three dollars in silver coin.*] For the first week.

DOUGLASS: You are now a member of the Douglass household, in good financial standing.

BROWN: Fine! And one other thing, Frederick. While I am here I wish to be known in public only as "Nelson Hawkins." I want John Brown to be thought still in the Territories. Though Kansas is won, still there's a price on my head some enterprising young scamp might be ambitious to collect.

DOUGLASS: Ha! I shall turn you in at once! [*They laugh.*] As you wish, John. I shall inform the entire household at supper.

[*The outside door opens and a child's voice cries, "Momma! Momma! We're back!"* DOUGLASS *smiles and looks up expectantly. In runs* ANNIE DOUGLASS, *a vivacious little six-year-old, followed by* SHEILDS GREEN, *a stockily built Negro with a bundle of papers under his arm.*]

ANNIE: [*Sees her father and runs to him.*] Oh, Poppa! Guess what I've been doing! Me and Sheilds. I helped Sheilds take out the papers!

DOUGLASS: [*Lifts her in his arms.*] You did? Well now, aren't you Poppa's big, big girl!

ANNIE: Yes, I am! [*She gives him a hug, then giggles.*] Oh, Poppa, your whiskers. They tickle! [*She squirms around in his arms and for the first time sees* BROWN *across from them. She abruptly stops her laughter and her eyes grow big with wonder.*]

DOUGLASS: [*Setting her down.*] John, this is the light of my life, my little Annie.

BROWN: Well, she's quite a young lady now, isn't she!

DOUGLASS: Annie, this is Mr. ... Mr. Hawkins. Say how-do-you-do like Poppa's big girl.

ANNIE: [*Steps forward timidly and gives a little curtsey.*] How de do? [*Then rushes back into her father's arms.*]

BROWN: And how-do-you-do to you, little lady!

DOUGLASS: Mr. Hawkins is going to stay with us for a while, Annie. Is that all right with you?

ANNIE: [*Considers—suspiciously.*] Doesn't he have a house of his own?

BROWN: Yes, I have, Annie. But it's a long way off.

ANNIE: [*Bolder now.*] Do you have a little girl?

BROWN: Why, yes—in fact one of my girls has the same name as you. Annie. Only she's a big girl now.

ANNIE: Bigger than me?

BROWN: [*Smiles.*] Yes, a little. But you'll soon be grown up and married, too. You just wait and see!

DOUGLASS: Hold on there! Don't go marrying off my baby so soon.

ANNIE: [*Her timidness dispelling, she leaves her father's arms and moves toward the stranger.*] You got whiskers, just like my Poppa. Do they tickle too?

[DOUGLASS *laughs and winks at* SHEILDS, *who stands in the background, watching the proceedings with a wide grin.*]

BROWN: Well, I don't know. Do they? [*He bends down and juts out his chin.*]

[ANNIE *reaches out and tugs gently at his beard.*]

Uh-uh, careful!

[*They laugh as* ANNIE *jumps back, startled.*]

DOUGLASS: Well, how about it, Annie? Has he passed the test? May he stay, or shall we turn him out?

ANNIE: [*Considers this idea for a moment—then joyously.*] No, no! He can stay! He can stay!

DOUGLASS: Good! It's all settled.

BROWN: [*With a little bow.*] Much obliged to you, ma'am!

[ANNA *enters from Off Left.*]

ANNA: I thought I heard another woman in here!

ANNIE: [*Running to her.*] Oh, Momma, Momma! I helped Sheilds with the papers! I helped with the papers!

ANNA: You did, sweetie? Well, that's nice. And did you meet our guest?

ANNIE: Oh, yes! He's got a little girl, too, with the same name as me, and his whiskers tickle just like Poppa's.

DOUGLASS: A dubious compliment!

ANNA: All right, dear. Suppose you run on upstairs now and get yourself ready for supper? Make sure you hang up your coat.

ANNIE: All right, Momma. [*She curtsies to* BROWN.] 'Scuse me, please. I have to go now. [*She runs over to* SHEILDS.] Can help you again sometime, Sheilds?

SHEILDS: Yes, honey. Anytime you want.

ANNIE: [*As she runs off and up the stairs.*] Gee, Momma, I'm sc hungry I could eat a whole hippopotamus!

DOUGLASS: [*To* BROWN.] Now you see where all our money goes. To buy her hippopotamuses!

[BROWN *laughs.* ANNA *returns to her kitchen, and* SHEILDS GREEN *starts to follow.*]

DOUGLASS: Oh, Sheilds! Come, I want you to meet our guest er—Nelson Hawkins. [*To* BROWN.] This is Sheilds Green sometimes known as "the Emperor"!

BROWN: [*Extending his hand.*] The Emperor? Am I in the presence of royalty here? Glad to know you, Mr. Green [*He shakes hands vigorously.*]

SHEILDS: Glad to know you, suh.

DOUGLASS: Royalty in a sense. Because of his great strength Sheilds's master nicknamed him "The Emperor"—used tc point him out to his guests, laugh and make fun of him Now it's Sheilds's turn to laugh. Not agreeing to be whipped one day, he left his master with a wrenched arm three loose teeth and a dislocated collar bone.

BROWN: Well, well! Now that's an odd going-away present And you reside here in Rochester now, I take it?

SHEILDS: Yes suh.

DOUGLASS: Sheilds has made his home with us since his escape.

BROWN: Good! We'll be seeing a lot of each other then, Mr Green. I have an idea you may fit into our scheme quite handily, too, if you've a mind to. I shall need a number of men like you—strong, courageous, unafraid.

DOUGLASS: Tell us, what is this scheme of yours? [*He motions them toward seats.*]

BROWN: All right. Now is as good a time as any. [*He reaches for his bag, and withdraws a large rolled parchment.*] All the while I was in Kansas, Douglass, I have been thinking, planning, praying over this thing. Kansas was but an interlude, an opening skirmish. It has given me a hard core of trusted men, baptized in fire and blood, who will follow me anywhere. And now ... now the time has come to carry the war into Africa itself, into the very heart of the Southland. [*Unrolling the parchment, he lays it over the table Down Right.*] Here. Will you be so good as to hold one edge for me, Mr. Green?

SHEILDS: Yes suh. I got it, suh.

BROWN: Now. If you will look carefully, Douglass—and you too, Mr. Green—here we have a map of the States from New Hampshire to Florida, and Maryland to Missouri. Now: here are the Allegheny Mountains sweeping from the North clear through to Alabama. Do they portend anything to you, eh?

DOUGLASS: I don't quite know what you mean. They form more or less a natural chain from North to South, but —

BROWN: Exactly! These mountains are the basis of my plan, Douglass. I believe these ranges to be God-given, placed there from the beginning of time by some divine pre-arrangement for but a single purpose—the emancipation of the slaves. [*He pauses, eyes shining.*]

DOUGLASS: Go on. Explain.

BROWN: Look here, at the Blue Ridge Mountains of Virginia. These ranges are full of natural forts, where one man for defense would be the equal to a hundred for attack. Now, I know these mountains well. My plan, then, is to take a force of men into the Virginia hills. There I will post them in squads of fives along a line of twenty-five miles. Now, when these are properly schooled and drilled in the arts of mountain warfare, it will then be possible to steal down to the plantations and run off slaves in large numbers. Think of it, Douglass! Think of the consternation among the

Virginia slavemasters when they see their slav disappearing into the hills!

DOUGLASS: [*Weighing it all.*] Yes ... yes, I can imagine.

BROWN: Not only for the good of delivering these peop from their bondage, you understand—though that is course the paramount end. But the prospect of valuab property which is disappearing in the middle of tl night—ah! Here, Douglass, we attack the slave system its core, and that is its pocketbook. [*Springing up.*] O Douglass, you and I know that eloquent appeals to men emotions, their reasons, their sense of justness and fa play have little effect if the evil you would have the discard is the means of their bread and syrup. They m turn a deaf ear to God himself, but once you remove tl monetary profit from their vices, take away the means l which they gain their filthy dollars, they will desert it as in fear of plague and seek other means more economical secure to furnish their tables.

DOUGLASS: [*Has been listening carefully.*] Yes ... yes, there much truth in what you say. But ... suppose you succe in running off a few slaves. What is to prevent them fro merely selling their slaves further South?

BROWN: Ah! That in itself would be a show of weakne Besides, we would follow them up. Virginia would be on the beginning.

DOUGLASS: But they would employ bloodhounds to hunt yc out in the mountains.

BROWN: That they might attempt, but we would wh them—and when we have whipped one squad, th would be careful how they pursued again.

DOUGLASS: And the slaves themselves? What would becon of them once you had liberated them from their bonds?

BROWN: We would retain the brave and the strong in tl mountains, and send the rest north into Canada by way the Underground Railroad. You're a part of that operatio

Douglass, and I'm counting on you for suggestions along that line.

DOUGLASS: I see. But won't it take years to free any appreciable number of slaves this way?

BROWN: Indeed not! Each month our line of fortresses will extend further South—Tennessee, Georgia, Alabama, Mississippi—to the Delta itself. [*He points them out on the map, which* SHEILDS *now holds, gazing in wonder.*] The slaves will free themselves!

DOUGLASS: And those you retain in the mountains. How do you propose to support this growing band of troops?

BROWN: We shall subsist upon the enemy, of course! Slavery is a state of war, Douglass, and I believe the slave has a right to anything necessary to obtain his freedom.

DOUGLASS: [*Thoughtfully.*] Now, if you were surrounded, cut off ... if it's war, then you must not underestimate the enemy.

BROWN: True, that's true, but I doubt that we could ever be surprised in the mountains so that we would not be able to cut our way out.

DOUGLASS: Perhaps ... still, if the worst were to come?

BROWN: [*Impatiently.*] Then let it come! At least we will have been doing something. Action—action is the basis of reform, and long ago, Douglass, I promised my God I had no better use for the means, the energies and the life He gave me than to lay them down in the cause of the slaves. [*Turns to* SHEILDS.] Mr. Green. You've been silent. Let us hear from you.

SHEILDS: [*Admiration in his voice.*] You're Cap'n John Brown, ain't you?

BROWN: [*With an amused glance at* DOUGLASS.] Why, yes—yes I am, Mr. Green.

SHEILDS: Jus' call me Sheilds.

BROWN: All right, Sheilds.

SHEILDS: I'm not a what-you-call eddicated man, suh. M Douglass here's jus' now learnin' me readin' and writin' ain't much to offer, I knows, but when you gits ready send them mens into the mountains, please let me kno I'd powerful like to be one of 'em, Cap'n Brown.

BROWN: And so you shall, Sheilds, so you shall! [*He strides* SHEILDS *and shakes hands vigorously. To* DOUGLASS.] Ther you see? My first recruit! I'll have to write Forbes abo this. Oh, I haven't told you about Forbes, have I?

DOUGLASS: Forbes?

BROWN: Yes. Colonel Hugh Forbes. By an extraordina stroke of good fortune, Douglass, I've met a certa Englishman, a military man who has engaged in several the revolutionary movements of Europe. I've verified th he fought with old Garibaldi himself. I've engaged th man as drillmaster for my troops.

DOUGLASS: Drillmaster?

BROWN: Yes. I have induced Colonel Forbes to join me an supervise the proper training of a fighting force. I consid it very fortunate that I could persuade him.

DOUGLASS: Where is he now?

BROWN: In New York, writing a military manual for the u of our troops.

DOUGLASS: Why, it all sounds so incredible! An Englis drillmaster and a military manual ... ! I know yo accomplishments, John. You were successful in Kansas b personally leading a small band of men. But now all th talk of a drillmaster and a special manual —

BROWN: But you fail to realize the scope of the missio Douglass! This is to be no minor skirmish, this is war an war demands extensive preparation. You can see ho important it is to make allowances now for whatev might arise in the future. Douglass ... [*Intensely.*] Douglas I've spent years perfecting this plan in detail. I've teste my methods under fire. Believe me, I know whereof speak!

DOUGLASS: [*Slowly.*] Yes, in the past you've proved that beyond all question, John.

BROWN: Then you're with me, Douglass?

DOUGLASS: [*Turns away—thoughtfully.*] Your plan at best is risky, very risky. If it fails it may undo a great deal of work that's been built up over the years ... even set off a spark that might destroy us all. But there is one thing that cannot be denied: you have not just talked about slavery, you are doing something about it. And against such odds ... We cannot rely upon time and the kindness of men's hearts to free our people, John. You have proved your worth as a fighter, and you have my support.

BROWN: [*Goes to him—in emotion.*] Oh, Douglass ... Douglass!

DOUGLASS: What can I do to help you?

BROWN: All right. I shall need men to add to my force, brave men and strong—like Sheilds here. I need your aid in assembling them.

DOUGLASS: John, do you know Harriet Tubman?

BROWN: No, but I've heard of her. The "Conductor" of the Underground Railroad.

DOUGLASS: She is now in Canada, resting at a settlement of fugitive slaves. I will take you to her. She will find you all the men you can use.

BROWN: Good.

DOUGLASS: And what of money and supplies?

BROWN: Yes—though I do not grudge the sums I spent in Kansas, now my funds are nearly gone. I intend to solicit contributions from antislavery men of means.

DOUGLASS: Tomorrow you shall meet another, a wealthy millowner who often has aided in the operation of the "Railroad." He will be most anxious to help.

BROWN: Splendid! I shall write to others in Boston,

Philadelphia, and New York. I'll have them communicate with me here, as "Nelson Hawkins."

DOUGLASS: And I can reach leaders among the slaves from Virginia to Mississippi. When you are ready to move, they will know you are coming.

BROWN: Oh, Douglass! Douglass! [*He grasps* DOUGLASS *by the shoulders.*] I knew I could count on you! It's coming ... I can feel that it's coming! As Moses led the children of Israel from Egyptian bondage to the land of Canaan, so shall we lead the children of Africa from Southern bondage to the land of Canada. It is God's will. Together—together we will free the slaves! [*He stands with arms outstretched toward* DOUGLASS *and* SHEILDS *as*

CURTAIN

ACT TWO

SCENE 1

TIME: *Several months later. Noon.*

At Rise, ANNA DOUGLASS *is discovered tidying up in the hallway. She comes down into the parlor for a quick look around, then starts to leave, when she spies a hat resting on a chair. She picks it up and examines it; it is of curious military design. She glances ominously toward the closed study door then drops the hat back onto the chair in disgust. Off Right the front door opens and* LEWIS *enters, whistling gaily.*

LEWIS: Hello, Mother.

ANNA: Oh, that you, son? You're home early. I ain't fixed dinner yet.

LEWIS: Oh, that's all right. There was nothing going on at the office anyway. Where's Dad?

ANNA: [*Indicates the study.*] In there. That man is here again.

LEWIS: What man?

ANNA: That soldier man. You know, Captain Brown's friend. Colonel somebody.

LEWIS: Oh, you mean Colonel Forbes.

ANNA: That's the one. He's in there with Fred.

LEWIS: What's he want this time?

ANNA: I don't know, but I'll bet it's money. Fred's keepin' the old man's funds for him and he has to handle his business when he's gone.

LEWIS: But Captain Brown's not ready to move yet. He's still out raising funds. Doesn't seem right to be paying Colonel Forbes for doing nothing.

ANNA: That's what I been tellin' Fred! But he says the old man insists. Says he'll need Forbes and he'll be ready pretty soon now.

LEWIS: I hope he knows what he's doing.

ANNA: So do I, Lewis. Every time Fred talks to him he just says, "God'll take care of everything." 'S if God ain't got enough to do already.

[*The front door slams and* ANNIE *runs in, shrieking.*]

ANNIE: Momma! Momma!

ANNA: My gracious! What's the matter baby?

ANNIE: Quick, Momma, I have to hide!

ANNA: Hide from what, Annie?

ANNIE: From Bobby and Henry. They're after me!

ANNA: Bobby and Henry? What are they after you about?

ANNIE: We was playin' slavery, an' I'm the slave. Only I ran away!

[LEWIS *grins and shakes his head, exiting toward the kitchen.*]

ANNA: Oh ... well, you better get away quick then, 'fore you get caught. That'd be just terrible, wouldn't it?

ANNIE: No, it won't be so bad. Jackie's playin' Mr. Hawkins and he always helps me get free again.

ANNA: Oh, I see. Well, your poppa's got company in the liberry and I hate to turn you out. But you better go back outside and play. [*She guides* ANNIE *toward the hallway.*]

ANNIE: All right, Momma. But if they catch me, they're gonna sell me off to the highest bidder!

ANNA: Oh? Well, if that happens, I'll come out an' see if I can't buy you back with some gingerbread and cookies. Run on, now.

[ANNIE *starts out but then, glancing out the hallway window, she squeals and comes running back.*]

ANNIE: Momma, Momma! They saw me! I have to get away! I have to get away! [*She dashes off toward the kitchen.*]

ANNA: [*Following.*] Lawd-a-mussy! I don't know what I'm gonna do with you ...

[*As they leave the study door opens and* DOUGLASS *enters, followed by* COLONEL HUGH FORBES. FORBES *is a tall, once-handsome man in his thirties with a harried, hungry look about his eyes.*]

DOUGLASS: [*Is frowning.*] I'm very sorry, Mr. Forbes, but that is the state of affairs and I don't see that there's anything more to say. Now, if you'll excuse me, I have quite a bit of work to do.

FORBES: Now, just a minute, just a minute here! Am I to understand, then, that you refuse to discharge these obligations?

DOUGLASS: [*Displeased.*] I am under no obligation to you whatsoever, sir.

FORBES: Well, perhaps not you personally, Mr. Douglass, but you *are* acting for Brown. And I tell you that he is behind on my salary. Again! Now really, old chap, just how much do you fellows expect me to put up with? I have tried to be patient, man, but even my endurance has its obvious limitations. Why, so far I think I have been rather agreeable about this whole thing, and —

DOUGLASS: [*Smoldering.*] Oh, you have, have you? And I suppose you were just being agreeable when you wrote this letter to George Chatham demanding by return mail a check for fifty dollars! Mr. Chatham is not responsible for your salary, Mr. Forbes. Nor am I. From here on you will have to make your arrangements personally through Captain Brown, or not at all. Now again, I am asking that you excuse me. I have more important matters to attend to.

[LEWIS *appears at the dining room door and stands listening.*]

FORBES: Important matters! What is more important than my salary? Really, Mr. Douglass, I am amazed at your apparent lack of understanding. Can you possibly fail to appreciate that I am in a rather unique position here? That a word from me in the proper ears would spell the end of this whole scheme? The end of Brown and you and all the rest?

DOUGLASS: So now it's out! At last!

FORBES: [*Daring.*] Yes, at last, if you couldn't get it before! Where do you think you'd be, any of you, if it weren't for me? Why, this whole thing constitutes in essence a conspiracy—a conspiracy against the peace of Virginia and a plot against the government. All I'd have to do would be go to Washington and seek the proper authorities, and it would be a bad day for you, sir!

DOUGLASS: [*Flaring.*] Bad day for me indeed! Mr. Forbes, if you think you're going to blackmail me—or John Brown either, for that matter—you've got quite a surprise coming. I'll not give you another cent of his money. You may go where you like and tell whom you please, but you'll not intimidate me one whit! Now, I'll thank you to leave my house.

FORBES: [*Placatingly.*] Now, now—there's no need for haste. You needn't upset yourself so, Mr. Douglass. I —

DOUGLASS: We will speak no more about it, sir!

FORBES: Take until tomorrow to think it over. After all, only two hundred dollars.

DOUGLASS: Take your hat and get out. Before I feel compelled to assist you!

FORBES: [*Indignant.*] Now, really, I — ! [*He draws himself up with arrogant dignity.*] Very well. You force me to take action. I have tried to reason with you, I should have known that that is impossible. And I am not in the habit of being insulted by … by …

[DOUGLASS *removes his spectacles, calmly.* FORBES *turns and beats a hasty exit.*]

LEWIS: [*Steps into the room.*] We can stop him! I'll catch him before he gets around the corner — !

DOUGLASS: No, Lewis, let him go! I must reach the old man at once—I want you to go to the telegraph office and get off a message. Here, take this down. [*He looks around for paper and pencil, but* LEWIS *withdraws his own.*] To Nelson Hawkins, Esquire. Care of Gerrit Smith, 17 East Locust Street, Peterboro, New York …

LEWIS: I've got it. Go on.

DOUGLASS: "Return at once. A wolf has upset the pail."

CURTAIN

SCENE 2

A few nights later.

Gathered in the room are DOUGLASS, BROWN, CHATHAM, LOGUEN, SHEILDS, *and another gentleman to be identified as* SANBORN. *They appear to have been having a conference, but now they have paused and are finishing up refreshments of cake and coffee.* LEWIS *is circulating with a plate of cake slices, but everyone seems to have had enough.* ANNA *has the coffee service and pours another cup for one or two of the guests. Several light up cigars or pipes, and the room begins to take on the air of a political caucus. At length,* SANBORN *puts down his cup and calls the meeting to order. He is a mild, cultured gentleman with a Boston accent.*

SANBORN: Gentlemen. Gentlemen. It's getting very late. Shall we get on with our business?

[*There are ad libs of "Yes. Quite so. By all means."*]

All right. [*He turns to* BROWN *who sits near the fireplace facing the others, as if in a witness chair.*] Captain Brown, we have all listened earnestly to your arguments in favor of continuing with your plan. I think I can speak for all of us here when I say that we greatly admire your spirit and have implicit faith in your capability. We have supported you before, and are most anxious to do so again, in order to advance the day of freedom for our enslaved brethren.

However—and here I speak not only for myself but also the committee I represent—however, we cannot afford to ignore this new and most distressing development. A trust *was* misplaced. The man *has* gone to the authorities—Senator Seward himself telegraphed me in Boston and asked me to get to you right away. He is trying to keep it quiet, but still for all we know, right now we may be under the watchful eye of federal agents merely awaiting the opportune moment to pounce!

Under these circumstances it seems that your plan is doomed to failure if you insist upon pursuing it now. You have convinced us in the past that you are worth supporting. We have subscribed funds and promised supplies and arms and ammunition. We do not withdraw them now!

[*There are ad libs of disagreement from the others.*]

BROWN: Mr. Sanborn, I do not concede that now is a less favorable time than in some distant future. We can do it still! We must not be made timid by the first dark shadow that falls across our path. A swift blow, a swift blow now, gentlemen, before they get a chance to believe the scoundrel — !

[SANBORN *frowns and shakes his head firmly.*]

CHATHAM: But why not, Sanborn, why not? If we could get things rolling now, catch them off their guard — !

SANBORN: You mean let them catch us off our guard! And remember—they've got Forbes with them now. He knows the whole plan in detail.

BROWN: If you will only leave that matter to me—I have those who can be put on his trail. Forbes will get what traitors deserve!

[*There is a disapproving murmur.*]

SANBORN: That is simply impossible, Brown. In the face of what has happened, it's sheer madness!

LOGUEN: Careful ... careful, Captain.

CHATHAM: Well, John, I'm not so sure that that's at all advisable ...

SANBORN: You should never have taken the man into your confidence.

DOUGLASS: Well, I think we've *all* been fools not to have seen through his game from the very first. But still, Frank, it seems so ... tragic to have to postpone the entire operation now.

CHATHAM: Of course! What's the matter with Gerrit and Higginson and the others on the committee, Sanborn? Are they getting cold feet because of a handful of stupid men in Washington, or have they been this timid from the very first — !

SANBORN: Now, now, Chatham, there's no need to go too far over the matter. From the first we've had to consider that we could all be prosecuted for conspiring to violate the Fugitive Slave Law and a score of other such measures. But we all take our chances in this work and regard it as our Christian duty, and I'm sure none of us regrets a single action or dollar spent up to now.

CHATHAM: Well, good. Who was it said: "We must all hang

together, or most assuredly we shall all hang separately."

[*There is a little light laughter.*]

LOGUEN: [*With a frown.*] Well, gentlemen, it is all very well to joke about it, but I for one am behind Captain Brown one hundred per cent. I protest against any postponement. If the thing is postponed now, it is postponed forever—because Forbes can do as much evil next year as this. I believe we have gone too far to turn back now!

BROWN: [*Encouraged.*] Aye, Reverend Loguen! And I tell you, sirs, that I can do it. I have the means and I will not lose a single day now. I tell you we can be freeing slaves a week from tonight in Virginia.

CHATHAM: What? So soon?

BROWN: Absolutely, sir! [*Rises.*] There is no need for delay. I would have been in Virginia now were not Harriet Tubman lying ill in Canada. But she can send me others who know the "Railroad"'s route as well as she. I and my men will free the slaves, and hers will lead them out.

CHATHAM: But with so small a band? I thought you needed scores —

BROWN: General Tubman will dispatch a good-sized force to me as soon as I have need of them. And when the first blow is struck the slaves will rise throughout the countryside. Men from the free States will come down and join. An army will form, consolidate and march southward. Oh, I tell you, sir, it can be done and I can do it now! [*He pauses, trembling with the emotion of it.*]

[*And all eyes turn toward* SANBORN. SANBORN *meets* BROWN'*s gaze gravely, then slowly and firmly shakes his head. There is a pause as the others register their disappointment.*]

But my men will fall away ... everything that I have been building in my lifetime will come down to nothing, nothing ... [*He sinks to his chair.*] You don't know what you're doing ... you just don't know ...

SANBORN: We know how disappointed you are, Captain

Brown, and we regret it exceedingly, believe me. But we cannot listen further. Our hearts are still with you, but I believe it is pretty well decided. [*Turns toward* DOUGLASS.] Frederick ... ?

DOUGLASS: I ... no. No, Frank, I have nothing further to add to what I've already said.

SANBORN: All right. Captain Brown, this is what you must do. You must stay low, let time pass. The alarm will die down, the suspicions. Then you will return and strike, and we shall be behind you. In the meantime, tell us no more of your plans. We will trust you with our money, but we can aid you no further for now. Go back to Kansas and wait. Time must pass.

[*There is silence.* BROWN*'s eyes are smoldering but he does not speak.* SANBORN *rises, signifying that the conference is at an end, and the others follow suit.* SANBORN *turns to* DOUGLASS.]

We must thank you, Frederick, for receiving us so graciously on such short notice.

DOUGLASS: That's quite all right, Frank. I'm only sorry that I can't put you all up for the night.

CHATHAM: Oh, we have plenty of room at our place. I'll take good care of him.

SANBORN: That's very kind of you, George.

DOUGLASS: [*One last try.*] Stop by tomorrow, unless you have to hurry back.

SANBORN: [*Smiles and shakes his head.*] I'm afraid I'm catching the early Boston train. So I'll say goodbye now. Until the next time. [*He grasps* DOUGLASS*'s hand, then turns to leave.*]

[*He stops, seeing* BROWN *still sitting brooding by the fireplace, but* BROWN *abruptly turns away, refusing to say goodbye, and* SANBORN *continues out via the hallway.* CHATHAM *follows.* LOGUEN *puts a sympathetic hand on* BROWN*'s shoulder before passing on.* DOUGLASS *accompanies them all to the door as* SHEILDS *stands looking after, flashing hostile eyes at the departing guests.*

ANNA *and* LEWIS *reappear and gather up the cups and saucers. They exit.* SHEILDS *seats himself dejectedly by the table and gazes with sympathy at* BROWN, *who continues to sit in defeated silence, solemnly regarding the fire.*

Presently DOUGLASS *returns. He pauses near the archway, then comes slowly Down and sits, drawing his chair nearer the fire. For a moment he does not speak.*]

DOUGLASS: [*Quietly.*] I'm sorry, John.

BROWN: [*Stirs and smiles weakly.*] It's all right, Frederick. You told me how it would be.

DOUGLASS: Perhaps it *is* better to wait.

BROWN: [*Sighs.*] "There is a tide in the affairs of men,
Which, taken at the flood, leads on..."

I am at my tide, Frederick. Despite what they say, I cannot turn back now.

DOUGLASS: You don't mean that. Another year, a few months perhaps —

BROWN: [*Shakes his head.*] I cannot delay further.

DOUGLASS: Surely you can't mean that you're going on with it now.

BROWN: It will be now or never.

DOUGLASS: [*Alarmed.*] Has all this tonight meant nothing to you?

BROWN: Oh yes, yes. It has meant a great deal. They have failed me at the first small sign of difficulty. I cannot afford to leave them that opportunity again—I will proceed without them. It means altering my plans somewhat, but I have already prepared for that. You see, Frederick, I leave nothing to chance.

DOUGLASS: [*Sympathetically.*] You're tired, disappointed ...

BROWN: For twenty years this plan to free slaves has held me like a passion. It will be desperate, perhaps, but it will be holy. For I was created to be the deliverer of slaves, and the time is now.

DOUGLASS: [*Goes to him.*] Come up to bed, and we will speak more of it tomorrow.

BROWN: No, my friend. There is no time to waste in sleeping now.

DOUGLASS: Now, really, John, you're taking this too far. After a good night's rest things will look different in the morning.

BROWN: Morning must find me on my way. I am leaving tonight.

[SHEILDS, *sitting silently on the other side of the room, sits up at this, and listens intently.*]

DOUGLASS: Leaving? But what can you do now, alone?

BROWN: I still have my band, Frederick. I must get them word immediately—listen to this. [*He takes out a telegraph sheet and reads.*] "The coal banks are open. Old miners will come at once." Ha! They'll know what I mean. And where.

DOUGLASS: But what about arms, supplies— ?

BROWN: I already have enough cached away in a warehouse in Pennsylvania with which to begin. Once we reach Virginia, we'll live off the land. As for arms, there will be all we can use just waiting for us at Harpers Ferry. Once there, we can begin our operations without want of —

DOUGLASS: Just a minute! Did you say ... Harpers Ferry?

BROWN: Yes.

DOUGLASS: There is a United States Government Arsenal at Harpers Ferry.

BROWN: Of course! That is what I mean. We shall seize it first. With its store of weapons and supplies we can arm our forces as they expand, equip Harriet Tubman's men as they come, supply the slaves for miles around.

DOUGLASS: Brown! What are you thinking of?

BROWN: [*Speaking fervently now.*] Can't you see it, Frederick? The word traveling from lip to lip ... the slaves rallying to the call ... the mountain passes sealed with bullets ... liberty spreading southward like a trail of fire! ...

DOUGLASS: John!

BROWN: The nation roused —

DOUGLASS: Do you know what you're saying?

BROWN: The chains dropping —

DOUGLASS: It's mad. It's madness, I tell you!

BROWN: Free men rising from the muck of enslavement! —

DOUGLASS: [*Shouts.*] John!! Listen to me. You cannot do it!

BROWN: [*Slowly realizing what* DOUGLASS *is saying.*] What ... ?

DOUGLASS: It is impossible, insane! You must not even think of it.

BROWN: You're ... going to fail me, then? You too, Douglass? I'm counting on you to help me, Frederick, are you going back on me, too?

DOUGLASS: [*Taking him by the arm.*] Sit down. Sit down, John.

[*They sit.*]

Do you believe I'm your friend? That I want to do what's right?

BROWN: I believe you, Frederick.

DOUGLASS: Then listen to me. I have helped you as much as I could. I intend to help you further, when the right time comes, in your great slave-freeing raids. But what you are saying now is wholly different.

BROWN: Wherein is it different? This is greater, that's all, greater. We shall free more slaves and free them faster.

DOUGLASS: But don't you realize what you'd be doing? You can't attack Harpers Ferry. You'd be attacking the United States Government. It would be treason!

BROWN: [*Eyes flashing.*] Treason! Government! Laws! Blast them all to hell! I answer you back, Douglass. I answer you back with humans and right! I answer you back there is a higher law than all!

DOUGLASS: John, you're living on earth—you're dealing with men.

BROWN: [*Defiantly.*] I deal with God!

DOUGLASS: Oh, I see! You deal with God. And is it God who counsels you to rash, inopportune action? Is it God who calls you to dash away your talents and your usefulness in a single ill-considered stroke? And what of the slaves themselves — you want to help them, you say. Why then do you think of doing the very thing that will harm them most? Why bring the nation's anger on them? *You* may defy the federal government, but they cannot.

BROWN: But we will rouse the nation behind them! It needs rousing. It's cursed. It's dying. It needs to be startled into action.

DOUGLASS: Oh, can't you see, John? By running off slaves from southern plantations, you attack the slave system without endangering retaliation by the whole nation. Aye! There will be many who will approve and come rallying to your support. But if you start by attacking Harpers Ferry your blow is not at slavery itself. Your blow is against the whole nation, and will bring down on your head—and the slaves—the panic and condemnation of thousands whose sentiment would otherwise be with you.

BROWN: I cannot concern myself with public opinion just now. Action! Action is the only means to reform. You know that Douglass ... you've said it yourself.

DOUGLASS: Yes, John, yes—but must we have action, any action, at so great a price? Tell me. Tell me, John: is there ever any justification for such unprovoked violence, even in pursuit of a righteous cause?

BROWN: Yes! Yes, by God, I believe there is. If we cannot persuade the nation with words to purge itself of this curse, then we must do so with weapons. This is war, I tell you, and in war there must often be sacrifices made to expediency.

DOUGLASS: Be careful, John! Think now of what you say. Some day *you* may be sacrificed to *their* expediency.

BROWN: I am thinking. And I am unafraid. In God's good time, as we seep southward, those of good faith will see their trust was not misplaced.

DOUGLASS: You'll never get South, John! Not if you insist upon starting at Harpers Ferry. I know the area—it's like a steel trap. Once in you'll never get out alive. They'll surround you, hem you in!

BROWN: [*Defiantly.*] They surrounded me in Kansas! They never took me there!

DOUGLASS: They'll hurl all their military might against you!

BROWN: We'll cut our way through! We'll take prisoners and hold them as hostages.

DOUGLASS: Virginia will blow you and your hostages to hell rather than let you hold the arsenal for an hour!

BROWN: I'm not afraid of death! Is that why it's insane, Frederick? Because we may spill a little blood?

DOUGLASS: We're talking about freeing slaves, John! Not throwing lives away in a hopeless insurrection — !

BROWN: But this is the way to free slaves—all of them not just a few! [*Intensely, with great passion.*] It must be by blood! The moral suasion of Moses and Aaron was in vain, even with the abetment of the locusts and the boils. Not till the shedding of the blood of the first born of Egypt was there release for Israel. Through blood out of bondage, Douglass! Without the shedding of blood there is no remission of sins —

DOUGLASS: John! Do you think you are God?

BROWN: [*Stops, momentarily stunned.*] God? ... God is different things to different men, Frederick. To some He is a separate entity, dispensing wrath or reward from philanthropic heights. To some He is watchdog conscience, gnawing at the marrow. To me ... God is simply the perception and the performance of right. And so I am a little bit of God. Or trying to be.

DOUGLASS: [*Starts to speak, then sighs.*] I cannot argue with you further, John Brown. I see I cannot hope to change your mind.

BROWN: Then you're coming with me, Frederick?

DOUGLASS: I cannot.

SHEILDS: [*Interrupting from the background.*] Wait for me, Cap'n Brown! I'm goin' up to get a few things.

DOUGLASS: [*Turning.*] What? Sheilds ... ?

SHEILDS: Yes, Mistuh Douglass. I believe I'll go wid de ole man. [*He turns and goes upstairs.*]

BROWN: Come with us, Frederick. I need you.

DOUGLASS: I cannot.

BROWN: Douglass! I will defend you with my life.

DOUGLASS: John —

BROWN: I want you for a special purpose. When I strike the bees will begin to swarm and I shall need you to help me hive them.

DOUGLASS: You have changed your plan. I cannot go with you now.

BROWN: Will you fail me then? Will you fail your people? [*Suddenly smoldering.*] Or are you so far removed from slavery that you no longer care!

DOUGLASS: [*Taken by surprise.*] What — ?

BROWN: [*Tauntingly.*] Have you carried the scars upon your back into high places so long that you have forgotten the sting of the whip and the lash?

DOUGLASS: John, that's not being fair! Don't —

BROWN: [*Like a whip.*] Or are you afraid to face a gun?

[DOUGLASS *gasps as if struck. Then, catching himself, he grasps the back of a chair for support.*]

DOUGLASS: [*Slowly.*] I have never really questioned it before, John. If it would do good ... if it would do good, this moment I would die, I swear it, John! But I cannot cast away that which I know I can do for that which I know I cannot do. I have no right to do that. I should rather fail you, John, than feel within myself that I have failed my people. For them ... I believe it is my duty to live, and to fight in ways that I know can succeed.

[BROWN *stares at* DOUGLASS *for a moment, then turns and starts for the stairway. Reaching it, he pauses and turns to* DOUGLASS.]

BROWN: I shall miss you, Frederick ...

CURTAIN

SCENE 3

A few weeks later. Early morning.

Except for a faint glow from the fireplace, the room is in darkness. Breaking the stillness rudely is the sound of someone knocking at the door, excitedly. There is a pause, and the knocking resumes, louder than before. A pause, then again. This time a light appears from the top of the stairway, and ANNA*'s voice is heard calling: "Yes, just a minute! Just a minute!" Then* LEWIS *is heard saying, "I'll go down, Mother, you stay up here."*

LEWIS *appears descending the stairway with a candle, a pair of trousers pulled on hastily over the bottom of his nightshirt. He goes Off to the door.*

LEWIS: [*As he unbolts the door.*] All right, just a minute.

[*The door opens.*]

Yes?

VOICE: [*Off.*] Are you Lewis Douglass?

LEWIS: Yes.

VOICE: Fred Douglass's boy?

LEWIS: Yes, I am.

VOICE: Then this here telegram must be for you.

LEWIS: Telegram? For me?

[ANNA *appears on the stairway with a light. She descends halfway, peering toward the door. She is in a nightgown with a shawl thrown over her shoulders, and her hair hangs down in a braid.*]

VOICE: That's right. Telegraph operator asked me to drop it by to you right away. Urgent.

LEWIS: Why, thanks. Thanks very much, Mister — ?

VOICE: Oh, that's all right. You don't need to know my name, it's better that way. You just get to what that wire says.

LEWIS: Hey, wait! Wait a minute, mister.

VOICE: [*Farther away.*] Good night!

ANNA: Lewis! What is it, son?

LEWIS: [*Closes the door and returns.*] It's a wire, Mother. It's addressed to "B.F. Blackall, Esq."

ANNA: That's Mister Blackall, the telegraph operator.

LEWIS: [*Opens it hastily and reads.*] "Tell Lewis, my oldest son, to secure all important papers in my high desk at once." That's all it says. Not even signed.

ANNA: It doesn't have to be, you know it's from Fred.

LEWIS: Gee, Mother, do you think he's in trouble?

ANNA: I don't know, son. But I been on pins and needles for the past two days now. The high desk, did he say?

LEWIS: Yes, Mother.

ANNA: Then he must mean those letters and papers he been keepin' for Captain Brown. Come on, son. [*She heads for the study.*]

LEWIS: Oh!—but the high desk is locked. And Poppa always keeps the key with him.

ANNA: [*Turning.*] Then look in the kitchen and get a knife or something. Lewis, hurry!

LEWIS: All right. [*He goes.*]

[*From the stairway comes a small voice crying, "Momma...?"* ANNA *looks up and sees little* ANNIE'*s face peering from between the banisters.*]

ANNA: Annie! What you doin' out of bed?

ANNIE: [*Affecting baby talk.*] Big noise wake me up. Peoples talkin' and bangin' on doors.

ANNA: Now you know you ain't supposed to be gettin' out of your bed in the middle of the night, even if the Walls of Jericho is tumblin' down! And you with such a cold.

ANNIE: But I'm scared, Mom-ma ...

ANNA: Not half as scared as you're gonna be if you don't put your little behin' back in that bed!

[ANNIE *begins to cry.* ANNA *goes to her.*]

Now, now there, baby. That's no way to do. There ain't nothin' to be afraid of. [*Takes her in her arms.*] Hush, now, everything's gonna be all right.

LEWIS: [*Re-enters with a chisel.*] This ought to get it open, Mother!

ANNA: All right, Lewis. You go ahead. You know what to take out?

LEWIS: Yes. Yes, I know. [*He goes into the study.*]

ANNIE: Mom-ma, where's Poppa?

ANNA: Poppa's in Pennsylvania, honey, tendin' to some business.

ANNIE: When's he coming home? I miss him.

ANNA: I know you do, darlin'. So do I. He'll be home soon, though. Maybe tomorrow or the next day.

ANNIE: Is Sheilds coming back with him?

ANNA: [*Quietly.*] I don't know, honey.

ANNIE: Mr. Hawkins?

ANNA: No ... no, I don't think so, baby. You come on here, now, 'n let me tuck you back in like a nice little lady, 'fore you catch your death of —

[ANNIE *sneezes.*]

There! You see? [*She rises and starts upstairs with* ANNIE *in her arms.*] Now you just come on and go right back to sleep. There's nothin' for you to be afraid of, an' nobody's gonna wake you up again ... [*Her voice trails off as they move from sight.*]

[*Knocking begins at the door again.* LEWIS *comes out of the study, startled, a bunch of papers in his hands. The knocking repeats. After a hasty look around,* LEWIS *stuffs the papers into his waist, arranges his nightshirt over them, and starts for the hallway. Remembering the library door, he dashes back to close it, then on to the Front.*]

LEWIS: [*Breathlessly.*] Who is it?

CHATHAM: [*Off.*] It's George Chatham, Lewis.

LEWIS: [*Relieved.*] Oh! [*He opens the door.*] Come in, Mr. Chatham, you gave me quite a start.

CHATHAM: [*Enters, removing his hat.*] Thank you, my boy. Now, where's Frederick?

LEWIS: Oh, he's not here. He's away on a trip to Pennsylvania.

CHATHAM: I know, Lewis, but he's due back tonight, isn't he? Have you had no word from him?

LEWIS: Well, yes. But he didn't say when he was coming. Just told me to take care of a little business for him, that's all.

CHATHAM: But I just left Reverend Loguen. He said he was looking for Frederick tonight. I even went down to meet the train, but he wasn't on it.

LEWIS: Well, I'm sorry sir. Is something the matter?

CHATHAM: Yes, by God, there's a great deal the matter! This attack on Harpers Ferry has stirred up a regular hornet's nest. I've got to see your father to find out what's going on.

ANNA: [*Appears at the head of the stairs.*] Lewis? Who is it?

CHATHAM: [*Turns.*] It's George Chatham, Mrs. Douglass.

ANNA: [*Descending quickly.*] Oh, Mr. Chatham. What is it?

CHATHAM: Oh no, don't become unduly alarmed. I bear no bad tidings. I just came here looking for Frederick.

ANNA: He's on his way home?

CHATHAM: Why, yes, didn't you know? Loguen had a telegram from Philadelphia. He should have arrived on the twelve-forty. Perhaps he'll be in on the three-oh-two.

ANNA: Oh, well, I'm so glad. I been near 'bout worried to death, wonderin' where he was and what's goin' on.

CHATHAM: You're not the only one, Mrs. Douglass. This thing has set everybody back on their heels.

LEWIS: Uh—'scuse me. [*He heads for the study.*]

ANNA: Go 'head, son ... Well, what do you think, Mr. Chatham. Have they got much of a chance?

CHATHAM: I'm afraid it looks bad, pretty bad right now, Mrs. Douglass. So far the Captain's still managed to hold the Arsenal with his little band. But Buchanan's ordered in government troops, you know.

ANNA: Aw-aww ... !

CHATHAM: They've got the place surrounded. It'll take a miracle to get them out now. [*Shakes his head in grudging admiration.*] Oh, that Brown, that Captain Brown! Even if he fails, you've got to give it to him. We told him no, but he went right ahead anyhow. And the sheer nerve of it all —Harpers Ferry! Well, God help him.

[LEWIS *returns from the library with a sheaf of letters and papers.*]

LEWIS: Here, Mother. What shall I ... [*Conscious of Chatham's presence.*]

ANNA: [*Distressed.*] Oh, I don't know, Lewis, I—out in the woodshed! Hide them under the eaves!

LEWIS: Good! [*He dashes out.*]

ANNA: [*Impatient for something to do.*] I ... I think I'll go on back and fix up a little somethin' to eat. I know Fred'll be near 'bout starved when he gets off the train. Sit down, Mr. Chatham, and make yourself 't home.

CHATHAM: No, thank you, Mrs. Douglass. I'm going to run on back to the telegraph office to catch the latest news. Then I'll meet the train and look for Frederick.

ANNA: All right, but at least you ought to stop and take a cup of tea. It's gettin' pretty chilly out, and you know you're gettin' too old to be chasin' aroun' in the middle of the night like some young buck.

CHATHAM: Thank you, Mrs. Douglass. But if I were a young buck I'd be out chasing around for different reasons than am now!

[*From Off Right the front door is heard to open.* CHATHAM *and* ANNA *move to the archway.*]

ANNA: Fred!

[DOUGLASS *enters, carrying a traveling bag. He removes his hat as* ANNA *runs to greet him.*]

DOUGLASS: [*Surprised.*] Anna, my dear. What are you doing up so late? And George!

CHATHAM: Hello, Frederick, I'm so glad you're back. What happened? — I met the train, you weren't on it.

DOUGLASS: No, I got off in the freight yard and walked home as I often do.

CHATHAM: No matter, as long as you're here. Frederick—this Harpers Ferry business. Did you know about this?

DOUGLASS: Yes. Yes, I knew.

CHATHAM: But Frederick! This wasn't the plan. And even if it were, I thought we'd decided —

DOUGLASS: You're perfectly right, George. I tried to talk him out of it, but to no avail. I even went down to Pennsylvania, caught up with John in an abandoned stone quarry near Chambersburg. We argued on and on. But the old man was like steel ... !

CHATHAM: So you couldn't stop him, eh? Oh, that's just like him—stubborn as an old mule. A magnificent old mule! Tell me, Frederick. How much longer do you think he can hold out?

DOUGLASS: [*Looks at them both quickly—they haven't heard.*] The arsenal fell an hour ago. It's all over now.

CHATHAM: What!

DOUGLASS: Yes. The Army troops, under a Colonel Robert E. Lee, they stormed the place. John and his men fought bravely, but it fell.

CHATHAM: Frederick! And the Captain?

DOUGLASS: They took John alive, though they say he's badly wounded. One or two escaped but the others are all killed or captured.

ANNA: Have mercy! ... And Sheilds? How 'bout Sheilds, did you hear — ?

DOUGLASS: Yes, Anna, they have him, too. According to reports, Sheilds was on the outside when they surrounded the place. He could have gotten away! Instead he slipped back in, said he had to go back to the old man.

ANNA: [*Turns away.*] Poor Sheilds ...

CHATHAM: Well, that's that. So it's all over.

ANNA: Oh, Fred—what will they do with them now?

DOUGLASS: It doesn't take much to imagine. If they're lucky, they'll get a trial first. And that's where you can help, George, if you will.

CHATHAM: [*Eagerly.*] Yes?

DOUGLASS: We may have a slight chance of saving them if we

act right away.

CHATHAM: All right, Frederick. You just point the way.

DOUGLASS: Good. Now first we have to contact Sanborn and Gerrit Smith and Higginson and the others. We'll have to hire a lawyer, the most brilliant legal mind we can obtain.

CHATHAM: [*Beginning to make notes.*] All right. Just give me a list and I'll get off wires at once.

[*From Off in the hallway comes a banging at the door and a* VOICE *crying: "Douglass! Douglass!"*]

DOUGLASS: [*Looking up.*] What's that?

[ANNA *scurries to the door and opens it.*]

ANNA: [*Off.*] Why, Rev'n Loguen!

DOUGLASS: [*As* LOGUEN *enters.*] Loguen! What's all the excitement?

LOGUEN: [*Breathing heavily.*] I've ... I've just heard —

DOUGLASS: About John and the arsenal? Yes. We're just mapping plans for their defense. In the next few days we have to rally support from all quarters, perhaps even go to Virginia ourselves, and —

LOGUEN: Virginia! In the next few days *you'll* be as far away from Virginia *or* Rochester as the fastest ship can sail!

ANNA: What!

DOUGLASS: What does this mean?

LOGUEN: It means you've got to get away, Douglass. At once! They're after you.

DOUGLASS: Who?

LOGUEN: Federal agents!

CHATHAM: But what for?

LOGUEN: They found papers in Brown's knapsack, some of them letters from Douglass. They've issued a warrant for his arrest!

CHATHAM: But Frederick wasn't there! They can't —

LOGUEN: They *have,* I tell you. Listen, Douglass. I've just come from Selden's house, the Lieutenant Governor of the State.

DOUGLASS: Yes?

LOGUEN: Selden summoned me half an hour ago to tell me the governor's office had just received requisition from the governor of Virginia for "the deliverance up of one Frederick Douglass," charging him with "murder, robbery, and inciting servile insurrection." *And* two United States marshals—with no less than President Buchanan's authorization—have been secretly dispatched from Buffalo and should arrive here before dawn.

ANNA: Tonight!!

LOGUEN: That's right!

DOUGLASS: Well, I expected they might send someone here. But so soon! [*To* ANNA.] Did you get my message? Did you see to the papers?

ANNA: Lewis is takin' care of them right now.

DOUGLASS: Good. Well, let them come. [*He turns back to* CHATHAM *and his notebook.*]

ANNA: [*Goes to him.*] Fred. Fred, listen. If they're after you you've got to get away!

LOGUEN: Don't you understand, Douglass? You can't stay here.

DOUGLASS: [*Smiles.*] But I wasn't *at* Harpers Ferry. And now that my papers are secure —

LOGUEN: And you actually think they'll stop to consider that? Listen—Selden has instructions from Albany. He will have to surrender you if they find you here.

DOUGLASS: But we must help John and Sheilds and the others —

LOGUEN: Right now you have to help yourself! Or you'll be in the same jailhouse they're in.

CHATHAM: But Frederick wasn't involved in this thing,

Loguen. Why should he —

LOGUEN: [*Exasperated.*] That's not the point, George! Just once let them get their hands on him. Just once let them get him down to Virginia —

CHATHAM: [*To* DOUGLASS] But you can prove, can't you, that —

LOGUEN: What do you think he can prove at the end of a rope?

[CHATHAM *halts.*]

Listen now. I have Jim Mason standing by down at the smithy's shop with his team and rig. With a little luck he can get you over the border by sunrise. You'll be safe in Canada for a few days, and by then we can arrange for your passage to England.

DOUGLASS: To England!

LOGUEN: Yes, Douglass, yes! Once they find out you're in Canada, don't think for one minute they won't try to bring you back.

DOUGLASS: You're right, of course, Loguen. But ... [*He looks with concern toward* ANNA.]

ANNA: You go 'head, Fred, don't you worry none about us.

CHATHAM: I'll look out for them, Frederick. They'll be safe, believe me.

[LEWIS *has returned quietly and stands in the background, his joy at seeing his father back giving way to bewilderment as he catches on to what is being said.*]

DOUGLASS: [*With a wry smile.*] And so this time you've come for me, eh Loguen? ... And Jim, Jim Mason's standing by again with his rig, for me ... Well, I've been a fugitive before ... hunted, running like a beast ... pursued by human hounds.

LOGUEN: [*Nods.*] I know the feeling well, Douglass. Now — [*Indicates that it is time to go.*]

DOUGLASS: [*Shrugging him off—bitterly.*] Then tell me, Loguen

—how long this night? How long this dark, dark night when no man walks in freedom, without fear, in this cradle of democracy, no man who's black? How will it happen, what will we have to do? Nat Turner tried it with guns, and he failed. Dred Scott went to the high courts, and they hurled him back into slavery. Old John said it must be by blood, and tonight he lies wounded in a Virginia prison. When will it end, Loguen—how long this night?

LOGUEN: [*Slowly.*] Douglass, this I believe as surely as God gives me breath to speak it: no man lives in safety so long as his brother is in fear. Once arouse consciousness of that, and there will be those living and those dead, there will be guns and blood and the high courts, too ... But it will come. I may not be here to see it, Douglass, but it will come.

DOUGLASS: How often do I wonder. [*He turns to go, sees* LEWIS.]

LEWIS: Poppa!...

DOUGLASS: [*Reaching toward him.*] Hello, son.

LEWIS: You're going away?

DOUGLASS: You'll have to take care of the family for me, Lewis. You're the man of the house, now.

LEWIS: [*Choking up.*] Poppa, I — !

DOUGLASS: Now, now, son. In front of your mother?

LOGUEN: I hate to rush you, Douglass, but —

[*From the stairway comes* ANNIE'*s voice, asking, "Poppa?"*]

DOUGLASS: [*Looking up.*] Yes, Annie darling!

[ANNIE *races down the stairs and leaps into* DOUGLASS'*s arms.*]

ANNIE: Oh, Poppa! You're back, you're back.

ANNA: [*Aware of the time.*] All right, now, baby. It's back to bed for you, before you catch any more cold.

DOUGLASS: [*Concerned.*] What? Has she been sick?

ANNA: Only a little cold, Fred. Here, Annie. Let's go bac[k] upstairs.

ANNIE: [*Hugging* DOUGLASS *more tightly*.] I don't wanna! wanna see Poppa some more!

ANNA: Now, Annie. That's no way for a little lady to ac[t] You'll see Poppa again — [*She stops*.] Again ... Come on honey. Kiss Poppa goodnight.

ANNIE: [*Kissing him*.] Goodnight, Poppa. See you in th[e] morning.

DOUGLASS: Yes... yes, dear. In the morning. [*He lets her down.*

LEWIS: [*Sensing the situation*.] Here, Mother, I'll take her up.

ANNA: Thank you, Lewis.

[ANNIE *sneezes*.]

Be sure and tuck her in tight, now.

LEWIS: I will. [*He turns to his father*.] Poppa, I —

[DOUGLASS *indicates for him not to say any more in front o[f]* ANNIE. LEWIS *turns and goes upstairs with* ANNIE.]

ANNIE: [*As she goes Off*.] Goodnight, Poppa. Goodnight Momma.

DOUGLASS: [*Watching her*.] Goodnight, dear ... !

ANNA: [*Goes to him*.] Fred —

DOUGLASS: Now I'll be all right, Anna. Take care of yourself.

ANNA: [*Her arms around him*.] Oh, Fred! Be careful!

DOUGLASS: I'll send you word as soon as I can. Maybe I won'[t] have to go very far or stay very long. Maybe —

LOGUEN: [*He and* CHATHAM *are in the hallway*.] Douglass — Time grows short.

DOUGLASS: Yes, Loguen, I'm ready. [*He starts for the door*.]

[ANNA *runs to him again and they embrace. He breaks away quickly and goes out, giving a last glance up the stairway.* CHATHAM *precedes him, carrying* DOUGLASS'S *bag*.]

LOGUEN: [*To* ANNA *as he follows.*] If anyone comes ...

ANNA: [*Nods her head.*] I know. I know what to say.

[*He exits, and the door is heard to close.*

ANNA *stands at the window for a moment, fighting back the tears. Then she comes slowly back into the room. She goes quickly to the lamps and blows them out, leaving herself just a candle. Then she pauses, looking in the fireplace. Taking up a poker, she stirs the dying embers and sings softly to herself:*]

"Didn't it rain, children ...
Rain, oh my Lord ...
Didn't it ...
Didn't it ...
Didn't it —
Oh, my Lord, didn't it rain..."

[*There is a sharp rap at the door.* ANNA *looks up, frightened. The knock sounds again, crisply.* ANNA *goes to the archway and looks toward the front door. The knocking sounds again, lower and more insistent.* ANNA *lifts her head, draws her shawl about her shoulders, and strides bravely toward the door with her candle, as*

CURTAIN

ACT THREE

TIME: *Six months later. Early evening.*

LEWIS *is seated at the table at Right, going over a ledger book with pen and ink. There is a stack of North Stars on a chair nearby. From Off Right, at the front door,* ANNA *is heard talking with a caller.*

ANNA: [*Off.*] All right. Thank you, thank you very much. I hope you enjoy it. Goodbye ...

[*The door closes and* ANNA *enters. She sighs happily.*]

Well, that's another one. Here Lewis, put this with the res
[*She gives him a bill and some change.*]

LEWIS: Fine! Say, we could use you at the office. You'r
getting to be our star salesman.

ANNA: [*Smiles.*] My, the word certainly got around in a hurry
I don't know how many times today I've answered that
door to folks wantin' their copy.

LEWIS: Same way at the office. Guess they really missed
while Pa was gone.

ANNA: That's what everybody says. But there's a lot of peopl
comin' by who never took it before. [*Proudly.*] I sold nin
new subscriptions today.

LEWIS: That's fine! Well, I'm certainly glad we're back i
business again. Though I still can't get over them callin
off that investigation all of a sudden.

ANNA: Well, what with the election campaign comin' up
there wasn't much else they could do. By the way, then
folks out in Chicago. Them Republicans. Have the
nominated anybody yet?

LEWIS: Last I heard this afternoon, Senator Seward o
Massachusetts was still leading on the second ballot. Bu
Abraham Lincoln of Illinois was coming up strong.

ANNA: [*Frowns.*] Poor Mr. Seward certainly has worked har
for it. Well, soon's you find out you better go in there an
tell your father. That's all he's been studyin' 'bout all day.

LEWIS: But isn't that newspaper man still in there?

ANNA: Mr. Tilton? Yes, son. Seems he came all the way u
here from New York to get Fred to write some articles fo
his paper.

LEWIS: Oh?

ANNA: Yes, and then — [*She breaks off as the study door open*
and DOUGLASS *enters, frowning.*]

DOUGLASS: [*Searching about among papers, books, etc.*] Anna
what did you do with that little book I use for keeping

names and addresses in? I can't find it anywhere.

ANNA: Well, I don't know, Fred. I haven't bothered it. Lewis, you know what he's talkin' about?

LEWIS: Why, no. No, Pa, I haven't seen it.

DOUGLASS: [*Annoyed.*] Well, somebody must have moved it! I always keep it in the lower right hand drawer of my high desk, and now it's not there. Anna, are you sure ... ?

ANNA: [*Calmly.*] Now, Fred, you don't have to holler like that at me!

DOUGLASS: What? Oh—oh, I'm sorry, I ...

ANNA: When did you have it last, do you remember? Have you looked in all the drawers? Try all your pockets? How 'bout upstairs? Here, let me go see — [*She starts for the stairway, but halts as* DOUGLASS *feels his pockets and withdraws a small book.*]

DOUGLASS: [*Slowly raising his eyes.*] I'm ... sorry, Anna.

ANNA: That's all right, Fred. [*Pause.*] Now don't stay 'way from your guest.

DOUGLASS: Huh? Oh, yes. Yes ... [*He goes back into the study, closing the door.*]

ANNA: [*Shakes her head.*] Lawd-a-mussy!

LEWIS: Mother, what's wrong? Do you think he's sick?

ANNA: Well, Fred ain't really sick, not like you usually think of somebody being sick.

LEWIS: Then what is it?

ANNA: I don't know just how to explain it, son. But there's somethin' pressin' on his mind. Somethin' heavy. Yes, I guess Fred is sick, Lewis. Sick somewhere in his soul. He's not the same since he's been back.

LEWIS: Mother, do you think maybe it's because ... because of Annie?

ANNA: [*Softly.*] That may be part of it, son. Fred loved that child more than anything else in the world, and when she died—especially with him away in Europe—I ... I guess a part of him died, too. I know it's the same way with me.

LEWIS: [*Comfortingly.*] Mother ... do you think maybe if I talked to him ...

ANNA: No, Lewis. Leave him alone. When he's ready to talk about it, he will.

[*The door knocker sounds.*]

Lord-a-mussy! I been answerin' that door all day.

LEWIS: You sit right down now, I'll get it. Probably another one of those subscribers. [*He goes to the door.*]

ANNA: All right, Lewis. If you need me I'll be back in the kitchen. [*She straightens up the newspapers and goes out Left.*]

[*The study door opens and* DOUGLASS *appears, ushering out* THEODORE TILTON.]

DOUGLASS: ... And believe me, Mr. Tilton, it is with great reluctance that I must turn you down.

TILTON: [*Somewhat in annoyance.*] Yes, and it is with great reluctance that I must leave without getting what I came for. [*Stops and turns.*] You know, Douglass, the first time we met I was impressed, greatly impressed. Completely aside from considerations of race, I thought: "Here is a man of whom the whole nation should be proud!" And now I find you here, twiddling your thumbs, as it were, sulking in the wake of your exile because of this Harpers Ferry business —

DOUGLASS: Mr. Tilton, it is well known that I was not present at Harpers Ferry. Perhaps I should have been, but the fact of it is I had no part in the matter.

TILTON: But do you deny you had dealings with John Brown? I was at the trial, I saw the letters and documents, I —

DOUGLASS: [*Electrified.*] You were at the trial?!!

TILTON: Why, yes. I covered the sessions personally for my paper ...

DOUGLASS: Then you saw John Brown before—before ...

TILTON: Yes, Mr. Douglass. I was there.

DOUGLASS: Tell me ... tell me, Mr. Tilton. I ... [*He indicates a chair.*]

[TILTON *sits.*]

TILTON: [*Solemnly.*] The old man was quite a brave soul ... His conduct and deportment during the trial were commendable—even the prosecution had the greatest respect for him, you could tell .... Of course, they did rush things a bit. Brown's wounds hadn't healed before they dragged him into court ... But his mind was clear and his tongue quite sharp. When the counsel they appointed to him tried to introduce a plea of insanity, he rejected it himself, told the court in booming tones that he considered it a "miserable artifice and pretext," and he viewed such a motion with contempt ... And then, after the verdict, when they asked him if he had anything to say ... he rose erect, though it must have pained him terribly to do so ... and he said —

DOUGLASS: [*Staring into space.*] "... Had I so interfered in behalf of the rich, the powerful, the so-called great ... every man in this Court would have deemed it an act worthy of reward. To have interfered in behalf of His despised poor, I did no wrong, but right."

TILTON: [*Nods his head.*] It was ... well, little short of magnificent.

DOUGLASS: [*Whispers.*] John! ...

TILTON: I tried to get to see him afterwards. But they kept him under heavy guard, barred all visitors except his wife ...

DOUGLASS: Mary ... poor Mary.

TILTON: President Buchanan ordered a detachment of federal troops in to guard the town, three hundred strong, under Colonel Robert E. Lee—he's quite famous now, you know, they say he'll be made a general for sure. All Charlestown became an armed camp ... the army troops, State Militia with cannon, volunteers, even fresh-faced cadets from Virginia Military Institute. Ha!—every so often some young fool would cry out, shoot at a branch in the dark, and the whole lot of them would scurry around in the night like terrified idiots!

DOUGLASS: And ... then?

TILTON: [*Starts to speak, then rises, shaking his head.*] I cannot talk about it. I'd never seen a hanging before, and I hope to God I shall never see one again. [*Turns.*] But you, Douglass ...

DOUGLASS: Don't ... don't. [*To himself.*] I know the old man was wrong, but I should have gone with him anyway ... Sheilds! Did you see Sheilds Green? The Negro they called the Emperor?

TILTON: No. I did not stay for the other trials. But, of course you know ...

DOUGLASS: [*Turns away.*] Yes, I know.

TILTON: When I learned that you were back from England, i excited me! Here is a man so brave, that even with the shadow of a congressional investigation stalking him, he comes home to continue the fight—I must have articles, a whole series of writings from this man for my paper, said! And then your letter, turning me down ...

DOUGLASS: You give me more credit than I am due, Mr Tilton. I came home at this time only because of death in the family.

TILTON: Oh, I'm sorry to hear that. But still, why not back to the struggle?

DOUGLASS: [*Evasively.*] I ... need time to think, I—if I could have brought my family to England, I might have stayed there ... Slavery ... this whole situation, Mr. Tilton Frankly, I'm beginning to think it's ... hopeless.

TILTON: [*Stunned.*] Hopeless ... ? Hopeless ... ? [*Begins with sadness and builds toward anger.*] So ... the great Frederick Douglass creeps home, tail between his legs. The man who argued so bravely the philosophy of reforms lies in earnest struggle is tired of struggling himself. "If there is no struggle, there is no progress," he says. "Those who profess to favor freedom, and yet depreciate agitation, are men who want crops without plowing up the ground. They want rain without thunder and lightning ... the ocean without the roar of its many waters." And now this sterling writer, this august philosopher declares the situation hopeless. He writes words of fiery revolution to others, and after he persuades them, *he* sinks to the ground, exhausted and faint!

DOUGLASS: [*Stiffly.*] So ... you read my paper?

TILTON: Every issue you sent me! And I must say I was taken in like a perfect fool. Even started echoing your sentiments on the editorial pages of my own paper, causing me to lose circulation by the thousand and forcing me into debt to raise funds for its continued existence. Hah! And now I find my inspiration, my dauntless messiah has lost his faith. Behold ... ! He heals the blind, and when they see enough to follow him, lo! the man is blind himself!

DOUGLASS: [*Calling a halt.*] Mr. Tilton! [*Turns away.*]

TILTON: [*Emotion subsiding.*] No matter, no matter! ... The newly enlightened will carry aloft the brazier even if it does burn the hands a bit. As a matter of fact, I shall be surprised when I reach New York if my plant is still standing.

DOUGLASS: Why so?

TILTON: Oh, I'm quite the radical abolitionist these days, you should see! I've passionately eulogized John Brown, attacked the federal government as a pro-slavery bunch of horse thieves, and called President Buchanan a pig-headed ass in inch-high headlines on the front page! Oh, you should just see the stack of lawsuits filed against me.

DOUGLASS: You are either very brave or very foolish.

TILTON: Who cares — I've been having fun! [*Impishly.*] And

besides, I'm right. Why, have you even taken a close look at a picture of Buchanan's face? ... But I see you are in no mood for jest. Well, can't say I haven't tried. No harsh feelings, I hope?

DOUGLASS: No. No, of course not.

[*There is a knock at the door. Presently* ANNA *appears, going to answer it.*]

TILTON: I'll be going now. Got to get back down and start beating the drums for the election campaign. If you should change your mind, and decide to help me make a little music, don't hesitate to join the band, eh?

DOUGLASS: If I should, I'll let you know —

TILTON: No—no, no promises now one way or the other. If you come to the point where you must, you will.

[ANNA *comes on with* GEORGE CHATHAM.]

Well ... Chatham!

CHATHAM: [*Carries an odd-shaped bundle which he leaves in the hallway.*] Mr. Tilton! Why, I didn't know you were in town. Hello, Frederick.

DOUGLASS: Hello, George.

TILTON: I didn't expect to be, but I ran up on a little editorial business. How's Ellen and the girls?

CHATHAM: Oh, fine, just fine. You're not leaving, are you? I just —

TILTON: Yes, I'm afraid I must. My mission was fruitless and I must go on back. What's the latest on the convention, have you heard?

CHATHAM: Yes, they've just finished the second ballot and are getting ready for a third. Our man Seward's still leading. Perhaps he'll take it on the next ballot.

ANNA: And how about Lincoln? I thought he was pressin' pretty hard.

CHATHAM: Oh, I wouldn't give him a second thought. He's

gained a few votes, true, but they'd never be so stupid as to nominate such an idiot!

TILTON: Well, Lincoln might not be as bad as we expect. He has already distinguished himself in debate with Stephen Douglas, and as for the "rump" candidate, Breckinridge, I don't think we'll have to worry much about him. So pluck up, George!

CHATHAM: Well, if they do nominate Lincoln, I shall have the greatest difficulty in resigning myself to the necessity of supporting him, hayseeds and all. Why the man's simply impossible! "Honest Abe" they call him. Sounds like a used-carriage dealer.

TILTON: Now, now, George. Just because the man is not of solid New England abolitionist stock is no reason to give him up for lost. He may prove his worth, in time.

CHATHAM: [*Hands together.*] Let us pray ...

TILTON: [*Laughs.*] On that, I'll take my leave! Goodbye, Chatham. [*Bows.*] Mrs. Douglass. [*To* DOUGLASS, *who starts to see him out.*] No, that's all right, I can find my way to the door. And Douglass! ... [*Extends his hand —sincerely.*] I'm leaving my first drummer's chair open. Just in case ... [*With a wave of the hand he is off, escorted to the door by* ANNA.]

CHATHAM: [*Smiling.*] What's all this, Frederick? Are you going in for musicianship these days?

DOUGLASS: No ... no, George. I'm afraid I'd play out of tune. Now, what have you come to see me about?

CHATHAM: Well, two things, really. The first I think you already have some idea of.

DOUGLASS: [*Turning away.*] Yes. Yes, I know.

CHATHAM: Then what is it, Frederick? Yesterday at your office I asked you to join with us in our rally tonight at Corinthian Hall. But tonight I hear you have tendered your regrets. Is this true, Frederick?

DOUGLASS: Yes. It's true.

CHATHAM: But Frederick! Why are you refusing us now, when we need you most? We haven't had so good a chance in years to upset the slaveholders' stranglehold on the Presidency. We have to stir up all the support we can get.

DOUGLASS: I know all that, George, you don't have to —

CHATHAM: Then you'll do it, Frederick? The whole town will be so glad to see you. You know, you've become quite a celebrity since you've been gone.

DOUGLASS: Oh. And why?

CHATHAM: Why, why, you ask! Why, because *l'affaire* John Brown has captured the hearts and imaginations of the whole North! It's fired the flame of liberty and turned many a pussyfooting ne'er-do-well into an ardent Abolitionist! John Brown's gallows has become a cross. And all Rochester is proud to know that you helped him, that you believed in him when other less hardy souls failed him. That you had to flee the screaming, anguished wrath of the Virginia slavers because of your part in the undertaking.

DOUGLASS: [*Stricken.*] Is that what people think?!!

CHATHAM: Why, you're a hero, man! Rochester's own representative in John Brown's great venture.

DOUGLASS: George! ... George ... [*Suddenly.*] I cannot speak for you tonight. That's all.

CHATHAM: But Frederick. I told the Rally Committee I'd come here personally, and —

DOUGLASS: [*Curtly.*] You should have consulted me before making any such promise.

CHATHAM: [*At first, taken aback. Then challenging.*] Frederick ... what's wrong?

DOUGLASS: Wrong? Why—I'm tired ... I haven't been feeling too well, lately. Yes, I've been ill.

CHATHAM: Frederick ... we've been friends for a long time. Ever since you first came to Rochester and started your paper.

DOUGLASS: Please! Please, George, I'd be the first to admit that I owe you a great deal, but don't try to use that to force me to do something I am not agreed to doing.

CHATHAM: That's not it at all, Frederick! I meant that I had come to believe the two of us could sit down and talk openly and fairly with each other. But it is hardly honorable of you, is it, to hide behind such a paltry excuse? You, who have braved storms and mobs and defied death itself in bringing your message to the people?

DOUGLASS: [*Turns to him.*] George, I cannot speak for you. I can no longer stand upon a platform and address an audience as I have in the past.

CHATHAM: Why, Douglass, you're one of the ablest public speakers I've ever known.

DOUGLASS: Able or not, I am not worthy.

CHATHAM: Not worthy? Why, who—if not you, of all people —who can lay claim to greater right?

DOUGLASS: I have forfeited my right! I have failed to live up to the confidence placed in me.

CHATHAM: Douglass! ... You're talking riddles!

[DOUGLASS *turns despairingly, and starts into his study. His hand freezes on the doorknob, then, resignedly, he closes the door and turns again to face* CHATHAM.]

DOUGLASS: George ... you mentioned that the people of Rochester think of me as a hero, their own representative in John's great venture. You know as well as I do that it isn't true.

CHATHAM: Frederick, I have always known you to be a man of the highest dedication to the cause of liberty, and —

DOUGLASS: We're not talking about past reputation, George, and we cannot base supposed fact upon such schoolboy idealism as dedication to a cause! The question is: was I or was I not an accomplice of John Brown in his raid on Harpers Ferry on October 16, 1859?

CHATHAM: Listen, Frederick, I —

DOUGLASS: Why, you have me sailing under false colors, cloaked by the public imagination in a role of glory that is as false to me as if I played Romeo upon the stage. [*Turns.*] Shall I tell you the truth of the matter? Shall I —

CHATHAM: But Frederick, I don't see —

DOUGLASS: Well, I'll tell you whether you want to hear it or not! [*He wheels about and paces, the Prosecuting Attorney, his own conscience on trial.*] George, that night after you and Sanborn and the others left, John told me he was going on with it, that he was going to start at Harpers Ferry. I argued against it, but in vain. When he implored me to go with him, I told him I thought it was more important for me to speak and to write, to stay alive for my people, than to take the chance of dying with him at Harpers Ferry. And so I let him go, alone—except for Sheilds Green ... . But George ... I have discovered that it is possible for a man to make a right decision, and then be tormented in spirit the rest of his life because he did not make the wrong one. There are times when the soul's need to unite with men in splendid error tangles agonizingly with cold wisdom and judgment ...

Then in London, when the news came ... how brave the old man was ... how steadfastly he refused to name or implicate anyone ... how he died upon the gallows, it came to me in a rush that John, in his way, had succeeded! In splendid error he had startled the sleeping conscience of the nation and struck a blow for freedom that proves stronger every hour.

And now you come to me and ask me to play the hero. To accept the plaudits of the crowd for my "gallant alliance" with a man who was wrong in life, but in death has scored a victory—a victory you propose me to take the bows for.

CHATHAM: Frederick, you must hear me —

DOUGLASS: Don't you see, George, that I cannot do it! John believed in his mission and however wrong he was he gave his life for it. But what have I done, except talk about it—I who have *been* a slave!

CHATHAM: [*Rising.*] Frederick, you're torturing yourself! Don't —

DOUGLASS: I will not go on masquerading as a crusader, a leader of my people, a brave warrior for human rights!

CHATHAM: Will you stop a moment and listen!

DOUGLASS: You are in the presence of a fraud! I resumed publishing my paper because I must feed my family, but do not believe that I can stand on a platform and look an audience in the eyes with this burning inside me: "*Are you afraid to face a gun?!!*"

CHATHAM: [*Takes* DOUGLASS *forcibly by the arm—shouts.*] Frederick, I demand that you be quiet!

[DOUGLASS *grasps the back of a chair, his energy spent.*]

[CHATHAM *speaks gently.*] That's it. Listen. There is a second reason I came to see you tonight, Frederick. It is to fulfill a request.

DOUGLASS: [*Wearily, as in delirium.*] Request ... request ... what kind of request?

CHATHAM: [*As he secures his package from the hallway.*] Early this winter I made a trip to North Elba. There, by a great boulder in which he himself once carved the letters "J.B." is where they buried Captain Brown. I talked to his widow, Mary, a proud, fierce-eyed woman whose composure made me half ashamed of my tears. When she learned I was from Rochester, she gave me something to give to you, Frederick. [*He takes the package to the sofa.*] I told her you were in England, but she smiled and said you would be back. You had a job to do, she said, and she knew you would be back to finish it. [*He undoes the canvas and withdraws a tarnished old musket and a torn, bespattered*

American flag.] She asked me to give these to you personally, Frederick. That John wanted you to have them. [*He carries the musket to* DOUGLASS, *who slowly reaches out for it, then suddenly cringes, folding his hands.*]

DOUGLASS: His ... musket?

CHATHAM: Yes. [*He takes the musket back to the sofa and lays it down, carefully. Then picks up the flag and drapes it over the musket.*] And the flag he carried with him to Harpers Ferry ... [*Fumbles in his waistcoat.*] He gave her a message for you, there in the prison, while he was waiting. [*Withdraws a folded piece of paper.*] Here ...

DOUGLASS: [*Takes it slowly, and reads; barely audible.*] "Tell Douglass I know I have not failed because he lives. Follow your own star, and someday unfurl my flag in the land of the free." [*He bows his head, his shoulders shaking silently. Then slowly, haltingly, he makes his way toward the sofa.*]

[*Dimly, from a distance, comes the sound of the booming of a drum.* CHATHAM *goes to the balcony window and looks out. He turns and watches* DOUGLASS, *who, having reached the sofa, bends over to touch the flag and musket.*]

CHATHAM: [*Softly.*] It's nearly time for the rally, Frederick. They are marching from the square. [*Comes to him.*] Come, Frederick. Will you join us?

DOUGLASS: [*Quiet now. When he speaks his voice is steady.*] You go on ahead, George. I'll be along in a moment.

CHATHAM: [*Understandingly.*] All right. All right.

DOUGLASS: But ... I must tell them the truth. I did not go with John.

CHATHAM: [*Nods admiringly.*] You tell them, Frederick. You tell them what you must.

[*He goes to the hallway just as* LEWIS *comes rushing in from outside, where there is excitement in the air. The drumbeats are nearer and there are voices.*]

LEWIS: [*Joyously.*] They're coming! They're coming! It's a

torchlight parade!

CHATHAM: Well, let's see it, son! Let's see it!

LEWIS: And the convention's decided. The candidate is chosen!

CHATHAM: [*Stops.*] What! Who is it, Lewis?

LEWIS: Lincoln!

CHATHAM: [*Astonished —roars like a wounded bull.*] *Lincoln?!!* We cry out for a leader, a savior, a knight in shining armor! And who do they offer us? Barabbas!

[ANNA *comes quickly down the stairs.*]

ANNA: Lord-a-mussy! What's goin' on out here!

CHATHAM: It's a torchlight parade, Mrs. Douglass. Come! [*He guides* ANNA *and* LEWIS *out, then stops and turns for a moment, puffing his cheeks indignantly.*] Lincoln! [*He stomps out.*]

[DOUGLASS *stands gazing down at the flag and musket.*

Outside the excitement has increased and now a bright flicker of orange and yellow light dances in from the street, bathing the hallway with bobbing shafts of light. The booming drum is very near now, and amid the accompanying babble a VOICE *cries, "There's Fred Douglass's house!"* ANOTHER *takes it up: "Yeah, where is he?" And* ANOTHER: *"We want Douglass! We want Douglass!"*

DOUGLASS *stirs and turns his head to listen.* ANNA *rushes back into the room excitedly.*]

ANNA: Fred! Where are you, Fred! They callin' for you! For you, Fred! [*She pauses Upstage, arm extended.*] Well, come on! They callin' for you!

DOUGLASS: [*Lifts his hand.*] I'm coming, Anna.

[ANNA *goes back off.*

A fife and drum corps has approached and now swings into Battle Hymn of the Republic, and the voices take it up, singing:

"John Brown's body lies a-mould'ring in the grave..."

DOUGLASS *picks up the flag. He folds it. He holds it against his breast for a moment. Then laying it over his arm, he draws himself to full height and strides manfully off to the door, as*

CURTAIN

THE END

WILLIAM BRANCH
(1927-)

Son of an A.M.E. Zion minister, William Branch has used the theatre to raise important moral issues concerning racial justice. He was early attracted to the professional theatre when in his freshman year at college he joined the national cast of the hit Broadway black drama, *Anna Lucasta,* for its Chicago run. Branch graduated from Northwestern University in 1949 with a degree in speech and served a three-year stint in the United States Army.

His army experience probably inspired his first play, *A Medal for Willie* (1951) about the hypocrisy of making a hero of a small town black man who died fighting for his country. In life Willie had faced the usual discrimination and indignities to which poor blacks were subjected in those days. Blacks, engaged in all their country's wars in defense of democracy, deserve more than medals and the panoply of drums and colors on a single day to mark their heroism. It is time they enjoyed nothing less than their full democratic rights.

Branch's next play, *In Splendid Error* (1954), was one of his major works for the stage. It was produced at the Greenwich Mews Theatre in New York where it ran for four months to mixed reviews, though the critics for *The New York Times, Saturday Review,* and other papers found it stimulating with certain scenes containing a good deal of spirit and force. Production of these two plays and others in the 1950s made Branch one of the leading black playwrights of the decade.

Branch attended Columbia University, from which he gained a Master of Fine Arts in playwriting, and later he held a one-year fellowship at the Yale University School of Drama. He is the author of some ten plays that have been produced in the United States, Europe, Africa, and the Far East. He has also had a distinguished career as a writer and director for national television and has written for motion pictures. For his work in these areas he has won awards, citations, and an Emmy nomination. He has also held teaching appointments at a number of prestigious institutions in America and abroad including the University of Ghana, the University of Maryland, Smith College, and Cornell University.

Source: *Dictionary of Literary Biography, Vol. 76: Afro-American Writers 1940-1955.* Trudier Harris, ed. Chapel Hill, NC: University of North Carolina, 1988.

I, MARCUS GARVEY

(AND THE CAPTIVITY OF BABYLON)

by

Edgar White

MARCUS MOSIAH GARVEY
(1887-1940)

The Jamaican Marcus Garvey was arguably the most prominent black political leader anywhere in the world in the decades following the First World War. Where other leaders drew their following from the educated middle class, Garvey set out deliberately to mobilize a mass movement among the poor, working-class blacks in America. These were the new industrialized workers who had come from the southland to northeastern factories during the war years. Torn from their southern roots, Garvey offered them a vision of a proud and mighty race and they flocked to his movement in tumultuous numbers.

Garvey was born in Jamaica, the West Indies, and though his formal schooling ended at the elementary stage, he had a passion for books and reading. Forced by family circumstances to find work at an early age, Garvey started out in a printing shop, a chance encounter that would serve him well in future years when he published his own newspapers. After taking part in an unsuccessful printers' strike, Garvey moved to Costa Rica and Panama where he edited newspapers for the colonies of Jamaican migrant workers. His love of reading and his early experience of publishing gave him a respect for the printed word as a means of communication.

In 1912 Garvey went to London and established contacts with African nationalists. Reading deeply about African and black history convinced him that he was called to be a leader of his race. He returned to Jamaica and organized the Universal Negro Improvement Association (U.N.I.A.) through which he hoped to promote racial pride and concerted action. In 1916 he took his new organization to New York where, fired by his passionate oratory, it grew rapidly, amassing a national membership estimated at two million. With membership contributions, Garvey acquired Liberty Hall in Harlem as U.N.I.A. headquarters, started a black steamship line for trade and travel among black communities, and set up a corporation to stimulate the growth of black-owned businesses. He also published the movement's paper called *The Negro World*. By August 1920, Garvey was able to hold in Harlem his first massive international conference at which he declared Africa to be the ancestral home of black people and called for that continent to be freed of white rule. Thus while the powerful western European nations were intent on carving up the continent in the aftermath of world war, Garvey was inviting blacks to return to their homeland and claim it as their own.

The appeal of Garvey's racial politics to his global mass following made him a threat to European and American imperial interests. His independent spirit and disdain for the integrationist ideology of the colored American middle class created enemies among the black intelligentsia, while his lack of a proper business organization to manage the affairs of the U.N.I.A. contributed to the collapse of his financial ventures. In 1922 he was charged with mail fraud, found guilty, and in 1925 sentenced to a five-year term in Atlanta Penitentiary. Released two years later, he was deported to Jamaica where he began publishing a weekly paper, *The Black Man*, sought political office unsuccessfully, and tried to revitalize his U.N.I.A. movement. In 1934 he moved back to London and continued to rally his faithful supporters by travelling abroad to speak at meetings and by publishing a journal until his death in 1940. He was named the first national hero of Jamaica.

The Caribbean playwright Edgar White has chosen to write about Garvey, but there is more than regional affinity in the connection. Like Garvey, White too is a West Indian emigrant who hails from the island of Montserrat and makes his home in New York or London. A thoughtful black nationalist, White has written plays, poems, and novels, his underlying theme being the plight of the black man in a white dominated society. His drama is presented in a series of short, telling episodes that epitomize the restless energy of his hero's life: the physical and emotional hardships Garvey endured, the slights and threats and reverses suffered, and always the fear for the safety of his wife and children.

Garvey allowed none of these obstacles to divert him from his mission, which he saw with increasing clarity. He continued to publish and to attend and speak at meetings when possible. His indomitable spirit and powerful exhortation: "Up You Mighty People!" brought hope, dignity, and a sense of community to masses of black people in the Caribbean, Latin America, the United States, Britain, and Canada. Their joyous response to Garvey's message is reflected in the playwright's use of heightened prose, poetry, music, and song to weave a striking tapestry of Garvey's life for the stage.

Source: *Dictionary of American Biography*, No. 22, Supplement Two. Robert L. Schuyler, ed. New York: Charles Scribners Sons, 1958.

CHARACTERS

[*in order of appearance*]

Marcus Garvey, a black leader
Indiana, his sister
Wallace, her lover
Hamil, an Indian grocer
Mr. Jenkins, a missionary
Amy Jacques, a young girl
Auntie, her Nanny
Minister of Information in Jamaica
West Indian Archie, a Garvey supporter
Amy Jacques Garvey, Garvey's wife
F.B.I. Agent
K.K.K. Attorney
Newspaper Editor
Margret, an old Jamaican woman and Garvey's housekeeper
Mr. Tyler of *The Gleaner* newspaper
Chorus
Musicians

ACT ONE

1912-1916, London and Jamaica

ACT TWO

1916-1927, The United States

ACT THREE

1927-1938, Jamaica, Canada, London

SEQUENCE OF ACTS AND SCENES

ACT ONE 1912-1916:
THE FORMATIVE YEARS—LONDON AND JAMAICA.

Prologue: Garvey's voice on tape recording: "There is no height to which we cannot climb ... "

SCENE

1. Indiana's house in Bayswater, London.
2. Garvey in the city.
3. Indiana's house six weeks later.
4. The formative years and journalism.
5. A street scene.
6. A view of the times.
7. The Christian Aid Society.
8. Garvey's return to Jamaica, 1914.
9. The British official.
10. Amy, the debutante.
11. Garvey reflects and writes on Jamaica.

ACT TWO 1916-1927:
YEARS OF TRIUMPH—THE UNITED STATES.

Prologue: Garvey's voice on tape recording: "The Negro fights himself too much..."

SCENE

1. Garvey in America, 1916.
2. Harlem.
3. The Harlem riots. Garvey is shot.
4. The hospital.
5. The Harlem office.
6. With Amy after being wounded.
7. The first U.N.I.A. Convention, Harlem, 1920.
8. Birth of the Black Star Line. Garvey is arrested.
9. Amy at a Rally for the Appeal.
10. Garvey and Amy before the Trial.
11. The Trial.
12. Prison: three aspects.
13. Deportation.

ACT THREE 1927-1938:
THE MOVEMENT IN TRANSITION AND THE LAST YEARS: JAMAICA, CANADA, LONDON.

Prologue: Garvey's voice on tape recording: "Mr. Chairman, Ladies and Gentlemen, Fellow Citizens of the British Empire ..."

SCENE

1. The Return to Jamaica
2. Garvey and Amy at home.
3. Dockworkers rally against United Fruit Company.
4. Garvey's political platform: a recording.
5. Garvey's house, six months later.
6. After the election.
7. London, 1937: South Kensington.
8. Canada, 1938: the U.N.I.A. Convention.
9. London, 1938: depression and revival.
10. Garvey visits the Caribbean Islands.

Epilogue: Garvey's voice on tape recording: "When I am dead ..."

ACT ONE

1912-1916: THE FORMATIVE YEARS—LONDON AND JAMAICA.

PROLOGUE

[*Garvey's voice on tape recording:*]

There is no height to which we cannot climb by using the active intelligence of our minds. Mind creates, and as much as we desire in Nature, we can have through the creation of our own minds. Being at present the scientifically weaker race, you must teach in your homes and everywhere possible the higher development of science *par excellence,* for in science and religion lie our own hope to withstand the evil designs of modern materialism. Do you understand me? I said: Do you understand me?

SCENE 1
INDIANA'S HOUSE IN BAYSWATER, LONDON.

[MARCUS GARVEY, *age 25, has just arrived in London. It is a rainy, winter's night as he knocks at the door of his sister's house. Sound of knocking growing more urgent.*]

INDIANA: Coming. [*She wraps a robe about her.*] Yes?

GARVEY: Sis?

INDIANA: Oh God, Marcus. Jesus, you soaking wet. Come in, man. You don't even have a coat.

GARVEY: I'm all right.

INDIANA: Give me your suitcase. God, this thing heavy.

GARVEY: Just books.

INDIANA: Take off that jacket before you catch your death. But how you could come so. You don't know what England give in winter?

GARVEY: I had to leave fast, Sis. I didn't have time to plan.

INDIANA: So what happen. I thought you was in Panama.

GARVEY: I went back to Jamaica to try again.

INDIANA: But what wrong with you, Marcus. You can't understand to leave the people them politics alone? Is fool you fool. Them kill you if you talk too strong.

GARVEY: Things hard back there, Sis. No work, no food. Those who find it take anything. They crush the Unions.

INDIANA: I don't care about Union. Is you I care about.

GARVEY: You don't understand, Sis. Things so bad that I've seen people march on the prisons and beg to be arrested so they could eat.

INDIANA: You joking. People beg for jail?

GARVEY: I'm telling you. It's the truth. And when I tried to organize they set fire to the newspaper.

INDIANA: God, I glad I reach England, Marcus. People too wicked back home.

GARVEY: But there is some who can't reach, Sis.

INDIANA: They just like crab in a barrel. I can't worry for everybody. Is just me family I care for. [*Pauses.*] You hungry, Marcus?

GARVEY: Those tired, them hungry. [*He starts to cough.*]

INDIANA: Here, drink some tea. You going to have to get use to this cold.

GARVEY: So you like it here, Sis?

INDIANA: Me could manage. Make do until I could do better, you understand. [*She studies him as he drinks the tea.*] So what you make up your mind for do?

GARVEY: I don't know yet, really.

INDIANA: You have money?

GARVEY: Ten shillings. Dr. Love gave it to me.

INDIANA: Ten shillings! What you could do with that?

GARVEY: Well, we'll find something.

INDIANA: And where you go stay?

GARVEY: I thought ...

INDIANA: Listen, Marcus. I have a man friend and it wouldn't really be convenient for you to stay here too long.

GARVEY: You mean that fellow Wallace.

INDIANA: Yes, is him yes, and so?

GARVEY: Nothing.

INDIANA: I know you don't like him. Mother don't like him either. Well, make me tell you something, me don't care who like him and who don't like him. I like him, right?

GARVEY: All right, Sis.

INDIANA: Just so you understand.

GARVEY: I understand.

INDIANA: Jamaican people too damn fast for get in your business. Drink you tea before it get cold.

GARVEY: Yes, ma'am.

INDIANA: You can stay here until you could do better. You going to have for sleep here upon the chair. It's not too bad as long as the fire going. I tief little coal from where I work. The old woman never miss it. Anyway, with as much money as them have, they could stand it. I have lots to ask you about mother and them, but it could wait. I have to get up at five tomorrow. People here don't make joke with time. England not easy, brother, but you'll soon see. Sleep good. [*She kisses him.*]

GARVEY: Sleep good, Sis, and thank you.

SCENE 2
GARVEY IN THE CITY.

[*Photographs of London in 1910's flashed on screen.*]

GARVEY: London, the dirty city. Where the dust settles deep down in your chest alongside poverty. I had to see you, London. I had to come and learn. I come in search of a lion but all I found was a senile old man which they called the empire. A senile old man who was still choking the world.

[*Pause.*]

Hell is a place much like London.

I made a mistake and came in Winter.

There was little snow, dampness in the rooms, but it was the eyes which crucified me.

Eyes like my sister's.

Really my mother's eyes, but younger.

She worked as a chambermaid that year.

She would bring me what food she could steal.

I attended classes when I could and tried to learn the speech of the mother country.

'What is it you want, Marcus?'

'What is it you really want?'

'You should find work in a kitchen,
Washing dishes or clean the floor,
At least that way you could eat regularly.'

But always the eyes watching,
cutting through my clothes like the dampness.

To understand Britain you must understand cricket. You must understand little boys who play with power, making up the rules as they go along. You must attend parliament every day and watch them play with the world.

[*He begins to dress as he speaks.*]

I wore thick flannel drawers, and a shirt which was soon worn at the cuffs and neck. My sister knit me two sweaters which I tried to hide with a jacket, first of wool then of tweed.

Still I am cold.

It takes courage to get out of bed.

It takes madness to go out of doors.

I read much of the night but I must be careful of wasting candles.

And always the eyes are watching.

I read DuBois, and Johnson, and Booker T. Washington. I want to know how they knew when they were ready.

I go to Hyde Park on Sundays to watch the speakers. Some have a gift. I must learn that gift.

My sister says I should join a church. There is always safety in a church, she says. The black mass has so much religion and no salvation.

I've been to Spain, I've been to Ireland.

God is what we're given but hope is what we take.

My sister says I should find a woman,
ease my moods and keep thought at bay.

[*He walks about stage.*]

I see them, the women, moving like dark ravens through this city.

Walking under the gas-work fires,
the long skirts to hide the winter from their legs.

Too poor for love, girl. Love is for those who know where they live and how. I know nothing except hunger. Hope and hunger in a constant circle. Too poor for love, girl.

[*Remembering.*]

There was a time, a girl of ten. An English girl but she played like any boy.

We climbed fences and ran by Roaring River. When my mother baked she would eat and laugh out louder than any boy. There was no difference in us, but then her father said 'We will go away soon to England and it would not be good if you still played with niggers.'

And this he said in my hearing.

And then he took her way beyond my seeing.

And I swore never again would a white man have cause to call me nigger for love of his daughter, sister, or wife.

Too poor for love, girl, and with my fingers I touch darkness.

SCENE 3
INDIANA'S HOUSE SIX WEEKS LATER.

[GARVEY *seated reading beside gas heater. His sister,* INDIANA, *enters with her boyfriend* WALLACE. WALLACE *is carrying a bottle. They are laughing.* GARVEY *looks up annoyed.*]

WALLACE: [*Kissing her.*] I want to love you up all night.

INDIANA: You too rude. [*She suddenly sees Garvey.*] Marcus, you still up?

GARVEY: Just doing a little reading.

WALLACE: How you going, Garvey boy? [GARVEY *doesn't answer.*] I say how you going?

GARVEY: All right, Wallace, all right.

INDIANA: Marcus, you wasting light again. Why you can't read in daytime. Anyway is bad for you eyes.

GARVEY: Just want to finish this chapter.

WALLACE: What you reading? [*He takes book from* GARVEY's *hand.*] "Up from Slavery." Some heavy stuff here, boy. So you find work yet?

GARVEY: No, I —

WALLACE: So you just a read, read, read.

INDIANA: Morning, noon and night he reading.

WALLACE: So what you want do, come a teacher?

GARVEY: You wouldn't understand, Wallace.

WALLACE: Why I'm not bright like you—right?

GARVEY: I didn't say that.

WALLACE: Why you don't become a preacher.

GARVEY: I don't want to be a preacher.

WALLACE: But you want to eat everyday, though. You want that all right.

INDIANA: Is true, you could make good money as a preacher.

WALLACE: He don't like money, do you, Garvey?

GARVEY: I want to do something to help my people.

INDIANA: Which people that?

WALLACE: You can't even help yourself, you want to help people.

GARVEY: Look at the black man—what do you see? Where i his army, where is his nation, his history?

WALLACE: Bugger me if I know.

GARVEY: When you build a man you must start with a hear and a brain. The heart is Africa, that's where the puls starts. That's why I study.

INDIANA: You're a dreamer, Marcus. [*She kisses him.*]

WALLACE: Sure, you could dream when you have somebod paying the bills, feeding and clothing you. [*Looks a* GARVEY.] Ain't it, Garvey?

GARVEY: What you trying to say, Wallace?

WALLACE: Me, I not trying to say nothing.

GARVEY: [*Getting angry.*] Yes, you are. You're trying to accus me of living off my sister. I won't let a little drunken wor like you insult me.

INDIANA: Marcus.

WALLACE: What I want to know, Mr. Leader-of-the-blac man, is how long you planning to stay here? I can't fa straight when I come in this house. You always here.

INDIANA: Wallace, go inside let me talk to my brother.

WALLACE: No. I'm tired of him putting on airs like he's som big professor. He can't even find work.

INDIANA: Wallace, please.

WALLACE: All right, all right, but it's him or me, you going t have for make a choice. [*He exits.*]

GARVEY: Sis, I don't know how you could live with someon like that, the man is an —

INDIANA: I don't want you talking about him, Marcus. He good to me. He has his funny ways but he tief a little lov out of my heart. He make me feel good. Anyway is not fo you to tell me who I should love. You come here aft them chase-you-way from Jamaica and now you try to te me I should worry about my people. Well, he is the onl people I want to understand.

ARVEY: Yes, I guess so.

NDIANA: I'm not like you. I can't think big thoughts about how the world should be. Me just know how it really be. All I know is I need a man for love me. When I wake up in the morning I want him there side of me. Before I go off to scrub the white people them floor, I need to know that somebody love me. You're different. It seem like you don't need nobody. All you want is books and politics. You just like father, mad and silent; you going dead poor just like him.

ARVEY: Father believed in something.

NDIANA: I don't know what he believe or don't believe. I just know he was mad out him rass.

ARVEY: I don't want to hear it.

NDIANA: Cause it true. If mother didn't cook and sell few cakes, we would all have starve. You think he would have care.

ARVEY: He cared.

NDIANA: I see you coming just like him. Well, I'm not going let you destroy the little happiness I have.

ARVEY: Wallace? That's happiness?

NDIANA: Whatever it is, it's mine and I want to keep it. Please try to find some place because—well, you see the situation. This place not big enough for three different kind of minds. You know them kinda way.

ARVEY: I know.

NDIANA: [*Turning from him.*] You a good man, Marcus, you not wicked. I wish you all the best but—I want you find somewhere else. Leave me and my man in peace. I 'fraid to lose him.

ARVEY: Don't worry, he's not going anywhere, and if he does it won't be because of me.

INDIANA: [*Starts to cry.*] What chance all you give me? Eve
time you see me with a little joy you want take it from m
Just like father. Look what happen when I did save up n
little bit of money for so long. Just when I was ready f
leave Jamaica didn't he just drop down dead to spite me?

GARVEY: Come on, girl. You can't blame that on him.

INDIANA: Well, he bad-mind enough for do it. Anyway is n
had to take the little money bury him. I wanted to cry o
and say: let the Government bury him. So you tief his la
from him; is you send him mad; let you bury him.
wanted to push his coffin right in front t
Governor-general yard, but me too shame so I bury him.

GARVEY: We couldn't of done that and still hold our head u

INDIANA: You all right. You could just sign up for some shi
go all over God world when you ready. What about m
Now I find a way you want come along and cau
contention.

GARVEY: I'll go now. [*He kisses her.*] I just wish you all t
best.

INDIANA: [*Turning away from him, afraid to face his eyes.*] Wa
good, Marcus. Mind you don't end up like father. Do
dream so hard.

SCENE 4
THE FORMATIVE YEARS AND JOURNALISM.

GARVEY: [*Excited.*] I've always loved journalism. No, not tru
I've always loved printing. I love ink. There's a power
words but mainly when they're seen. I see that as a peop
we've known talk. Talk is what we do on plantations. Ta
is what we do while waiting on the lash. It comes easy to
people who don't exist.

[*He pauses and makes a motion of his hand.*]

There's a mystery. As a people we must see ourselves
print.

We must have images. LA PRENSA.

When I feel most alone, when I feel that I cannot see my face, I publish a newspaper.

Perhaps it's only a small bell but it keeps away the big bell of death which is hideous to hear.

I met a man. A man of newspapers and ideas. His name was Mohammed Ali. The man saw countries and history such as I never saw. The *Africa Times and Orient Review.* That was a paper. He showed me what the power of print could be. It made clear what was happening all over Africa. I could see the pattern of rape and plunder. Before I thought only of what happened to the Caribbean but now I saw with new eyes.

When the Chinaman leaves China, no matter where he goes in the world, he always works and thinks of China. He is a Chinaman. The Indian leaves India but he is always of India. But what of the black man? Where is his allegiance? Where is his army, his nation, his god? He alone considers himself a West Indian, a black Englishman, a black American, but never an African.

Then I thought, we must start somewhere. When you build a man, a new man, you start from the heart first, and the heart is Africa.

[*Slow drum rhythm.*]

But how to do it? A newspaper is one thing but it is not enough. I think sometimes that I was born too late. If perhaps I was born in the time of Toussaint L'Ouverture. If I had a country like Haiti behind me. But that's idle dreaming. Slavery takes a different form now. I look at Jamaica and I see no whips or chains evident. Those who suffer don't know why they suffer. Those who conquer us now are no longer riders of horses. We have entered the twentieth century, the time of the *new man* but it's still the same *old man* who is on our necks. But how to cut him out? How to cut the wound and excise that poison pus which is everywhere in the black world?

A sickness unto death, Lord, and no physician comes.

I read so much now that my eyes become a blur. All m waking hours I search for the answer to one questio Sometimes even in my sleep I ask: How did a race, one s great, so in harmony with the world and the univers about it, how did we black people end up [*He pauses, look at his hands and then up to audience.*] *here,* in this void?

How did they go about bringing us to our knees?

How in the Caribbean, how in South Africa, how in th Congo?

And the answer comes slowly and many-layered, but comes. It was not through divine mystery, not throug predestination, but through deception, cruelty, an plunder, systematic plunder. Thank you, England, you'v taught me all you can.

There's nothing more I can get from you now.

SCENE 5
A STREET SCENE.

[GARVEY *walks from his room to the Indian grocer,* HAMIL.]

HAMIL: What will you have today, Garvey. Is it good wit you?

GARVEY: Cold, my friend, cold.

HAMIL: It's not cold yet, my friend, wait until next month.

GARVEY: What is that smell, Hamil?

HAMIL: Smell, what smell? Oh, maybe it's the cats.

GARVEY: Can't you do something with them?

HAMIL: What can one do? We need them to keep the ra away. Do you know how many rats there are i England?— in London, never mind England. It will be th plague again, you watch. [HAMIL *picks up his newspaper*

There will be war soon, Garvey.

GARVEY: A pound of saltfish, please, Hamil.

HAMIL: You watch, before the year is out there will be a war.

GARVEY: You mean a civil war with Ireland?

HAMIL: No, no, my friend, it is not Ireland I'm speaking of. It's a world war that I mean.

GARVEY: England says she doesn't want to get involved in a world war.

HAMIL: My friend, where there is a war, there is money; where there is money, there is Britain. You watch. Maybe you better get two pounds of saltfish just in case.

GARVEY: That's all right, I don't think the war will reach this week. One pound will be enough, Hamil.

HAMIL: [*Wrapping package of fish in paper.*] How do you find this England, Garvey?

GARVEY: Cold, my friend, cold.

HAMIL: When they see you on the street, when they see that you're not white, the rich cough into their gloves, the poor cough in your face [*He pauses as he hands* GARVEY *the package.*], but they all cough, my friend. You understand?

GARVEY: I understand.

HAMIL: When this war comes, you know, this war which they say will never happen.

GARVEY: Yes.

HAMIL: They will ask us to fight.

GARVEY: No, my friend, they will not ask, they will *tell.*

HAMIL: And still when they see us —

GARVEY: They will cough.

SCENE 6
A VIEW OF THE TIMES.

GARVEY: [*Excited.*] Today I sold an article.

Eight shillings, for an article.

Eight shillings.

[*A pause.*]

Enough to buy a new shirt. Enough to make a visit to the tailor shop, let the Jew stop the draught which enters my trousers.

I look at this England, this mother country of the empire.

I look at the East End where families huddle together until death.

A place where the children keep watch over each other's sleep to drive away the rats.

The young men die by thirty or end up in workhouses, prisons or asylums. I ask myself why is it that the poor are always so short in size.

Why?

I ask myself where does all the money go which they grind out of the colonies?

I know one thing clearly.

If empires can rise, so too they can fall.

There was a time when if a man said Rome would be no more, they would look at you with eyes wide and sad as my sister's. They would look at you and say that you must be mad.

And yet — where are the Caesars?

They say that the sun will never set on this empire but I'm here to tell you that I have seen the end.

I have seen the number of the beast.

And in your end is my beginning.

[*He exits. The drum rhythm builds.*]

SCENE 7
THE CHRISTIAN AID SOCIETY.

[GARVEY *goes to the relief agency in an attempt to get money to return to Jamaica. He speaks with a* MR. JENKINS, *a one-time missionary.*]

JENKINS: [*He looks up and produces a big British smile.*] Mr. Garvey? Come in, won't you. Have a seat. Now, how may we help you?

GARVEY: Well it's as I said on the form —

JENKINS: I'm sorry I can't hear you. Can you speak up.

GARVEY: [*Louder.*] Yes. It's as I wrote in the form, I'm requesting a temporary loan to assist me in my return passage to Jamaica.

JENKINS: Oh yes, I see. Well, what exactly do you do?

GARVEY: As I said there on the form [*Points to form which* JENKINS *is holding.*] I am a journalist.

JENKINS: I see, a journalist. How very extraordinary. Are you a Christian, Mr. Garvey?

GARVEY: Well yes, I was raised a Christian.

JENKINS: And what faith?

GARVEY: Well, my mother was a Catholic.

JENKINS: I see.

GARVEY: About this loan, I've already raised half the passage myself. I merely need —

JENKINS: Do you consider yourself a practicing Christian, I mean do you believe?

GARVEY: Do I believe? Well yes, I believe in the presence of hell. I mean that much I know clearly. As far as heaven goes, well of that I have no knowledge.

JENKINS: But you say you are certain there is a hell.

GARVEY: Well, I've lived that all my life. I've seen it with my eyes. In Jamaica, in Latin America, in Colombia where the children have tin for eyes. They work in the mines from age eight to whenever death comes, and their brothers take over.

JENKINS: I see. Do you think you would be interested in doing Home Missionary work in Jamaica? I think conditions would be quite favorable for someone like you. That way your passage would be no problem, you see.

GARVEY: Missionary work for the church?

JENKINS: Well, yes.

GARVEY: I don't really think that I could honestly commit myself to something like missionary work for the church, you know.

JENKINS: Well, why not?

GARVEY: Because the church in the Caribbean has been more of a problem than a help. No, I don't really think I could do that.

JENKINS: Well, apparently you don't wish to return to Jamaic very badly, Mr. Garvey.

GARVEY: [*After a pause.*] Not that badly, Mr. Jenkins. You see, think you charge a bit too much for your help. I'll get back to Jamaica on my own. [*Turning away.*] Thank you.

JENKINS: Mr. Garvey, you say that the church has done more harm than good. I don't feel that you have taken into account the fact that we have given to many of your own people, a reason for living. A meaning, if you will.

GARVEY: You can't have meaning on an empty stomach.

JENKINS: We have given aid as well.

GARVEY: And what if people do not believe.

JENKINS: Then we try and teach them to believe.

GARVEY: And tell me, what does the church do when i witnesses cruelty and injustice?

JENKINS: We do all that is humanly possible, short of violence

GARVEY: And what if you saw a man cheated by his employers. The man complains and the police club him to the ground.

JENKINS: I would ask questions.

GARVEY: I asked questions and they put me in jail.

JENKINS: I would publish —

GARVEY: I published, and they set fire to my office and burned my papers.

JENKINS: I would appeal to the government.

GARVEY: There is no government for a black subject.

JENKINS: Well ... I would pray.

GARVEY: Back to square one.

JENKINS: Square one?

GARVEY: We have been praying.

JENKINS: Jesus said that when he comes again —

GARVEY: We will all be dead, quite dead, and until then the wicked will flourish. Well, I can't wait quite that long. Thank you. Good day. [*He exits.*]

JENKINS: Good day. With these people, men are always more of a problem to convert than the women. [*He shakes his head.*]

SCENE 8

GARVEY RETURNS TO JAMAICA, 1914. EN ROUTE HE STOPS OFF IN PANAMA.

POEM IN PANAMA

Nosotros los ninos del azuca,
Esperamos para la azuca

Yo voy a colon,
Madre de dios,
Yo voy a colon.

Nosotros esclaves de la tierra,
Nacimos trabajor bajo de la luna,
Nacimos trabajor bajo de la sol.

Nosotros los ninos del azuca,
Y siempre cierca de la muerta.

(We are the children of sugar,
For sugar we live.

I am going to Colon,
Mother of God,
I am going to Colon.
We are slaves of the land,
Born to work under the moon,
Born to work under the sun.

We are the children of sugar,
And always near death.)

[*Slide of Jamaica flashed on screen. Voice on tape recording. An old Jamaican voice full of silence and history.*]

VOICE:

When Garvey come back to Jamaica he was a different man.

I don't know really how to say it.

It was like he was seeing vision.

When he left, we had all say:

Well the government a-chase him now.

All the while we feel say he

just a jester and shape a style.

But when he come from England

all of we that look 'pon him say:

This man different, he not shouting no more

is like he know well what he have for do for sure.

And when the man a-speak

there was a kind of trueness there

and that was the summer of 1914

and the world was afire.

Come, Marcus, we ready for you now.

[GARVEY *enters. The* CHORUS *of musicians answer him.*]

GARVEY: Lord, I'm frightened, I don't know where to start.

CHORUS: Speak the words and your soul shall be free.

GARVEY: But I don't yet know ...

CHORUS: Speak the words and your soul shall be free.

GARVEY: Well, you must start somewhere.

You build from where you stand. [*He clears his throat.*]

My friends, my brothers, if anything that I say here today makes any sense to you, remember that it is really yourselves speaking through me. I'm only putting in some order the things

I've heard you say in the streets, in the rumshops, in the fields where you work and in the churches where you pray.

You say it is not enough!

It is not enough to work every day and reap no reward for your labor.

It is not enough to bear children and watch them come from nothing and perish with nothing.

It is not enough to work land and never own it. To be a stranger always in the very place where you're born. An Englishman can come from abroad and walk one end of this island to the next like a god, but there are places where we who are born here cannot go, except to work as a footman or a laborer.

It is not enough.

All of us have family that have emigrated to other lands in search of opportunity. Few find it. Brothers, fathers, sons, who labor in Panama, or Costa Rica. They work like beasts, they live in filth. If ever you speak of exploitation, they beat you in the streets. They throw you in prison. The British Consulate says that we are the children of Cain. We have no rights. If you don't like it, they say, then go home. But go home to what?

Home to the Dungle. Home to the barrack-yards, the shanty towns, the same people in power who want to keep us in bondage.

It is not enough.

The Caribbean is based on an aristocracy of skin. The white man created the mulatto. Look around you, my brothers. Do you see any dark-skinned people in any positions of power?

Are we truly the children of Cain?

Are we to be despised because we remind the world too much of Africa?

When they needed our strength they looked to Africa. Could there ever have been a Great Britain without Africa, India, andAsia?

When they needed our minerals, gold and silver and diamonds, they looked to Africa.

When they needed our science they looked to Africa.

So how then can they despise Africa?

[AMY, *a light complexioned girl, enters while* GARVEY *speaks. She is walking with her maid whom she calls* AUNTIE.]

AUNTIE: Come along, girl. This not for you.

AMY: I want to hear what he has to say. He's a good speaker, isn't he, Auntie?

AUNTIE: In the first place, we shouldn't be here among these quashie people. They come from the bush.

AMY: From bush?

AUNTIE: From country. These people them never bathe. If you

don't watch good you could catch lice. You don't see how they smell like goat. Your people wouldn't like to know me bring you here.

AMY: But Auntie, we won't stay that close.

AUNTIE: However close you stay by them is too close. In the second place, these people should be working. You can't make speech and work the same time. Them too damn lazy.

AMY: But Auntie, they have a right.

AUNTIE: In the third place, if you don't watch yourself one of these man will try and trouble you.

AMY: Trouble me?

AUNTIE: Rub-you-up and leave you when you belly swell.

AMY: But we just listening —

AUNTIE: And in the fourth place, I have to go make number one, so come make we go home right. [*Takes her hand.*]

AMY: Yes, Auntie. But he is a good speaker, isn't he. [*They exit.*]

GARVEY: [*Continuing with his speech.*] In a world of wolves, one must go armed. The greatest defensive weapon in the world for the black man is race first. They say we are a people who love to gamble. Well then, let us gamble on ourselves. Trust in ourselves, think for ourselves, stand up for ourselves.

SCENE 9
THE MINISTER OF INFORMATION.

MINISTER: Come in, come in, Garvey, sit nuh, man.

Make yourself comfortable. What you drinking? You not drinking!

Have a sweet drink, man. Now, Garvey, I've been reading those things you write in the paper.

Articles? Yes, of course, articles. Some good things in there, man. You handle the language nice. A lot of style. You does write them yourself?

Good man, very good.

Look, man, you say somethings here about the need for a Negro organization. [*He scans a newspaper.*]

Where is it now? Oh yes, Universal Negro Improvement Association.

Listen, don't you think it would kind of make more sense to call the thing Colored Improvement? This Negro business is kind of a touchy subject, you understand. There's few people on the island who would follow that kind of thing.

Now, you know, I only have the best interest of our people at heart.

Is not what you say, Garvey, it's the way you say it.

You seem to be a chap with good sense, why don't you go home and consider.

When you change your mind, you come and see me again and then we shall see about letting you publish your newspaper.

There's a good fellow.

SCENE 10
AMY, THE DEBUTANTE.

[AMY *is being dressed by her maid. She is preparing for a garden party. Her hair is well brushed. The maid offers her the choice of two dresses. She steps out of one dress and into another.*]

AMY: [*To maid.*] No, Auntie. I think I'll wear this one, thank you. [*To audience.*] My teacher in second standard was named teacher Biddy. I was her favorite. I was always at the head of the class. I did well at Math and Composition and when they called me to recite I would never stammer. I was good at piano and needlepoint. I never learned to cook because they said there was no need to. And when I was sixteen my father called me into his study. You are a very special girl, he said, and you must save yourself for a very special man. You should continue with your piano and your singing and not worry your pretty little head too much about the world. But I want to worry my pretty little head, Father, because you see, I don't like the piano. I think I want to study Law.

Law, he said, oh no, not Law.

Yes, I said, Law.

Well, then, perhaps you should go to England, he said, I have contacts there.

I think I would like to go to America, I said.

Oh, you shouldn't go there, you have relatives there who would not want to see you.

And why wouldn't they want to see me, Father?

Because they are passing.

Passing for what? I asked.

Passing for white, he answered.

And so I stayed home for another year and went to garden parties and drank pink lemonade and tea.

[*Pause.*]

And waited.

SCENE 11
GARVEY REFLECTS AND WRITES ON JAMAICA.

[*On the wall is a map of the Caribbean.*]

GARVEY: [*Shaking head in disbelief.*] In the Caribbean, spelled with one R and two B's. Something about this place which paralyzes thought.

Too much rum and talk. Too much blood in the soil. Too much history.

It's funny the way that the powers-that-be choose to deal with me. Before I left for England, when I was organizing unions, they'd curse me and hunt me down. Now that they see I have a following they no longer curse me. Now they listen and shake their heads and say:

'Yes, Marcus, of course. You think we should build a school, a trade school for the people. Sure, Marcus, a good idea, a very good idea. We need an agricultural school like that college in America, Tuskegee. A fine idea.'

But nothing happens. More meetings, more dinner parties, more drinks passing.

We are with you. The church is with you. The governor is with you. But where is the money?

The government is glad that ninety per cent of the people are illiterate. Good, keep them that way. As long as they stay in their rumshops and drink the liquor which is owned by the top families, everything is fine.

And don't complain, Marcus Garvey. Your name has even appeared in *The Gleaner*. Quite an achievement for a little black boy from St. Anns.

[*A pause.*]

And the trade winds pass on afternoons and tickle the cotton dresses of the women. And they look so good. Why trouble yourself, Garvey. Just fall asleep with the others here in the Caribbean, spelled with one R and two B's.

Here where slavery is an art form.

But you see those mountains. From a child I loved them.

Wondrous green mountains.

[*He points in a circular movement.*]

You can follow them all around in a circle and they take you to a place they call North America.

[*Slowly.*]

North America.

[*Slow drum rhythm.*]

All of this is one large country.

The maps don't tell it because even the maps have been taught to lie.

North America, South America,
Caribbean spelled with one R and two B's. And yes, this too is mine.

BLACK

ACT TWO

1916-1927: YEARS OF TRIUMPH AND TRAGEDY—THE UNITED STATES

PROLOGUE

[GARVEY'*s voice on tape.*]

The Negro fights himself too much. His internal racial conflicts constitute the puzzle of our age. My experience has been one where the Negro keeps up a continuous fight against himself. He never agrees with himself for long. He never permanently constructs. We now realize that the system takes us nowhere.

SCENE 1
GARVEY IN AMERICA, 1916.

[GARVEY *moves to that part of his room where posters of the* U.N.I.A. *are on the walls. Stage lighting illumines the first National Conference poster.*]

GARVEY: When first I reached the place they called America, it was with a kind of hope and a kind of fear. There was a man I wanted to meet there, Washington, but he died on me. Time kind of cheated me there. I had plans but God had some other plans.

The thing now was what to do. To go or to stay.

I thought maybe a month would do it; give me what experience I need.

I went about the country watching the black leaders: New York, Philadelphia, Baltimore.

I visited thirty-eight states and everyone the same. Those who have keep, the rest starve.

The people were ready to stand, the people are ready when the leaders are ready but —

I did not mean to stay in America, it just happened.

I came to talk to leaders but the leaders had no ears, only bellies and mouths filled with smiles. So I talked to the people instead.

I've heard so much about this Harlem. The rumor was that it was easy to die in Harlem. That you had to watch how you walk and who you talk to.

But how do you talk to people.

[*He begins to walk to the front of the stage.*]

This isn't Jamaica.

But a street is a street and so —

[*He begins his address.*]

Hello, my friends, I won't take much of your time. I want to speak with you about something called freedom and something called respect.

The two usually go together and the absence of one usually means the absence of the other.

Freedom is the thing we fought for. The black man has fought for America, the black man has fought for England. We went forward to help in the Great War which they said would never happen. We fought and we died. We never led because they said we were not intelligent enough to lead. We could never be officers, but we could *die*. Dying is a thing which, as black people, we know well how to do, but for what do we die?

The war is over now and what have we as a people won?

Is there any black man here today who could say that this world is any better for him now? Two hundred thousand black soldiers.

Have the Ku Klux Klan given us more respect because we fought in the war?

Are there better jobs now?

Are your families living in better housing?

I have been deceived, you have been deceived. We as a people have been deceived.

[GARVEY *suddenly falls to the floor. A woman comes forward and rubs his face with her kerchief. She wears the fashionable dress and coat of the period. She helps him to his feet. He looks at her with genuine surprise. She walks away.*]

GARVEY: Sometimes I get so involved with thought that I forget that there is such a thing as the body. If you do not feed it occasionally, and give it some sort of rest, the body gets even with you. It has a way of reminding you who is boss. You must be careful, Garvey. You can't fall in the street because then you'll just be one other dreamer among the damned.

SCENE 2
HARLEM.

GARVEY: I like this Harlem. It doesn't frighten me. There's life here. Not the despair like I found in the East End of London. Not the paralysis like Jamaica. You could die, yes, but hell, at least there's a chance. [*A pause.*] When you talk you have to talk to an eye, or maybe a smile. Anything which is recognition. You must know when you've touched that place where everyone really lives. That place where to see is to know. Then you deceive deception [*He smiles.*] with *truth*. There's a man named Archie. He's an island man, too, and I know they call him a pimp and a gangster but there's something clean to him. [*A man in this thirties, wearing a brown, pin-stripe suit and panama hat enters.*]

WEST INDIAN ARCHIE: I'm going to tell you, Garvey. Me like the way you talk, you know. It different. You not like the rest. I not too much for the book and thing, but me like it when you say black man should stand up. It make sense. But now, look at Harlem. All of we black people, here, right, but what is it we own? The only thing there is Madame Walker and she beauty salon. Not that it is a bad thing, I mean you does see some sweet girl working there. But what else is we own? Italian man, Jew man, Irish man, they run the shops and we only buying. Dutch man own the houses. If we even die, is they we must go for bury us. So where is this power you talking about?

GARVEY: The leaders must raise the consciousness of the people.

ARCHIE: [*Laughing.*] The leaders. You could forget it, brother. You're it. You better understand that and move on your own. You set up a little meeting place here and you see what happen. They try and tief it from you. You do the work and they get the glory. Preachers and politicians, they all the same. Is you one, Garvey, you may as well deal with it.

GARVEY: I want to try and open some more branches of the U.N.I.A.

ARCHIE: Go on, no. I'm with you.

GARVEY: And we need a good newspaper. A newspaper can reach places that one man can't.

ARCHIE: A newspaper good. All me read is the racing page

really, but I'd like to see a strong black paper. Something different from *The Amsterdam News* society page and thing. But tell me now, what do you intend to do about all these white people who run Harlem?

GARVEY: I'll appeal to the people to open their own shops.

ARCHIE: Appeal! [*Laughs.*] Well, you go on and appeal, brother. I have a next way to do things.

GARVEY: No violence. The police would love an excuse to shut us down.

ARCHIE: No, no violence. You don't worry your head. You just go on with your paper and thing. I go deal with it. Just like a woman, gentle persuasion.

SCENE 3
THE HARLEM RIOTS.

[GARVEY *is shot. Heavy rhythm, sound of police sirens.*]

GARVEY: Gentle persuasion. Not a shop window was left unbroken. Not true, one window, a Chinaman who owned a laundry put up a sign in his window "ME COLORED TOO."

Our organization, the U.N.I.A., is said to be a racist organization.

Why? If the Jew can have pride and respect for his race, why can't we? If he can dream of Zion, why can't we? Africa is our mother, then why should her bastard children not go in search of their mother?

Why is it that when the white man says "go back to Africa" it is all right, yet when we say "repatriation" we are called racist?

Why shouldn't a black man marry a black woman? She is beautiful, she is the queen of the earth.

All through history black people have been enslaved

because of the white man's fear for his woman. So what is the threat now?

The truth is that it was not sex that was the fear, it was and it is economics.

[*A woman comes forward and addresses* GARVEY.]

WOMAN: Mr. Garvey, what do you mean when you say race first?

GARVEY: What I mean is that the question of race is the greatest problem facing the world today. The majority of the world is not white, it is black. Yet the white minority controls the destiny of the black majority. This is said to be an act of God, but I do not believe God could be so cruel. Do you believe he could?

WOMAN: [*Blushing.*] No, I can't believe that.

[*A man suddenly rushes forward with a gun and shoots* GARVEY. *The role should be played by the actor who was the* MINISTER OF INFORMATION.]

WOMAN: [*Screaming.*] God, they've shot Garvey, they've shot Garvey.

SCENE 4
THE HOSPITAL.

INDIANA: Marcus. Dem no kill you? Mek me see where dem shoot you. It hurt? Me hear say you are head of big organization now. Is true? Then you could give people work. Wallace, come in here.

WALLACE: How you, Marcus? Me hear 'bout you back in Englan' you know. It hurt? Not too bad, eh? Look, when I tell people you use to live wid we back in Englan' nobody nah believe it. So ah tell you sister, come let we go America.

INDIANA: Me know you was here and that you might need me.

WALLACE: You show him de ring?

INDIANA: No, not yet.

WALLACE: Show him! Show him!

INDIANA: We married now.

WALLACE: So listen, old man, maybe you could find a little something for me to do, eh? Look, ah wouldn't ask except for yuh sister sake. There is lots a tings I could do, you know. Ah been practicing speaking. Yes, "If fishes were wishes, then fences could fold."

INDIANA: Marcus, who the girl downstairs? The one wid the March woman eyes?

WALLACE: Leave 'im, 'im want to sleep.

INDIANA: Is all right. You can sleep now Marcus, we here!

SCENE 5
THE HARLEM OFFICE.

[GARVEY *with* WEST INDIAN ARCHIE *and the woman,* AMY.]

ARCHIE: You sure, you all right.

GARVEY: Don't worry, I'm fine.

AMY: I thought he killed you.

GARVEY: So did the newspapers. I can use the publicity. You see [*He shows them headlines.*] he only did me a favor. A blessing in disguise.

ARCHIE: Don't worry, we go deal with him.

GARVEY: I don't think anyone is going to take care of him anymore. It seems that he committed suicide.

ARCHIE: You should carry a gun.

AMY: Do you believe he really committed suicide?

GARVEY: Put it this way, I believe he's really dead.

ARCHIE: You need a bodyguard.

GARVEY: [*Looking at Amy.*] I need a secretary more than I need a bodyguard.

AMY: Do you really need a secretary?

GARVEY: I get over ten thousand letters a week in the post. What do you think I need?

AMY: My God!

GARVEY: I could use him, too.

AMY: What about your wife?

GARVEY: She doesn't like to type. What's your name?

AMY: Amy Jacques.

GARVEY: Amy?

AMY: Yes, Amy, just like your wife.

[GARVEY *looks at her and smiles.*]

ARCHIE: Look, I'm going send some friends to kind of keep an eye on things, okay.

GARVEY: Archie, you good and I thank you, but when the time comes no friend on earth could stop it. I can't keep looking over my shoulder. Besides, I never like to look back.

[GARVEY *walks forward and the two others exit.*]

GARVEY: Lord, we've not yet spoken but now I think it's time to speak. Forgive me if I do not fall on my knees, Lord. We have been on our knees too long. But when you turn away the captivity of Zion, we were like them that dream.

Give me strength, Lord.

I'm not afraid, I've seen death and beyond death.

I know that there is no dying.

For I have spoken with the enemy at the gate.

SCENE 6
WITH AMY AFTER BEING WOUNDED.

GARVEY: You know, Amy, it was funny when I saw the gun fire at me. I didn't even hear the sound. It was like I wasn't there for a while. I was back in Jamaica and someone else was standing here. All I heard was voices.

AMY: I remember I screamed.

GARVEY: But it wasn't just your voice, it was many voices. I was back at Roaring River, and the water was full of blood and the sound of water was the screaming of slaves and they kept calling: Garvey! Garvey! and all that I could think was what a waste. What a total waste if I were to die now before I've even started. What a waste to have done so much preparation for a thing which would never come. And I knew then that I couldn't die. There would be no sense to it. Do you know what I mean?

AMY: I know.

GARVEY: It's like training years for a race then someone trips you at the gate. And then I wondered, how many black people died before the world ever knew their face. How many, how many voices in Roaring River like duppie? How many spirits? Well, the world will know *this* face. I will not die, I will not go mad, I will not vanish, until — I'm ready.

SCENE 7
THE FIRST U.N.I.A. CONVENTION, HARLEM, 1920.

[*Garvey addressing audience. He dons his hat and gown.*]

GARVEY: My friends, my brothers. We are sharing a moment of history. You know sometimes people ask me what it is I plan on doing. I tell them I *am* doing what I plan on doing. We as a people must stop looking to some future miracle and realize that the miracle has already started. We ourselves are that miracle. Look around you. See one another. Is it not a miracle that so many of us could come together with One God, One Aim and One Destiny? Now some people say of me that I hate white people. That's ridiculous. I don't hate Lenin, I don't hate Trotsky, I don't hate DeValera. He's an Irishman who is leading his people to Freedom. Trotsky and Lenin are dealing with freedom. Anyone who fights against oppression, I'm for them, because they are for truth.

The time has come. I'm not speaking of what we will do. I'm speaking of what we *are* doing. *Now* is the time.

[*Behind him* WEST INDIAN ARCHIE *and* AMY *unfold the Red, Green and Black flag.*]

My friends, we have appealed to the League of Nations and they only laughed. We came to them with grievances and they told us that we could only appeal through our government. But where is our government? And who speaks for us?

We as a people must speak for ourselves. Through the Red, Green, Black of our consciousness.

Red, the color of blood which we have shed.

Black, the color of our race.

Green, the vegetation of Africa. Africa redeemed!

[*The sound of heavy rasta drumming.*]

SCENE 8
BIRTH OF THE BLACK STAR LINE.

MUSICIANS:

Garvey take a little boat
and he make it float,
Him take it from the dry, dry land,
Him take it from the dry, dry land.

Some have greed and some of them have power,
None of them know the day or the hour,
When the son of man shall come,
When the son of man shall come.

Garvey take a little boat
and him make it float,
You know he's there upon the Black Star Line,
Meditate upon the Black Star Line.

[GARVEY *and* WEST INDIAN ARCHIE. GARVEY *walks to the map of the world which is on the wall of his room.*]

GARVEY: You know, Archie, two-thirds of the world is water.

ARCHIE: No fooling, and here I can't even swim. You planning on taking a cruise? You could use a rest, you know. Man have for just rest sometime, Garvey.

GARVEY: Time enough to rest when you're in the grave. We've been resting too long. No, it's not a cruise I'm talking about. You know, I've been trying to find a way of getting our newspapers to Africa.

ARCHIE: Yesterday Garcia was saying that they not letting them pass in Cuba no more.

GARVEY: They're banning them everywhere. The British Consulate has alerted all the customs. We can't send it by post any more. They think they've got us. [*Laughs.*] But the sea —

ARCHIE: Hey man, I have some friends, merchant seamen —

GARVEY: Right. Black seamen go everywhere in the world.

ARCHIE: That's a good idea, Garvey. Damn, you bright for true.

GARVEY: And not only can they smuggle in the newspapers but they can bring back reports on what's happening all over Africa, the Caribbean and Europe. I don't want words of the Press, I want to know what men see with their eyes.

ARCHIE: You know something funny. There's not a place in this world you could go that you don't find at least one

West Indian. I don't care if it's the North Pole, there's always one. Is like we could live anywhere, withstand anything. We a funny people, boy. Tell me Garvey, when you think of God do you see a white man or a black man.

GARVEY: [*Smiling.*] When I think of God?

ARCHIE: Yes, God. I'm serious now.

GARVEY: I see a black man, Archie, a black man.

ARCHIE: [*Grabbing* GARVEY *and kissing him on the cheek.*] Thank you, me know me can't mad. When I think of God is a black man me see. Not that blonde Jesus man they does paint on church calendar. A man black like me. And when he laugh, he does laugh like me when I have money in me pocket and a woman in me bed. And when he grieve, he grieve the way I grieve when me feel the lash of life. But make me tell you, Garvey. If I was God, I would have never let man suffer so. I would never be cruel so. Come to think of it, I don't think a black man could be so damn cold—no, maybe them right,

God *must be* a white man. [GARVEY *looks at him.*]

I go see this thing, right Garvey?

[*He exits.* GARVEY *moves forward and addresses a rally.*]

GARVEY: My friends, brothers in the struggle. There are some who think that once you have achieved wealth that all life's problems vanish. It's a beautiful thought. [*Pause.*] There are some middle-class blacks here who hope to buy their way into the American dream. The problem is that the minute you try to travel abroad the reality of prejudice enters. There is no means of transport whereby we are not reminded we are a second-class people.

The time has come for us to own our own vessels. Our own means of transport. Even in Africa we are discriminated against by shipping companies. We are four hundred million strong. Why must we beg anything? We have a black country, Liberia. Why should we not make that our base? There are those who say we are mad. Is it mad to labor for our own cause instead of someone else's? Black people have been willing to die for everyone else's country, everyone else's but our own.

I ask you, where is our Zion?

[*As* GARVEY *is leaving the rally, a white man steps out of the audience. He is an F.B.I. agent. The actor should have been sitting there throughout the play. He steps forward to the stage.*]

F.B.I. AGENT: Are you Marcus Garvey?

GARVEY: [*Turning slowly towards this man.*] You have said it.

F.B.I. AGENT: Federal Bureau of Investigation. You are under arrest.

GARVEY: [*Sees* ARCHIE *is about to attack and restrains him.*] No, it's all right, Archie. [*Turning to* AGENT.] On what charge?

F.B.I. AGENT: Fraudulent use of postal service and incitement to riot.

GARVEY: I demand the right to see my lawyer.

F.B.I. AGENT: [*Handcuffing him.*] Tell it to the District Attorney. Come on. [*They lead* GARVEY *away.*]

SCENE 9

AMY AT A RALLY FOR THE APPEAL.

AMY: My friends, as you know they have arrested our leader. This should be nothing strange to us. They are merely continuing a pattern of worldwide repression from South Africa to the southern states of America. By arresting him, they hope thereby to arrest our cause. You see, it is not only Garvey in jail, it is each and every one of us. They are trying to discredit him. We are not allowed our heroes. The burden is now on us. More than ever we must show them our determination not to abandon the struggle which Garvey stands for! The liberation of black people, everywhere. We must not wallow in self-pity. Garvey does not need pity, he needs help.

CHORUS: One God, One Aim, One Destiny!

AMY: We have tried to raise bail for him. For an ordinary man, a bond of five hundred dollars would suffice. But Garvey for them is no ordinary man. They are asking fifteen thousand dollars.

CHORUS: What! Fifteen thousand!

AMY: That's right, fifteen thousand dollars, and it must be in cash as no bonding house will touch the case for fear of being blacklisted. We must not rest until every cent of that money has been collected. Next, we must rally, we must petition, we must demand publicity for this trial. The minute the eyes of the world leave the case, he will be a dead man, of that I am certain. They are holding him in the Tombs prison, and I assure you the name means just what it implies. I'm sorry I cannot stay any longer but I have to address rallies in ten cities over the next forty-eight hours, so please forgive me if I appear a little tired. I beg of you, please contribute whatever you can. Don't fail Garvey and don't fail yourselves.

CHORUS: Yes, Sister. [*Cheering.*]

AMY: I thank you.

SCENE 10

GARVEY AND AMY BEFORE THE TRIAL.

GARVEY: Well, Amy, you seem to have done a wonderful job.

AMY: It wasn't a job. Just forget it.

GARVEY: I can't forget it, ever.

AMY: Well, you better deal with this court case. These people seem pretty serious.

GARVEY: They are serious. They want to put me away. It seems that I've caused them a few problems since I've become international.

AMY: What does your lawyer say?

GARVEY: He says I should plead guilty on technical grounds.

AMY: And?

GARVEY: And nothing. I'm not going to plead guilty. I'm not guilty so why should I plead guilty, technical or not. The only thing I did wrong was stand up.

AMY: We know all that, Marcus, but what are you going to do? You're going to need new lawyers.

GARVEY: I'll be my own lawyer, plead my own defense.

AMY: Do you think that's wise, Marcus?

GARVEY: No.

AMY: Then why?

GARVEY: Things have to be said and I think I'm the best one to say them. After all, it is my honesty which is on trial; well then, who better than me to defend it?

AMY: And what if you lose?

GARVEY: I can't lose — I have right on my side.

AMY: Ha-ha!

GARVEY: Don't be so cynical.

AMY: Again I say, and what if you *lose*?

GARVEY: Well, in that case you better marry me so that you can take charge of my papers.

AMY: [*After a shocked silence.*] That's a hell of a proposal.

GARVEY: Well, I'd like to give you June, moon and spoon, but I really don't have the time.

AMY: I'm not asking for June, moon, spoon, but you could say a quiet "I love you." That would suffice.

GARVEY: Well, that goes without saying.

AMY: No, it doesn't go without saying.

GARVEY: Okay, Amy Jacques, I love you, and please pass the ammunition.

AMY: What do you love—a secretary, a typist, an accountant,

or a second-in-command?

GARVEY: [*Grabs her.*] Come here, girl.

SCENE 11
THE TRIAL.

ATTORNEY: [*Dressed in a long white sheet of Ku Klux Klan.*] The State accuses Marcus Garvey of willfully and knowingly using the United States Postal Authority for purposes of fraud. And that Marcus Garvey did knowingly and with criminal intent use the mails to promote the sale of Black Star Line stock in a venture which was hopeless.

GARVEY: Your Honor, I shall prove beyond a shadow of a doubt that I at no time attempted any act of fraud either against the Government of the United States or against my people. Every one of the prosecution witnesses, I will prove, has been paid by the F.B.I. to give false evidence. What I attempted to do was form a people's cooperative venture whereby the people could for the first time own some small part of an enterprise which was of their own making. For once let the people have some control of their own destiny. I stand before you and this honorable Court for judgment, and I do not regret what I have done for my organization or my people. Whatever I have done I've done from the fullness of my soul. We had no monetary consideration but only the good we could do for our race for this and succeeding generations.

I have respect for freedom, the freedom of every race. I believe the Irish people should be free, I believe the Jews should be free, and the Egyptian and the Indian. I believe also that the black man should be free. If you say I am guilty, I go to my God as I feel, with a clear conscience and a clean soul, knowing I have not wronged even a child of my race or any member of my family.

I ask no mercy, I ask no sympathy. I ask justice only.

[*Light dims on* GARVEY *and rises on* AMY.]

AMY: Justice! For four weeks the trial went on. The faces kept parading. One by one, Marcus, you exposed the lies, the deceit and the lack of concrete evidence. Then it was over. Guilty! The sentence was five years' imprisonment. Five years. And I died then but I couldn't die completely because you were watching.

SCENE 12

PRISON: THREE ASPECTS.

ONE:

GARVEY: [*Pacing.*] I should have realized that there was no way in the world they would set me free. The F.B.I. had spent over five million dollars in espionage in order to get me. They attended every meeting, followed me everywhere, checked all my correspondence. When they joined forces with the British Government, there was no way they would have let me walk out of that courtroom a free man. It's up to you now, Amy. You will have to see that my notes are put in order for a book. You will have to find the publisher. If none will deal with it, you'll have to publish it yourself. It's important now that the organization does not fall apart. You will have to become President in my absence. I know it's a lot to ask but I'll have to ask it. I hear that Firestone Rubber is buying land rights in Liberia. It's just a means of making sure I'm kept out. A ninety-nine year lease. You must do what you can to make the people aware that when they lose the land, they lose the power. Ninety-nine years and a million dead souls.

TWO:

GARVEY: Lord, out of the depths I call to thee. My father died in the poorhouse: shall his son die in prison?

Appeal — denied.

Appeal — denied.

Appeal — denied.

They're determined that I stay locked up forever.

And when the Lord turned again the captivity of Zion w were like them that dream. Then were our mouths fille with laughter.

MUSICIANS: [*Playing and singing softly.*]
Be not afraid,
one of the thieves was saved,
Be not too proud,
one of the thieves was slain.

THREE:

[GARVEY *walks to chair that he uses as a desk on which to writ To the side of stage is a dimly-lit outline of* AMY *undressing. H writes a love poem for* AMY *from detention.*]

GARVEY: Suppose ... suppose we had only dreamt the days c slavery

captivity would only be a word then

and the four hundred years which it took to make you, gi

(first the whips and then the poverty) only dream.

Assume instead that I accepted

first this night and then your body.

Renounced, all plantations

and the Middle Passage.

Withdrew pain and carved out silence,

and sucked your nipples

which are two cities in exile.

And what if tonight there were no history

only lovers

in Harlem

in Kingston
in Brixton
in Freetown
and I came *quite* inside you
beyond all the kingdoms of coming.

SCENE 13
DEPORTATION.

[*The white prison* WARDEN *reads a letter of clemency while in the background* GARVEY *prepares to leave prison. He is given a brown paper bag tied with string. He stands in a crumpled suit. The* WARDEN *speaks with a strong Southern accent.*]

WARDEN: Whereas it has been made to appear to me that the ends of justice have been sufficiently met in this case by the imprisonment already served: I, Calvin Coolidge, President of these United States, do hereby commute the sentence of the said Marcus Garvey to expire at once. Signed, Calvin Coolidge, President, November 18, 1927. [*He looks at* GARVEY.] Well, son ...

GARVEY: I'm not your son.

WARDEN: Looks like you about to get a free trip home. You lucky they ain't made you serve the full five years.

GARVEY: I shouldn't have had to serve five days.

WARDEN: Well, ain't my decision. I'm just a government employee. Anyhow, you never done nothing to me, I ain't got no quarrel with you, seems you a mighty fine speechifier. Should a been a preacher, you'd a been better off, know what I mean.

Still, kind of strange the way they lock you up and let everybody else go. Seems like you ain't guilty of nothing.

Worse they could say was that you was robbing niggers, and that ain't bothered nobody before. [*A pause.*] Anyhow, you about to be deported.

GARVEY: Deported? The pardon didn't say anything abou deportation.

WARDEN: No, it didn't say nothing but the Immigratio Department sure did. It seems like they want you out o here for good.

GARVEY: I'll fight it, I'll appeal the decision.

WARDEN: Yeah, sure, of course you could appeal, this is a democracy. But I'll tell you, Garvey, you got some peopl mighty worried 'bout you. They not go rest until you lon gone from this here United States. [*He hands him a package.* Well, good luck. They have an armored convoy waitin outside to take you to New Orleans and put you on th first boat out of here.

[*Drum rhythm builds.* GARVEY *steps out in exile.* AMY *i waiting for him. They touch palms together. He turns from he to audience of supporters.*]

GARVEY: My friends, some would have you believe that b getting rid of me the problem will go away.

But the problem will not go away.

I may go away, but not the problem.

There is no power on this earth great enough to stop

Africa becoming free,

Asia becoming free,

Latin America becoming free,

The Caribbean becoming free.

[*A pause.*]

Because you shall see,

And to see is to know.

BLACK

ACT THREE

1927-1938: THE MOVEMENT IN TRANSITION AND THE LAST YEARS: JAMAICA, CANADA, LONDON.

PROLOGUE

[GARVEY'*s voice on tape recording.*]

Mr. Chairman, Ladies and Gentlemen, Fellow Citizens of the British Empire: I am here this evening as the President General of the Universal Negro Improvement Association, an organization of eleven million Negroes in Africa, the United States of America, South America, Central America, Canada and the West Indies, to present to you the claim of our race upon your civilization.

SCENE 1

THE RETURN TO JAMAICA.

MUSICIANS:

Chi Chi Birdo!
Some of them a holler,
Some a bawl.

Chi Chi Birdo!
Some of them a holler,
Some a bawl.

GARVEY: I returned to find Jamaica just as I left it, asleep and hungry. Too asleep to know that they're hungry. The people were fire and the Government ice.

[*The* EDITOR *of The Gleaner newspaper does a small mime of betrayal. He moves about the stage showing crocodile teeth and makes the movement of a monkey. He then addresses the* CHORUS *of musicians who are celebrating* GARVEY'*s return.*]

EDITOR: Why are you honoring him. You know he's been in prison. He's a charlatan, a gangster.

MUSICIANS: Man, go way!

EDITOR: [*Addressing* GARVEY.] Well, Garvey, I see you're back. I hope you'll keep yourself quiet. We've had reports on you. I think you could be very dangerous for this island.

GARVEY: Dangerous?

EDITOR: We have no color prejudice here.

GARVEY: You've still got your pink tea garden-parties, your colonial clubs. *The Daily Gleaner* hasn't stopped lying for England. You haven't changed, so why on earth do you think I should?

EDITOR: Careful, that's libel. We'll be watching you, Garvey Watching you well close.

SCENE 2
GARVEY AND AMY AT HOME.

AMY: Look, I'm not complaining. I knew what I was getting into. But please, Marcus, just understand that I'm tired very tired.

GARVEY: You'll soon feel better.

AMY: All I'm saying is don't get involved in the politics here so soon after coming back.

GARVEY: I'd like to rest, Amy, believe me, but I hear the voices and I see the waste, and I can't rest.

AMY: They don't want change; just as long as they've got their salt fish when night comes and their rum to drink, they don't give a damn.

GARVEY: You can't lose faith. You can never lose faith.

AMY: And do you think they appreciate what you try to do? They all betray you, even your own family.

GARVEY: I don't deal with the past, Amy, I never look back. If I did I would get bitter or go mad like Bedward. We can't afford to waste our energy in revenge.

AMY: Eighteen people testified against you, people that you tried to help.

GARVEY: Eighteen, what's eighteen? We had thirty-five

thousand members. That's not a bad percentage. [*He laughs.*] Even Christ lost one out of twelve. You have to deal with the young, that's the only hope.

AMY: Well, you'd better deal with your own young—the doctor says I'm pregnant.

GARVEY: [*Jumping up.*] What! Praise God. [*He swings her round.*] A new soldier.

AMY: Careful, careful, my darling, he's not quite a soldier yet. [*A pause.*] The doctor says I need lots of rest or I'll lose the baby. I'm very anemic now.

GARVEY: Don't worry, Amy, you can do it, I know you can.

AMY: It's not a race, Marcus.

GARVEY: We'll call him ... [*Thinks.*] Marcus!

AMY: That was very difficult to arrive at.

GARVEY: Well ...

AMY: And what if it's a girl? [*They both say it together.*] Amy, of course. No thank you. [*They laugh together until they hear a voice calling from outside. It is the voice of an old woman named* MARGRET.]

MARGRET: Mr. Garvey! Mr. Garvey!

GARVEY: Yes?

MARGRET: Mr. Garvey, sir, Mr. Herbert say I should come see you. He say you could help me.

GARVEY: Come in, what's the matter?

MARGRET: [*Seeing* AMY.] Sorry for trouble you, but me don't know what for do.

GARVEY: What happened?

MARGRET: It's me son, Robert, sir. Is me last son. He just eighteen, sir, and because he complain when them want cut him pay, them want say he a-lead strike.

GARVEY: Who says?

MARGRET: The company, sir, the fruit people them. And so

them lick him, so them lash him till he near dead. God, he me last son. If he gone, what me for do?

GARVEY: Where did this happen?

MARGRET: There by the dock, sir. Me nearly dead when me see him. Them mash up him face, sir. Them warn him never strike no more, never.

AMY: And what did the others do?

MARGRET: Not a Jesus thing, miss, them never lift a finger for help him.

AMY: [*Giving* GARVEY *a long meaningful stare.*] I see.

MARGRET: Mr. Garvey, sir, what me for do? Me already lost two good son in Panama and now them want take me last.

GARVEY: Where is he now?

MARGRET: In me yard but them want for lock him way. Them say him dangerous. Oh God, oh God, I tell him Backra no love we quashie, mind you tongue, never tell them how you feel. But no, he too proud.

AMY: Will you have some ginger tea?

MARGRET: I don't want trouble you, Miss Garvey.

AMY: No trouble, come.

GARVEY: Yes, go with her, I'll see what I can do.

AMY: [*With anxiety.*] Marcus.

GARVEY: Yes?

AMY: Walk good. [*She touches him.*]

SCENE 3
DOCKWORKERS RALLY AGAINST UNITED FRUIT COMPANY.

[GARVEY *addresses the rally.*]

GARVEY: This is no country for young men.

The young flee because there is no chance here.

The young flee and with them our hope.

Do we hate ourselves so much?

A VOICE: Yes, Garvey.

GARVEY: We need a party here for the people who have nothing and expect more.

We have a right to jobs, to work.

We have a right for our children to be educated.

Again I say, this is no gift, it is a right.

We who labor for this place, we who bring our energy and our hope from the mountains into the city of Kingston and yet get nothing for it except betrayal at the hands of the United Fruit Company, these alien people.

Who is it in this Government who speaks for us except God.

We must stand and fight as one family.

If we eat, we eat together.

If we starve, we starve together.

If we strike, we strike together.

Toward one destiny. Then our young will stay.

EDITOR: [*Coming forward.*] So you back at it again, Garvey. I warned you.

GARVEY: Here we stand with clean hands and faces, a good British child.

EDITOR: I tell you, we had no trouble here until you come. Jamaica is a paradise. Who want to leave can leave. You too provocative, Garvey, that's your trouble, too provocative. You don't know to leave things rest.

We don't want any politics that will mash-up the Caribbean.

The Press will bring you to your knees. Watch!

GARVEY: You know what's wrong with you, journalist. You believe in nothing and you do less. You believe in nothing except alcohol and a pay-check.

Your weapon is the typewriter and the newsprint and you destroy dreams and give the lie to hope for whichever master employs you.

And what you hate most of all is that a month after you're dead no one will even remember your name. [*He walks off.*]

EDITOR: And you think they'll remember yours? Who the hell will remember Marcus Garvey? You're a mad man, you hear me. You mad. They should send you to the asylum like Bedward. [*Realizing suddenly that he is alone and screaming in the street, he fixes his jacket and tie and exits.*]

SCENE 4
GARVEY'S POLITICAL PLATFORM.

ANNOUNCER'S VOICE: [*A recording.*] The Peoples' Political Party will have a meeting tonight.

GARVEY'S VOICE: If elected, I shall do everything in my power to make effective the following:

1. Representation to the Imperial Parliament for a larger modicum of self-government.

2. Protection of native labor.

3. A minimum wage for the laboring and working classes of the island.

4. A law to protect the working and laboring classes of the country by insurance against accident, sickness and death occurring during employment.

5. A law to encourage the promotion of native industries.

6. Land reform.

7. The creation of a Legal Aid Department to render advice and protection to such persons who may not be able to have themselves properly represented and protected in the Courts of Law.

CHORUS: [*Singing.*]
One step forward,
Two steps backward
Down in Babylon.
One step forward,
Two steps backward
Down in Babylon.

SCENE 5
GARVEY'S HOUSE, SIX MONTHS LATER.

[AMY *has given birth to a son.* GARVEY *has not yet arrived and it is now two days after the birth.* AMY *is in bed at home being attended by the same woman of the previous scene who came to* GARVEY *for help.*]

MARGRET: You all right?

AMY: I feel much better, thank you, Mrs. Wright. How is the baby?

MARGRET: The boy him fine, ma'am, he sleeping good.

AMY: Have you heard anything from my husband?

MARGRET: He send word to say you mustn't worry. He soon come.

AMY: Mustn't worry, he'll soon come.

MARGRET: Oh, there's a gentleman to see you, a Mister Tyler of *The Gleaner*.

AMY: To see me? I wonder if something happened? Show him in please. Just a minute. [*She straightens her head tie and tries to make herself presentable.*] All right, show him in, Mrs. Wright.

MARGRET: Yes, Ma'am. [*She exits and returns with* TYLER, GARVEY'*s enemy.*]

TYLER: [*Bringing flowers for* AMY.] Thank you. It was good of you to see me. Congratulations on the birth of your boy.

AMY: Thank you. Mrs. Wright, can you put these in a vase, please.

MARGRET: Yes, ma'am.

AMY: That's very kind of you, Mister Tyler, but I'm certain you didn't come simply to congratulate me, did you.

TYLER: It's about your husband, Mrs. Garvey. May I call you Amy?

AMY: No, you may not. What about my husband, Mr. Tyler, is something wrong?

TYLER: Well, not yet. You see, he's making speeches again and getting a lot of people quite confused.

AMY: Confused?

TYLER: He has them striking for more pay. They won't get it. The Company can hold out much longer than they can. Half a loaf is better than no loaf, and a bird in the hand is better than ...

AMY: Yes, yes, I know all that, Mr. Tyler. What is it you want from me exactly.

TYLER: I'd like you to talk to him before it's too late. You know he's trying to run for office. He doesn't have the kind of diplomacy and tact necessary for politics.

AMY: You mean he doesn't lie?

TYLER: He'll never win, he has too many enemies and he's making more every day. They're already saying he's a communist. I really think it would be to his advantage if you make him think again about this business. You know he's not going to be young much longer. He has responsibilities now he's a father. There's no pension fund for retired revolutionaries, you know.

AMY: Mr. Tyler, my husband is not about to be influenced by anyone except himself and his conscience. I'm afraid I really can't help you. Now, if you'll excuse me, I'm very tired.

TYLER: Well, I hoped that you at least would see sense,

especially now — [GARVEY *enters.*]

GARVEY: Amy?

AMY: Marcus.

GARVEY: [*Looking at* TYLER.] What is he doing here?

TYLER: Hello, Marcus.

AMY: He just stopped by to congratulate us.

TYLER: Yes, that's right. You just getting back?

GARVEY: Get out.

TYLER: Well, I was just leaving. Please consider what I said, Mrs. Garvey.

AMY: I have no need to.

TYLER: Well, suit yourself.

GARVEY: Get out, I said.

TYLER: Take it easy, old man, I'm going.

GARVEY: And never let me find you in my home again. I don't mind dealing with filth out in the streets but not where I live. This is where I come to rest.

TYLER: A word of warning, Garvey: stay out of politics if you want to stay out of prison.

GARVEY: [*Suddenly producing a twelve-inch long machete.*] Get out of my house, I said.

TYLER: Aiyee! You're mad. [*He flees.*]

AMY: Garvey.

GARVEY: It's all right, Amy.

AMY: Where in God's name did you get that thing?

GARVEY: A farmer in St. Ann's gave it to me. He told me mind how I go. Don't worry, I'll leave it for young Marcus. [*He kisses her.*]

AMY: You saw him?

GARVEY: He looks strong. I knew it would be a boy.

AMY: You mean you're glad it's a son and not a *daughter.*

GARVEY: Don't say that. It would be a child, whether boy or girl.

AMY: And why weren't you here, Marcus?

GARVEY: You know I would have been if I could. I sent word.

AMY: Yes, 'Mustn't worry, soon come.' And what now, Marcus?

GARVEY: Well the strike is going well. I think they'll hold out.

AMY: I'm not talking about the strike. I'm talking about your family.

GARVEY: That's what I'm talking about, only it's a much larger family, I mean.

AMY: You couldn't even be here for the birth of your child.

GARVEY: There have been many births, Amy, and many deaths. And there will be many births and many deaths. But if I, his father, can't make any more hope for him in this white man's world, as they call it, then why bother. You see why I can't stop working now.

AMY: [*Screams.*] There are others!

GARVEY: [*Rising from beside her on the bed.*] If not me, who? If not now, when?

SCENE 6
AFTER THE ELECTION.

[GARVEY *is at home; the old woman,* MARGRET, *now his housekeeper, tries to cheer him up after his defeat.*]

MARGRET: Well, Mr. Garvey, sir.

GARVEY: I tell you, you mustn't call me 'sir'. I'm just like you.

MARGRET: No sir, you not like me, you could read and write. Everybody love to hear you. They say you a-come from God. [*A pause.*] I sorry you lose the election, sir. Is *you* me vote for.

GARVEY: I'm sorry, too, Margret, believe me.

MARGRET: Anyhow, me no really deal with them people. The Government not going count you vote right. Once them see you coming from a different way, them plot 'gainst you. Jamaican politics well heavy. When them see you poor, them dash way you vote.

GARVEY: Well, I'm going to try and appeal to the Governor for a recount.

MARGRET: Appeal ... yes, well, that good, sir. I wish you luck. Appeal, yes. [AMY *enters excited*.]

AMY: Marcus, I hear they're after you.

GARVEY: Well, they won't bother now, I've already lost the election. That's what they wanted.

AMY: They want more than the election. They want you locked up and this time it won't be for a few months. I think you'd better leave Jamaica, Marcus.

GARVEY: I won't run from them.

AMY: Marcus, what good is it going to serve? You know how much we've already spent in fines. Every time we appeal, we lose. They say that you've attacked the Courts and called them all corrupt.

GARVEY: Well, they know it's true.

AMY: You can't do that in Jamaica, Marcus. It would have been different if you'd won and had the party behind you. Now you're alone and no one is going to back you.

GARVEY: I might have lost but the People's Party will continue. There's no way they can hold back the tide now.

AMY: Please, Marcus, let's get out of Jamaica before it's too late. I know what I'm saying. They even want to throw you off this property.

GARVEY: They took my father's house from him. I won't let them steal mine.

MARGRET: Excuse me, sir, me no mean for jump in you

business but what Madam say is right. Me hear them talking in the market. Them say them mean for kill you, sir. Them feel say is you cause the people for rise up. Is you one they 'fraid. Them mean for stop you, sir. Is best you go way now, come back when things not so hot. You must think 'pon you family.

[GARVEY *looks at them.*]

SCENE 7
LONDON 1937: SOUTH KENSINGTON.

GARVEY: It was so that we entered the city.
Night didn't betray us,
only the wind in the secret places
and the banks shut tight
like the churches.
To enter now this London,
the city of sadness.

[*He calls* AMY.]

Amy! [*He coughs.*] Amy!

AMY: [*Enters wrapped in blanket.*] Shh. Quiet, you'll wake the kids. God, it's cold.

GARVEY: [*Coughing.*] It's not cold. The British climate is good for you, it builds character.

AMY: Builds character, does it? I guess that's why you came down with pneumonia last year.

GARVEY: A lady wouldn't mention it. [*He laughs and coughs.*] You look like an Indian.

AMY: I don't care what I look like, I'm warm.

GARVEY: Come here. [*He holds her.*] Has anything changed back home in these two years?

AMY: Nothing. People are still poor and they try to forget it by gossiping about how dark our kids are. They say I should have married a man with fairer skin.

GARVEY: If they spent less time dealing with other people's business and more time in revolution, they wouldn't be in the mess they're in.

AMY: God knows that's true.

GARVEY: Maybe you should have married another man. Life would have been much easier.

AMY: Well, it's not too late.

GARVEY: [*Jumping up.*] What? You want licks?

AMY: [*Laughing.*] Would you really care?

GARVEY: [*Avoiding the question.*] I want you to take a letter to the President of the United States.

AMY: [*Takes out pad.*] What do you want me to say? "Dear Franklin, having wonderful time. Wish you were here. Love to Eleanor" ...

GARVEY: Don't be flippant. "Mr. President" will be fine. [*He becomes serious.*] I have made repeated attempts to gain re-entry into the United States. I have decided to make a direct appeal to you.

AMY: [*Putting down pad.*] Marcus, they are not going to let you back into America.

GARVEY: I know that but I like sending letters, it gives me a feeling of hope. Why not? We know how to read and write, don't we? Might as well make use of it. Three-quarters of the world is illiterate, we might as well make use of the gift we have. Sure, why not write the President, write to God if we can. I came from nothing, what have I got to lose?

AMY: All right, Marcus. "Dear Mr. President, I have tried repeatedly to apply for a visa to enter the United States. The" [*She suddenly stops.*] Marcus, he sounds like he's coughing again. I'd better go see.

GARVEY: You fuss over him too much.

AMY: [*Already on her feet.*] He's not been well. This country is bad for him. [*She exits.*]

GARVEY: Here we sit with clean hands and faces ... [*Coughs again.*] Lord let me keep my will, please don't take that from me. [*He reads the letter from the pad and continues.*] "Applications for visa. I have submitted countless letters to the State Department. I only wish to enter America as a private citizen. I feel that I have that right as I have at no time, either by thought, word or deed, done any harm to the United States Government. You are perhaps aware of the circumstances of my departure. It should be evident by now that I am innocent of the charges which were made against me."

[AMY *re-enters.*]

AMY: Marcus, his fever is worse. I think I'd better take him to hospital.

GARVEY: No, no hospital.

AMY: Marcus, the boy might get pneumonia.

GARVEY: If they find out he's my son, they might kill him.

AMY: Marcus, please, do you want the burden of his death on your shoulders?

GARVEY: Amy, understand I have a lot of enemies. They would do it from spite.

AMY: We have no choice. We can't just sit here.

GARVEY: [*Considers quickly.*] You're right. There's no place to hide. All right, take him but use your name. Tell them he's Marcus Jacques. He might have a chance then.

AMY: I'll get him ready.

GARVEY: And Amy, don't leave him. If they say he'll have to stay overnight, you must stay with him. I don't trust them.

AMY: Yes, Marcus. [*She exits.*]

GARVEY: [*Alone.*] They have ways, they have ways of breaking you. [*He slams his fist on the desk, sits down, destroys the letter to the President and writes instead.*]
Forgive, O Lord, our errors,
Help me to all forgive,

And save us from life's terrors,
And peaceful let us live.

[*He laughs mockingly.*]

And peaceful let us live.
And peaceful let us live.

SCENE 8
CANADA, 1938: THE U.N.I.A. CONVENTION.

[GARVEY *comes slowly to front of stage thinking about his words carefully. He turns and looks behind him; for the first time* AMY *is not beside him.*]

GARVEY: Thank you for the warm welcome you've given me here in Toronto. It was very kind of the Mayor to allow me to speak. Of course, I should have liked to be allowed to live here, but then one can't have everything. Canada is a land [*Pause.*] that slaves ran away to when they could. My friends, when we appeal to the League of Nations for repatriation and nationhood, they merely laugh. When Germany makes a statement and reinforces it with arms and machinery, they do not laugh, they listen, and that, my friends, is the difference. The simple truth is that if you do not own land you own nothing. We have died in Europe. We have died in America, as we have died in the Caribbean, and yet we still do not own the land. That is why I say we must invest in Liberia, in Sierra Leone, in Nigeria. It is time we see to our own destiny. Our own defense. Europe would not want Africa unless she saw limitless possibilities of exploitation. It is time we see to ourselves. No one can protect us but ourselves. It is now time for the darker races of the world to take ascendancy.

Are you ready?

Let no man, let no power on earth turn you from your goal: freedom.

CHORUS: Freedom, freedom.

SCENE 9
LONDON, 1938: DEPRESSION AND REVIVAL.

[GARVEY *enters house and finds* MARGRET, *the housekeeper. He has been away on a speaking tour of Canada.*]

MARGRET: Welcome back, sir.

GARVEY: Margret, how are you? Where's Amy and the children?

MARGRET: She gone way, she take them.

GARVEY: Gone? Gone where?

MARGRET: Home to Jamaica, sir.

GARVEY: Home to Jamaica?

MARGRET: She say I must look after you. She couldn't help, sir. The doctor say if the boy stay here he go grow up a cripple. His foot get bad, sir. Them say it come from the fever. He need sun. No sun in England, sir.

GARVEY: She should have waited.

MARGRET: She try and reach you in Canada, sir. Please don't be vex.

GARVEY: [*Sitting down with coat and hat still on.*] I had no choice, Margret. I had to go to Canada. I had to address over twenty thousand people. I had to choose between them or my family.

MARGRET: She understand, Mr. Garvey. Take off your coat. I fix you some nice ginger tea and sweetbread. [*She exits.*]

GARVEY: Not even my family am I allowed. God, what price must you pay to be free? How much?

CHORUS: [*Singing.*]
Be not afraid,
One of the thieves was saved.
Be not too proud,

One of the thieves was slain.

[*Refrain.*]
Man and God,
One of them was saved.
Man and God
One of them was slain.

How shall I go on?
Only say the word.
How shall I go on?
Only say the word.

[GARVEY *is seated with chairs arranged in Masonic order.*]

GARVEY: I, Marcus Mosiah Garvey, being of sound mind — [*He pauses.*] Well, pretty sound anyway.

MARGRET: [*Enters, excited, holding a newspaper.*] Mr. Garvey, Mr. Garvey, sir. Them a-say you dead.

GARVEY: Really? Strange, I don't remember dying.

MARGRET: So them a-say. Look. [*She shows him the paper.*]

GARVEY: [*Reading.*] "Mr. Marcus Aurelius Garvey died here in London yesterday of a heart attack. Mr. Garvey was reputed to be a fervent Pan-Africanist and colored leader. He died here in exile in a West Kensington flat, number 2 Beaumont Crescent." Eager, aren't they. Amazing how nice people are to you when they think you're dead. [*Under his breath.*] The son of a bitch.

MARGRET: Lord, don't joke so, sir. I nearly drop with fright when I read it.

GARVEY: It's a great honor, Margret. How many men get to read their own obituary. [MARGRET *bends over and starts to rub her stomach, then stretches.*] What's the matter?

MARGRET: Wind, sir. I have it too bad.

GARVEY: The news send the wind up you?

MARGRET: You take it for joke, sir. I feel these people too damn wicked. Write something like that. [GARVEY *gets up and rubs her back.*]

GARVEY: You feel better?

MARGRET: Yes, thank you, sir.

GARVEY: Good, I want you to send a telegram to Amy. I know she'll be worried. [*He scribbles message.*] "Reports of my death slightly exaggerated. Not to worry. Love always, Marcus." [*He gives* MARGRET *the note and some money.*] And send her this ten pounds for the children. She'll know I'm all right. Dead men don't send money.

MARGRET: Yes, sir.

GARVEY: Mind how you go.

[MARGRET *exits and* GARVEY *sits. Slow drum rhythm builds.*]

GARVEYS VOICE: [*On tape recording.*] The West Indian Negro, educationally he has, in the exception, made a step forward, but generally he is stagnant. The West Indies in reality could have been the ideal home for the Negro, but the sleeping West Indian has ignored his chance ever since his emancipation. [AMY *enters in silhouette. She addresses him while looking out into the audience.*]

AMY: Marcus, they say if you come back to Jamaica they'll kill you.

GARVEY: But I will come.

AMY: In South Africa, they're keeping watch on the harbors. They say they'll shoot you and drown you in the sea.

GARVEY: But I will come.

AMY: In Kenya they fear you. In the Gold Coast, in Guinea, the police wait.

GARVEY: But I will come.

AMY: In America they have their orders. They've banned you in St. Vincent, in St. Kitts, in Barbados.

GARVEY: But I will come.

AMY: Trinidad, Grenada, St. Lucia.

GARVEY: You'll have to find them,
The young men from darker places.
You'll have to find them,
The ones who still have questions in their eyes.
Find them where they meet
Along the sides of the road
Or in the rum-shops and bars
Where they whisper together.

You'll have to find them,
Because me they will not let live.

You'll have to find them,
The young men from darker places
Who understand.

SCENE 10
WHEN GARVEY CAME TO ANTIGUA.

[GARVEY *visits the Caribbean islands. A poem to be spoken by the actor who plays* WEST INDIAN ARCHIE.]

WHEN GARVEY CAME TO ANTIGUA

It was a day like so. We get word from the sailors that he was coming to Antigua; still the government didn't want we to know.

And when we see the ship, *The SS Lady Nelson*. He had just stopped in St. Kitts. And when we see it coming into harbour we jump like beast.

Harbour bell ringing like mad, but this time it was not to take us to bondage, or to tell the death of some black man. This time the bell ringing to tell we that hope reach.

It was like Zion come.

Man, I tell you, you want to see woman. Everybody dress and go down to the pier. Who work left work. Who sick not sick no more because they must see this man.

We did hear that them lock him way in the jailhouse, but jail not strong enough to hold him.

And when he talk is like we talking. And the sound that come from him, man, it is like it coming from the earth self, it so strong.

And he said we who never own anything, not the land we work, not even the children which come from our seed, we will someday own the earth.

And when we labor, we'll not be weary because it will be for ourselves and those who come after.

And when we go down to the sea with our nets
We'll know why we go.

EPILOGUE

[GARVEY'*s voice on tape.*]

When I am dead, wrap the mantle of the Red, Green and Black around me for in the new life I shall rise with God's grace and blessing to lead the millions up the heights of triumph with the colors that you well know. Look for me in the whirlwind or the storm, look for me all around you, for with God's grace, I shall come and bring with me countless millions of black slaves who have died in America and the West Indies, and the millions in Africa to aid you in the fight for Liberty, Freedom, and Life.

BLACK

THE END

EDGAR B. WHITE
(1947 -)

Edgar White was born on the small West Indian island of Montserrat and brought to New York at age 5. The sudden transfer from rural setting to big city life was a difficult adjustment for the youth. It is probably responsible for his unique artistic vision which gives his work a special place in black theatre. His first play, entitled *The Mummer's Play,* was written when he was only sixteen and already it displayed the author's erudition and the fantastical reach of his creative imagination. It is about two struggling black artists who take their frustrations to an equally befuddled St. Peter, and it was produced at Joseph Papp's Shakespeare Festival Public Theatre in New York in 1965. This production inaugurated a healthy relationship between the young writer and the off-Broadway theater which has staged no less than six of his plays.

In 1964 White enrolled in City College of the City University of New York and later transferred to New York University from which he graduated in 1968. In the next eight years, he wrote and had produced in New York some fourteen plays, six of which were published by William Morrow in two collections, *Underground: Four Plays* (1970) and *The Crucificado: Two Plays* (1973). By this time White had also published three books of fiction, had taken up a writing fellowship at the Yale University School of Drama, and had become artistic director of the Yardbird Theatre Company of Harlem.

White's plays, many being short episodic pieces, are not literal examinations of racial conflict. The author's talent is for the oblique, ironical statement, and he boldly alludes to other literatures and cultures in dealing symbolically with the dramatic tensions inherent in his work. He has currently made his home in London where the Black Theatre Cooperative has staged several of his plays including *Trinity—The Long and Cheerful Road to Slavery* (1982), three short pieces that explore the consequences of slavery and colonization on Africa and the Caribbean, and *Like Them That Dream* (1983) dealing with the racial situation in South Africa. At this writing White is in Jamaica to attend the premier of his new play, *The Three Kings.*

Source: *Dictionary of Literary Biography, Vol. 38: Afro-American Writers After 1955: Dramatists and Prose Writers*. Thadious M. Davis and Trudier Harris, eds. Detroit, MI: Gale Research Co., 1985.

PAUL ROBESON

by
Phillip Hayes Dean

PAUL ROBESON
(1898-1976)

The controversy that plagued the mature years of Paul Robeson reached beyond the grave. When Phillip Hayes Dean's play premiered in New York and London, protest notices appeared in the press and placard-bearers on the streets before the theatres. They contended that the play did not deal justly with the real Robeson. Whether this charge is true or not is not the issue. As we have stated earlier, a playwright may take liberties with actual facts, may emphasize or minimize particular events, alter time sequences, include or exclude whatever he considers important to present his own distillation of his hero's life. What matters is how successful he is in convincing audiences in the theater that he has captured a particularly germane essence, an enlightening vision, of a unique individual.

The facts concerning Robeson's early life are indisputable, if astonishing. He quite simply excelled in everything he undertook. Born at Princeton, N.J., he was the youngest in a family of eight children. His father, a runaway slave, had worked his way through Lincoln University to become a Protestant minister who eventually settled in Somerville, N.J., as pastor of the St. Thomas A.M.E. Zion Church. His mother, a schoolteacher, was of mixed ancestry. When Robeson was six years old she was tragically burned to death in a household accident.

In his senior year at high school, Robeson gained top marks in a competitive examination for a full scholarship to Rutgers College (now Rutgers—The State University). At Rutgers he found himself to be the only black in the student body. Strong, tall, and handsome with a deep, resonant voice, Robeson overcame initial racial hostility by his personality no less than by his remarkable achievements as scholar and athlete. By the time he graduated from Rutgers four years later in 1919, he had been elected to Phi Beta Kappa in his junior year; had won the debating championship in each of his four years at college, and was valedictorian of his graduating class. In sports, Robeson at six foot-three inches and weighing 240 pounds was considered to be one of the great college football players, being named "All American" twice, in 1917 and 1918. He was also an outstanding all-round athlete, having won thirteen varsity letters in football, baseball, basketball, and track.

Robeson entered Columbia University Law School in 1920. To finance his law training he played professional football on weekends and sang occasionally in New York City night clubs. He received the LL.B. degree in 1922 but never practiced law. Instead he was drawn to the theatre and the concert stage, encouraged by a Columbia chemistry student named Eslanda Goode whom he married in 1921. She continued to influence his work until her death in 1965.

As with college, Robeson's professional careers in the theatre and concert hall can be measured by a number of memorable achievements. His first major concert, given at the Greenwich Village Theatre in New York City in 1925 and with a program comprised wholly of Negro spirituals and worksongs, was a ringing success. Supporting him on the piano was his friend Lawrence Brown, who would continue as his accompanist, arranger, and musical advisor for over thirty years. A two-year concert tour of the United States, Great Britain, and Europe followed.

For the next twelve years Robeson traveled extensively, expanding his repertoire to include folksongs of other nations and cultures, with special interest in African and Asian cultures. To fully understand the meaning of these songs, he studied the languages in which they were written, eventually acquiring proficiency in reading and speaking over twenty languages including Chinese, Hebrew, Russian, Gaelic, and several from black Africa. He also made over 300 recordings; occasionally adding to his program popular contemporary pieces. One of these was the song he made famous around the world: "Ol' Man River." It had been written for him in the operetta *Show Boat* (1928) and to hear him sing it was a profoundly moving experience for audiences everywhere.

On the dramatic stage, too, and in films, Robeson made his mark. Although not formally trained for the stage, he scored several dramatic triumphs: as Brutus Jones in *The Emperor Jones* for the Provincetown Players in New York City in 1924; as Crown in *Porgy* (1927); and in London as Yank in *The Hairy Ape* (1931) and Lonnie in *Stevedore* (1936). But the role that brought him the highest accolades was Othello, first performed by him in London in 1930 and then in a production by Margaret Webster for the American stage in 1942. After out-of-town tryouts the production opened in New York City in October 1943 for an unprecedented run of 296 performances, the longest of any previous Shakespeare play on Broadway. The critics were almost unanimous in their praise; Robeson was magnificent in the part. Robeson also had leading or featured roles in eleven motion pictures before he refused to act in any more commercial films, stating his discontent with the type of roles he was asked to play. The one exception was that of a Welsh coal miner in *The Proud Valley* (Supreme, 1941), which was his favorite film.

Throughout his artistic life, Robeson was a fearless and outspoken advocate for oppressed peoples and minority groups. He supported workers' parties, joined progressive organizations, lauded colonial independence movements, and gave numerous benefit concerts—e.g., in London for Jewish refugees from fascist countries. He went to Spain and sang near the front lines for republican soldiers fighting Franco's fascist forces in the civil war. He had been invited to visit Moscow by the celebrated film director Sergei Eisenstein and he arrived there from London via Berlin in 1934. Hitler's stony-faced storm-troopers outside his Berlin hotel reminded him of a lynching party; in contrast he was immediately impressed with the openness and warmth of his welcome in Moscow and with the apparent lack of racial prejudice. He made many friends among Jewish artists and intellectuals.

As spokesman for the oppressed, Robeson was accepted as art of the popular front against fascism during World War II. Iowever, when the "Cold War" heightened in the late 1940s nd Robeson continued to voice his admiration of the Soviet Jnion, he was soon targeted as a communist or communist ympathizer by the House Committee on Un-American ctivities which had generated communist hysteria through ts public hearings of the "Hollywood Ten." Later Senator AcCarthy would intensify the issue by claiming communist nfiltration in the United States Government. Robeson's assport was withdrawn in 1950 thus preventing him from ccepting engagements abroad, stores stopped carrying his ecords, and he was frequently denounced in newspaper ditorials. State Department briefs justifying the government's ction claimed that during his concert tours abroad, Robeson ad repeatedly criticized the conditions of Negroes in the Jnited States, that he was the recognized spokesman for large ections of Negro Americans, and that he had been for years xtremely active politically on behalf of independence of the olonial people of Africa.

Robeson's passport was restored in 1958 after a lengthy egal battle through the federal courts. For eight years his overnment had effectively prevented him from earning a iving. Robeson left the United States and remained abroad ıntil 1963 when he returned to America. He had become ill on visit to Russia in 1959 and had been in and out of hospitals ince then. In a series of entries in his *Bulletin of the Center for oviet and East European Studies*, Nos. 17-20, 24, and 26, Herbert Aarshall, a Robeson admirer and former artistic associate, rgues that Robeson had finally become convinced of the talinist Terror that had wiped out so many of his old friends nd colleagues. The burden of this discovery was unbearable nd caused his breakdown. On returning home Robeson nnounced his retirement from all public appearances. He vent into seclusion until his death in 1976.

Playwright Dean has written a full-length mono-drama bout his hero. Observing that Robeson's most popular nedium was the solo, concert stage performance of spirituals

and folksongs, Dean has appropriated that medium as th
format for his drama, even to the point of having a silent bu
supportive pianist taking the role of Lawrence Brown
Robeson's longtime accompanist. It is an appropriate concep
to hear the story of Robeson's life recounted by his stag
character, periodically interspersed with well-known song
from his repertoire. But it places enormous demands on th
actor — considerable histrionic skill to cope with fast changin
moods and situations, vocal flexibility, concentration an
energy — for there is no "down time" to allow an actor to re
unobserved during a performance. The spotlight is kept o
him relentlessly and if he has done his job well, at the end w
are left with a composite image of a magnificent artist,
committed fighter for social justice, and a compassiona
human being that is quite overwhelming.

Sources: *The National Cyclopedia of American Biography, Vo 58*. Clifton, N.J.: James T. White & Co., 1979. Also *Curren Biography,* Charles Moritz, ed. New York: H.W. Wilson Co 1976.

CHARACTERS

Paul Robeson
Lawrence Brown

ACT ONE

Carnegie Hall	Paul and Audience
Philadelphia	Marian
Somerville	Pop
Trolley Car	Mr. Pillgard and Ladies
Rutgers	
I. Waiting Room	Paul
II. Cafeteria	German Lady
III. Winants Hall	Glee Club
IV. Audition	Hans Mueller and Dr. Hoffman
New York Hospital	Reeves, Ben and William
Somerville	Pop
Rutgers	Coach Sanford, Big Red Flanagan and the Team
Pop's Church	Paul at the Coffin
New York	
I. Harlem	Paul and Larry
II. Van Vechten's Mansion	Van Vechten and Essie
III. Wall Street	Essie, Mr. Hayden and Miss Minnie
IV. Paul's Apartment	Paul and Essie
V. A Friend's Party	Paul and Essie
VI. YMCA Theatre	Dora Williams
VII. Provincetown Playhouse	Mr. and Mrs. Jerome Kern and Gilpin

ACT TWO

Russian Border	Customs Officer and Civil Guard
The Kremlin	Soviet Artists, The Impassioned One and a Spanish Artist
Battlefield Hospital	Abraham Lincoln Brigade
London	Lord and Lady Barclay, British Intelligence
Africa	Tribesmen and Ebo Women
Voyage to America	Paul
Statue of Liberty	Paul
Broadway	Paul

Washington, D.C.	President Truma
Kansas City	Concert Audienc
Peekskill, N.Y.	Audience, Police, FBI, a Mo
Interlude	Paul and Larry Brow
Washington, D.C.	Mr. Walters and House Un-America Activities Committe
Mother Zion	Ben's Congregatio
Philadelphia	Paul and Audienc

ACT ONE

An ebony grand piano stands in center stage. A leather piano benc sits before the keyboard. On downstage right and left sit six chairs three on one side and three on the other. These suggest the overflo seating for a concert. Upstage center of piano, the sculptured bust o Paul Robeson sits on a pedestal. It is lighted dramatically.

The concert light comes up, and the ACCOMPANIST *enters from stag right with music under his arm. He sits at the piano and prepares hi music on the rack. Then, he plays a stately introduction, and th recorded version of "This Little Light of Mine" begins, th* ACCOMPANIST *blending with it.*

[*Taped.*] This Little Light
of Mine, I'm gonna let it shine,
This little light of mine, I'm gonna let it shine,
This little light of mine,
I'm gonna let it shine —
Let it shine,
Let it shine,
Let it shine —

[*At the end of the first verse, the pianist continues playing, as we hear the voice of* PAUL *on tape.*]

[*Tape.*] Ladies and gentlemen — this is Paul Robeson. I'm sorry I can't be with you tonight in Carnegie Hall. That's why I prepared this tape. I am deeply honored that my keness by my friend, Antonio Salemme, will be dedicated onight in this great hall. I can think of no finer birthday present for my seventy-fifth year than this gathering of my riends — and I thank you.

salute my friends of all nations.

want you to know that I'm the same Paul, dedicated as ver to the world-wide cause of humanity for freedom, peace, and brotherhood. As Joe Hill says in the song, "I'm with you still."

Light comes up on PAUL *and comes down on bust.* PAUL *is in white tie and tails. He is sitting on one of the chairs.*]

just couldn't go to Carnegie Hall. I called Lawrence Brown, who was my accompanist for so many years, and I old him I just can't go. I'm settled now here in Philadelphia with my sister Marian. She's a retired schoolteacher, you know. She dug out one of my old concert suits. I said, "Oh, Marian, for *you*, I'll wear it, medals and all, but I just can't go to Carnegie Hall."

The bust in the ceremony tonight was my second modeling experience. In 1924 I posed for another sculpture by Tony. It was a nude bronze, life-size. Tony called it "Negro Spiritual." It depicted me singing "Deep River." How many of you have ever posed like this for two months, naked, singing "Deep River"?

[*Assumes pose of The Thinker.*]

The chap who sat like *this* had it easy! But like this [*Poses as in Negro Spiritual.*] singing "Deep River."

So, if you see the statue, you'll know what it's singing!

The Art Alliance of Philadelphia refused to show it — Seems the woman in charge convinced the Board that they couldn't be responsible for arousing the public by exhibiting the figure of a naked colored man in Rittenhouse Square!

So, they sent Tony a telegram asking him to replace the

statue with something else. Tony sent them a life-siz *female* nude—which they gladly accepted. As far as *I* coul see, she wasn't singing a thing.

The little song on the tape—"This Little Light of Mine"— chose it because it was my father's favorite.

Pop!

It seems such a long time since I really talked with Po Over fifty years, I guess.

There was one conversation we never could finish—abou my brother Reeves.

[*To Pop.*] Aw, Pop. how could you pretend one of you sons didn't exist? Reeves did exist. He was your son, too.

[*To audience.*] Ben had written that he saw Reeves i Harlem—said he was in a bad way. I wanted to go up t Harlem and look for Reeves. I could visit Ben's nev church. And Pop could come up, too, and after Ben' service we could all three walk around Harlem and loo for Reeves and bring him home.

[*To Pop.*] Aw, Pop, don't change the subject!

[*To audience.*] I remember the night Pop put Reeves out— "Trouble's going to follow you all the days of your life Reeves—I can't have you setting a bad example for Paul."

Reeves was not a bad influence. Only horrible thing h said to me was, "Kid, you talk too much."

All he ever told me to do was to stand up and be a man Don't take low from anybody and if they hit you, hit 'en back harder.

[*To Pop.*] I know what the Bible says, Pop, but Reeves wa your son, too! You always said you saw yourself i *me*—Pop, you were in all your sons!

[*Trolley music.*] Did you hear a trolley? That's the trolley carrying me from Somerville, New Jersey, t Rutgers—year of our Lord 1915.

[*To Pop.*] Pop, when I get settled I'm going to go up t

Harlem and look for Reeves and bring him home. I had to say that, Pop, before I went away. Perhaps it has something to do with starting out on my own. Look, Pop, here it comes! See who the conductor is! Mr. Pillgard—no, Pop, you take care of *yourself!* I'll be fine!

[*Piano plays "Git on Board" as* PAUL *gets on the trolley. He uses chair as suitcase.*]

Bye, Pop!

[PAUL *turns to woman on trolley.*] Mornin', ma'am!

[*To another.*] Mornin'—Yes, ma'am. Rutgers.

[*He sits.*] Mr. Pillgard—do me a favor? Ring your bell.

[*Trolley bell.*]

Yes, sir, it is the big day. Thank you, sir. Yes.

Mornin', Mrs. Littlejohn! Yes, Ma'am! I sure *can* use your prayers!

Yes, Mrs. Gray, I got your nicely washed and pressed shirts in my suitcase. Thank you, ma'am.

[*To audience as old man. Music: "Swing Low, Sweet Chariot."*]

They are domestics going off to work in kitchens around town. I've known these people all the days of my life. Some of them are members of my father's church. Many times I'd been with him in their homes, when he was there to give them spiritual comfort. And many times we were blessed with a good meal.

Uh-oh, do you hear that woman laughing? That's Mrs. Carol-Smith. Now she's looking at me, and do you know what she's thinking? Why isn't her son going off to college? Why is he sitting up there in the penitentiary? She always said that *I* was a child of destiny. That's just how she put it—"child of destiny."

She once said that she knew I wasn't going to be anybody's yard boy or handyman, and I asked her how she knew. She said, "Well, you just clean a yard too well, son. And that's a sure sign you're meant for better things.

Nature smiled on you."

I didn't know what I was going to be. Maybe a ministe like my father. Or a teacher, like my mother. And I wis she could be here now. I bet she'd be so happy. You kno Pop always said Mrs. Carol-Smith looked something lik her.

Well, I guess she doesn't really. It was just Pop's way o drawing a picture of my mother. He always did that. H said that one looked like her—that one talked lik her—that one down there ironed like her.

Just Pop's way of helping me see her.

You see, I was six when she died. A coal from the stov ignited her dress and she burned.

[*Music out.*]

And here I am on my way to college. That's a wonderfu word—college!

[*Music changes: "Git on Board."*]

The last one to get off the trolley was Mrs. Leslie. She cam back, took my hands, and placed them on her stomach and then she got off without saying a word.

[*To Mr. Pillgard.*] Mr. Pillgard, did you see what Mrs Leslie did?

[*To audience.*] Mr. Pillgard said she was most likely expect ing a child—kind of a gesture of blessing— transferrin good fortune.

'Bye, Mr. Pillgard!

[*Music changes: "The Banks of the Old Raritan."*]

[*To audience. Picks book off of piano.*] That first day I set foo on campus—it was the greenest place I'd ever seen. No that Somerville isn't green—but not like *this*. The ivy tha covered the buildings looked like it'd been polished by hand!

[*Piano plays clock chiming eight.* PAUL *sits down in waitin room.*]

They asked me to wait in the hall for my appointment with Dean Roberson—yes, Roberson! R-O-B-E-R-S-O-N. Quite similar give or take an R.

I guess there was a lot of "What to do with Robeson" that day—because there was no room assignment.

[*He laughs.*] Do you know what I was thinking about that first day? Booker T. Washington, the day *he* went off to school.

Well, it seems the head of the school was a good Christian white lady and she took one look at Booker T. and handed him a mop and pail—said she'd be back in a while. Well, old Booker T. rolled up his sleeves and went right to it. He was getting everything. The corners, the cracks in the ceiling, a cobweb or two—just everything. And as I say, she was a good Christian, and she knew how to look for dirt.

[PAUL'*s number is called. He jumps up.*]

Number twenty-six! That's me!

When she couldn't find any, you know what she did? She let ole Booker T. into her school. And he and that mop and pail went on to found Tuskeegee Institute, one of our finest colleges, and most likely one of the cleanest.

"Registrar's Office." Now, signs like that call for a special face. You see, my brothers and I invented a whole trunkful of "faces for special occasions." This one calls for William's intelligent Negro face.

[PAUL *makes "intelligent" face, and crosses stage right—he enters Dean Roberson's office and is surprised by the dean's appearance.*]

[*To Dean Roberson.*]

Excuse me for staring, Dean Roberson, but you remind me of someone my father *used* to know. Woodrow Wilson.

You see, before we moved to Somerville, we lived for a

while in Princeton, and Woodrow Wilson was president of Princeton University. And he and my father were both Presbyterian ministers.

Oh, no, no ... my father isn't Presbyterian any more. He's got his own church. It's uh ... Methodist, and Episcopal, and you might as well add African and Zion, too. Because it's actually called St. Thomas African Methodist Episcopal Zion Church.

Yes, I learned a great deal from my father. Books everywhere. He taught me Latin and Greek and diction. My father's a graduate of Lincoln University, sir. Yes, he is quite a scholar.

How does my father spell his *name*? R-O-B-E-S-O-N.

I can't say *why* he might have changed it, sir.

Problems? Reservations by whom? ... Oh, Mr. Ackerman, my high school principal! I can imagine what *he* said. He was always taking the colored students who had discipline problems and placing them in gym classes all day. Freddie Pearson spent his whole four years of high school in gym. Came time to graduate, he didn't have enough credits. But, boy! Did he have muscles!

He was always trying to encourage the colored students to drop out of school and get jobs.

Oh, but he *did*, sir. He'd even get the jobs for them. The girls he'd place in private homes and the boys always ended up shining shoes in barbershops downtown.

Well, yes, sir, he did once. He said he had a job for me, but I just said, "No." You see, Dean Roberson, I like school. Well, yes, I tried to tell the other students what he was doing, but then he really did have reservations about me.

No, sir, I never thought of myself as a troublemaker. Thank you, sir! ...

[PAUL *stands and begins exit. He is stopped by a question by the Dean.*]

The state oratory contest? ... Yes, sir, I won third place. Really? *You* were one of the judges? [*Pause.*] I was hoping for at least second place.

Well, it was a speech by Wendell Phillips on Toussaint L'Ouverture. My brother's favorite.

No, sir ... I wasn't trying to be belligerent. Yes, sir—"My children, France comes to make us slaves." ... Huh? ... Oh—like I did in the contest?

[PAUL *takes a new stance at the piano. The* ACCOMPANIST *plays a phrase from "La Marseillaise."* PAUL *delivers the speech melodramatically.*]

"My children, France comes to make us slaves! God gave us liberty: France has no right to take it away. Burn the cities, destroy the harvest, poison the wells, show the white man the hell he comes to make."

[*To audience.*] Well, I guess it was a bit strong.

[ACCOMPANIST *plays clock chiming nine.*]

By the end of the day, I knew I was in good hands. The major they recommended for my field of study—agriculture.

I was housed temporarily in a small single room in Winants Hall.

When I got settled, I set off to find what this fine institution had to offer in the way of "eats."

[PAUL *is on campus grounds. He tries to question a passing student.*]

Oh—excuse me. [*Pause.*] Sorry.

[*He is rebuffed. He turns in another direction.*]

Say, I'm a new Negro student here. Could you kindly direct me to ...

[*He is given the cold shoulder.*]

Oh my! I say, but you also seem to have that lean and hungry look. I am the Prince of Morocco—could you kindly direct me to the ca...

[*He is ignored again.*]

Excuse us, sir—my name is Rufus—Rufus, the new bus boy ... no, no ... could you kindly direct me to where the dirty dishes are? ... Oh, that way? Thank you.

[*Music: "The Banks of the Old Raritan."* PAUL *puts foot into the cafeteria, then freezes.*]

When I set foot in that cafeteria, everything stopped.

[*Music out.*]

And I just stood there, waiting to see if they'd all just get up and leave. Did you eat in the same room with a Negro? Or did you just walk out in righteous indignation?

While they were trying to decide what protocol to follow, I walked over to the steam table—it seemed like a mile.

[PAUL *has now moved behind the piano, which serves as steam table. He uses his book as a tray.*]

The white-haired lady serving the food said (German accent), "Ve don't serve colored food."

[PAUL *walks away, then changes his mind and returns to address the cook.*]

Oh! You mean—you don't serve food to the colored?

"Ve don't served colored food."

Oh, that's all right, I'll take the *white.*

Breast of turkey, of course, And the cauliflower looks good. Mashed potatoes. And can't go wrong with milk and coconut cake! Would you make that a la mode, please? Vanilla, of course. Oh, no, no, no ... I only use salt!

[*To audience.*]

I kept thinking of something my brother Reeves told me. "Never show fear," he said. "If they see fear in your eyes, you've lost the upper hand. Always keep a rock handy."

[*Music: "The Banks of the Old Raritan."* PAUL *walks to center stage and pauses.*]

I'll tell you one thing—if any of you are planning to dine at Rutgers, I cannot recommend the white food! And after having a good look at it, I can't recommend the colored food either.

[*He continues walk across stage. He sits on stage left. He is in his dormitory room.*]

But you know, I paid for my little victory that very same night. I'd forgotten—at Rutgers there was one thing lower than being Negro or freshman! Negro freshman!

[*Music: "Old Black Joe."* ACCOMPANIST *sings,* PAUL *listens.*]

ACCOMPANIST

Gone are the days
When my heart was
young and gay
Gone are my friends
From the cotton fields
away,
Gone from the earth
To a better land I know,
I hear their gentle voices
callin'
Old Black Joe.

Gone are the days
When my heart was
young and gay
Gone are my friends
From the cotton fields
away,
Gone from the earth
To a better land I know,
I hear their gentle voices
callin'

PAUL

Isn't that lovely? Right outside my door, the famed Rutgers Glee Club. Singing one of my favorite songs. But after forty-six times! In the middle of the night. Not so lovely. For freshmen it's called hazing, for a Negro it's called something else!

The tenors aren't bad though.

Baritones are good.

The basses [*Gestures indicating so-so.*] need help. [PAUL *sings with* ACCOMPANIST.]

[PAUL *finishes song alone.*]

Poor Old Joe.

They sent me a scroll. It said—"Dear Poor Old Joe of Winants Hall—since we can't beat you, why don't you join us?" That's just what I tried to do—I auditioned for Dr. Hoffman.

[ACCOMPANIST *plays introduction to "Jacob's Ladder."*]

And one of the boys from the Rutgers Glee Club played for me.

[PAUL *is auditioning for Dr. Hoffman, director of the Glee Club. He and his* ACCOMPANIST, *Hans, are onstage alone.*]

We are climbing Jacob's Ladder,

We are climbing Jacob's ...

[*He is interrupted by Dr. Hoffman. He peers into the dark auditorium.*]

Excuse me, Dr. Hoffman. Oh, Paul Robeson. Thank you, sir. Hans, he wants it again—lower.

[*Hans plays in a lower key.*]

"We are climbing Jacob's Ladder.
We are climbing Jacob's Ladder
We are climbing Jacob's Ladder
Soldiers of the cross ... "

[PAUL *comes to the downstage area.*]

I'm sorry, Dr. Hoffman—I didn't hear you ...

Oh, it's a Negro spiritual, sir. I learned it in my father's church ...

The Junior Choir ... Before that, sir, I was in the Sunshine Band ...

Oh, the Sunshine Band, sir. That's the choir for little children. But when I sang in the Senior Choir, they let me solo. I've been singing all my life, sir!

No, I never had any formal training. Just sang, sir.

Oh, you're not accepting me?

Might I ask why, Dr. Hoffman?

No. No, sir. No—I've never been told I have a pitch problem.

Oh,—you know, I never would have thought of that —

I suppose I *would* stick out, sir.

[PAUL *retreats to his room. To audience*.]

Of course, in my heart I was hurt and humiliated. But Pop always said, "Go with your *head* and not your heart." He said, "Reeves went with his heart and that's what always got him into trouble."

[PAUL *experiments with pitch pipe, blowing notes and then matching the notes. He does this several times*.]

I *know* what Reeves would've told him.

"I'm not off pitch! Your Glee Club's off pitch—and you're off pitch! Put that in your pitch pipe and smoke it!"

[*Music: "Jacob's Ladder."*]

Reeves was a free spirit. He didn't trust the intellect. He always said, "We're all in a prison locked in the brain!"

Reeves was a rebel—even when he was little he was always getting into fights. Later on, he had this little bag of rocks he carried in his pocket. Anytime anybody would insult him, he always let'm have it! We were always bailing him out. Police would say, "Here come those Robesons again!"

So when Dr. Hoffman turned me down, something in me wanted to hit back ... with a rock.

[PAUL *raises a fist. Music out.* PAUL *takes out a pitch pipe and experiments with it again.*]

In spite of my pitch problem, I was getting straight As. It was these grades that caused Dean Roberson to take a special interest in my progress. And he was still fascinated by the similarity in our names. He was so fascinated he even arranged for an appointment with a Dr. Howard Merton from the University of North Carolina. Dr. Merton was a geneticist. [*Pause.*]

You see, Dean Roberson surmised that because of my intelligence, it had to follow that my blood was white. And then, there was the unresolved matter of our names.

Well, there *was* mixture in my background, on my mother's side, the noted Bustill family. The blood of the Bustills was African, Cherokee, and white Quaker stock, going all the way back to the early days of America.

But I wasn't about to tell *that* to old distant cousin Dean Roberson — let alone some strange doctor from North Carolina. So I refused to be tested.

Dean Roberson called me into his office. Said [*Southern accent.*], "I was wonderin' and my grandmother was wonderin' too, if the Robesons came from North Carolina? Because the Robersons had a plantation there."

I said, "Dean Roberson, my father didn't just come from North Carolina, he escaped from North Carolina."

[PAUL *blows on the pitch pipe. Singing.*]

"There's a man goin' 'round takin' names.
There's a man goin' 'round takin' names.
He has taken my brother's name,
And has left my heart in pain —
There's a man goin' 'round takin' names —"

[*Music continues.*]

On a November day in 1916, I got a call from William— now, Dr. Robeson. He said Reeves was in the hospital and that I'd better come quick. I took a jitney— they call them taxis now. The driver charged me a whole nickel.

When I arrived in the corridor William and Ben were standing in front of Reeves's room.

[PAUL *crosses center.*]

There's a line from Shakespeare: "Let us not burden our remembrances with a heaviness that is gone."

That's hard not to do. Reeves was the first person to die who was close to me. I really didn't know my mother, but Reeves I knew and loved.

I wanted the world to stop—just for a moment—and acknowledge that my brother was gone. But somehow the world seemed not to notice that.

So I made up my mind right then that when it came time for them to take *my* name, the world was going to pause for a moment and say, "Paul Robeson has left this earth!"

[*Music: "Amazing Grace."* PAUL *is in his father's church.*]

I found Pop in his church, sitting in a pew, mending some old hymnals.

[PAUL *leans on back of pew and talks to his father.*]

Hello, Pop. You feelin' okay? ... Oh, you're feelin' fine? ...

Oh, that's good ...

No, I just took a couple of days off from school ...

Yes, Pop, there *is* something wrong ...

[PAUL *holds back his tears.*]

Oh no, not me ...

No, not Ben ...

Not William ... Pop, will you please stop mending that hymnal? [*Pause.*] It's Reeves, Pop. He died this morning. We want to bring him home now.

[PAUL *rises. To audience.*]

The hymnal Pop was mending he suddenly tore into shreds. At that moment I saw my father become a very old man.

[*Music out. To audience as old man. Music: "Ma, He's Makin' Eyes at Me."*]

1916—the year Woodrow Wilson became President by promising to keep us out of the war. One month after his inauguration we were in the war. Elementary politics!

[*Music out.*]

I returned to school and decided to enter another political arena. I loved football, still do.

[*Music: Football fight song.*]

No Negro had ever played for Rutgers, and I wanted to be the first.

[*Music out.*]

But Coach George Foster Sanford, a Yale man, said [*Imitating a New England accent.*], "I don't want the extra burden of a Negro on the team. I'm trying to build Rutgers into a football power, and if a Negro on the team causes dissension, then—I don't want a Negro on the team. Period! I think it would be better for you, and the team, if you turned in your uniform."

And I said, "Coach Sanford, you might as well tell them to turn in their uniforms! Why don't I just try?"

[PAUL *takes a three-point stance.*]

Well, on the first play of the scrimmage, I went out for a pass, a simple buttonhook play. I remember beginning my pass pattern—[*Begins pass pattern.*] and that's all I remember.

[*Comes downstage and kneels.*]

How many of you have ever seen the cleats on the bottom of football shoes?

Oh, today they're plastic, but, in 1917, little steel spikes. As I lay unconscious on the field, several of my teammates ground those spikes into my fingers—when I woke up my hand was on fire. Four of my fingernails were missing. My shoulder dislocated, my nose broken.

It was so bad, they had to send for my brother William.

[PAUL *mimics William.*]

And William says, "If you want to quit school, okay, but Pop and I wouldn't like to think you were yella."

[PAUL *to William.*]

Yella? What do you mean—yella! Would you rather see me get killed? Look at my face! It never *was* much to look at! But it's a mess now! And, William, did I ever tell you that some of the players wear gloves, so's not to touch the ball after *I* do?

Why don't I transfer to Lincoln University? You liked it there, so did Pop ...

Oh, lose my scholarship?

All right, can't afford it!

All right, don't miss your trolley. And, Dr. William, if I get killed, I want a simple service in Ben's church.

[*To audience.*]

You know, I didn't mind the broken nose, or being called yella! But those fellows were saying, "You're a Negro and you're scared of us and you're gonna run." Well, they weren't just insulting me, they were insulting my whole family—my whole race!

[PAUL *to Coach Sanford on football field.*]

Coach Sanford, I think I could be your best end. I just may turn out to be your best all-around player. I can block and hit and tackle and run. You've been watching me. Coach Sanford, I want that uniform!

[*To audience.*]

Ten days later, I was back on that field.

While I was healing, Coach Sanford suggested who was responsible for my hand—Big Red Flanagan, second-string quarterback.

[PAUL *is on the football field.*]

On the third play of the scrimmage, Big Red called a sweep around my end, and I was waiting for him. Two key blockers were knocked out of the play, and there was Big Red coming right at me. When he saw me, panic spread across his face.

[PAUL *mimes tackling Big Red.*]

You could hear the sound of leather meeting flesh and bone as I dropped my left shoulder and smashed it into his groin. I lifted and tossed him—and you could hear the dull thud as his body hit the ground. Whomp! And I thought I killed him and so did the team.

[PAUL *backs off.*]

They started to surround me, but Coach Sanford pushed his way through and said, "Let him alone! Practice over! Clean up! You, too, Robeson—you're on the team! Period."

[*To audience.*]

What? Big Red Flanagan—just knocked the wind out!

[*Music: College fight song.*]

The season of 1917, Rutgers did real well. Well, pretty well. [*Pause.*] Took first place.

Pop did a lot of traveling back and forth on the trolley in those days. His congregation always knew where he'd been on Saturdays—his sermon was short and raspy on Sunday. He left all of his fire and brimstone up there in the bleachers.

[PAUL *looks up at the balcony. Points to seat.*]

The seat right up there. One time my father got so excited he actually popped a collar—never could find the button.

Look at him up there.

[*Shouting to bleachers.*]

Hi, Pop! Some game, huh?

[*To audience.*]

His hair looks all gray from here. What is he now? Seventy-three? *No.* It can't be! [*Pause.*]

Nothing gave Pop a bigger kick than reading about his son in the sports pages—because there was always a line in there about him. Something like " ... and he is a minister's son."

And of all the nicknames the sportswriters started calling me, guess what Pop's favorite was? *The Black Phantom.*

Then it happened. Our team lost its best supporter—a telegram from Ben. "Come home. Pop's gone."

[*Music: "Takin' Names."*]

I caught that little trolley, knowing that every house, every bit of landscape I'd be seeing for the last time. I went directly to the parlor and sat with my father.

[PAUL *picks up chair and places it to end of piano, where he sits. He addresses his dead father.*]

Pop, we won the last game. Your son caught the winning pass. Your son made All-American. And when we returned on the train, the whole school turned out to greet us. And, Pop, when he stepped off the train, guess what they did? They put a wreath on his head—and lifted your son onto their shoulders and carried him all the way back to the campus ... where we all sang together.

[PAUL *is in tears.*]

Aw, Pop—why did you have to go and die? [*Pause.*]

Pop, I'm All-American now, the first in the history of Rutgers. And I'm all over the front page of the Somerville *News*. And, Pop,—you're there, too.

It says, "Paul Robeson, son of the Reverend William Drew Robeson of this town."

[PAUL *stands. To audience.*]

My father never feared death. His eye was always on perfection. And now, I knew he was at home. [*Pause.*]

But I'll always see him in the bleachers—cheering!

[*Music stops.*]

Hi, Pop. I'm glad you were my father.

[*To audience.*]

Strange, isn't it, how every man thinks the current he's in is the whole ocean and it isn't! Every move I made in my life has led me to ever-widening currents.

Pop had been my rudder until then; now he was gone, and I was facing a mighty big ocean that I had to chart for myself.

[PAUL *comes downstage with chair and addresses audience.*]

How many of you out there are lawyers?

[*He looks into audience.*]

Congratulations! Anybody from Columbia University Law School? Well, I'll tell you, not easy.

In our first class in constitutional law, our professor said, "Look at the man on your left and look at the man on your right; in three years, neither will be there."

[PAUL *is in a Columbia University classroom. He takes a note pad from the book.*]

Shall I continue, Professor? Thank you, sir!

[*Addressing classmates.*]

So, gentlemen, of all the forces that have acted in strenghthening the bonds of our union and protecting our civil rights from invasion, the Fourteenth Amendment is *the* vital part of American constitutional law, and through *it* ... the American people shall develop a higher sense of constitutional morality.

[PAUL *answers a question posed by his classmates.*]

What? No. Gentlemen! The Fourteenth Amendment does not grant any new rights and privileges—it merely strengthens the ones that exist, assuring the disadvantaged citizen, particularly the American Negro, the American Indian, and oriental Americans, that no state, particularly the southern states, can arbitrarily abridge those rights.

[*The jeering from his classmates becomes unbearable. He stops because of frustration. To professor.*]

Please ... Professor! Can I handle this? Thank you, sir.

[*He takes off his jacket. Menacingly to classmantes.*]

All right! All right! Every time I get up for one of these exercises you fellows start your stamping your feet—whistling, making your catcalls! You act like this is a minstrel show! Well, if that's the case, you'd better start paying me!

And if any of you think I am not capable of collecting, try not paying up!

[*Takes fighting stance.*]

Rest assured, gentlemen from out of state! You won't have to confront me in your courts!

As you well know, the American Bar Association still excludes Negro lawyers. But you will have to confront these issues in your courts or someone will have to confront them outside your courts on your streets. Really!

[*To audience. Music: Vamp "Git on Board."*]

I found that college men in those days didn't have much in the way of social awareness. The First World War changed all that. It certainly did for me.

A wave of young Americans flooded into Europe to make the world safe for democracy. Many black men among them.

My brother Ben enlisted, joined the 369th, and became a chaplain in that "war to end all wars."

[*Music: "Hot time in the Old Town Tonight."*]

Then the war was over and that wave came rushing back to our own shores, the young black men, filled with their achievements and expectations, hit New York in a shower of ticker tape and confetti, which seemed to confirm their expectations about democracy here at home.

And they marched triumphant.

[*Music out.*]

Until they hit the Mason-Dixon line.

[*Music: "Beautiful Dreamer."*]

That's when newspapers were filled with stories about Negro servicemen returning home from the war, returning home to the South, to be castrated, lynched, tied to trees and burned to death—and sometimes in the uniforms of their country. In Waco, Texas, a colored man was buried alive while a crowd of men, women and children cheered.

The tide of blood swept back to the North again ... to St. Louis, to Kansas City and Chicago. Men who once butchered meat for the nation now slaughtered each other in the streets.

[*Music out.*]

They called that summer "The Red Summer of 1919."

[*Music: "Git on Board."*]

It's hard to describe how I felt then [*Touching his heart.*]—inside. Helplessness, frustration, anger. Especially when our first antebellum southern President, my father's good friend Woodrow Wilson, had said, and I quote—"We are handling the Negroes in exactly the way they ought to be handled." Unquote.

The great Jamaican Marcus Garvey didn't think so. He organized an exodus back to Africa!

I felt the battle was here and I moved to Harlem.

Harlem—the Mecca for the new Negro.

It was the Jazz Age, and Harlem was the capital.

[*Music: "Sweet Georgia Brown."* ACCOMPANIST sings under dialogue.]

If Paris had its Jazz Age with its "Lost Generation," we had the Harlem Renaissance with the "Found Generation."

Negroes were developing new ideas in all fields—alternatives to the present economic, cultural, and political systems.

Everything from rent parties to rent strikes. Here we had our uptown Union Square—the Hyde Park of Harlem, where street-corner orators stood on ladders and preached the gospel according to the new Negro.

[*Music: "Black Bottom."* ACCOMPANIST *sings.*]

Black Bottom sure's got 'em—
Black Bottom sure's got 'em ...

Yeah, *that* was the sound of Harlem.

[*Crosses to center.*]

There were advertisements that went—"Hurry up to Harlem. Home of the happy feet. Barbaric dancing at its best."

They were doing the black bottom.

[PAUL *dances the black bottom up stage to piano. He pickes up top hat from piano, pops it out, and puts it on.*]

And they were doing the cakewalk ...

[*He dances the cakewalk downstage, and then goes into "The Apache Twosome."*]

The closest I came to scrimmage after Rutgers was the night I dislocated my shoulder at the Savoy Ballroom doing "The Apache Twosome" with Ruby LeBeau.

They did everything at the Savoy.

And it was there that black and white first danced together. And female couples were allowed.

[PAUL *crosses to piano—he sits on bench with* LARRY. *They sing "Nobody Knows You."*]

Nobody knows you, when you're down and out.
In your pocket not one penny,
And your friends, you haven't any.
Soon as you get on your feet again
Everybody is your long-lost friend.
Mighty strange, without a doubt.
Nobody knows you when you're down and out.

[*Music: "St. Louis Blues."*]

Ethel Waters first introduced W.C. Handy's "St. Louis Blues" to Harlem, at the Cotton Club.

And then the white owners of the Cotton Club refused to let W.C. in to hear his own music.

[*Music out.* ACCOMPANIST *stops playing and frowns.* PAUL *laughs.*]

That's right! They'd accepted his music but not him.

That's how the white millionaires sponsored the Harlem Renaissance. They came attracted by the glitter and glamour and they stayed to absorb all the good energies and ideas, and the promise of a Harlem Renaissance that should have been, was never fulfilled.

Oh yes—Harlem has its millionaires, and millionaires sure *had* Harlem!

There was one I grew quite fond of though. Carl Van Vechten!

Carl was music critic for the *New York Times,* and he gave wonderful parties.

[*Music: "Vienna, My City of Dreams."* PAUL *crosses up to piano.*]

His mansion was always filled with intellectuals, athletes, jazz musicians, artists, and entertainers.

[PAUL *is at a party at Carl Van Vechten's. He leans on piano with a drink in his hand.*]

My first time there—I wasn't really comfortable at first. But then I started to listen ... and I realized these people had wonderful, exciting minds. And then word got out that a famous athlete was in the salon.

That's how they called it—"salon."

And then one breathless little thing walked up to me and asked me for my autograph. When I signed my name, she looked at it and said, "Paul Rob-e-son? Who's he? I thought you were Jack Johnson."

No, I'm not Jack Johnson. My name is Paul Robeson. They call me "Robey."

[PAUL *spies Essie on the stairwell. He points to Essie and speaks to* LARRY.]

See that girl dressed in the rose fringe coming down the stairs? She winked at me when I was hanging up my coat. Did you notice? *She* winked at *me.*

[*To Mr. Van Vechten.*]

Mr. Van Vechten, who is the rose fringe?

And Carl said, "Eslanda Cardozo Goode. The first black pathologist/chemist, Columbia Presbyterian Hospital. Quite bright."

And I said, "Yes, and for a pathologist, she's also quite pretty. See how the light catches those almost alabaster cheekbones?" He said, "Yes, she got them from her mother. The Cardozos were of African, Jewish, and Spanish blood."

[*Talking to Essie.*]

I beg your pardon, Miss Goode, am I who? [*Pause.*] Yes, ma'am, I am, and never let it be said that the great Jack Johnson ever refused a waltz.

[*Music: Crescendo.* PAUL *dances with Eslanda, he winks at the audience, finishing downstage. Music out. To audience.*]

And she said she lived with her mother, and yes it woul be all right for me to see her home, even though I wasn' really Jack Johnson. Not only was it all right to see he home, but we all three sat down to some of the best roas chicken I'd had since leaving Somerville.

It was 3 a.m. and Eslanda insisted on walking me back t the subway. She said she didn't want me to get lost in strange neighborhood.

She really wanted to ask me if I thought her mother woul make a good mother-in-law. I thought, "There's somethin wrong with this young lady."

Perhaps it was the combination of late meals an microscopic slides. Or the strange combination of gene After all—an African, Spanish, Jewish, Sephardic marrie to an African, Cherokee, white Quaker—in an Africa Methodist, Episcopal, Zion Church. I decided I woul never see her again.

[PAUL *has crossed and sits down. Music: Hungarian melody.*]

No dessert for me, Eslanda. Too rich!

I know we can always eat at your mother's house. Bu Essie, between you and me, I don't need "When are yo going to get a job, Robinson?" My name is Robeson.

Tell her what my name is!

You told her *what*? Where did you get the idea we wer engaged?

[*Raises his voice.*]

What? I don't care if there *is* a cute little apartment o 125th Street. I am *not* talking loud. Finish your desser What's so funny? Essie, we are not getting married. This i the Last Supper!

[*Music: "Wedding March." To audience.*]

We were married on August 17, 1921. My brother Be performed the ceremony.

[PAUL *is marching down the wedding aisle.*]

Coach Sanford was there, other friends from Rutgers, my sister Marion came down from Philadelphia. Mother Goode, of course was there. And Eslanda took my breath away—she was dressed in Spanish lace.

Our only honeymoon was the jitney ride to our new home—that's right! The cute little apartment on 125th Street.

The rent was eighteen dollars a month.

[PAUL *crosses to stage left and sits.*]

Eslanda continued her work at the hospital while I finished my law studies. When I was admitted to the New York bar, Coach Sanford arranged an appointment to a Wall Street law firm—Hayden, Hartford, Hubbard, and Hoyt.

[PAUL *crosses stage right to his office at H, H, H, and H.*]

My first office was a little cubicle way at the end of the hall.

It was used mainly for storing old legal records. But somehow, they managed to get a desk and chair in. I was the only Negro in the firm, except for a Miss Minnie Peterson, the lady who cleaned.

[*At his desk.*]

I wasn't there long before I realized that all the secretaries in my department were quitting. It seems they refused to take dictation from me. The only time I ever saw Hayden, Hartford, Hubbard, or Hoyt was when they dragged some client back to my office to discuss ... football.

[PAUL *studies book.*]

But during the months there, I devoured all those old legal volumes—and from them develped some pretty good legal presentations. They were that good they were given to young white lawyers to use in court.

Then I was assigned to research this one case that involved a wealthy client of the firm who had just died.

In his will he named as recipient to a Mississippi property

a Negro servant who had been with the family a long time and nursed him through his illness.

The family wanted to contest the will on the grounds that he was incompetent at the time he signed it, and they even implied coercion on the part of the servant.

So after I finished the research on the case, I decided I had to take it to Mr. Hayden.

[PAUL *crosses center and addresses Mr. Hayden.*]

Mr. Hayden—sir, due to the nature of this case and the nature of the research done on this case, I think it best that the lawyer who did the research should handle it in court.

And Mr. Hayden said, "Paul, I have it on good authority from the Lawyers Club that New York judges are very reluctant to decide cases in favor of Negro lawyers."

I said, "Sir, I've confronted this kind of hostility all of my life."

He said, "Paul, to defend a will with a Negro recipient is difficult enough, without adding a Negro lawyer to that defense."

He said, "Paul, your briefs are brilliant, but I cannot jeopardize this case by letting you handle it in court."

[PAUL *nods and excuses himself. He crosses back to his office. Angrily slams book down on the floor.*]

I felt like I was practicing law about as much as Miss Minnie was.

[*To Miss Minnie.*]

I'm sorry. Oh no, no.

[PAUL *picks up the book and lifts his feet for her to clean.*]

Go ahead about your work ...

Miss Minnie, when I came in this morning, you were singing. But when you saw me, you stopped and looked at me so strangely. And you're doing it right now ... why?

She said, "It just don't make sense."

And I said, "What don't make sense?"

She said, "After all that education and your bein' in here with nothing to do but talk about football."

Miss Minnie, you're a smart woman. Of course it doesn't make sense, because it was all a joke. Hayden, Hartford, Hubbard, Hoyt, *Robeson*. There's not an *H* in my name—anywhere.

[PAUL *stands.*]

Do me a favor, don't clean up this office. Clean it out!

And don't you ever stop singing.

Do you know anybody who might want to buy a used Phi Beta Kappa key? Sorry!

[*Crosses stage left. He is at home. To Essie. He is very upset.*]

Eslanda, it's just like my brother Reeves said, "We are *all* in prison." Yes, Essie. A prison.

What? No, I will not. I said I will not!

[*Shouting.*]

No, I want to be of service in court. And I will not just hang up a shingle someplace. My God—for what—divorce cases! I am prepared for more than that.

Look at these hands! Look at them! This morning when I left the office a little man pushed in front of me on the subway, and, Eslanda, I almost hit him. You know, I could have *killed* him ... What do you mean I've got to do something?

Essie, I don't know what I'm going to do, but I need time. It's time out!

[*Music: "What'll I Do?" to audience.*]

You know, being out of work has a lot of little disadvantages, too. I got on Essie's nerves more and she sure got on mine. So we went out more to friends' houses.

Like this one night we were at a friend's house. It was a party. People took turns telling jokes, doing a dance, singing songs.

[PAUL *is at a party.* ACCOMPANIST *sings "What'll I Do."* PAUL *stares pensively into space.*]

What'll I do with just a photograph to tell my troubles to?
When I'm alone with only dreams of you that won't come true
What'll I do?

[*Music out.*]

ACCOMPANIST:

It's your turn, Paul.

[*Music: "Drink to Me Only with Thine Eyes."*]

PAUL:

Well, I didn't feel like singing. I didn't feel like doing anything! I looked at Essie. Looked at her face and suddenly the words of a sonnet came to my mind.

[*Music out. To Essie.*]

When, in disgrace with fortune and men's eyes,
I all alone beweep my outcast state,
And trouble deaf heaven with my bootless cries,
And look upon myself, and curse my fate,
Wishing me like to one more rich in hope,
Featured like him, like him with friends possessed,
Desiring this man's art and that man's scope,
With what I most enjoy contented least;
Yet in these thoughts myself almost despising.

[*He looks at Essie.*]

Haply I think on thee; and then my state,
Like to the lark at break of day arising
From sullen earth, sings hymns at Heaven's gate;
For thy sweet love remember'd such wealth brings
That then I scorn to change my state with kings.

[*To audience.*]

And then on the way home, Eslanda kept saying how well I'd done. She said, "The room was so still." She said, "Something drew them in. You never know where that quality can lead you, Paul."

It was like having a layer fall away from me.

There comes a time when a wife becomes your mate. It doesn't happen when you walk down the aisle. There's nothing you can do to make it happen: but there does come that time when your wife becomes your mate. It doesn't mean she understands you any better. I guess it starts to happen when she helps you to take off that first layer.

And that night—as we crossed Broadway and 122nd Street, Eslanda Cardozo Goode became my mate.

And then she started getting telephone calls in the hall—from a certain Dora Williams. Dora Williams had been at that party.

Dora Williams was the director of the Harlem YMCA amateur theater group. They were rehearsing a new play called *Simon the Cyrenian*, about the Negro who carried the cross for Jesus. The noted actor Charles Gilpin was to have played the role, but he was called out of town on a paying job in *The Emperor Jones*.

[*To Essie. He laughs.*]

No, Eslanda, your dramatic arts is not for me!

Yes, I know the sonnet was great, Essie. It's a great sonnet. Well, tell your Dora, not for me!

[*To audience.*]

I met Dora on stage. I swear I saw tears in her eyes as she said, "Congratulations. *You* are going to carry the Cross for Jee-sus."

And right then and there Dora began my education in the theater. Upstage—Downstage. Stage Right—Stage Left. Tormentor. Teaser.

[PAUL *picks up chair Stage Right and uses it as a cross.*]

And one heavy, heavy, heavy, heavy Cross.

There was one very serious problem. The role called for the actor to whistle. Now, I've done a lot of things in my life. But there's one thing I never could do.

[*He tries to whistle, and fails.*]

Nothing comes out.

And Dora is standing there saying in a very businesslike manner, "All right, Robey. Are we going to get the whistle or not?"

And I said, "Dora, I will get the Cross up the hill for *you*, but even for Jesus I cannot whistle."

And she said, "Well, what are you going to do? We can't just have a hole in the play."

And then Essie, bless her heart, came up to the apron of the stage and she said, "Let him sing."

And Dora said, "I didn't know he could sing. Sing what?"

And I said, "What else? 'Were You There When They Crucified My Lord.'"

On opening night, there was a line toward the end of the play.

[PAUL *is onstage opening night. Music: "Were You There."*]

"Daughters of Jerusalem, weep not for him, but weep for yourselves and your children, for if they do these things in a green tree, what shall be done in the dry?"

Then Jesus said to Simon:

"If any man will come after me, let him take up the Cross and follow me." And Simon said, "I will bear this till he comes into his own light—"

I got the Cross up that hill, and then I turned to the audience.

[PAUL *puts chair on piano. It is the Cross. He sings.*]

Were you there when they nailed him to the Cross?
Were you there when they nailed him to the Cross?
Oh, sometimes it causes me to tremble, tremble, tremble.

Were you there when they nailed him to the Cross?

[*Music out. To audience.*]

And then, you know what I did? I swear, to this day I don't know what possessed me. Now, the play wasn't over yet, but I turned to the audience and took my first honest-to-God bow—right there under the Cross!

[*He bows.*]

And as if that wasn't bad enough—I stood up and sang another one.

[*Music: "Joshua Fit the Battle." Segue into "Swing Low, Sweet Chariot."*]

I think I sang about four songs before they stopped me.

Because I was not prepared for that feeling. But it was the most natural feeling I'd ever felt—in my life!

Now you've all heard the expression "Grab the brass ring." Well, what happened to me that night was like grabbing the brass ring, kicking off, and being swept off the earth.

[*Music out.*]

Do you know who was in the audience that night? Sitting in the third row? Right next to my wife, Eslanda, for some strange reason—Eugene O'Neill.

Mr. O'Neill had a play about a young Negro lawyer married to a white girl. It was called *All God's Chillun Got Wings.*

That play caused quite a stir. The daily critics protested that "A Negro playing a white girl's lover on the stage would destroy the American theater."

Do you know what the producers did for me? Hired me a bodyguard. That's right. I was an actor only one night in a Harlem basement, and already I had a bodyguard. His name was Pete Washington. Old Pete took one look at me, he goes, "Whew! I'm supposed to protect him, that big ape? He ought to be protecting *me*!"

And the Ku Klux Klan of Georgia got into the ac
naturally. They wrote Mr. O'Neill a letter warning hir
that his son would be killed if that play went on. O'Nei
wrote his answer in two short words. So the play went on

It became quite a success.

And then one night O'Neill came backstage and askec
when *All God's Chillun* closed, if I would go on the roa
and replace Mr. Charles Gilpin in *The Emperor Jones*—h
said Mr. Gilpin had started to drink a lot and wa
changing dialogue.

Oh, you know, there are people to this day who believe
created the role of *The Emperor Jones*? No, for the record,
was the great Charles Gilpin.

After my final performance of *The Emperor Jones* a ver
special group of people came onto the stage.

[PAUL *is onstage after performance. To guests onstage.*]

I should know you!

And then he took off his hat! Big Red Flanagan.

[PAUL *holds his side.*]

Yeah, I think of you too, every time it rains.

Oh, Mr. and Mrs. Kern—Mrs. Kern, please. [*Offers her seat.*]

Larry—Mr. and Mrs. Jerome Kern—Lawrence Brown.

Yes, I'm afraid this was our last show.

Oh yes, my wife and I saw your *Showboat* last month. W
loved it. You are taking it to London?

Oh ... I think I'd like that. But I'd have to talk it over wit
Essie of course.

And I'd like to discuss the lyrics with Mr. Hammerstein.

I really loved the show, but there's something about th
lyrics ...

[*He is interrupted by Mr. Kern.*]

Yes, I'm aware of the great opportunities in England for someone such as myself—So I'll drop by on Tuesday—fine—thank you, good night.

[*Mr. and Mrs. Kern exit stage right.* LARRY *points out Gilpin to* PAUL. *He is onstage. To audience.*]

After all the other visitors left, one man remained. Mr. Charles Gilpin. I didn't recognize him at first. He was older, and so tired.

He mumbled his congratulations, and left. And it's with me still—all the things I didn't say to him.

Sir, I am sorry. I didn't want to take your place. I never did.

Why couldn't you leave that stuff alone? Look at yourself. You had no right to do this to yourself. We needed you. The Negro people need the great ones like you. We owe a place to the ones who come after us. We owe them a place.

Will I be the next ex-nigger of the year? No! They'll not do that to me. I'll not be found staggering through Harlem—chasing a ghost of what I might have been.

They'll not do that to me.

[*Lights fade center while music under finales with "Ol' Man River."*]

ACT TWO

[*Larry enters with score and sits at the piano. Piano and tape begin on cue. On the tape we hear* PAUL *singing "Ol' Man River." After finale* PAUL *enters Stage Right and addresses the audience as the Old Man.*]

As they say, in America, the London production of *Showboat* was a "smash hit." It certainly opened new worlds for me, concert stages, debating circles. I was in constant demand in the music chambers of the British aristocracy.

[*Music: Minuet.*]

Oh, Lady Margaret, good afternoon ... *but* you are looking well.

[*To audience.*]

Most singers are susceptible to English weather. It is being said here that I am susceptible to English aristocracy. And when they wanted to be rather crude about it, English *female* aristocracy. I guess what made the gossip so intriguing was the incomprehensibility of such attractions. And I must say, I didn't understand it fully myself. For instance ...

[PAUL *takes position at the piano and sings. He is at Lord and Lady Barclay's. Music: "Drink to Me Only."*]

Drink to me only with thine eyes
And I will pledge with mine
Or leave the kiss within the cup ...
And I'll not ask for wine ...

[*Music out.* PAUL *crosses stage left and fans woman who passed out.*]

There was this one English lady, every time I'd get to a certain line in the song she'd faint. I can't say that I understand it, but certainly noticed it ... even came to expect it.

[*To Lady Barclay.*]

Oh yes, Lady Barclay, she's done it again! Something about the line, "kiss within the cup."

[*Lady Barclay introduces* PAUL *to Mr. Hamilton.*]

Oh, friends of yours from America—how do you do, Mr. Hamilton? Oh, charmed, I'm sure. Over here on holiday? The Republican party ... Chairman. I see.

[*To Lady Barclay.*]

Yes, Lady Barclay ... the last time I saw Essie she was in the library refereeing a debate between the Socialist views of Mr. Bernard Shaw and the grand old Republican party views of Mrs. Calvin Coolidge.

I wonder if Essie will survive? Lady Barclay! If you do see Essie tell her that I'm ready to leave. Presently. Thank you.

[*To Mr. Hamilton.*]

Yes, Mr. Hamilton ... I beg your pardon, sir ... No, I don't think of myself as an exotic here. I can assure you, I am not here at this function as an exotic. Because here, sir, you see, unlike in our own country, I am considered an artist, an athlete, and, most importantly, a scholar. Now if you will excuse me ...

[PAUL *decides to leave Mr. Hamilton but he is stopped by a question.*]

No, I don't entertain the idea of returning to America. I'm often asked that question by Americans visiting over here. "Paul, when are you going to go back to America?" My standard answer for some time now has been, "Why? What for?"

[PAUL *is amused by Hamilton's response.*]

My people need me? Mr. Hamilton, at this point in my career, I am only beginning to discover how I may be of help to my people ... Yes, I'm aware that my films are shown in America. And I am also aware that they are distributed only in Negro neighborhoods ...

Hollywood ...?

[PAUL *pulls up a chair next to Mr. Hamilton and sits.*]

Mr. Hamilton, I'll put it to you this way. In Trafalgar Square there is a large likeness of me in electric-light bulbs. And it says, "Paul Robeson in *Sanders of the River.*" Now I ask you, sir ... is Hollywood prepared to offer me anything like that? I can tell you what I would be offered—silly little parts in silly little films.

Oh, really ... You are prepared to guarantee me a Hollywood career. And what, sir, would I have to *do* for that? ... But, Mr. Hamilton, I'm not Republican ... Yes, I'm a star ... but I rather fancy the ideas of Mr. Roosevelt over the ideas of Mr. Hoover.

And I'm not certain if anyone could or should deliver the Negro vote. Mr. Hamilton, perhaps this won't make any sense to you at all, but in Somerville, New Jersey, wher Negroes go to the bank to cash their checks, and withdraw their money, they always seem to walk away with old worn-out dollar bills. And how my father would grumble that he'd have to hurry and spend quickly before it disintegrated into antiquity.

But here, when I go to the Bank of England to draw out some of my pounds and shillings, I always seem to walk away with brand new, crisp sterling notes. Which *can* last in your wallet forever.

[PAUL *is distracted by Essie's entrance.*]

Oh, Essie! Good day, Mr. Hamilton ... I do hope you enjoy your stay here. And if you have any difficulty getting tickets to my concerts, do give me a ring and I'll see what I can do.

[PAUL *stands and crosses stage left. He is at home, dictating to his secretary.*]

May 3, 1934—Dear Ben: Thanks for the letters. It's hard to believe that Eslanda and I have been here for a full seven years now. We rented a beautiful home in Hempstead from the former Ambassador to Turkey. To further impress you, dear brother, I am not writing this letter, I am dictating it to my secretary, Cyril. Oh yes, put your name in ... Cyril Bunting—put your name in!

Here's our schedule for the week:

Monday—supper with George Bernard Shaw.

Tuesday—luncheon for Mrs. Calvin Coolidge at the Savoy. I would have loved to have invited Bernard Shaw too, but I've learned from Essie one doesn't invite the Socialist Shaw and Republican Coolidge to the same function. Not a done thing.

Wednesday—is matinee, but Eslanda is entertaining members of the Labor party.

Thursday—late supper with Lord and Lady Barclay.

Friday—Ben, I'm meeting with two incredible chaps, African students—Jomo Kenyatta and Kwame Nkrumah— yes, Cyril, that's N-K-R-U-M-A-H at the African Students' Union.

They've made Eslanda and me both members of their union. You might say, Ben, Africa can truly be called the "Dark Continent" only by virtue of the fact that its history is lost. We're so used to seeing Africa through the eyes of Western culture, when it is most accurately seen through the eyes of oriental culture.

That is why I'm finding it so much easier to speak and sing in Swahili, Russian, and Chinese than it was to speak and sing in German and French.

And there is a very important thought here. With the coming of the Renaissance to Western culture, something happened to Europe. Reason and intellect were placed above intuition and feeling.

The result being a European race that conquered nature and now rules the world.

But as science advanced, the art of the West declined.

So the question is, "To what end does the West rule the world if all art dies?" Or as Jesus, the Easterner, put it—"What does it profit a man to gain the whole world if he loses his own soul ... "

Thank you, Cyril. See you at the theater.

[*Crosses to pick up book from piano. Then crosses back stage right. He is engrossed in his schedule book. He calls to Essie, who is in the other room.*]

Essie ... we're finished now ... what, darling? The date of the Georgia Tech football game? Are you still writing that "bloody" book?

[*To audience.*]

I love the word "bloody."

[*To Essie.*]

So, what are you doing, another chapter on the heroic exploits of the "Black Phantom of Rutgers U.?" And don't you dare title your book that! If you do I'll denounce you in the London *Times*.

Essie, darling, you know you're just the last person in the world to write a book about me ...Why? Because you know nothing about me.

So stop trying to make me your hero, Essie. Stop that "child of destiny" nonsense! I don't want to live up to anybody else's heroic images of me.

Here's a chapter for your book; when the Georgia Tech football team vowed to stomp the "Black Phantom" to death, what do you think the great hero did? Ate soap—to drive his temperature up, so that he could be admitted to the hospital. The only reason I played the game at all was to make All-American. Put that in your book!

You can title that chapter, "Looking Out for Your Future." I'm not so dumb, you know. You think I'm your little tin angel, don't you, Essie. No faults!

You couldn't imagine, could you, Essie, for instance, that I would be unfaithful to you, Essie?

Oh, you could!

You mean you've been listening to the gossip?

If it were true? Oh, Essie, if it were true. If I slept with half the women I'm accused of, I'd probably be on display in the British Museum of Natural History ... probably pickled. Like this!

[PAUL *assumes the pose of Negro Spiritual.*]

Oh no, no, no, Essie, I only brought it up to make a point. Not to start a debate about fidelity.

Please!

I just wanted to talk about the concert tour.

[PAUL *checks through schedule book.*]

So—France, Belgium—a command performance in Holland for Her Majesty the Queen ... Scandinavia, Russia.

Now before Russia, I want to spend a day or two in Berlin. I want to find out what happened to Maria.

And I can't reach Max. Max Schumann. He used to arrange my concerts there. He doesn't seem to answer any of my letters and neither does Maria ...

You know Maria. His daughter ... 1930.

Oh, you never met Maria! How could you? She never came to any of the concerts.

And you weren't there that night when Max came back to my dressing room and asked me to do him a favor.

He wanted me to come home with him and meet his daughter. She was about twelve at the time.

Max sat me down in the living room and gave me a drink.

[PAUL *is in the home of Max Schumann. He sits.*]

And then he asked me if I would listen to his daughter play. [*Pause.*] He excused himself from the room. I could hear him in the hall, encouraging her to go in and play for me. I thought, "She must be a very shy child"—but it was more than that. The door opened and in she walked ... she was only three feet tall ... she was a dwarf. She didn't even look at me. She walked straight to that piano and sat down and began to play. Her little hands could barely reach the keyboard.

But, Essie, you should have heard the music coming out of those little hands. The sorrow, the pain as they struggled across the keyboard.

[*To Maria.*]

What's your name? ... Maria? That's a very nice name. Tell me, Maria, have you been playing long? ... You play very well for someone so ... young.

Do you enjoy playing? ... Good! That's very important—that you enjoy it.

Do you like concerts? ... What? ... You've never been to a concert! Why ... What are you afraid of! ... Well ... people stare at me too! ... Why? Well, because ... I'm very tall.

That used to worry me a great deal when I was little ... What do you mean how little? Oh, you know, little ... compared to where I am now. Very little.

People would say, "Paul, how tall are you going to be?" And I'd say, "I don't know." And I'd ask my pop. I'd say, "Pop, I don't want to be too tall, because I don't want people staring at me."

And my pop would set me on his lap, and he'd tell me the story of the giraffe and the rabbit...

What! You never heard the story of the giraffe and the rabbit? Well ... maybe it's because it's an American story. Well, come here ...

[PAUL *takes Maria by the hand and leads her to a chair.*]

There was this giraffe ... now you know how tall giraffes are. And this little rabbit. They were very good friends! Well, they were walking down the road one day, and it was a very long walk, so they became very hungry. They decided to look for something to eat. Pretty soon they came to an apple orchard. And this orchard had a very high fence around it. That old giraffe walked over to the fence and he was just tall enough to stick his head over the fence and eat some apples.

But the little rabbit was too short. So he said, "Hey, Mr. Giraffe ... why don't you drop a couple of those apples down here for me. I sure would like to sink my teeth into one of those apples."

And the old giraffe said, "Ho, ho, ho, little fella, that's the price you pay for being too little."

So they walked down a bit further and they came to a peach orchard. And this peach orchard had a big, high wall around it. The old giraffe walked right over to that wall. [PAUL *imitates giraffe.*] Ho, ho, ho ...

But guess what—the wall was too high ... that's right! Even for him. But right at the bottom of the wall there was a little hole just big enough for the rabbit to crawl through. And the rabbit was through that hole like a shot.

Pretty soon he could hear the giraffe's voice on the other side of the wall, "Hey, little rabbit, why don't you kick a couple of those peaches out here for me. I sure would like to sink my teeth into one of them peaches."

And guess what the rabbit hollered back? [*Maria answers him.*]

That's right! "That's the price you pay for being too tall."

I guess my pop was telling that story to show me if you keep going on down that road you'll soon come to an orchard that's right for you.

Yes, it would have been better if they shared—but that's not part of the story—it's an *American story.*

Little Maria. Tell me, *little* Maria, would you do me a favor, a favor for *big* Paul? Would you accompany me in a song?

[PAUL *walks Maria to piano.*]

You know, your daddy told me you have all my records and that you know all my songs. O.K., let's try your favorite.

[*Music: "Congo Lullaby."* PAUL *laughs.*]

Oh, that one!

[PAUL *sings while Maria plays.*]

My little black doll
Curl up in your nest of love
The moon is a charm to keep you from harm
So sleep at my chest.
So sleep, little one ...
Till darkness is by.

Little Maria, you know ... when I come back to Germany, and I will come back someday, I think I'd like you to play that song in my concert.

Oh no, Larry won't mind, not for one song. Now, you practice real hard, and when I come back to Germany I want you to play that song in my concert. And I'll give you billing. It'll say:

"Paul Robeson sings 'Congo Lullaby' accompanied by Maria Schumann."

[*Music out. To Essie.*]

And then she ran out of the room to tell her father.

[*Piano refrain: "Congo Lullaby."*]

Eslanda and I did return to Germany that year, 1934.

[*Metronome ticks in the background. Music out.*]

I had wired Max hoping he would meet the train. Even the train station seemed different. People moved around me furtively and in hostile silence ... Brown Shirts, Hitler's storm troopers, were everywhere. Nothing furtive or silent about them.

[*Essie spots Max.*]

Where, Essie? ... Is that Max?

[*Shouting to him.*]

Max!

Max! Have you been ill? You remember Frau Robeson. If I had seen you in the streets, I wouldn't have recognized you. So where's Maria? ... Who took her away? ... Where did they take her? ... Max, who took Maria away? ... You're not making sense, Max!

Get back on the train? We just got here ... What will they accuse you of?

[*To Essie.*]

I'm sorry, Essie. He's not making sense.

[*Max runs away.* PAUL *calls after him.*]

Max!

[PAUL *turns around. Storm troopers are surrounding him.*]

I beg your pardon. Who are you? ... Herr Krugger ... You came to do what? ... Well, thank you very much, I don't need an escort to the train.

Are these men with you? Would you please tell your friends I don't like people getting behind me.

[*Storm troopers curse in German.*]

Watch your mouth! Yes, I speak German, but I'm telling you in English, watch your mouth! ... You!

No, my wife is not German. As a matter of fact she's not even white. If it's any business of yours, she's Negro.

There's no need to ask her, I just told him.

If any of you lay a hand on my wife, I swear I'll kill one of you. Even if you put a bullet in my brain I'll live long enough to get my hands on at least one of you. Preferably you, Herr Krugger ... and I swear I will kill you.

[*Turns to Essie.*]

Essie, let go of my arm, Essie, I want both my arms free!

Now, just walk slowly back to the train.

Don't walk too fast ... I don't want those animals to think they smell fear.

[PAUL *and Essie return to the train.*]

Turn the light out, but leave the shade up. Until the train pulls out, I want to keep my eye on them.

[*Metronome out.*]

No, Essie, don't turn on the lights. I just want to sit here in the darkness. Because we might as well get used to it ... the world is moving into darkness.

[*Piano refrain—"Congo Lullaby."* PAUL *flinches.*]

Oh, my God ...

[*To Essie.*]

I just thought I saw a reflection in the window ... What? A little girl's face on a dwarf's body with the eyes of a woman as old as the Cross.

[*Music out. Music: "Meadowlands." The train stops.* PAUL *and Essie are at the Russian border.*]

Are we stopping ... Must be on the Russian border ... So much ice on the window I can hardly see out ...

[PAUL *wipes ice from train window.*]

[*To Essie.*]

Essie, better get the passports ready ...

Essie, we are in the middle of nowhere.

Essie, do you see what I see? Through the smoke of that campfire there—what are those people doing out there?

[*Essie points out two unusual-looking Russians.*]

Where, Essie ... those two over there?

Yes, I would say they do look a little like they're part Negro, but they're armed, Essie, all of them.

Essie, that man and woman over there they have their children with them. They're armed, too.

[*To customs officers at the door.*]

Yes, just a minute!

[PAUL *wipes ice off the train window. He peers out. To customs officers who just entered.*]

The passports? ...

Yes, here they are ...

Yes, I'm Paul Robeson. And this is my wife! ... But I am Paul Robeson! ... To Moscow. To do a concert there. What's wrong? ... Aren't they in order?

[*An officer touches* PAUL *and he jumps away.*]

Mister, please—don't grab me like that.

If you want me to go somewhere you just say so. I speak Russian ... All right, where do you want me to go? Why must my wife come, too?

[PAUL *and Essie step down from the train.*]

It's cold out here. What do you want of me?

[*They warm themselves by the campfire.*]

And he said, "Your passports are not in order. SING! If you are the real Paul Robeson, sing! These people have heard all of his records and they will know." One of the men with African features waved a record in the air. He also yelled, "Sing!"

[*Music: "Sanders of the River."*]

So there on the frozen plains of Russia on an arctic Christmas Eve, to prove my identity, I became a people's artist. I sang a work song from tropical Africa to a group of Afro-Asian Russian peasants standing guard on the border.

[*Music: The Moldau.* PAUL *and Essie are in Moscow, greeting crowds that have come out to see him.*]

When we arrived at the station that Christmas morning, there were little children there to greet us bearing flowers for the giant man from America.

As we moved down the broad Moscow streets the people of Russia stood and waved, and cheered, and threw flowers and kisses, and called "Tovarich, Tovarich, Tovarich, Tovarich." "Friend!"

[PAUL *greets them back.*]

"My friends!" Maie Tovarichee.

I couldn't help but notice the vast diversity of ethnic groups.

[*Music out.* PAUL *points them out.*]

There's a Georgian, a Ukrainian, a Moldavian, the Tartars and among them the Uzbeks—Asians and Afro-Asians.

Twenty-five years ago the Uzbeks had been classified as a backward people. Now they stood as equals with their fellow countrymen. Cheering me!

And I knew that I was undergoing an experience I never had before. Always there was the tension ... even in England. The tension that comes with being Negro in a white society. For the first time in my life, I felt that I could lay down that sword and shield.

[PAUL *is in a reception hall at the Kremlin. Music: The Moldau.*]

At a reception given for Essie and me in one of the great halls of the Kremlin, I met the great first artists of Russia; Sergei Eisenstein, the great film maker; Konstantin Stanislavski, head of the Moscow Art Theater, proponent of the new socialist realism.

We toasted each other with crystal glasses as old as the stars as they spoke glowingly of how their art was helping to portray the workers realistically in depicting the achievements of the proletariat in building socialism.

[*Music out.*]

And then there was the isolated Vsevolod Emilevich Meyerhold who moved from corner to corner in the great hall. Always half hidden by shadows. Student of Stanislavski, teacher of Eisenstein, brilliant theatrical innovator, but ... leader against the new socialist realism. He was accused of formalism, which they considered bourgeois, decadent.

Already it was being whispered that he was an enemy of the Revolution.

[PAUL *turns to stage right door.*]

The doors of the great hall opened and Señora Maria Cordova, the Impassioned One, burst into the room. She had been one of the great silent film actresses of Spain.

She froze and looked directly at me.

She walked to the center of the great hall, took a kerchief and placed it over her head, and shaped it into a bandanna. Now she pantomimed a Negro woman working in a field. Suddenly she stopped—her face contorted with fear.

Then she loosened the bandanna and tied it under her chin—now she was a Spanish peasant toiling the earth. Again she stopped and her face contorted with the same fear.

She moved to Eslanda and me ... "Federico."

Federico Garcia Lorca? Oh yes, I am familiar with your countryman. He spent some time in my country living in Harlem ... writing about my people there. His poems about Harlem show a great sensitivity and a deep empathy ...

Well yes, that's what I experienced when I read his poetry ... a great sense of humanity. What struck me about his art is its purpose—to embrace all mankind with love.

The line, "I damn all those who ignore the other half, the half beyond salvation."

Señora Cordova backed to the center of the room. She stood silently. She crossed her hands as if they were bound. She raised her head slowly. "Federico ... the beast has killed Federico."

Then she collapsed. Stanislavski rushed to her aid. Even Meyerhold left the shadows to assist her from the room.

[PAUL *comes downstage and addresses audience.*]

The Spanish poet Federico Garcia Lorca had been executed in Spain by the Fascists.

His execution would shock artists and intellectuals throughout the world. There would be telegrams, letters, protests, demonstrations.

[*Music: "The Four Insurgent Generals."*]

So Eslanda, Cordova, and I followed the crimson sun to the land of the poet. Larry Brown joined us in Barcelona.

We witnessed the siege of Madrid; saw Spanish villages reduced to rubble by German and Italian aerial bombardment; saw fields torn up by mechanized cavalry.

The nazi-fascist juggernaut was using Franco's rebellion against the Spanish Republic as a laboratory for modern warfare.

What was most shameful to me was the way that Franco was using the black Moroccan cavalry as an instrument of terror and destruction, evoking racist feelings as old as the Crusades.

But help had come. Volunteers had come from the ranks of workers and artists. They had come from many lands; Germans to oppose Germans; Italians to resist Italians.

Brother against brother. They had come from Yugoslavia, Canada, Ireland, from all over the world to form the International Brigade.

[*Music out.*]

And a new feeling grew within me, when I met the men from my own land. They were called the "Abraham Lincoln Battalion."

When I sang for them my heart was filled with admiration for those young white Americans, and how proud I was to see my own people, some of the first to volunteer, fighting along with them.

[*Music: "Ol' Man River."* PAUL *addresses Republican soldiers at a hospital site.*]

Where are you from, soldier? ...

You saw *Showboat*. Where? ... In London. Did you like it? ...

No, *I* thank you!

But, you know, I don't sing it that way any more.

No, you see, the original lyrics were:

Niggers all work on the Mississippi
Niggers all work while the white folks play.

And for London, as you know, I changed it to: "Darkies all work..." But now I feel much more like:

There's an old man called the Mississippi
That's an old man I don't want to be ...
What does he care that the world got troubles
What does he care that the land ain't free.

[*Crossing the stage.*]

Must keep laughing instead of crying.
Keep on fightin', until I'm dyin'!

[PAUL *addresses a blind soldier.*]

Where are you from, soldier? He's blind. Touch his arm! Where are you from? ... Omaha, Nebraska ... It must seem far away now, doesn't it, soldier? ...

What? ... Where was I born?

You know, one of your commanders asked me that yesterday, and I heard myself saying Princeton, New Jersey, but that's not quite right.

Because I began to *feel* life intensely when I saw the reflection of a little girl that I loved in a window ... and knew that she was dead.

That's when I felt born.

I felt born when I saw through the smoke of a campfire a pathetic huddle of Russian peasants guarding the border. That's when I felt born! And I feel I am being born with you here today ... on this blood-soaked soil of Spain! And I give you my promise — *to take my stand with you!*

[*Music out. As old man to audience.*]

And in my heart, I literally meant—take my stand with

them—on the lines.

But they didn't hand me a rifle—they did something else. They gave me a medal. A little three-pointed gold star. And I said, "Why me? What have I done to deserve it?"

Why not that man there ... that lost a leg yesterday or that man there who will never see again!

They said, "No! You take this medal, and you go on singing, Paul."

"Please, tell them why we are here ... why we are fighting here, and why we are dying here." And I accepted the medal.

[*Music: "Drink to Me Only with Thine Eyes."* PAUL *is in England at the Barclays'.*]

Which brings me to the point of my asking to see you, Lady Barclay, and you too, Lord Barclay. I want to enlist your aid in arranging a series of concerts throughout the British Isles. The proceeds, sir, to go to the Spanish Relief Fund. Really? I didn't know you felt that way, Lord Barclay. But you must know that Franco is being backed by the armed might of Hitler and Mussolini ... Oh, you do! You see them as mere bounders? Uncouth fellows, you say? The type you wouldn't invite to tea, you mean?

Lord Barclay, I really can't believe I heard you correctly, sir, certainly you don't wish them Godspeed? What is academic—No, I didn't see the newspaper.

[*To Lady Barclay.*]

Yes, sir, it is a medal they gave me on the battlefield near Madrid ...

No, sir, it is not heavy, and, Lord Barclay, I never saw myself as carrying the Cross ... except in a little play a long, long time ago. But I do see Spain as a crucifixion.

[*Music: "Los Cuatros Generales." To audience, takes paper from piano.*]

Madrid has fallen. So now the dress rehearsal for World

War II was over and upper-class England was rather pleased by what the dictators were doing. After all, the nazi-fascist partnership was out to save the great houses of Europe from the menace of communism.

I left the aristocracy and went out among the common people of England because they were the only ones who would be able to stand up to the holocaust that was to come.

[*To audience at concert.*]

In Germany and Italy there is no longer any nonsense from labor. NO! Business is going ahead better than usual without labor unions. As for war, well, that was all nicely taken care of by Prime Minister Chamberlain when Czechoslovakia was sacrificed to Hitler. And it could have been stopped in Spain. Just as Mussolini could have been stopped when he marched into Ethiopia. And it could have been stopped in Germany when Hitler unleashed the Nazi terror against the Jews ...

And I gave twopenny concerts for the workers. And at those concerts I talked. I kept talking. People began saying, "What's happening to Robeson? Why doesn't he just sing?" Lady Barclay's friends put it more elegantly. They said, "Paul, if you want to go on living in England, why don't you just *shut up*!"

But I couldn't. They kept warning me to stay out of British politics. I didn't know that I was in British politics—I thought what I was into concerned the whole world.

I got to talking about Africa, but when I got onto the subject of colonialism, that's when I knew how deeply into British politics I had gotten.

[PAUL *is at home.*]

Yess, Essie ... who is at the door? ... British Intelligence?

[*Essie enters with British Intelligence.*]

Good afternoon, gentlemen. Won't you be seated. Would you have tea? Essie, a pot of tea, please. And I think these are three-lump gentlemen.

So, what can I do for British Intelligence.

Yes, you know ... I thought I recognized you, you've been at several of my concerts.

Enjoy them?

Yes, sir, I am painfully aware that Hitler has invaded Poland. I suppose it's just a matter of days before England declares war on Germany ...

Dissention?... Me ... I take it you mean my speaking against colonialism ... Yes, I am acquainted with Kwame Nkrumah. But if you are implying he writes my speeches for me, the answer to that is no.

Yes, I've written several articles tracing the roots of fascism to the Renaissance ... Oh no, no. I haven't made a bridge between fascism and colonialism, but I suppose such a bridge could be made.

Desist? ... Desist from what? ... My concerts or my talking during my concerts? ... I see. What if I choose not to? ... I am aware the government has been given certain emergency powers. But, gentlemen, as long as there are issues to be addressed, I must seek platforms from which to address them. And if I can't find them here then I will find them elsewhere. I thank you, and good day.

[*To Essie.*]

Essie, I want you to book passage for yourself for America. I'm going on to Africa.

[*To audience.*]

I wanted to get there before the marching jackboots set fire to the whole world.

[*Old man to audience.*]

So I went to Africa. I walked the land of my ancestors. My pride in Africa ... grew with my learning ... It impelled me to speak out again against the scorners of African culture and African self-determination. As I moved across Africa, I wrote articles and sent them back to British publications and American periodicals.

As I moved, the colonial arm of the British Intelligence moved with me and they cautioned me. Here was the white man in the land of my ancestors cautioning me. Telling me that I was a guest. Proclaiming, as it were, that I was an intruder.

Nonetheless, I moved among the people—talked with them; bathed myself in the eternal rivers that once bathed my fathers; breathed the air that circulated back through the centuries; warmed myself in the hot African sun.

One day, a blind old Ebo woman traced the contours of my face and whispered through warm tears, "You are one of the boys that went away."

[*Music: "Takin' Names."*]

The cold hand of death touched my shoulder. A telegram. "William died suddenly, Ben."

I knew I could not get there in time for the funeral, but William was on my mind as I stumbled down to the sea to a vessel that would take me to America through the Middle Passage of the Atlantic.

[*Music: "Shenandoah."*]

One evening I walked out on deck and stood there alone in the cold moonlit night looking out at the dark Atlantic. I could feel the chill rising up from the cold sea. It seemed that I was shivering inside. I could feel a chill inside my body ... Beyond my flesh and bones ... even beyond my blood.

The large white waves rose up in anger and struck the ship in the bow and then fell back into the sea. Over and over again they struck the bow and fell back into the sea. And I could hear in those large white waves the wail of men, women and children ... Slaves, who had been cast into the sea along the route of the Middle Passage.

There is a line from the Holy Bible that speaks of the seas

giving up their dead. It had come to pass. The Middle Passage was giving up its dead to me.

And at that moment, I knew what my voice was. I knew what those low basso notes were. The wails of all their voices rising up through me from the bottom of the sea.

I knew that I had to use that voice wherever there were those who want to hear the melody of freedom or hear the words that might inspire hope and courage in the face of despair and fear.

[*Music out. Music: "The Star-Spangled Banner."* PAUL *points to stage right indicating the Statue of Liberty.*]

There she is ... Desdemona. Ah yes ... I've always thought of that Lady with the Torch as Desdemona. Lady of light!

[*To the Statue of Liberty.*]

Will you let me play Othello to you, Desdemona?

[*To audience.*]

It had never been done before, you know. No African had ever played that African in America.

Are you ready, America?

[*Music out.*]

I'll not shed her blood
Nor scar that whiter skin of hers than snow
And smooth as monumental alabaster ... but that is the cause!

What is the cause? ... Here was a Negro, a general,

A Negro general with power over white men.

A perfect man!

What is the tragic flaw of this perfect man?

Othello said, "Haply, for I am black."

Is that his tragic flaw—the fact that he was black?

Iago had duped this Renaissance Venetian society into accepting the color of a man's skin as a tragic flaw in his character. No, the flaw was not in the man, but in the society. By playing Othello, I could help Americans look inside themselves—look into the deepest fabric of American society and see that its tragic flaw was racism. That was the cause!

It is the cause, it is the cause, my soul.
Let me not name it to you, you chaste stars!
It is the cause.

I guess America was ready for an African Othello. Because we became the longest running Shakespearean production in the history of American theater.

[*As old man to audience.*]

And we thought we were making progress, but during that run President Franklin Delano Roosevelt died.

[*Music: "Hail to the Chief."*]

That black riderless horse walked so slowly down Pennsylvania Avenue, leading the cortège that carried the dead FDR and with him the hopes and dreams of the American Negro people. Behind him walked the man from Missouri. We didn't know much about the man from Missouri, but we found out.

I had been to the South on several occasions to do concerts and help organize unions. The conditions I saw throughout the South were unthinkable.

Shortly before I arrived in Greenville, Mississippi, three young Negro boys hardly more than children had been taken out of their homes and lynched. I viewed the bodies. They were mutilated. And again American Negro servicemen were returning home from World War II, returning home again to the South to confront terror.

So I led a delegation to Washington to protest the lynching.

President Truman agreed to receive the committee and I was the spokesman.

[*Music out.* PAUL *addresses the President in the White House.*]

Mr. President, why can't you use your executive power to force an anti-lynching law? Mr. President, because you find lynching personally abhorrent means nothing to the millions of American Negroes in the South who are afraid of another "Red Summer of 1919!"

Mr. President, the mood of the Negro has changed, and whether he's smiling at you or not—he wants his freedom! And he will have it! And if this government will not protect him, then he is prepared to protect himself.

[PAUL *is stopped by Secret Service.*]

You can assure your Secret Service men that I am not armed! Mr. Truman, I meant no offense to the office of President, but sir, if this country continues to ignore the plight of the Negro, our society faces certain dismemberment.

You know, the press was more upset by the fact that I shook my finger in the face of the President than by the conditions I came to protest. But a commission was formed. It recommended some positive actions and we were hopeful, but when those recommendations were presented to Mr. Truman, he failed to implement them. And the battle had to go on.

I went on to Kansas City to do a concert there. I walked out onto the stage ...

[PAUL *is at the Kansas City concert. Music: "Drink to Me Only with Thine Eyes."* PAUL *scans the crowd.*]

Just a moment, Larry.

[*Music out.*]

Could we have the house lights, please.

[PAUL *walks out to the apron.*]

Ladies and gentlemen, I came to Kansas City to sing. I am finding it quite impossible to do so! I shall have to refuse to sing for you tonight! I am beginning a policy of never singing in places where my people are barred. So if you can find one Negro in this hall tonight, I will sing. [*Pause.*]

Do you see one? Now, isn't that odd? Isn't it odd—that none of them would come to hear me sing? Isn't it?

[PAUL *begins exit but is stopped by a shout from the audience. He addresses him.*]

Beg pardon, sir. Ungrateful? To you? ... Sir, I owe you nothing! What I have, I worked for! I'm not your symbol! You let one Negro through in a generation and you flaunt him before the world to hide your mistreatment of sixteen million others like him! And then you expect me to be grateful to you.

Oh, sir!

[PAUL *replies to shout from audience.*]

There's that word you love to shout—communist! I should think you'd be tired of shouting it. I'm sick and tired of hearing it. I'm for peace! I'm violently anti-fascist. I'm against fascism in all of its disguises, and I will not sing for such an audience tonight or any other night. I'm sorry, Larry.

[PAUL *exits. Larry closes piano, takes his music, and leaves. Music:* PAUL *re-enters, singing.*]

In Salt Lake City, I says to Joe
Him standing by my bed
They framed you on a murder charge
Said Joe, "But I ain't dead"
Said Joe, "But I ain't dead."

How far must a man travel before he can be treated like a human being?

After my Kansas City concert, I was invited to the Paris Peace Conference, and that cost me my right to travel. So Larry and I went right up to the Canadian border to sing a concert there. And you don't need a passport to go to Canada—unless you are Paul Robeson. I stood on the American side and the Canadians stood on the other side and I sang there ... under the Peace Arch.

[*Music: "Joe Hill."*]

From San Diego up to Maine
In every mine and mill
Where workers strike and organize
He said, "You'll find Joe Hill"
He said, "You'll find Joe Hill."

[*To audience.*]

Anybody know where Peekskill, New York, is? I'll never forget it. I was almost lynched there! I'd gotten through Berlin, the siege of Madrid ...

A crowd of local citizens whipped into a frenzy by newspaper editorials that claimed that little Peekskill was being invaded by the "Red Horde" and anything that happened to Paul Robeson was Paul Robeson's own fault.

[*Music out.* PAUL *addresses Peekskill audience.*]

Ladies and gentlemen, we all came here to Peekskill to sing and to speak out in the name of peace, because atomic warfare is unthinkable. No one in his right mind wants war with the Soviet Union.

There are those that see my struggle for peace as some kind of international conspiracy. I am not and never have been involved in any international conspiracy, and I do not know anyone who is.

[*To offstage. He is given a message.*]

Yes, young man, what is it?...What?

I've just been informed that there is a mob forming ... perhaps the state troopers will be able to contain them and maybe not.

So if any of you feels you must leave, please do so. It's me they're after, and I don't want anyone else hurt on my account. No, I'm not running anywhere. Here I stand and no fascist-minded people are going to drive me anywhere.

[*Music: "Joe Hill."* PAUL *sings.*]

"The copper bosses killed you, Joe,
They shot you dead," says I.
"Takes more than guns to kill a man,"
Says Joe, "I didn't die."
Says Joe, "I didn't die."
I dreamed I saw Joe Hill last night,
Alive as you and me
"Why, Joe, you're ten years gone," I says.
"I'll never die," says he.
"I'll never die," says he.

[*Music out. To audience.*]

You know there were about two thousand state troopers there to keep the peace. Why didn't they try to stop the lynching?

[PAUL *shrugs.*]

But you know who tried to stop it, though. A young white GI, not a part of our group, saw a black man being beaten to death, and he yelled, "Hey! That ain't the American way!" And he wades in. He gets hurt, but he saves the man's life!

So ... after Peekskill, my royalties stopped.

[*Piano.* ACCOMPANIST *sings "Nobody Knows You."*]

Rutgers disowned me, they even removed my name from the All-American list from 1917 and 1918! Oh yes, the All-American was now Un-American!

And would you believe it got worse? It did.

In 1952, the Soviet Union awarded me its highest honor, the Stalin Peace Prize.

They refused to let me travel abroad to receive it, but when it arrived in New York with the twenty-five thousand dollars that came with it, the IRS was there, of course—the first to take its cut.

The press has always viewed my relationship with Russia as something rather sinister.

When Khrushchev denounced Stalin at the Twentiet Party Congress, they were at it again.

I said, "If that is true, then the Soviet peole are going t have to deal with that. Just as America would be bes advised not to worry so much about Russia and b concerned about the abuses done to my people here."

And then Russia sent troops into Hungary. They were at i again!

I said, "I am against nations who cross the borders of othe nations to do injury and harm to people."

I take no sides politically when I see one man bloody th head of his fellow man.

Don't ask me about Hungary and Stalin ... ask me simpl about men who bleed, and I'll tell you I grieve for them.

But that didn't sell! All that my tormentors wanted to hea was that Paul Robeson denounces Russia ...

[*Music out.* LARRY *comes in singing "Takin' Names."*]

There's a man going 'round takin' names
There's a man going 'round takin' names
He had taken my brother's name
And he has left my heart in pain
There's a man going 'round takin' names.

LARRY: Paul Robeson, will you please come forward?

[PAUL *moves downstage center.*]

LARRY/CHAIRMAN: Please be seated at the table and identif yourself by name, residence, and occupation.

[*Music out.* PAUL *sits.*]

PAUL: My name is Paul Robeson. I live at 16 Jumel Terrac New York City, and I'm an actor and singer by occupatio and law on the side now and then.

CHAIRMAN: Are you appearing today in response to subpoena which was served upon you by the Hous Committee of Un-American Activities?

PAUL: Oh yes!

CHAIRMAN: Mr. Robeson, did you file a passport application on July 2, 1954?

PAUL: Gentlemen, I have filed about twenty-five in the past few months.

CHAIRMAN: When applying for this passport, were you requested to submit a non-Communist affidavit?

PAUL: Sir, I considered this issue very thoroughly with my counsel and my family and friends. I wouldn't think of signing such an affidavit! It is a complete contradiction of the rights of American citizens.

CHAIRMAN: Are you now a member of the Communist party?

PAUL: Oh please, please, please —

CHAIRMAN: Please answer, Mr. Robeson!

PAUL: You know, I really thought I was here about some passport. All right—it's a legal party I believe, like the Republican party or the Democratic party!

CHAIRMAN: Was your Communist party name John Thomas?

PAUL: My name is Paul Robeson, and what I have to say I have said as Paul Robeson in public all over the world, and that's why I'm here today.

CHAIRMAN: Are you now a member of the Communist party?

PAUL: Do you want to come to the ballot box when I vote and see?

CHAIRMAN: You are directed to answer the question!

PAUL: In 1946 in California, I stated for the record that I was not a Communist! Since that time, I have refused to answer that question, and I refuse *now*, Mr. Chairman, because my vote is nobody's business!

CHAIRMAN: You are directed to answer the question, Mr. Robeson!

PAUL: In the first place, gentlemen, wherever I've been—and I've been many places—the first to die in the battle against fascism have been the communists, and I have laid many wreath on many a communist grave. And that is no criminal—and in the second place the Fifth Amendme has nothing to do with criminality. Therefore, I invoke th Fifth Amendment ... Mr. Walters, is it not?

CHAIRMAN: Yes.

PAUL: The Pennsylvania Walters? The author of all the bil designed to keep all kinds of decent people out of thi country?

CHAIRMAN: No, only your kind.

PAUL: Colored people like myself, from the West Indies an so on?

CHAIRMAN: We are trying to make it easier to get rid of you kind, too. Mr. Robeson—are you a Communist?

PAUL: I am not being tried today for whether or not I'm Communist. I'm being tried for standing up and fightin for the rights of my people who are still second-clas citizens in this country. You want to shut up every Negr who has the courage to stand up and fight for the rights o his people and ...

CHAIRMAN: Mr. Robeson!

PAUL: Do just try to be fair with me—for the rights of hi people, for the rights of workers—and I've been on man a picket line for workers around the world and for you Pennsylvania steel workers, too, and that's why I am her today. And could you please let me read my statement?

CHAIRMAN: Let *me* read a statement *you* made about th Soviet Union: "The Soviet Union is the only country I hav ever been in where I felt completely at ease."

PAUL: I suffered no prejudice as I am feeling here today.

CHAIRMAN: What prejudice are you talking about? You were graduated from Rutgers valedictorian and Columbia Law School—and I remember seeing you play football at Lehigh.

PAUL: We beat Lehigh. That's right—Big Red was on my team!

CHAIRMAN: Mr. Robeson, while in Paris in 1949, did you not state that the American Negro would refuse to fight if the United States went to war against the Soviet Union?

PAUL: I was invited to the Paris Peace Conference and I wasn't asked there to sing. I was asked to talk ... to about two thousand students from all over the colonial world. I remember saying "I find it inconceivable for American Negroes to go to war on behalf of those who have oppressed them for generations against a country like Russia, which acknowledges the full dignity of the Negro."

CHAIRMAN: Are you now or have you ever been a member of the Communist party?

PAUL: On many occasions I have publicly expressed my belief in the principles of scientific socialism, my deep conviction that for all mankind a socialistic society represents an advance to a higher stage of life ... that is, a form of society which is economically, socially, culturally, and ethically superior to a sytem based on production for private profit. The development of human society from tribalism to feudalism to capitalism to socialism is brought about by the needs and aspirations of mankind for a better way of life.

CHAIRMAN: I'd like to read a statement by Thomas Young, a Negro publisher: "Mr. Robeson is now so far out of touch with Negro thinking in his everyday emotions, he can no longer speak authoritatively about or for the race."

PAUL: Mr. Chairman, could I please protest the reading of this. If you have Mr. Young here, so that I can cross examine him, and I can, O.K., but otherwise, why can't I read my statement?

CHAIRMAN: No, you may not! Why did you not stay in Russia, Mr. Robeson?

PAUL: Sir, that is a very important question. Because my

father was a slave *here* and I have many cousins who are sharecroppers *here*, and I have never been able to measure my success in terms of myself. And that is why my own success has not meant all that it really should mean—really! And I have sacrificed literally hundreds of thousands, if not millions, of dollars, for what I believed in.

CHAIRMAN: Will the photographers desist in taking pictures; it's rather nerveracking.

PAUL: It's quite all right, I'm used to it. I have been in moving pictures and I can pose and I can smile but I cannot smile when I'm talking to you.

CHAIRMAN: The reason you're not in Russia, Mr. Robeson, is because you are promoting the communist cause in this country.

PAUL: [*Interrupting.*] Can I read my statement?

CHAIRMAN: No, you cannot read that stuff!

PAUL: [*Reads statement amid shouts and gavel.*] I will say before this committee that you will not silence me in speaking out against the injustices done to my people. You can brand me a Communist, and I will still speak out!

You can turn the Negro leadership against me, which you've done, and I will still speak out for the Negro people.

You can take my passport away and force me to live off the charity of my brother Benjamin—and I will still speak out.

You won't stop me from crying out!

And if you finally succeed in socially, economically, and politically assassinating me, don't think you'll stop me!

Because, it's not just me, it's the Negro people whom I echo! And if you do silence my voice by making me a non-person, there will be another voice—and another—and another!

CHAIRMAN: I've endured all of this I can. The meeting is

adjourned!

PAUL: I think it should be. I think you should adjourn this forever!

[*Music: "Down by the Riverside."* PAUL *sings. Music out.*]

I want to thank the people of Mother Zion for coming out this afternoon and spending the whole time with us. This is the end of a rather long journey. I want you to know that the hard struggle for my right to travel is over now. My concert career has practically been re-established all over the world ... Oh, yes, it is official.

And this is why *I* applaud you—because without you, this couldn't have happened. Not without the strength and courage and help and the prayers of those of you who raised your voice in protest—your voices were echoed—to the miners in Wales and Scotland, to the docks of London and Liverpool, to Africa.

And finally to the House of Commons in England itself, creating a groundswell that became an earthswell of all the common peoples of the earth.

I've been waiting for this afternoon, just to come back and say thank you—I want to say thank you to my brother Benjamin. I wish my sister-in-law were here. And say thank you to my family and to say thank you to the children. Because the children know, as I've said many times, every struggle I've been engaged in—everything I've done—has been to try and see that my grandnephews, my grandchildren, that *your* children—we all, everywhere, of all races, all creeds—can walk this American earth in unity.

[*Piano plays introduction to "Jacob's Ladder."*]

Please join us!—please join us! We are climbing Jacob's ladder:

We are climbing Jacob's ladder,
We are climbing Jacob's ladder,
We are climbing Jacob's ladder,

Soldiers of the Cross.

Please join us!

Ev'ry rung goes higher an' higher,
Ev'ry rung goes higher an' higher,
Ev'ry rung goes higher an' higher,
Soldiers of the Cross.

Rise an' shine an' give God the glory,
Rise an' shine an' give God the glory,
Rise an' shine an' give God the glory,
Soldiers of the Cross.

[*Music out. Music: Trolley bell, then "This Little Light of Mine."*]

Pop!

The years are falling into place now. I have discovered there are two forces in the world. Evil and the struggle against evil. And where I have found evil, I have struggled against it. And it has been that struggle that has kept my hope alive. My hope for America. My hope for Russia. My hope for all the nations of the world.

My hope for mankind itself.

And I am taking all those hopes now and passing them on to you.

[*Music: "Ol' Man River."*]

Soft you! A word or two before you go,
I have done the state some service, and they know't;
No more of that. I pray you, in your letters,
When you shall these unlucky deeds relate,
Speak of me as I am. Nothing extenuate,
Nor set down aught in malice. Then must you speak
Of one that loved.

[*Music: "This Little Light."*]

I really wish I could have been with them this evening in Carnegie Hall. They called afterwards and said it went rather well and I would have been proud. But I just ouldn't go.

PAUL'S *voice merges with tape.*]

3ut always remember, I'm just Paul now, and other men nd women are carrying on my work. May their lights hine, bringing love and brotherhood to all mankind.

thank you and I wish you a good night.

THE END

PHILLIP HAYES DEAN

Phillip Hayes Dean was born in Chicago, Illinois, and educated in the public schools of Pontiac, Michigan. In the late 1950s, he moved to New York City to pursue a professional acting career and made several appearances on Broadway. Though he wrote plays intermittently during these years, Dean did not emerge as a dramatist of considerable potential until 1971 when the Negro Ensemble Company produced *The Sty of the Blind Pig* at St. Mark's Playhouse, New York City, for 64 performances. For this play about a disintegrating black family in Chicago, Dean received the Dramatists Guild Award and a Drama Desk Award as the year's most promising playwright. The production was also selected by *Time* magazine as one of the year's ten best plays.

Prior to this success, Dean had had at least three earlier plays produced in New York. His one-act drama, *This Bird of Dawning Singeth All Night Long*, of a meeting between a white prostitute and a black woman who claimed to be her sister, was premiered by the American Place Theatre (APT) at St. Clement's Church in December 1968. In 1969 APT also mounted the two-act drama *Every Night When the Sun Goes Down* about an ex-convict who returns to his old haunts to arouse old cronies to destroy their environment. A third production was the single act *Thunder in the Index* at the Chelsea Theatre, Brooklyn, in 1969. It depicted a racial confrontation between a Jewish psychiatrist and his young, black patient.

Freeman (1973) marked another major accomplishment for the playwright. His protagonist is an ambitious black man, frustrated by being forced to compromise his principles in a pragmatic world, who burns down the community center which he views as a symbol of white power, and ends up in a mental hospital. The play was produced by APT and directed by Lloyd Richards. It was aired on National Educational Television during the 1976-77 season. Dean's mono-drama *Paul Robeson,* also directed by Richards and starring James Earl Jones as Robeson and Burg Wallace as Lawrence Brown, despite the controversy that attended its 1978 opening on Broadway, played for a total of 77 performances in New York and moved to London, England, later that year.

Source: Bernard L. Peterson, Jr., *Contemporary Black American Playwrights and Their Plays: A Biographical Directory and Dramatic Index.* New York: Greenwood Press, 1988.

ROADS OF THE MOUNTAINTOP

A Portrait of Dr. Martin Luther King Jr.

by
Ron Milner

MARTIN LUTHER KING JR.
(1929-1968)

That cold, grey December evening in 1955 Mrs. Rosa Parks of Montgomery, Alabama, heading home after a hard day's work as a tailor's assistant, refused to surrender her seat on a bus so that a white man could sit while she stood at the back. No one could have predicted that the ensuing year-long bus boycott by Montgomery blacks would bring to national prominence the then 26-year-old black Baptist pastor, Martin Luther King Jr., who was chosen to lead the protest. Before the boycott ended in victory with the outlawing of segregation on buses, King would be twice arrested, jailed, have his home bombed, would receive numerous threatening phone calls and letters, and have traveled across the country on speaking tours.

At the time the boycott started, King had recently accepted his first pastorate at the Dexter Avenue Baptist Church in Montgomery. He had come from a long line of Baptist preachers on both sides of the family and his father was pastor of the Ebenezer Baptist Church in Atlanta, Georgia. King had been a gifted child; sailing through public schools he entered Morehouse College at age 15 as a special student and graduated at 19. He then enrolled at Crozer Theological Seminary in Chester, Pennsylvania, receiving his B.D. degree three years later with highest honors and winning the Crozer postgraduate fellowship. King studied for his doctorate in systematic theology at Boston University. He received the Ph.D. degree in 1955. While in Boston, he met and married Coretta Scott, an Alabama native who had graduated from Antioch College, Ohio, and was attending the New England Conservatory of Music.

To sustain the bus boycott over 382 days, mass meetings had been held regularly two or three times a week in the city's black churches. It was during these meetings that King discovered his extraordinary powers of oratory. He could quote the Bible freely and he used its stirring imagery to reach out to poor blacks for whom, from the days of slavery, religion was a source of strength and comfort. During this period King also developed his philosophy for racial progress. Blacks needed political power which could be gained by increasing the number of registered voters, thus voter registration drives deserved full support. Blacks needed economic power and he urged his organization to seek a federal charter for a building and loan association.

Above all, King began to clarify his stand on non-violent resistance which would be his principal bulwark in the years ahead. He constantly urged his listeners not to retaliate against evil. The real goal, he argued, was not to *defeat* the white man but "to awaken a sense of shame within the oppressor and challenge his false sense of responsibility ... The end is reconciliation; the end is redemption; the end is the creation of the beloved community where all men would treat each other as brothers and equals."

King and 115 other black leaders met in Montgomery in August 1957 and formed the Southern Christian Leadership Conference (SCLC) with King as president. The intention was to extend the techniques learned in Montgomery through the South by using southern churches to enlist the black masses in the struggle for freedom. King published *Stride Toward Freedom: The Montgomery Story* in 1958 and the next year he made a pilgrimage to India to rededicate himself to the non-violent principles of Gandhi.

To devote more time to the work of the SCLC, King moved in 1960 to Atlanta as co-pastor of his father's Ebenezer Baptist Church. He joined the sit-in movement of black students at segregated lunch counters and helped them form the Student Nonviolent Coordinating Committee (SNCC). King was arrested at one of these sit-ins, taken to the state prison in Reidsville and put in a cell with criminals. He was released when John F. Kennedy, the Democratic presidential nominee, intervened. It is alleged that this episode won Kennedy the election by ensuring him the crucial black vote in November.

Once the new administration was installed, King pressed for a tough federal civil rights bill to wipe out segregation. He and his staff began to organize a series of well-publicized demonstrations in segregated cities either to force change or to show the nation and the world the violence to which segregationist officials would resort to maintain inequitable laws. Marching blacks were beaten, attacked by police dogs, had fire hoses turned on them, were arrested and jailed without fighting back as the television cameras recorded the savagery for national broadcast. When a young black deacon and a white minister were killed, thousands of ministers and lay preachers of all faiths came to Selma, Alabama, from all over the nation to join the march to the state capital. All of this activity was finally recognized in the passage of the 1964 Civil Rights Act and the 1965 Voting Rights Act.

In the spring of 1963 King had written his "Letter from Birmingham Jail" setting forth a manifesto for the nonviolent resistance movement. That summer he stood at the Lincoln Memorial in the nation's capital before a mammoth crowd of some 250,000 people who had joined the March on Washington for jobs and freedom. King delivered his electrifying "I have a dream" speech containing the following prophesy: "There will be neither rest nor tranquility in America until the Negro is granted his citizenship rights. The whirlwinds of revolt will continue to shake the foundations of our nation until the bright day of justice emerges." King firmly believed in the advent of the day of justice and ended his speech on a ringing note of faith and hope. At the end of the year his accomplishments and his vision had won him the Nobel Peace Prize and in January 1964 *Time* magazine named him the Man of the Year.

By 1965 northern cities were beginning to erupt in violence in the hot summers and against the nation's deepening involvement in the war in Vietnam. King decided to take his campaign for jobs and decent housing to Chicago where Mayor Daley was known as an entrenched hard-line politician who brooked no interference in city affairs. King felt that he needed to re-establish the efficacy of his nonviolent resistance philosophy which was beginning to lose ground to younger militants of the Congress of Racial Equality (CORE) and SNCC. They advocated black separatism and meeting violence with violence, using the slogan "Black Power" as their standard.

King moved himself and family into a Chicago slum apartment and began to organize the poor to demand their rights. Rents were held in "trusteeship" until property was repaired. Giant rallies and demonstrations were organized and in a short time Chicago was engulfed in a three-day race riot. In the midst of the Chicago movement, King was called away to Mississippi where James Meredith had been wounded by gunfire while attempting a solitary march to Jackson, Mississippi. King was involved in intense activity and negotiations to avoid another violent confrontation. In Chicago an unwelcome compromise was reached by King that summer in a bid to avoid escalating violence and the loss of liberal white and federal support for SCLC.

An advocate of world peace, King had denounced the Vietnam war which he saw as morally wrong and consuming valuable resources that could be devoted to domestic programs. His insistence on speaking out against the war, despite the advice of influential friends, made him a target for investigation by the Federal Bureau of Investigation (FBI). With the connivance of the Johnson White House, the FBI made a ruthless attempt to discredit King. His phone was illegally tapped, microphones were hidden in his hotel rooms, and scurrilous stories were circulated about his sexual indiscretions and financial misconduct.

Meanwhile King had become increasingly concerned about the nation's poor which embraced people of all races. He began preparations for a Poor People's Campaign which envisaged a march on Washington, D.C., of thousands of the inter-racial poor. In the midst of these preparations, King went to Memphis, Tennessee, to help black sanitation workers who were striking for the right to unionize. He was shot and killed on the balcony of the Lorraine Motel in Memphis. Subsequently, James Earl Ray, a convict who had escaped from a Missouri jail, was convicted and sentenced to life imprisonment for King's murder. On January 20, 1986, the nation observed its first annual Martin Luther King Jr. Day, a federal holiday that most states of the Union ratified.

In *Roads of the Mountaintop*, playwright Ron Milner begins his dramatization with King's acceptance speech of the Nobel Peace Prize in 1964. This is the apex of King's achievement so far—at 35 he is the youngest Nobel laureate ever—but the award also lays heavy responsibilities upon him and his associates to continue the struggle for social justice. While he stands at the mountaintop, King sees not only the Promised Land but the many roads he must still travel and the hardships he, his family and co-workers must endure before his mission can be accomplished.

In terms of format, Milner has surrounded his two principal characters, King and his wife Coretta, with a group of "Aides" who function in a number of ways. They act as King's fellow workers in the SCLC, but they also take other neutral and more menacing roles as the script requires, finally becoming pall-bearers at King's funeral. This device enables the rapid flow of events and keeps the stage peopled with a variety of figures, giving an impression of the restless energy of King's daily life.

Source: *Dictionary of American Negro Biography*, Rayford W. Logan and Michael R. Winston, eds. New York: W.W. Norton, 1982. Also *Dictionary of American Biography, Supplement Eight, 1966-1970*, John A. Garraty and Mark C. Carnes, eds. New York: Charles Scribner's Sons, 1988; and David J. Garrow, *Bearing the Cross: Martin Luther King, Jr., and the Southern Christian Leadership Conference*. New York: William Morrow & Co. Inc., 1986.

CHARACTERS

Dr. Martin Luther King
His Aides:
Ray
Abe
Josh
Harold
Aaron
Mrs. Coretta King
A Young Woman
Extras as needed

PLACE AND TIME

PART ONE
Selma, 1965

PART TWO
Chicago, 1966-1967

PART THREE
Memphis, 1968

SETTING

Stage center is an area which in Part One is a house in Selma; kitchen area stage left, dining room stage right. In Part Two, it is a slum flat in Chicago; bedroom area stage left, kitchen meeting place, stage right. In Part Three, it is a hotel suite, bedroom stage right, sitting room stage left.

Encircling and rising above this main area are playable flowing ramps, achieving a high point rear center. The ramps are the roads at the mountaintop. Downstage is an unobstructed playing area with, possibly, a speaker's rostrum in the far left and far right corners though light specials in those areas would make a cleaner, smoother, less repetitious effect.

PART ONE

SELMA, 1965

Set silhouetted against cyc-backdrop. REPORTERS' *voices in the dark.*

REPORTERS: [*Offstage.*] Dr. King?
Could you turn this way, please?
Into the mikes please, Dr. King.

[*Light up on* KING *coming into place three-quarters up stage right ramp. He wears dark suit, white shirt, tie; holds letter in his hand. Sense of popping flashbulbs.*]

KING: ... With this announcement, designating me as such for the year, 1964, I become the fifth American, and third member of my race, to receive the Nobel Peace Prize ...

REPORTER: [*Offstage.*] Also the youngest person to receive it.

KING: Yes. It fills me with deep humility and gratitude to know that I have been chosen as the recipient of this foremost of earthly honors. I do not consider this merely an honor to me personally, but a tribute to the discipline, wise restraint, and majestic courage of the millions of gallant Negroes and white persons of good will who have followed a non-violent course in seeking to establish a reign of justice and a rule of love across this nation of ours. This award also brings with it a demand for deepening one's commitment to nonviolence as a philosophy of life and reminds us that we have only begun to explore the powerful spiritual and moral resources possible through this way of life ...

[*He takes a step up the ramp, pauses.*]

We are also challenged to face the international implications of non-violence ...

[*He moves further up the ramp where he is met by the silhouetted forms of his wife,* MRS. KING, *and his top aide/buddy,* RAY; *the two help him into his robe, and place the impressive Nobel medallion around his neck. He moves to just left of the very pinnacle of the ramp/mountaintop. The sound of trumpets blaring, applause. He moves into light for acceptance speech.*]

I consider this award profound recognition that non-violence is the answer to the need for man to overcome oppression and violence without resorting to violence and oppression ...

[*There is applause; music: "We Shall Overcome." He moves back down the right side of the ramp, is joined by* MRS. KING, *as they wave to the crowds during a ticker-tape parade: Confetti falling, music of marching bands. He stops in light, representing rostrum of a black church in New York.*]

The last few days I have been on the mountaintop! And I'm reminded how Jesus took the disciples to the Mount of the Transfiguration, to see the glory of God's work. But after they had tarried there a while, amidst all the glory and wonder of God's handiwork, He led them back down into the valley of iniquity to get on with the work. Well, like the disciples I would like to stay up on the mountaintop! But like them, I must go back down to the valley! [*Applause.*] I must go back because my brothers and sisters down in Mississippi and Alabama can't register and vote! I've got to go back to the valley and *march* for our rights as citizens, and human beings! I must go back...

[*He waves; moves away to give* MRS. KING *robe and medallion, kisses her and, followed by* RAY, *comes marching down ramp to central stage. Lights change as* KING *crosses down left, to man sitting in dim light, loading and unloading pistol with shaking hands and labored breath; dim lighting and big hat hide the fact that he is the aide,* HAROLD.]

KING: [*Crossing.*] I must go back down into the valley of America's south, because even now in 1965, down here, some of us are still in slavery. [*He goes to sit on the floor in front of the man.*]

MAN: [*Loading gun.*] He rape her ... He kill her ... He take his knife and ... and cut away her woman parts ... Then he burn her ... Burn her ... He burn her ... [*Composing self;*

putting in more bullets.] Yes ... Yes ... That's why ... that's why, I either got to shoot him or myself. Shoot him, or shoot myself ...

KING: No, brother, no! You've got to let the law handle him!

MAN: The law? He the law and he the sheriff! They ain't take him to no jail! No court! No nothing! ... Let him just walk all over Cindy! And just on past me! 'Cause she say no more to letting him have his way with her! Tell him she love me! Gonna live as a decent woman with a decent man. And so he ... he do all that to her ... kill her. And kill me inside. Kill the last bit of man feelin' in me. So if Ah got to be dead ... might as well take him with me, or die trying ...

[*He snaps gun chamber into place.* KING *reaches out to touch his gun hand.*]

KING: No, brother, that's not the way.

MAN: Back off, Reverend King. Just back off now!

KING: No, brother, Listen: How come he can do that to you and Cindy? How come?

MAN: Because he's white! And we black! That's why!

KING: No, uh-uh. It's because he's recognized as a citizen and you're not! That's why!

MAN: Citizen?! What's that got to do with me and Cindy?

KING: Everything. How'd he get to be sheriff in the first place? His people voted him in. And voted in the judges who decide in the courts who goes to jail and who goes free. And that's what we've got to do: get our rights as citizens. Get our hands on that power. That vote! Then we'll decide who goes to jail.

MAN: Vote won't help Cindy. Or how I feel.

KING: Won't it? Won't she rest easier knowing Sheriff Lucas can't work his evil no more? Knowing this can't happen to no more little Cindys? So you kill him, then after they kill you—the same ones who voted him in, will vote in another one just like him. Then what can all the other little

Cindys growing up around here have to look forward to? But if you come with us, help us get that vote ... then that kind will be out of office. And the hundreds, thousands, of little Cindys growing up across the South won't have to worry, 'cause there won't be no more days like this.

MAN: [*A beat.*] Reverend King, tell me true now. You sure about this?

KING: Just as sure as I am that there is a God. And that He will one day establish a rule of justice and peace.

MAN: [*Pause.*] And how'm ah gonna feel, Reverend King? Gonna feel alive again? Like a man again?

KING: Just come with us, brother. And trust us. It's gonna be a new dispensation. You're gonna feel brand new from head to toe.

[KING *waves for* RAY *to come across and take the man off. He takes the gun, gives it to* RAY.]

MAN: Brand new? From head to toe.

RAY: Yes, brother. But we've got to fight for it. Not with violence. But a sure 'nough fight.

KING: [*As they leave.*] Yes, brother. We don't fight with guns. Fight with the power of love, and righteousness. With marching feet! And boycotts ... Yes, the power of withheld dollars!

[*Lights on young country woman, stage right; shabbily dressed, rags wrapped about her head, barefoot. Sits on edge of ramp.*]

GIRL: Dollars, Reverend King? Y'all got dollars?

KING: [*Crossing.*] Ma'am?

GIRL: Y'all's white bosses give y'all dollars? *Real* dollars?

KING: Uh, yes, ma'am. Those of us who have white bosses, or black ones, too. When we do real work, we receive real payment, real dollars, in return. [*Testing; incredulous.*] Don't you?

GIRL: Aw, naw, sur. Us don't need real dollars. Us got the certificates!

KING: [*Anticipating, pained.*] Your ... uh ... bosses ... give you ... uh, certificates, instead of money, dollars.

GIRL: Yes-suh. See, they let us stay in they shacks, on they land, long's we work they crops. Then see, they give us the certificates to get whatever we need from they stores. Then, see, they total up all the certificates after crop time and take out what we owe them, including rent for the shacks, of course. [*Laughs.*] Us always end up owing them. But they let us [*Laughing.*] go right on staying here. They don't know that we ain't gon' never catch up with what we owe. [*Laughs.*] Just stay right on, getting what we need with the certificates, living in the shacks! Uh-uh-uh, we sho 'nough foolin' 'em all right ... [*Chuckle.*]

[KING *sits wearily on floor, touching fingers to eyes.*]

KING: [*As to himself.*] Slavery ... right here now ... in nineteen sixty-five. Slavery. Plantation slavery.

GIRL: Reverend King, slavery been gone. Didn't y'all's bosses tell y'all? Way back in my great-great-great grandmammy's time! Way back. We been stayin' on here free ever since.

KING: [*Looks at her.*] Like this? For generations? Your mother and her mother, and her mother?

GIRL: Uh-huh. Some of the young foolish ones run off. Uh-huh, and we never hear from 'em again. You know why? [*Confidentially.*] Us bosses tell us about it. See them northern folks tell us coloreds all kinda' lies 'bout how good they is up there; get us to come running—then they catch us! An' grind us up! And turn us into dog food! Uh-huh. That's the truth, Reverend King. You stay down here, you hear? Don't you go fooling 'round up north now, hear?

KING: [*Drained, back to her; staring out past audience.*] Yes, my poor little darling, I ... I hear you. I hear you.

GIRL: [*Beams.*] You called me a darling. Why thank ya. Reverend King? Would you think bad of me if I asked something of you.

KING: No, dear. I could never think bad of you.

GIRL: Well, see, I've seen real dollars before, but I ain't never touched one, held one. [*He gets up, takes a dollar from his wallet.*]

KING: What is your name, sweetheart?

GIRL: Lilly. Lilly June.

KING: Well, Lilly June, I know you don't need no real dollar. But I want you to have this one. And I want you to keep it until we come back down here with the *new* freedom, you hear?

GIRL: Oh, yes-sur, I'll keep it all right. Show everybody. 'Ceptin' the bosses of cose. Reverend King? Gon' be a new freedom? Well, what was wrong with the old one?

[*She suddenly looks back as if hearing someone, waves furtively and quickly sneaks off.* KING *waves sadly; stands with lowered head. Lights on well-dressed man with brief case on stage right ramp. He holds hand up for recognition as if at meeting/rally/classroom.*]

MAN #2: Reverend King, what you've told us about the young girl with the dollar, and the umm man and the killer sheriff is indeed distressing to say the very least. But what I stand to express here this evening is that for some of us who have had the good fortune to be able to vote for a relatively long time now; and have also been equally fortunate in being removed from officers of the law giving free reign to KKK mentalities; those of us thus fortunate, have problems at once more obvious and more complex than those just mentioned. I am of course speaking of those like myself. And to quickly get to the point, both my father and my grandfather before him attained the position of president of a Negro institution of higher education. I myself was able to receive my doctorate from Princeton University, where I met my wife, who also received a doctorate. So I think I can state, without seeming to be boastful, that it is therefore not surprising that our eight-year-old daughter is unusually precocious and intelligent. Intelligent enough to perceive that her esteemed parents, so respected and applauded in our community, literally, physically, shrink in size before her very eyes, at the door of some white restaurant they fear to attempt to enter. These same two learned and articulate parents cannot explain to her why she cannot drink from the clean sanitary water fountains she sees white children drink from, but must instead consider those—those cisterns provided for those of our race. These same two doctors of learning who cannot adequately explain why from some inferior roadside diner she must be taken out while little white children have merely to cross the diner floor to the bathrooms. In short, sir, I join your marches and demonstrations, not for the right to vote, or to stay killer sheriffs—but to be able to look my intelligent and sensitive child in the eye. Something I don't think we have fully been able to do since the first time we took her walking downtown into the white areas. I thank you, sirs, for forcing me to a confrontation with my cowardice. Thank you.

[*He sits in chair. Moved,* KING *applauds him as he moves center. Lights and mood go somber, dark. Cast come to grave-site with black umbrellas, hats, veils, raincoats.* RAY *is perhaps the preacher, carrying the Bible.* KING *moves amidst mourners.*]

KING: And what was the young boy's name?

MAN #3: Emmett Till. Here from Chicago visiting relatives.

KING: And why did they … lynch him?

WOMAN: They say he whistled at a white woman. They say …

KING: Whistled at her? Was anyone punished?

OTHERS: No!!

KING: Did we receive justice?

OTHERS: No!

KING: Are we free here in the South?!

OTHERS: Lord a'mighty, NO!

KING: And what are we gonna do about it?

OTHERS: We're gonna march!
March, Martin, March! March, Martin, March!!
[*This becomes a chant.*] March, Martin, March!

KING: MARR—CHING!

OTHERS: MARR—CHING!

KING: BY THE THOUSANDS

OTHERS: THE THOUSANDS, THE THOUSANDS

KING: BY THE TENS OF THOUSANDS

OTHERS: THE TENS OF THOUSANDS

KING: MARR-CHINGG!

OTHERS: MARR-CHINGG!

KING: UNTIL!

OTHERS: UNTIL!

KING: OUR GREE-VON-SESS

OTHERS: OUR GREE-VON-SESS

KING: AND THIS EEEE-VOOL!

OTHERS: THIS EEE-VOOL, THIS EEE-VOOL

KING: ARE WITNESSED!

OTHERS: ARE WITNESSED! WITNESSED!

KING: UNTIL WE RECEIVE!

OTHERS: UNTIL WE RECEIVE, UNTIL WE RECEIVE!

KING: OUR BIRTH-RIGHTS AS CIT-UH-SONS!

OTHERS: OUR BIRTH RIGHTS AS CIT-UH-SONS! OUR BIRTH RIGHTS AS CIT-UH-SONS! OUR BIRTH RIGHTS AS CIT-UH-SONS!

ALL: [*As continual chant.*] The-right-to-vote-the-right-to- [*Calmer, slower.*]

KING: [*As others continue "right to vote" chant.*] Yes, and with that tool of citizenship ... [*Chanting continues.*] We'll vot out the evil that would keep us enslaved. And vote i righteousness.

ALL: Marching non-violently,
For Freedom, Justice, Equality.

[*They march to chant; then others back up, lowering chant. A spot picks up* KING *and* RAY *confronted by two southern* LAW OFFICERS *in cowboy hats. Others move off chanting low. Ensuing scene may be pantomimed without the* OFFICERS.]

OFFICER: Will you stop this here marching?

KING: No sir, we won't. Our conscience won't allow us to.

OFFICER: Well, then, you're under arrest.

[*They roughly bring him to a stool, down right, and force him onto it;* RAY *with him. He begins immediately to take out pen and paper and write notes.* ABE *is shown into cell, kneels by him at the stool.*]

KING: Now, Abe, you can't be soft now. You all didn't march today. We have to have a march every day; every day. Even march at night. Make sheriff Clark show his colors. Got to dramatize this thing. And he's our villain.

RAY: Best thing we've got: beating women and children with billy clubs right in front of the cameras. God bless him.

KING: Yes, we've got to give him more rope.

ABE: I know. See what *The Nation* wrote about you and him?

KING: [*Writing.*] Umm. What?

ABE: Said you're the best southern tactician since General Lee. And they said, like Lee you get a lot of help from the stupidity of your enemies! [*They laugh.*]

KING: But we've gotta keep it up. Now they trying to take the heat off by desegregating public facilities. The issue is voting. Keep that fact out front. Voting. Call President Johnson, ask him to send an emissary.

ABE: And a congressional delegation. Got you, Doc.

KING: Yes, we've got to get a voting-rights bill. Got to. Now get this letter out for me. Look here, written on Waldorf Astoria stationery.

ABE: We'll get you some more paper. Guess I gotta be going, Doc.

KING: God bless you, Abe. Get that letter out now ... [KING *goes back to notes, as light dims on him, picks up* ABE *center, for letter.*]

ABE: [*Reading.*] Dear Friends, when the King of Norway participated in awarding me the Nobel Peace Prize, he surely did not think that in less than sixty days I would be in jail. [*Chuckles, skipping on.*] ... revealed the persisting ugliness of segregation ... Good, Doc, good. This is Selma, Alabama. There are more Negroes in jail with me than there are on the voting rolls! [*Chuckles.*] Tell 'em, Doc. When reporters asked Sheriff Clark if a woman defendant was married, he replied, "She's a Nigger woman and she hasn't got a Miss or Mrs. in front of her name." This is the U.S.A. in 1965. We are in jail simply because we cannot tolerate these conditions for ourselves or our country. We need the help of all decent Americans. Right on, Doc.

[*He rushes off.* KING *puts on his coat, and leaves jail, waving at crowds as he stands with* RAY.]

KING: One suffers jail easily for the cause of justice! Where now? First to Washington to implore President Johnson for a voting-rights bill and federal registrars! Then back here and perhaps—back to jail.

[*Waving to applause, he starts out left. There is a gunshot. He turns as* ABE *and* AARON *come running across.*]

AARON: The state troopers, Doc! In Marion! They shot young Jimmie Lee Jackson!

ABE: He's—dying, Martin.

[*To funeral music,* KING *moves across center to light; speaks to followers in Brown Chapel in Selma.*]

KING: They say I'm the youngest man to receive the Nobel

Peace Prize. Well, Jimmie Lee Jackson was the youngest man ever to be elected to his church's Deacon board. Which says much of his character, his spirit. Well, we haven't lost him! No! Despair not! His hope! His spirit is still with us! And we are going to carry that spirit with us in protest to that courthouse! Yes, put on your marching shoes! Because we are having a memorial march! Now! Tonight!

[*As he starts out of the light, his aides,* RAY, ABE, JOSH, *and* AARON, *come to him for a quick heated argument.* KING *finally agrees and steps back into the light.*]

KING: Hold it! Hold it, now! Wait! I'm told that there are men with guns, snipers, snakes out there waiting to take my life. All right. All right. I've faced death before. And for Jimmie Lee Jackson, and all those like him, I will again. Many times. All right. I know you would, too. I know it. But they would use the night, the darkness, to cover their foulness. And we won't let them do that. No, we will use the expository glow of sunlight to let the whole world witness their evil. Yes, make them show themselves for the pitiful creatures they are! So, we will march this Sunday, on the Lord's Sabbath, March 7th! And we aren't going to the courthouse! We're going all the way to the Capitol, in Montgomery!

[*He leaves the light, leading* AIDES *across to center.*]

AARON: Going to Montgomery is a good idea.

KING: [*Wearily.*] But not on Sunday.

JOSH: What! But you said ...

KING: I know. But I promised my congregation at Ebenezer, in Atlanta, that I would come home and preach this Sunday. I'm going to Washington to speak to the President; then I'll keep my promise to my people.

JOSH: But Martin, we've got these people ready. One more day might take the fight out of 'em.

AARON: He's right, Martin. We know your church needs you.

But these people down here do, too.

KING: [*Sharply.*] And what about me?! My needs? I'm sick. Weak. I need to be at home a while. Meditating. Praying. At least for one day! My church doesn't need its minister half as bad as their minister needs them.

JOSH: [*After pause.*] Well, maybe the thing to do is, you go on and get your day of rest. We know you need it. And let us go on and march without you.

KING: [*Incredulous.*] Don't you understand? I *promised* to lead them. I *suggested* the march.

AARON: That's just it, Doc. John Lewis and Stokely Carmichael. Those young SNCC people, they started this Selma thing, remember?

JOSH: Yeh, and they ain't gonna be pleased at all with everything going when we go, and stoppin' when we stop.

KING: [*Exasperated.*] Lord spare me, *please.* [*Before he can reply angrily.*]

ABE: You know, Doc? Might not be a bad idea to let them march without you here. I mean, you're always saying that a part of our mission here is to get the people to see that they can do things for themselves, have the power themselves to change their conditions.

RAY: Sounds good to me. We'll be up in Washington, and knowing you, with the Lord's help, by Sunday you'll have the President involved down here. With all those Federal white folks observing, shoot, that march will probably go down like buttermilk in the summertime. [*Chuckles, smiles, breaks the tension.*]

KING: All right. Y'all go ahead. But keep in touch, now. I'll be home by then. Call me if anything starts to go wrong? Hear?

[AIDES *agree as they rush out to prepare.* KING *crosses on left to foot of ramp, where he is met by* MRS. KING. *They embrace, lights out as* KINGS *go off left. Lights up briefly for* AIDES *with picket signs, etc., beginning Selma march. They march off singing "We*

Shall Overcome." Lights up on KINGS, *down left. He is for the first time tieless and in shirt-sleeves, relaxed as he stands on porch breathing deeply; perhaps he wears smoking jacket.* MRS. KING *is also casually dressed. She comes to hug him from rear.*]

KING: Do you have any idea what it means to have you and the children to come home to? Do you know how good these moments are for me? How grateful I am?

MRS. KING: I know how good they are for me and the children. How grateful we are. [*They kiss.*]

KING: Yes ... but you know I have to get right back to Selma. They are probably marching right now.

MRS. KING: I know, you've got to go back. And this time I'm going with you.

KING: Coretta, it's going to be dangerous down there.

MRS. KING: I know. That's why I'm going. [*He starts to protest.*] Just hush, Martin. It'll be worse being here, waiting for word on what happened. Being like you are now: on pins and needles waiting for the evening news to come on. No. This time I'll be right there with you.

KING: [*Smiles.*] Woman, you're a wonder.

MRS. KING: To be with you, I'd better be. [*They kiss; he quickly breaks it.*]

KING: Is that the news coming on? It's about Selma. Come on, Coretta.

[*He literally drags her around toward audience and they pantomime turning volume up. The* KINGS *both come to feet staring stunned and pained off left, as if at T.V., as strobe-like effect combines with surreal music (say, mix of wild Pharaoh Sanders/Albert Ayler/Jimi Hendrix) to create sense of chaos and horror: screaming, sirens, etc.* AIDES *come running up center in disarray, panic.*]

AIDES: Martin!! Martin!! Did you see it?! Oh, God, Martin! Did you see what they did to us!?

ABE: Wearing gas masks, Martin! Gas masks!

RAY: Like creatures of war!

JOSH: Trampling us on horses, Martin! Horses!

AARON: Ten foot tall monsters raining down terror! [*He begins to reenact the beating with clubs; down on one knee, beating.*] Terror! Terror! Heads! Arms! Legs!

OTHERS: [*To him in memory.*] No no no, stop stop stop …

AARON: [*Continuing.*] Men! Women! Children! Riding over 'em! Beating 'em! Crushing! Crushing! Crushing. Like we were ants! Dogs! Beating! Beating! Beating! [*He gets lost in it; beating, crying. The others come to him, stop him, reassure him.* KING *crosses, followed by* MRS. KING.]

KING: Yes, we saw it. And so did the whole country.

MRS. KING: The whole world! T.V. and newspapers caught it all.

KING: It is themselves they beat into the dust! Segregation. The old southern ways! They're in their last days!

MRS. KING: The President is federalizing the National Guard, sending a contingent of troops!

ABE: What's he sending 'em now for?

KING: To protect our march to Montgomery. We're going back to Selma … back to Montgomery … We will finish the march in the name of Jimmie Lee Jackson. [RAY *comes in running with letters, papers.*]

RAY: There's money coming in from everywhere! Look at this!

KING: I sent out a call to ministers, priests, rabbis. To religious leaders all over the country to come down and make spiritual witness.

MRS. KING: Yes. The Bishop of Birmingham denied permission to 300 southern priests and nuns—and they're coming anyway!

JOSHUA: White priests and nuns?

MRS. KING: White priests and nuns.

RAY: Harry Belafonte is organizing entertainers from all over the world to meet us for a rally in Montgomery. Joan Baez, Sammy Davis ... A whole slew of 'em.

MRS. KING: Black and white ministers are coming down from all over the North.

KING: [*Putting an arm around him.*] Yes, Aaron, we're marching to Montgomery. And this time we won't be alone.

[*Group marches down front, then in place, to slow strains of "We Shall Overcome," singing tentatively. Voices come in over singing.*]

VOICE: [*Off stage.*] Ladies and gentlemen: The President of the United States.

JOHNSON: It is wrong, deadly wrong, to deny any of your fellow Americans the right to vote. We have already waited one hundred years or more. The time for waiting is gone. There must be no delay, or no hesitation, or no compromise. [*Applause.*] What happened in Selma is part of a far larger movement: the effort of American Negroes to secure for themselves the full blessings of American life. Their cause must be our cause, too. Because, really, it is all of us who must overcome the crippling legacy of bigotry and injustice. And We *Shall* Overcome.

[*Lights on group celebrating among themselves a moment, then resuming to a march; first, with more confidence; then, at a given point, slower, more apprehensively.*]

JOSH: There they are, Doc, waiting at the bridge. Just like before.

AARON: No horses this time ...

ABE: And no gas-masks ...

AARON: But they've got those clubs ...

RAY: Look at 'em, Martin, look at 'em. Moving back. Parting like the Red Sea!

KING: The red sea of hatred and bigotry, falling away. Praise God!

RAY: The red sea. Hello, Moses! [*Grabs* KING'*s hand. They are marching faster, more confident now.*]

KING: Better shake the Lord's hand. This is His work. Just look at all these people. Ever seen so many black and white people walking together before?

ABE: Down here? No.

KING: Rabbis, priests, ministers, nuns. Ever seen so many religions together before?

ABE: Down here? No.

KING: Just look at 'em all! Now, this isn't by *my* hand.

RAY: Well, Doc: God had to have somebody to work through.

KING: [*Waving.*] Yes sir! Glad to see you! [*To group.*] Isn't that Jimmie Lee Jackson's grandfather! How old is he?

JOSH: Seventy-two years old.

KING: Yeh? What's he saying?

MRS. KING: [*Listening.*] Rheumatism. Says he can't go but a little ways each day. But he's gonna' go that little each day.

AARON: There's old Levison and Rustin.

RAY: J. Edgar Hoover says they're communists.

MRS. KING: J. Edgar Hoover also says you're a degenerate, Ray. [*As others laugh.*] You too, Josh. And [*Looks pointedly at* KING.]

KING: My name is Jess. I ain't in that mess. Lord, my feet hurt.

MRS. KING: Ummm. Hmm.

[*Lights and positions change. The* KINGS *now are slightly before others. She is holding onto his arm.*]

KING: Montgomery, Coretta. Where it all started for us. Remember?

MRS. KING: You certainly ask silly questions. Of course I remember.

KING: E.D. Nixon. Is he here, today? And Rosa Parks? Isn't she supposed to meet us here, today?

MRS. KING: I think so.

KING: [*To others.*] This is truly an historical moment. Look we're passing the Jefferson Davis monument.

RAY: Well, I hope the Devil gives him the day off, so he can see us! [*All laugh ... marching.*]

KING: [*Chanting.*] What do we want?

OTHERS: Free-dommm!

KING: When do we want it?

OTHERS: Nowww!

[*Repeat sequence. Marching stops. Others applaud as* KING *moves down right into speaker's light.*]

KING: They told us we wouldn't get here!

RAY: Tell it, Doctor!

KING: But the whole world knows today that we are here, and that we are standing before the forces of power in the state of Alabama saying, "We ain't gon' let nobody turn us around"! Yes, we are on the move and no wave of racism can stop us! The burning of our churches, the bombings of our homes, the clubbing and killing of our clergymen and young people will not deter us. We struggle on with faith in the power of nonviolence. Our aim must never be to defeat or humiliate the white man but to win his friendship and understanding. The end we seek is a society at peace with itself, a society that can live with its conscience. That will be the day, not of the white man, not of the black man. That will be the day of man as man. [*Applause. Lights change.* KING *joins his group, leads them upstage toward house, singing.*]

WE HAVE OVERCOME
WE HAVE OVERCOME
WE HAVE OVERCOME TODAY
O' DEEP IN THE SOUTH
WE DO BELIEVE
WE HAVE OVERCOME

TODAY!

[*At the end of the song they go laughing into house. Mood and lights change as they sit casually, some on floor, in meditative air.*]

RAY: Well, God willing, maybe Jimmie Lee Jackson can rest a little easier now. He knows he didn't die in vain.

MRS. KING: We lost two others, too. Two white people down here trying to help black people.

KING: Yes, Mrs. Liuzzo. Came down from Detroit.

ABE: To be shot down on the highway, for riding with a black man.

JOSHUA: God rest them.

AARON: And Reverend James Reeb from Birmingham. He could have stayed safe at home, too.

MRS. KING: [*After thoughtful pause.*] Martyrs ... Isn't it awful that people have to die before we do what's right?

KING: Coretta, sometimes I think you're reading my mind. I was just thinking that same thing. I mean, we shake our heads at the so-called primitive people. The Aztecs and others. Making blood sacrifices: killing young virgins, pure young warriors; offering their blood to appease the gods. We shake our heads at them. But are we any less primitive today? No. Seems to me that all we've done is omitted the ritual. Still demanding martyrs, blood-sacrifice.

AARON: You got a point there, Doc. Would Johnson have passed the voting-rights bill at this time if Reverend Reeb hadn't been killed? A minister? A white minister?

ABE: Good question.

KING: Yes, and if we'd taken guns and fought we'd have been into a ritual just as old: war, open bloodshed. [*As others agree.*] Yes, and Stokely Carmichael, and these other young folks, talking about excluding whites from the movement. Hating. Fighting. Lord, can't they see? This is not about

black and white. It's about Good and Evil. About ... abo
... man's brotherhood. His evolution. Always has been. A
of history. Yes, and we got a little, little glimpse of the f
ture today. Remember, Abe? Aaron? When we took Bel
fonte and the Rabbi and the ministers to the airport? [*H*
moves to edge, as if looking out window.] Remember? All th
flights were jammed. Delayed. Thousands of demonstr
tors, crowded together on the floors, the seats, the stai
ways. And standing there, seeing them all: black an
white, nuns and priests, ministers and rabbis, lawyers an
shopkeepers, brimming with vitality in this—this kind
luminous moment of genuine brotherhood—I knew I w
seeing a—a—microcosm of mankind of the future.

MRS. KING: Beautiful.

ABE and RALPH: Amen. Amen.

KING: And Stokely and those other young folks, can't they s
how wonderful God is? What a marvelous spiritual to
He has provided here. This nonviolent confrontation
Evil? War, fighting, killing, confuses the issues. Blurs ev
ryone's humanity. But when violence goes up against no
violent love, violence soon loses its rationale, then
will—and in the end we are down to the pure issue, t
simple truth. God. How amazing is the divine desig
Gandhi in India was perfectly placed for the initial test, t
introduction. But we, black people, we are not only in t
lion's den, the belly of the whale, but all over the worl
When we pick up the torch of nonviolent confrontation
God. Oh, this isn't going to end down here, or in just th
country even. This thing is going to go all over the worl
All over the world. [*As the spot narrows on him, caught in h*
vision, the others stare at him in awe.]

END OF PART ONE

PART TWO
CHICAGO, 1966-1967

SETTING

Center area is now a Chicago slum apartment; being set up before audience by men in overalls, with paintbrushes, etc., with perhaps a KING AIDE *or two assisting/directing.* KING *stands dimly lit center; talking on phone with President Johnson; feeling obviously weary and harassed.*

KING: L.B.J. ... L.B. ... L.B. ... I am fully aware of that, sir, I ... with all due respects, sir. That would not change my mind on this Vietnam situation one bit. I ... Mr. President. Injustice anywhere is an unbalancing of justice everywhere. For me it is not merely rhetoric, sir, but a conviction. Yes ... you've always given me a hearing, sir. Yes, I am listening. But I don't hear anything that would change my ... Yes. That much I will do, sir. On my way through New York, I'll make it my business to stop at the U.N. and see the ambassador. Sir? Oh, she's fine, she's fine ... and how's Mrs. Johnson? Yes sir. You too, sir.

[*Hangs up. Cross fade to down center.* KING *picks up a dark trench coat and hat, moves into light; stands listening uneasily to uncomfortable conversation.*]

KING: [*After beats.*] Dr. Goldberg, I'm pleased to hear that the administration seeks not escalation of hostilities in Vietnam, but rather negotiations to end them. Most pleased. But I would ask you, sir—and I would ask the President as well: Is bombing the only way to negotiation and peace? When will America—herself born of a nationalistic revolution seeking freedom and independence—show understanding of, and get on the right side of, the spirit of revolutionary, nationalistic fervor, sweeping the third-world nations of today? Sir, I would offer myself as mediator. Perhaps my position as a Nobel laureate might lend some weight. I understand Dr. Bunche received his prize for negotiation, mediation, between

Israel and the Arab world. Perhaps I might embellish mine by mediating in Vietnam. [*He puts on his hat.*] I understand this much, Mr. Ambassador: All war is wrong. And this one is no exception. God bless you. Good afternoon.

[*Lights out. Lights up down-right,* KING *and* ABE *sit on suitcases, in crowded airport, awaiting delayed flight; they carry top coats/trench coats.* ABE *has various newspapers open.*]

ABE: [*Reading.*] Dr. King is already committed to a massive *unfinished* task in an area in which he has great influence civil rights. He can only dissipate that influence by venturing into fields that are *strange* to him. That's the *Herald Tribune* in New York.

KING: [*Getting to feet.*] Strange to him? Since when is violence and injustice strange to me? What did our friend, Max Freedman, have to say again?

ABE: [*Reading.*] Is he casting about for a role in Vietnam because the civil rights struggle is no longer adequate to his own estimate of his talents?

KING: [*Huffed.*] My own estimate of my talents, huh? I'm beginning to see their estimate all right. I'm supposed to sit down home somewhere on my porch, admiring my Nobel Prize all week; then on Sunday go preach about the evils south of the Mason/Dixon line? Didn't I buy some cigarettes? Oh, here they are ...

ABE: Martin ... those cigarettes ... [*Shakes his head.*]

KING: I know, I know. Don't you start on me, too. I only smoke 'em at times like this: sitting here waiting on this flight with nothing to do.

ABE: You been doing a lot of smoking ever since you got that call from President Johnson about your war statements. What did he say, Doc?

KING: He didn't say anything, directly. I can't seem to speak to him directly any more since I spoke out against the war. Basically the word he sent to me was that I should stay in the colored folks' place, civil rights—and leave the war to the "experts," the white folks.

ABE: Bet he wouldn't say that if you were draft age.

KING: [*Chuckles.*] That's a good point, Abe. Very good. Got to remember that one. [*A beat.*]

ABE: [*Gingerly.*] You kinda promised him you wouldn't make any more statements for a while, didn't you, Doc?

KING: [*Heatedly.*] Don't you start with that!

ABE: [*Surprised at the intensity.*] What, Martin?

KING: You know what! Lyndon Johnson, *President* Johnson, has made himself accessible to me and our concerns! He has talked to me frankly, and sincerely, man to man! Has listened to me. He has taken the correct stance, for the correct legislation, on every single civil rights issue. Every one!

ABE: [*Looking around for on-lookers.*] I know that, Martin. I understand the politics as well as you do.

KING: [*Lowering voice.*] Do you? Then you understand that I needn't be unnecessarily jeopardizing that relationship by publicly debating him on this war. Not at this moment. After all he has done, and is willing to do, for our rights, what is wrong with me holding my peace for a moment? Just—holding back, to give him more time on his plan to—to de-escalate the bombing, and—and—get to the negotiating table? What's wrong with that?

ABE: Nothing. Except you're smoking all those cigarettes. Martin? Do you really *believe* that's what he's doing?

KING: [*Shakes head, no; becomes animated, pained.*] Abe? Can't they understand that you can't speak out against wrong over here, and then shut up about it over there—without becoming a hypocrite? To yourself! Your beliefs! Everything you stand for! [*Catches self; smiles, and waves as to passersby.*] Yes ma'am! Thank you! And God bless you too ... Fine. Fine. [*He sits back down alongside* ABE. *In stage whisper.*] Can't let them see the Sunday morning preacher, acting Saturday night here in this airport.

ABE: Peace-prize winner disturbing the peace.

KING: Can't have that.

ABE: Nooo, J. Edgar might be looking.

KING: Probably is. [*A beat.*] Abe? Do you think there might be some truth in what they're saying about me? I mean, the SNCC youngsters call me "De Lawd" ...

ABE: So?

KING: What I'm asking is: Am I—sliding into an area of megalomania? Taking onto myself the—the Lord's mantle? Well, how can I—any man—really know that he is—called? Ordained?

ABE: [*Realizing seriousness; decides to lighten it.*] Well, let's play a little Socratic logic game.

KING: [*Rubbing hands together.*] Just the thing: Socratic logic game. [*It is an established group ritual. Sense of an old vaudeville skit.*]

ABE: All right. Now: is your ministry on the side of goodness and justice?

KING: I'd say so, yes.

ABE: All right. So is God on the side of goodness and justice?

KING: Assuming the existentialist and scientist haven't killed him: definitely.

ABE: All right. Then that means that you and the Lord are working for the same concerns. Working together, right?

KING: Sounds like it.

ABE: So, if you and God are in the same employ, and you being a mortal man, can't hire Him, then he must've hired you. Right?

KING: [*Tongue in cheek.*] Sounds metaphysically logical to me.

ABE: Well, if you're working for the Lord, what difference does it make if he called you for the job, or you walked in and asked for it? If you see something needs to be done on the job, you jump on it. Right?

KING: Jump on it.

ABE: Well, seems to me you're all right with the Lord.

KING: All right with the Lord. [*They slap five, laughing. Look up, listening.*]

KING: [*Getting up.*] That's our flight. [*Carrying suitcases, putting on coats, they start up center.*]

ABE: Martin? Why Chicago? I mean I know it's time for us to take our movement north. But why not L.A., or New York? Why Chicago?

KING: Two reasons: Chicago has the best grass roots organization. And Chicago has Mayor Daley.

ABE: Daley?

KING: Non-violent confrontation presents a drama between good and evil. It must have a strong villain. Someone to personify that evil.

ABE: Like Clark in Selma and Connors in Birmingham.

KING: And now Daley in Chicago. [*Lights change as they move up to flat.*]

[KING *and* ABE *are now in a Chicago kitchen, seated, with* JOSH *and young* HAROLD.]

HAROLD: I live here in Chicago, and I'll tell you: Daley won't be in front of no cameras beating nobody with no stick. His sticks are invisible. But we'll feel 'em all right.

JOSH: Looks like he owns every other preacher in town.

HAROLD: And just about all the politicians.

KING: That why Honorable Rep. Dickson's saying we aren't needed here?

HAROLD: You got it. This isn't going to be anything like Birmingham or Selma, Rev.

ABE: Rustin says it isn't the right time to go to his hometown, New York. And you say the same about coming here to your hometown. You all beginning to sound like the northern white folks.

JOSH: Yeh. We'll help you jump on those folks down south, but don't come up here in my neighborhood!

[JOSH *and* ABE *laugh, as* HAROLD *glares at them.*]

KING: Well, I can see we're ready for action. We've started snarling at each other already.

HAROLD: [*Half-joking.*] These two good ol' boys aren't bothering me. Just trying to hip 'em that the happenings happen different up here, that's all.

JOSH: Hip 'em. Uh-uh, done whipped out some Chicago talk on us. Hey now.

[MRS. KING *comes from left with* RAY; *she is carrying one suitcase, he two, all hers. She comes into flat, looks around as the* AIDES *get conspicuously busy.* KING *takes her bags from* RAY *and leads her into bedroom area.*]

MRS. KING: You can just *feel* the roaches!

KING: Coretta, we've come to call attention to these conditions. Now by moving in here ...

MRS. KING: I know, Martin, I know. We'll help reveal the situation. Dramatize it.

[*Looking around, she sits on bed, gets up quickly; they laugh as he comes to embrace and kiss her.*]

MRS. KING: Okay. But you know how the children are. They'll tell you exactly how they feel about it.

KING: I know. You keep those rascals off of me. Come on. [*He leads her back into the kitchen area.*]

KING: All right. Let's get our heads together before that rally.

JOSH: Where you wanna start? Unemployment? These slums?

ABE: Calling out the Mayor?

HAROLD: The youth gangs?

MRS. KING: They still sell these refrigerators?

KING: Coretta ...

MRS. KING: [*Absently; looking around.*] You're finding out what you have to deal with—and I'm finding out what I have to deal with.

AARON: Uh-huh. And speaking of that: people dealing with what they feel they should be; congratulations, Coretta, on your Women for Peace conference.

MRS. KING: [*Warily.*] Thank you.

AARON: You're welcome. And, Doc, you may as well know it now: I want some time out of this Chicago thing. The war is the evil I want to fight. I think even the Lord must have shifted priorities now. I don't think He can hear the crying over here so clear, with all the screaming and crying going on over there in the Mekong Delta.

ABE: Oh-oh.

KING: [*Bristling.*] I've got just one thing to say to that, Aaron. Now, every man has to answer to the dictates of his own conscience. So when you pick the time you go on out to that peace conference in California or wherever. But I have picked this time and this place. And all I ask is that for the time that you are here you focus here! Is that clear?

AARON: I can hear you very well, Doc. You don't have to raise your voice.

MRS. KING: [*Aside.*] Or the roof either.

KING: Coretta, Aaron, Lord, sometimes ... Dr. Spock wants me to make a world tour for peace! And come back and run for President with him on a Peace Ticket! You [*To* AARON.] want me to conduct peace rallies here! Josh wants me down south registering voters! Well, I can't be everywhere! Now *my* prayer, and *my* meditations, tell me the Lord wants me here in Chicago tending to these ghettos. So it is *this* part of the Lord's many works that we will be attending today—and that's all of that.

JOSHUA: [*Half joking.*] De Lawd has spoken.

ABE: Oh-oh, again.

KING: Joshua? You need to pray. You need to get your soul

right. Hear me? Don't fool with me, today.

MRS. KING: Well, my Lord, Martin. I think you need to re-read your Gandhi. There's such a thing as non-violent speech and attitude.

HAROLD: Amen, Sister King. The good brother needs to come down a little.

JOSHUA: Let the church say: Amen. [*Others are laughing now.*]

AARON: Let us pray for the brother!

[KING *smiles, accepting the reprimand.*]

KING: All right. Okay, here you go. [*He gets up in chair holding necktie up as if noose.*] Just pull the chair out! Lynch me! Lynch me!

ABE: Now he's a martyr.

RAY: Get him down from there!

[*Laughing, they all rush to pull him down, with ad libs; i.e.: Throw some cold water on him!/Yeh, cool him off ... Lights go black as they grab him. Lights almost immediately back up in tone and mood change.* KING *is seated at table facing* HAROLD *and* JOSHUA. *Others stand around table;* MRS. KING *is behind her husband.*]

KING: These gangs? What's their names? Rattlesnakes?

HAROLD: No, Rev. [*Chuckles.*] Cobras. Cobras. Vice-Lords. Blackstone Rangers.

KING: My God: Vice-Lords? Couldn't they think of anything more evil sounding? Vice-Lords? I'll tell you what. We'll go meet these gang leaders, and let them give us a little tour. Get the feel of things through their eyes; then go on over to that rally. Have I got my speech? You coming, honey?

MRS. KING: Hmmph. Even as cold as it is out there, you're not leaving me here by myself.

JOSH: By yourself? With all those policemen around?

HAROLD: And you know ol' J. Edgar is watching and *hearing* everything.

RAY: [*Looking under tables, lampshades.*] Yeh, J. Edgar? Where'd you put your doohickey this time?! Huh?! Testing ... test—tingg!

ABE: Uh, J. Edgar! We are about to leave now? Would you send two cars around, please?

[*Laughing, they leave flat-area. They move through darkness to meet light down center. Handing* HAROLD *his hat and coat,* KING *waves to applauding crowd, moves down front to speak.*]

KING: Chicago is an island of poverty in the midst of an ocean of plenty! So many people feel that the Civil Rights struggle is over because we have a 1964 Civil Rights Bill, and a Voting Rights Bill. They feel that everything is all right! Well, let them look around the big cities! Let them look around Chicago! Flourishing in its slums is a system of colonialism, not unlike the exploitation of the Congo by Belgium.

[*The* AIDES *come to separate lights waving fact sheets.*]

HAROLD: Chicago's 837,000 black people are so segregated that some school chidren thought Negroes were the majority race in America!

MRS. KING: Paying inflated rents for substandard housing!

KING: Conspiring to maintain inferior schools, preparing blacks only for unskilled jobs, thus perpetuating the old myth of Negro inferiority.

ABE: In the ghettos of Chicago thirteen percent of the work force is unemployed!

KING: A figure of major depression proportions. If the entire country had such an unemployment rate it would be viewed as an economic catastrophe!

MRS. KING: In ghetto stores prices are ten to twenty percent higher than in suburban stores.

HAROLD: Even when it's the same chain store!

JOSH: Call that the "color" tax.

RAY: Price you pay for being colored.

HAROLD: And in the main, the police turn their backs on black-on-black ghetto crime!

KING: And should, by the grace of God, one prove strong enough, or lucky enough, to break out of the cyclic trap of poor schooling, therefore poor job, therefore poor housing, and back to poor schooling; should one be strong enough to break all that—without succumbing to the seductive false-escapes of drugs, and alcohol—should one get by all that, still the white realtors will not sell a Negro a home in a better white area.

ABE: Even if you have the money.

KING: [*Beat.*] So tonight, I warn Mayor Daley. Warn him that I heard these same unattended frustrations and ills voiced by the people of Watts, a day after that rage had exploded in devastating violence. I say to Mayor Daley that should he turn the same deaf ears on these grievances as did Mayor Yorty out there in Los Angeles, then, God forbid, there will be the same terrible price paid here in Chicago! [*They leave, lights fading. Cross back up to the flat.*]

HAROLD: [*In dark.*] Well, we challenged the fat man all right.

JOSH: Yeh. What do you think he's going to do?

[*Lights up as group moves into flat.*]

KING: No matter what he does, I know what we're going to do.

MRS. KING: What is that, Martin?

KING: We're going to organize a slum union!

RAY: [*Considering.*] A slum union.

KING: Tell 'em about it, Aaron.

AARON: We'll organize the folks in these tenements and projects, and come up with some petitions for these landlords, some demands. And if they don't address those demands, we'll have demonstrations here in Chicago that'll make Selma and Birmingham look like a church auxiliary meeting.

HAROLD: Yeh, Reverend, demonstrations are fine. But the power, the threat, of a union is in a strike. And that's what we ought to do.

KING: How do you mean, Harold?

ABE: Oh, maybe it wasn't too soon to come to Chicago after all, huh, city-boy?

HAROLD: Hush, country. Grown folks talking.

KING: What kind of strike?

HAROLD: A rent strike, Rev. If the landlords don't meet our demands to fix these joints up, why we, the union, will collect the rent and use it for the repairs.

ABE: Deducting it from the rent.

JOSH: Now *that* will get their attention.

KING: Yes, and give us our drama, our confrontation ...

ABE: First with the landlords, and then the courts.

HAROLD: With Daley. In Chicago it's always with Daley.

KING: [*Continuing.*] Then when the newspapers and television pick it up ...

JOSH: Then the whole country will come rolling in here.

KING: Most importantly, the white folks of good will.

HAROLD: And good money ...

ABE: And prestige and power!

RAY: Yes, yes. Then it'll be all over but the shouting!

KING: All right. Let's get it started. Meet at eight-thirty this morning.

ABE: And hit the streets at ten, getting to the people.

HAROLD: And the preachers.

KING: Good! So, that's it. God bless you all. See you in the morning.

[*They call goodbyes to the* KINGS *and leave the two in the flat. The* AIDES *stand down center of the flat in silent discussion among themselves, as lights come up in the* KINGS' *bedroom. He sits on downstage side of bed. She stands behind bed on upstage side.*]

KING: [*Unlacing shoes.*] See you keeping your coat on too.

MRS. KING: Uh-huh. Not getting under those cold covers until you do.

KING: Won't be long.

MRS. KING: Tired? [*She gets on bed behind him on her knees, and massages his shoulder muscles.*]

KING: [*Pointedly.*] Not that tired. [*She smiles coyly. He touches, kisses her massaging fingers.*]

KING: I really appreciate you agreeing to stay up here with me. Bringing the kids. Can't tell you how much it means to me.

MRS. KING: Hush, Martin.

KING: Guess you're what they call a "trooper," huh?

MRS. KING: Just a minister's wife, that's all. It's just that your ministry is a little broader, and more unusual, than most. [*He chuckles.*] Most ministers' wives answer the phone and only have to talk about sick visits, and choir robes, and who's handling what fund-raiser. But when I answer ours it could be anything from Mrs. Gandhi to somebody wanting to know our position on Malcolm X and the administration's stand on Latin America. Lord, started out in a little church in Birmingham, and looked up and I was talking to Mahatma Gandhi; at the Taj Mahal, the White House; in Norway with a Nobel Peace Prize winner. La de da ...

KING: And in Chicago fighting Mayor Daley and these roaches.

MRS. KING: Hush. Don't mention those house insects.

KING: [*Chuckles; a beat.*] Well, how you getting along with those Women for Peace folks?

MRS. KING: Thought you didn't want to talk about Vietnam.

KING: I'm not talking about Vietnam. You'll hold down that corner for us right now. I'm talking about you dealing with all those Machiavellian women in that movement.

MRS. KING: Oh, I'm doing just fine. I watch them maneuvering, trying to use me, and I just step right up where I want to be. No more no less, huh. Sometimes I feel like telling those feminists and childniks, and whatever-niks, that if they really want to see some politics they should see the different women's auxiliaries at one of these black churches.

KING: [*Laughing with her.*] Yeh, I guess you can handle the kids here in Chicago all right. But we do have to hurry and find some appropriate schools up here.

MRS. KING: Can't be any harder than it is home in Atlanta.

KING: Coretta, don't now ...

MRS. KING: I swear I don't believe it. Being black in America is absolutely surreal. Your husband can be on the cover of *Newsweek, Time* magazine's "Man of the Year," Nobel Prize Laureate—but try to get your kids in a good school. And the white folks say, no. Say no, in your own hometown.

KING: Coretta, don't get started now. [*She has turned her back, crying, and lies on bed.*] Coretta ... don't cry, honey, honey, please ...

MRS. KING: [*Quietly.*] Can't help it, Martin. I don't mind so much for you and me. We can handle it. But when it touches the children then sometimes it's just too much ... too much. [*She cries, he tries to console her.*]

[*Lights fade and come up on* AIDES *crossing down left in dim light. ABE carries portable radio to his ear.*]

HAROLD: What's on the radio?

ABE: Quiet! Meredith in Mississippi.

JOSH: James Meredith? What's he doing?

HAROLD: Where you been Josh?

[*As they continue, lights up on stage left ramp, Meredith figure (could be* AARON *disguised) makes way up ramp wearing overalls, work cap, carrying sign: MARCH AGAINST FEAR!; sign also on his back (Find official photo for actual signs). Group now in shadow light, focus on Meredith.*]

He's making a one man march to Jackson, the capitol.

JOSH: By *himself*? In Mississippi? Damn, he's got guts. What's the point of the march?

ABE: Quiet! I can't hear.

RAY: March against fear he calls it. Wants those folks down there to stop being scared of those white folks. Stand up for themselves, register to vote.

HAROLD: What're they saying? What happened?

[*Shot rings out. Meredith figure falls, rolls off ramp, off stage. Lights out on ramp. Group rushes back toward apartment. They call for* KING; *he comes out of bedroom area in shirt-sleeves.*]

RAY: They shot James Meredith, Doc! In Mississippi!

KING: God help him. Is he alive? [*Rushes to pick up address book, going for phone.*]

ABE: Last we heard. He's in a hospital in Memphis. [*Lights down as* KING *dials. Lights immediately back up.* KING *hangs up phone.*]

KING: He's going to be fine. Listen: I'm going down there to the hospital.

HAROLD: Now? In the middle of all this?

KING: Hear me out now: Carmichael and Floyd McKissick are on their way down there; talking about continuing the march for him. [*As others grow silent.*] Figure we'd better have some non-violent representation down there. Don't you?

RAY: Yeh, they'll be down there talking that "eye for an eye, tooth for a tooth" talk.

ABE: Carmichael's got those Deacons for Defense set with their shotguns.

KING: Yes, and you can't tell defense from offense when everybody's got a shotgun. Honey, I'm sorry. [*He goes to her in the doorway.*]

MRS. KING: I know, I heard. Be safe. I'll be in Atlanta when you return. Hurry back. [*They kiss.* KING *puts on blue jean jacket, cap.* KING *and group leave flat, crossing down left. Lights out on flat and up down left.*]

KING: Josh, you come with me. Can the rest of you get this thing started here?

HAROLD: You insulting me, Rev.? This is my hometown.

ABE: Looks like you haven't been doing your homework.

HAROLD: Keep on. You gonna' get a non-violent knock out! [*They all laugh; others wish them well and go up and off.* KING *and* JOSH *go up on ramp. They go into march step on ramp; chanting:*]

KING: Whatta we want!?

JOSH: [*With off stage voices.*] Freee-dom!

KING: When do we want it?!

JOSH: [*With off stage voices.*] Now! [*Sequence repeated. Lights up on* CARMICHAEL *figure on stage right ramp. Can be* AARON *in sunglasses, etc.*]

CARMICHAEL: What do we want?

VOICES: [*Off stage.*] Black power!!

CARMICHAEL: When do we want it!?

VOICES: Within the hour!! [*Sequence repeated. At end of sequence,* CARMICHAEL *smiles over at* KING *and* JOSH.]

KING: [*As to crowd.*] We don't need men with guns on this march. We don't want violence or the *threat* of violence! Not on our side!

CARMICHAEL: [*To crowd.*] Facing a gun, you'd *better* have one! Violence is as American as apple pie. Remember "Don't Tread on Me?" Well, that's what these shot-guns say: Don't tread on us.

KING: Violence! Guns and Molotov cocktails are the tools of our oppressors! Righteousness, love, and reason are our non-violent tools! We didn't suffer beatings and jail and, yes, the death of comrades—and some of those who lost their lives, so that we might have better lives, were not oppressed blacks, but justice and brotherhood-seeking whites. Viola Liuzzo was not black. Reverend James Reeb, an Episcopalian Minister from Birmingham, was not black. No. Nor was Andrew Goodman, nor Michael Schwerner, two young Jewish men, who died right here in Mississippi, alongside young, black James Chaney! We did not suffer all that to end with a further divided nation! A segregated movement! Yes, we welcome whites! We invite all people of good will from all races, creeds, and faiths, from everywhere to join our ranks as we march non-violently toward a better world!

CARMICHAEL: Our kids don't believe black people can do anything without white people helping, leading us, because our grown people, our leaders, don't believe it themselves! I've suffered through all that right along with Dr. King. With SNCC I was there in Selma, when we tried to cross the bridge the first time. When they came with tear gas and horses. When I saw what was happening to the people I just started screaming, and I didn't stop until I came to myself at the airport. That day I knew I could never be hit again without hitting back. I've been to jail twenty-seven times! And I ain't going no more! The only way we can stop that white man from whuppin' us is to take over! We been saying freedom for six years and ain't got nothin'! What we gonna start saying now is "Black Power"! Whatta' we want?!

VOICES: [*Off stage.*] Black power! Black power! Black power!

KING/JOSH: [*Singing.*] Deep in our hearts
We do believe,
We shall overcome ...

VOICES: [*Off stage, growing louder.*] BLACK POWER, BLACK POWER, BLACK POWER. [*Drowns out* KING *and* JOSH.

CARMICHAEL *goes off triumphantly. Shaken,* KING *and* JOSH *start back down ramp.*]

JOSH: They didn't out-reason us, Doc; they just out-shouted us.

KING: I know, Josh. But they're our young people, our future. We can't lose them to this fatalistic violence. This—militant suicide. Gotta' show them that non-violence can win. Give 'em hope, Josh. That makes this Chicago campaign just that much more important.

JOSH: Amen.

[*Suddenly lights go to flashing red strobe effect; sirens, screams, reprise of Selma nightmare effect.* HAROLD *comes running up to* KING *with his suit coat (northern Chicago clothes).*]

HAROLD: It's a riot, Rev.! We better get out there! Try to cool things down!

[KING *pulls on coat and goes rushing center, under the sirens, bizarre lights, etc. He seems caught in a nightmare.*]

KING: No! No! This is not the way! No, listen! Listen to me!

ABE: [*On ramp.*] Over here, Doc!

[*He runs off.* KING *goes over that way; sound of falling glass surrounding him; he tries to avoid it, as he calls out.*]

KING: Listen to me! Listen! Please!! Hear me!

RAY: [*Ramp.*] Over here, Doc!

[KING *moves that way now, dealing with the nightmare, trying to shout it down. This happens a few times, being called from one place to another, spinning in horror and confusion.*]

KING: Give us your grievances! Let us deal with them!

[*Negro minister, complete with clergy collar, appears in light on ramp. Could be* RAY *in disguise.*]

MINISTER: It's Martin Luther King! These interfering outsiders! They're causing these riots! The mayor's anti-poverty program was just beginning inroads to the problem, when King shows up raising impatience! Why the Mayor received word that King's staff have shown these kids riot films. Just teaching 'em to riot! That's what they're doing!

KING: [*Incredulous.*] What?! What?!

[*Riot lights out. Spot on* KING *up center,* AIDES *framing him standing just beyond light.*]

HAROLD: Don't let these Chicago preachers bother you, Reverend. Some of them have changed The Lord's Prayer to say: "Give us this day our *Mayor* Daley bread."

KING: [*To audience.*] It doesn't bother me that they've blamed me for the riots, the violence. It doesn't bother me. I have stood for non-violence all my adult life. It doesn't bother me. Me and my God knows. It wasn't me who turned my back on the pain, the rage, and the frustration, simmering unattended in the slums of this city! We know who is to blame for the untended ills of the poor and the disadvantaged! The Mayor cannot claim innocence of our grievances. Did we not march, thousands strong, to his very door at city hall? Did we not put our needs on his desk? Did he listen to our cries? No! But I think he will hear us today. Because today we're coming out of the ghetto! We're leaving the reservation!

AIDE #1: We need better housing—so we're going where the better housing is!

AIDE #2: We need better schooling—so we're going where the better schools are!

KING: We aren't gonna march with any Molotov cocktails! That isn't our movement. No bricks, no bottles. We're gonna march with something much more powerful than all of that. We're gonna march with the force of our souls! We're gonna put on the breastplate of righteousness and the whole armor of God! And we're gonna march!

[*He leads his* AIDES *down front marching to up tempo version of "We Shall Overcome."*]

KING: [*Marching; as answering reporter.*] The existence of

injustice in society is the existence of violence, latent violence. No. We do not seek to precipitate violence. But we feel we must expose this evil even it if brings violence upon us. If we bring it out in the open, then this community will have to deal with it.

[*Lights change, slower version of song plays, as group moves slowly, apprehensively.*]

VOICES: [On tape.]
NIGGERS, NIGGERS, NIGGERS,
GO HOME NIGGERS, GO HOME MARTIN LUTHER COON!
NIGGER LOVERS, NIGGER LOVERS, NIGGER LOVERS
HATE, HATE, HATE, HATE, HATE, HATE, HATE.

[*Group ducks, as from bricks, shrink into protective circle.* KING *is hit on the head, falls.* AIDES *rush to pull him to his feet.*]

KING: No, no. I'm all right. Keep marching. Keep marching. I've been hit before. Keep on marching ...

[*The group moves on, the voices of hatred and bigotry growing louder. Some of the group are hit, fall, picked up, go on.* KING *gives a signal and the battered troop kneels to pray. Then* KING *rises, faces an unseen official.*]

KING: Sir? We have come for our share of fair housing. [*Lights change as group makes its tortured way back up stage: ducking, cringing, falling.* KING *steps out of group to unseen reporter.*] Yes, I have a statement. Did you see our young marshalls? Disciplined. Non-violent. Well, those are gang-members: Vice-Lords, Cobras, and Saints. Gang members touched by the power of non-violence. I'm very proud of them. [*Takes step, turns back.*] Also, the police did a commendable job. One other thing: the people of Mississippi should come to Chicago—to see real hate.

AIDE #1: Don't you feel something different about this up here, Doc?

KING: Different?

AIDE #1: From Selma and Birmingham, I mean.

AIDE #2: Yeh, nobody's out here but the black folks and the Jewish group!

AIDE #3: Uh-huh, where's all those people that came down there to stand with us?

AIDE #1: And where's the President?

AIDE #2: Busy with Vietnam.

KING: And there are some newspaper reporters here. But the networks aren't giving us the same coverage as before.

AIDE #3: Yeh, we're marching too close to the studios now.

AIDE #2: Yeh, we're just a footnote on the evening news nowadays!

AIDE #1: [*Ducking.*] Before this is over, we might be some footPRINTS!!

AIDE #2: Amen Brother!! Let's demonstrate a little faster!!

[KING *wearily moves out of light, up toward flat where his* AIDES *wait. He pauses, turns to field questions.*]

KING: Yes, I've heard of the Mayor's injunction. I understand it limits us to gatherings of only five hundred people. Within its jurisdiction. Well, we understand that the community of Cicero is not within that jurisdiction. Therefore, next Sunday, we march to Cicero. Yes, I know that's the worst possible place. The most insular and blatantly bigoted of the cloistered suburbs. Yes. And the most potentially violent. We are not accelerating for more publicity, but for more exposure. To expose this evil we will follow it into its deepest nest. If the harsh facts of the sub-standard existence of poor black Chicagoans, and what we have just experienced out here today, are not enough to move the Mayor and the consciences of people of good will—then perhaps a more dramatic exposure of this evil to the eyes of the world will give us redresses and responses instead of merely injunctions against victims. You're welcome. [*Takes a step; turns again.*] If they want a moratorium on the demonstrations, let them call a moratorium on injustice ... [*He goes into flat, moves wearily past*

AIDES *in kitchen. He goes into bedroom area; kneels in prayer.*] I'm tired of marching! Marching for something that should have been mine at birth! Tired of living every day under the threat of death ... [*Steps into light as if addressing audience/rally.*] I have no martyr complex! I want to live as long as anyone in this building! I don't march because I like it! I march because I must! And because I'm a man! And because I'm a child of God! [*He steps back as light fades and slumps to bed; falls asleep. Lights slowly up as* AIDES *rush in to wake him.*]

RAY: Martin! Martin!

AARON: Congratulations, Doc.

KING: Congratulations? For what?

RAY: Daley heard about our plans for Cicero.

HAROLD: He wants to meet with us, Doc!

ABE: We brought him to the table. He's ready to talk now. [KING *gets up to side of bed; prays, giving thanks. Lights fade. Lights up on flat;* KING *is now on other side of table, directly facing audience, weary, stoic.* AIDES *all are gathering suitcases, etc.*]

HAROLD: Well, we wrestled the fat man pretty good, considering ...

AARON: Considering that we didn't get a whole lot out of it.

ABE: [*Gesturing to* AARON.] Come on now: this fair housing agreement is better than anything they've had before.

RAY: Sure it is!

JOSH: And got these Savings and Loans promising to give, loan these families money for new houses. Now that's gonna make a big difference.

RAY: Sure it is!

KING: [*Rising.*] It really isn't very much, is it? [*He goes into bedroom, begins to close suitcase.* RAY *moves to doorway.*]

RAY: What you talking about, Doc? Shoot, it's just like down

South, ain't so much the winning as the fightin'. Once you show people they can fight, how to fight, well, shoot, they're on their way then. [*After a passing glance with the others,* HAROLD *goes into bedroom.*]

HAROLD: Tell you one thing we did get out of it, Rev. This Operation Breadbasket is the best thing to come down the chute. You watch, when I'm through, there won't be a store dealing in the black community anywhere in this city that doesn't also *hire* from the black community. You know, I"ll need your help on this, but we can go nationwide with it. Have nationwide boycotts against any firm that doesn't hire us in proportion to how much it sells to us! [*Others state agreement.* KING *stoically closes suitcase and starts out.*]

KING: I'm sure you'll handle it well, Harold. Let me know if I can be of any help. God bless you all. Yes, Harold, money and jobs are important, too.

HAROLD: Too? They're essential; central to all the rest.

KING: Perhaps. Anyhow, I'm sure you'll handle it well. [KING *leaves flat, walking slowly. Others call blessings to him, shake hands with* RAY, *go off right.* RAY *goes to catch up with* KING; *walks slowly with him down to edge of stage left ramp.* MRS. KING *enters and embraces stoic* KING, *waves to* RAY *who crosses, takes* KING'*s suitcase off, as he sits on edge of ramp. She returns.*]

MRS. KING: Martin? What is it? How long are you going to just—sit like this?

KING: Just two years ago, Coretta. Two years. I saw it there, after Selma, in the Birmingham airport. Remember?

MRS. KING: Yes, Martin, I remember.

KING: Like a garden. God's rainbow garden—white, brown, yellow, and red. All people. Blending. Communing. The final, ultimate truth: All races one race—the human race; with one concern—the humanity of all. It was right there. Visible. Functioning. And now in Chicago—back to business per usual. Every pot alone, every group standing on its own black bottom. The non-violent philosophy is lying in the dust and violence is rampant everywhere. [*Dry chuckle.*] And you know why? 'Cause they want to fight the easy evil. Win the quick battle. Fight the Klan, the Nazis, ignorant rednecks. But face your own neighbors, relatives. And worse yet, yourself; your own prejudice, your own greed. No, too steep a climb to that plateau, too deep a pit to reach that devil. Uh-huh. Want the sure, easy successes. Yeh, just like me.

MRS. KING: Like you? Oh, Martin, come on, now. You've been out there fighting every day.

KING: Naw, now. Don't try to sugar-coat it. You know what I'm talking about. That war. That war is wrong, immoral.

MRS. KING: I know that, Martin. We all know that. But you can't take it on.

KING: But to keep the—the—security of having President Johnson with me, I decided to hush up on that. Oh, yeh, much better to fight Daley than Johnson. Uh-huh. The easier struggle …

MRS. KING: Certainly better to fight one, than both at the same time. Just strategically more sound.

KING: Politically more sound. Not morally. And I'm supposed to be about morality, not politics. I was losing course. I had no chance of winning in Chicago. Because I was losing myself, Coretta, myself.

MRS. KING: Don't get all down on yourself, Martin. Things just didn't go as well this time, that's all.

KING: No, it didn't go as well.

MRS. KING: Martin, you are not Superman, now.

KING: No. Uh-huh. But we've got something in common.

MRS. KING: Oh? De Lawd and Superman?

KING: No, Coretta. I know where my strength and whatever gifts I have come from. From a sense of moral certitude.

That's the rock I stand on. As long as I know I'm on the path dictated by conscience and correctness, I'll stand against anybody and don't care about winning or losing, about what happens to me. Because the witnessing is half the victory. So, I've got it half-licked any way it goes. But I didn't have that certainty, that spiritual focus in Chicago. Mr. Johnson and Vietnam had the country divided, and divided me, too. There's a rock I cling to, a sense of moral certitude, and that's where the will and the power come from. I found out what it's like to walk alone, without God's guidance. And I don't ever want to know that fear and loneliness again.

MRS. KING: [*Concerned, going to him.*] Martin ...

KING: [*To reassure her and himself, preaching.*] Oh, but I'm back on the path now. Walking in the light. I'm a witness, Coretta. I've seen how God can take me, man, one as weak as me, and strengthen him and make him have an effect. The vision is a world without violence, without war, and the non-violence, the confrontational love of Jesus and Gandhi, can help bring that about. I'm supposed to be presenting that, going and telling it on the mountain.

MRS. KING: Hell, Martin, if you know where you made a wrong turn, just go back to that exit and get back on the right road. [*A beat.*]

KING: The war?

MRS. KING: The war and all the rest of it. You just can't stay lost like this. Standing around in your own shadow ...

KING: [*Struck by the image.*] My own shadow?

MRS. KING: Yes. Mourning your loss of space, like some fallen angel. You're just a man, Martin. You make mistakes. You've proven what you have to give. Without you there'll just be that trap of violence begetting violence you're always talking about. You're needed, so just quit moping and get back on your job.

KING: Listen to you. Who you ordering around, woman?

MRS. KING: Martin Luther King Jr., I believe.

KING: Woman, you're a wonder. Back on my job, huh? Yes, you're right. Raise my voice on what God gave me the vision to see. And the vision is a world without divisions, without violence, without war. They can't tell me my job. I know my job, and I'm back on it. And I know no one man can do it alone. But I'm gonna do my bit, shine my light, raise my voice. No matter who or what I might meet on that path. Yes, Lord. Yes, Indeed.

MRS. KING: Yes, Lord. Yes, indeed. Welcome home, Reverend King. [*She embraces him.*]

END OF PART TWO

PART THREE

MEMPHIS, 1968

SETTING

Center section is now a hotel suite; sitting room, stage left; bedroom stage right.

In silhouette, up left, KING *holding clerical robe;* AIDES *gathered in darkened area of suite. Taped voice speaks.*

VOICE: Dear, Dr. King, as you may have ascertained from my address and my heading, I am a Buddhist Monk here in Vietnam. Hundreds, perhaps, thousands of peasants and children lose their lives daily ... our land is unmercifully and tragically torn by war which is already twenty years old. I am sure that since you have been engaged in one of the hardest struggles for equality and human rights, you are among those who understand fully, and who share with all their hearts, the indescribable suffering of the Vietnamese people. The world's greatest humanists would not remain silent. You yourself cannot remain silent.

[KING, *almost ritualistically putting on mauve colored clerical robe, moves from up center to down; speaking as he moves through two dimmer lights to main light, down center.*]

KING: I am reminded of the words of the great Dante: The hottest places in hell are reserved for those who in a moment of moral crisis seek to maintain their neutrality.

HAROLD: So that's why he's decided to come out full against the war.

RAY: It's not just that. It's a matter of morality, of conscience.

ABE: It's been bothering him all along, his not speaking.

KING: [*At second light.*] I can't be silent. Never again will I be silent on this issue.

RAY: He saw that T.V. news story on those children being killed over there. Lots of things brought him out on this.

KING: [*In main light now.*] Since I am a preacher by trade, I suppose that it is not surprising that I have several reasons for bringing Vietnam into the field of my moral vision. A few years ago there was a shining moment in that struggle which I and others have been waging here in America. It seemed there was a real promise of hope for the poor—both black and white—through the Poverty Program. New hopes. New beginnings.

[*Lights off* KING. *Up on* AIDES *in sitting room of suite.*]

AARON: Doc actually told 'em that? That we've converted a civil war into a war with communists? And that we're testing weapons and methods over there like the Germans did?

ABE: Yep. And the facts bear him out.

RAY: [*Pacing.*] Of course they do.

HAROLD: [*Reading newspaper.*] No wonder the Jewish War Veterans cut loose on him.

AARON: What did they say?

HAROLD: Say that German reference is belaboring an ugly parallel. Say he's pandering to Ho Chi Minh.

KING: [*In light.*] But then came the buildup in Vietnam; breaking and eviscerating the programs for the poor as if they were idle political playthings. It became clear that America would never invest the necessary funds and energies in rehabilitation of the poor as long as adventures like Vietnam continue to draw men and skills and money like some demonic, destructive, suction tube. Devastating the hopes of the poor, particularly the black poor. Sending sons and brothers and husbands to fight and die in extraordinarily high proportions relative to the rest of society.

[*Lights down on* KING. *Up on* JOHNSON *at desk set on stage right ramp, on phone, glaring down at* KING.]

JOHNSON: I want it out on the wire services that this office says that King is taking up the communist line, right down the line, point for point. Get it out to everybody who'll publish it. Now, dammit!

[*Hangs up, furious; glares at* KING. *As his light fades,* KING *rises.*]

KING: Repeatedly we are faced with the cruel irony of watching Negro and white boys on our T.V. screens, as they kill and die together for a nation unable to seat them together in the same schools; together burning the huts of a poor village as we realize that they would never live on the same block in Detroit. I could not be silent in the face of such cruel manipulation of the poor.

[*Lights up on* AIDES.]

AARON: [*With magazine.*] Listen to *Newsweek* "abandoning his dream of an integrated America in favor of a country in which a race conscious minority dictates foreign policy." Wooo...

ABE: *The New York Times* says he's "white-washing Hanoi." Says the war and Negro equality are separate issues.

RAY: [*Bitterly.*] Separate but equal?

ABE: Says the place for his leadership is in the battlefields of the ghettos, not Vietnam. End quote.

[*Light on* KING.]

KING: I speak as an American to the leaders of my own nation: the great initiative in this war is ours. The initiative to stop must be ours. Let us extricate ourselves from this nightmarish conflict. Let us rededicate ourselves to the long and bitter—but beautiful—struggle for a new world. The choice is ours. And though we might prefer it otherwise, we must choose in this crucial moment of human history!

[*Lights out on him as he makes his way wearily back to bedroom set; taking off robe as* AIDES *continue in the sitting room. He sits forlornly, absently, on the bed, staring out at audience.*]

HAROLD: That one must have really hurt. He usually responds to the *Times.*

RAY: [*Angrily.*] Yeh, they hurt! *The Times* and all those—negroes!

AARON: Which ones this time?

RAY: Carl Rowan. Roy Wilkins. Whitney Young. Jackie Robinson. Senator Brooks. A whole bunch of 'em.

ABE: The NAACP's board passed a resolution against any effort to put the war and Civil Rights movements together.

AARON: Political statements. He should expect that.

HAROLD: Some of those guys change partners every time the music changes.

RAY: Well, he cried about it. Sat down and cried.

AARON: What? Why?

HAROLD: Johnson's got most of those guys wrapped around the federal pocketbook. Rowan especially. He knows that.

JOSH: Maybe he's just tired of it, dammit! Got these young black nationalists calling him a Tom on one hand! And these—these respectable Negroes on the other getting as far from him as they can. And—and —

ABE: Johnson looks like he's teamed up with ol' J. Edgar; turned him loose on us. That's where most of these communist stories are coming from.

RAY: Sure they are. Sure ...

JOSH: Yes, and he's human like anybody else. He gets tired, too!

HAROLD: Well, he's not going to take this sitting, is he?

ABE: Oh noooo. Just wait till you hear what he's got for 'em this time.

AARON: Yeh, what did he call this meeting for? I'm supposed to be at a Peace rally, right now. I see why he let me leave and join the Peace Movement now. This way he gets my services free! Ol' slick ...

[*They laugh with him.* KING *has composed himself, made his way to the bedroom doorway; goes in.*]

KING: Gentlemen? With an army of more than one-million strong, we are about to march on Washington!

HAROLD: Do *what*?

[*Everyone except* KING *is looking over the plans of his proposed campaign in Washington.* AARON *and* HAROLD *are extremely upset.*]

AARON: Doc? You're not really going to do this? You're not going to do this? You're just going to *say* you're going to do this, right?

KING: If I say it, I'm going to at least try to do it.

HAROLD: Doc, you're talking about declaring some kind of non-violent guerilla warfare against the capital of this extremely violent country.

KING: Johnson's the one who declared war. He's withdrawn from the one correct war, and declared two unholy wars. Declared a war on poverty, and now he's using half that

money to develop an army to put down the poor—shoul
they riot again. Then spending the other half of the mone
in Vietnam. He's gone back to business as usual; with poc
people being only the fuel for their machine with the thre
wings: capitalism, militarism, and racism.

AARON: Doc, except for racism, half the people don't eve
know what those words mean. But when the newspaper
get through with it, they'll have some weird idea of wha
you're talking about here. [*Reading paper.*] Phase one, se
up visible shanty towns in the capital, for explorator
demonstrations—whatever that means —

HAROLD: Now that sounds nice and simple: set up visib
shanty towns. But when an adverse media, and salty cop
National Guardsmen, and federal officers get in it—w
won't be setting up shanty towns, we'll be setting u
chaos and slaughter. Violence, Doc, violence!

KING: No, no. Well-rehearsed non-violent techniques wi
defuse the violence. But there will be arrests. We will fi
the jails.

HAROLD: And the hospitals too, Doc. The hospitals, too.

AARON: You're in Phase Two, now Harold. Let's see. [*Lookin
on sheet.*] Phase Two: Disrupt Government operations wit
non-violent sit-ins and demonstrations.

KING: Yes, like Birmingham and Selma, we'll fill the jail
keep up the pressure. They want to forget the poor. Swee
'em under the rug. Well, we won't let Congress do tha
We'll sensitize them to the malnutrition of those too poc
to eat, too poor for adequate health care. We'll pressur
and embarrass this fat-cat Congress before the eyes of th
country; the eyes of the world.

HAROLD: The war, Doc! The war! They don't care about th
eyes of the world when they're at war. And the eyes of th
country can't see anything but the old Red, White an
Blue.

AARON: There it is, Doc. There it is. Once they start wavin

that flag. That patriotism, that's all she wrote. Everyone on the right is with them, everyone standing on the left is against them, *and* with communism, and a fair target for assassination—[*Pauses, realizing, as the others do, what he is saying.*] Character assassinations ... Politics ... You know what I mean, Doc.

KING: Yes, I know, Aaron. You can say it. We've all faced it. The fear of death is one fear I have conquered. If a man has nothing he will die for, then he isn't fit to live. Well, gentlemen, I've got a lot to do to get started on this. [*Patting pockets as though for cigarettes, he goes back into bedroom area to get them.*]

HAROLD: Okay, Doc, look. Phase Three: National boycotts forcing businessmen to pressure Congress for our demands. We've already got the start of that with my Operation Breadbasket. Why don't we start with that one, Doc? Turn it all around?

KING: [*Coming out of bedroom, with unlit cigarette.*] Too easy for buy-outs if we start there. [*Pause.*] It's only after the poor have united in crisis, shown their will and power, that the threat and strength of the boycott will be real. And, gentlemen, this is to be a Poor Peoples' Campaign, not just a black people's campaign. We'll reach out in all directions; the southwest after the Indians; the west after the Chicanos; the Appalachians for poor Whites; and the ghettos for the Blacks and Puerto Ricans. This is bigger than just Negroes' rights. [*He leaves suite area starting down right.* AIDES *clamor out after him, calling.*]

AARON: But, Doc, even the labor unions haven't been able to really organize the poor across all class and racial lines! Even during the Depression!

HAROLD: When the Depression was over, so was the unity!

AARON: So how are you gonna do it!?

KING: The question now, gentlemen, is, are you with me? [*Turns to confront them forcefully.*] Are-you-with-me?

AARON/HAROLD: Yeh, Doc ... Yeh, we're with you.

[*As others stand around them, and lights fade on them,* KIN*
*moves towards center to light cigarette. Nightmare lights chang
to blue-green sense of riot lights. AIDES *in silhouette com
around ramp with newspapers as Social Commentators.]

AIDES: It's Martin Luther King, It's Martin Luther King, It'
Martin Luther King, He's the cause of the violence, He'
the cause of the riots! He's the cause!

SELMA ... BIRMINGHAM ... WATTS ... NEWARK .
CLEVELAND ... CHICAGO ... DETROIT ... [*Chanting*
He's the cause, etc.

AIDE #1: It was Martin Luther King's example ...

AIDE #2: Example of civil disobedience ...

AIDE #3: That sowed the seeds ...

AIDE #4: The fruit of which is being reaped in our cities toda
... [*"He's the cause" chant grows louder, faster, stronger.* KIN
*stumbles around under this psychological barrage, holding hi
ears, head; falls to knees, shouting.]

AIDE #5: The President will have 25,000 troops waiting for yo
in Washington! 25,000! [*Chant grows on.*]

KING: Nooo! I warned you! Begged! Pleaded! You do nothin
to change the conditions! Nothing! Then you hurl hate o
the product of the conditions—the Negro himself! Th
Negro himself! The Negro ... [*He is abjectly near sobs.*]

[MRS. KING *appears at foot of stage left ramp, other lights of
excepting spot on KING, *groggy, on his knees. Though the scen
*is played abstracly, without phones, it is a telephon
conversation which follows.]

MRS. KING: Martin? You all right, Martin? Martin, com
home, please.

KING: Coretta? Coretta? Where? Home? No, I don't want t
bring it there. No, mustn't bring it.

MRS. KING: What? Bring what, Martin? Are you awake
Martin?

KING: Death. Death is with me. Everywhere. Don't want it home ...

MRS. KING: [*Unsure of what she's heard.*] What? Martin? Martin, are you awake? Martin?!

KING: [*Becoming fully aware now.*] Oh, Coretta? So good to hear you. How are you, dear? The children? Are they well?

MRS. KING: Yes, Martin ... Martin? Come home. Please. We need you. You need us. Please, Martin.

KING: Home. Yes, yes, I'm coming home. [*He crosses over to meet her like a wounded soldier. She takes him into her arms and helps him off the stage.*]

[*As the* KINGS *go off stage,* AIDES *ring the ramps in silhouette; moving stealthily, menacingly, perhaps lying on stomachs as snipers, assassins.*]

AIDE #1: You'd better lock up Martin Luther King before this nation has a social revolution.

AIDE #2: The F.B.I. has documented fifty threats against his life.

AIDE #3: Some old boys I know in New Orleans have put some money on it. One $50,000, another one, $20,000. Lot of money for just shootin' a coon.

AIDE #4: Martin Luther King and his peripatetic parsons are plotting a new racial war. [*Chant, slow march, dirge.*] King, King, it's all King's fault. [*Repeats. Lights fade slowly as* AIDES *chant and march around like sentries guarding the power.* MRS. KING, *in clothes change, leads* KING *on stage into down left light. She is distraught, angry. He comes out in shirt-sleeves, tries to embrace her from behind. She pushes his hands away.*]

KING: Coretta. Come on, now.

MRS. KING: No, I don't want to hear any of that, Martin. No.

KING: Coretta, now, we have to talk about these things sometimes.

MRS. KING: No, Martin! Not now. No.

KING: All right. Just ... Just promise me that should...

MRS. KING: Martin ... [*She tries to go back into the house. He blocks her way. She turns back. He talks to her back.*]

KING: Should anything happen—You, and Ray, and what others are willing, will go on with the Movement. You will ...

MRS. KING: Yes! All right! All right! [*A moment of strained silence as she turns away again.*]

KING: [*Weary; sad.*] Coretta.

MRS. KING: It isn't fair, Martin. It isn't right.

KING: Coretta...

MRS. KING: [*Anrgily; brushing tears.*] I was there at the conservatory. In Boston ...

KING: Coretta ...

MRS. KING: Going to be a singer. Sing opera. Marry some doctor or something. I don't know. Then here comes Martin Luther King Jr. Whoever, whatever that was. Sometimes I wish to God I had never found out ...

KING: Coretta? What is it? What did I say?

MRS. KING: It's not what you say. It's what you do. How you live. How *we* live.

KING: Coretta, you know what my life is. What my ministry is.

MRS. KING: Yes. I know *now*. But I didn't know then, at the beginning. *You* didn't know. I had no idea of what it would cost us, Martin. Cost me. Cost the children!

KING: [*Looking around for them.*] Coretta. The children now, please.

MRS. KING: Your ministry. Yes. Everywhere you go; all over the world, you make things better for everyone but here it just keeps getting worse. The world gets more and more of you, and we get less and less! [*She turns away. He stands stunned, guilty, hurt.*]

KING: Coretta, honey, I'm sorry. I don't know what to do. To say. I ...

MRS. KING: [*Wiping eyes, shaking head.*] No, Martin. No. I'm the one who's sorry. I know what you have to do. It's just—sometimes I have to let some of it out somehow. That's all. I just have to ...

KING: [*Going to her.*] I know, honey. It's all right.

MRS. KING: You just don't understand, Martin.

KING: [*Embracing her.*] I do, honey, I do.

MRS. KING: No, you can't. This—fear. This awful fear. It just keeps growing and growing ...

KING: Shhh, honey. It's all right.

MRS. KING: [*Continuing.*] Ever since Montgomery. Even before they bombed our house—with our babies sleeping in there. Even before. Ever since it's been just mounting, building ...

KING: Hush, honey. Shhh, it's all right ...

MRS. KING: No. Sometimes when you leave this house I'm afraid to listen to the radio; watch the television. Everything inside me is trembling, shaking. And I—I can't let the kids see that, feel that. But sometimes, I think they know. Sometimes I don't know if I'm holding them up, or they're holding me. [*He turns her to him; kisses her; wipes her tears.*] Crying like a baby ...

KING: [*Whispering.*] It's all right, all right. Now listen: After we get this Poor People's Campaign started in Washington ...

MRS. KING: Aw, Martin, don't even start ...

KING: Naw. Listen, now. I mean it. I'm going to allocate, share responsibilities. Have regional headquarters and leaders. Aaron will have an area. Abe. Harold. And my area will be right here.

MRS. KING: Oh, Martin, please.

KING: Naw. Listen. I'm going to do more writing. Spend time

with you and the kids. Settle in here. Maybe do some lecturing for Dr. Mays over at Morehouse.

MRS. KING: Martin, any minute that phone in your office will start ringing with a call from anywhere in the world, and somebody will ask for help, and you know you can't say no.

KING: [*Grins; gives flirting, teasing kisses.*] I hope you can't say no ...

MRS. KING: Martin ... [*He brings her to passionate kiss; they quickly pull apart. She speaks into wings.*] Yes, Marty. Yes, Yolanda. Yes, your daddy wants to hear the President's speech. Don't you, Daddy. Come on.

KING: I sure hope it's a short one.

[*He plays with her hair, following her off. She knocks his hand down as they exit.*]

JOHNSON: I have concluded that I should not permit the presidency to become involved in the partisan divisions that are developing in this political year. Accordingly, I shall not seek, and I will not accept, the nomination of my party for another term as your president ... [*Lights fade on* JOHNSON. *Up on* KINGS *entering down left.* KING *in suit, carrying suitcase.*]

MRS. KING: Why are people calling here congratulating you on Johnson's resignation?

KING: I don't know. Wish they wouldn't. They say my position against the war, our fight over it, caused folks to examine his policies—to his detriment. He no longer had popular, grass root, poor folks' support. That's the lifeblood of a Democrat.

MRS. KING: You sound sad about it. After the way he turned on you?

KING: To his way of thinking, I turned on him.

MRS. KING: Utterly ridiculous. Your views remained consistent throughout. Remember what happened when you asked for federal assistance in Mississippi, to stop those folks from getting beaten and killed down there?

KING: [*Wearily.*] Yes, we got no help.

MRS. KING: I heard he said, "Let him call Hanoi for help."

KING: Umm. Sounds like him. Still, I feel sorry for him.

MRS. KING: What? After he left you in the hands of the Klan?

KING: Even so. He was basically a good man, Coretta. And he wanted so to be a great President. He would have been, too. One of the greatest of all. But that macho Texas upbringing got to him, I guess. He felt that to be liberal at home, soft on civil rights as the Republicans put it—then he had to be tough abroad, hard on communism. The war divided him just like it did the country. He never really understood that I could only be loyal to a moral correctness, not a political allegiance. I hear he says I tricked him, betrayed him.

MRS. KING: Ridiculous. Well, I hope you don't start worrying about that. You've got enough on your hands as it is. [*She looks back, off left.*] Yes! Daddy's gonna tuck you in ... [*Lights cross-fade as they move up left to children's bedroom area.* KING *is turning the lights out on their sleeping forms in the two beds.*]

KING: [*Looking around at children.*] Sometimes when I look at them, this whole thing gets very personal, you know? Now how could somebody deny them their humanness, their personalities, their brightness, just because it's encased in black skins?

MRS. KING: Wasn't it Dr. King who said: Judge them on the content of their character, rather than the color of their skin?

KING: And I'm going to do all I can to get that, too. [*He touches one, kisses another. Looks at them all.*] We've got to make the world look at them just a moment longer, see past the skin to the insides and see them as brothers, sisters, contributors. It's like their intelligence, their talents are the fruit of one peanut. But they're destroying all the peanut shells they see, regardless of the fruit. So, we've got to get respect, protection, for those black shells—so the fruit can be realized, shared.

MRS. KING: Yes, Martin, yes. Now let's let the little ones get to sleep, so they can grow. [*She takes his hand and leads him down in cross-fade, he picks up coat and suitcase as they cross. They move down left into light out on porch.*]

KING: [*Breathes deep.*] I'm so glad I came home. [*Hugs her.*] Feel like a new man. Joshua about to fit the battle ...

MRS. KING: Good. Just don't get to fittin' it too hard. After you and Ray take those days at the ocean—get your plans together—don't start driving yourself back into the ground again. You hear me, Martin?

KING: [*Waving across.*] Here comes Ray with the car ...

MRS. KING: Did you hear me, Martin?

KING: [*Kissing her quickly.*] Of course, of course. Bye, honey. Call you in a day or so. [*He crosses up right.*]

MRS. KING: After you come back from the island, where are you all going first?

KING: [*Backing across.*] Got a call from Lawson! May go down and give him a hand!

MRS. KING: James? Where is he?

KING: Memphis! Something with some garbage workers. I'll call you. [*He crosses up right and goes off.*]

[AIDES *as Sentries appear silhouetted on ramps again. This time they seem to be carrying clubs over shoulders, rifle-like. The clubs are actually rolled newspapers, which they open to read, point to as references when they "fire" their verbal/media "shots." They pace like coiled soldier-cats.*]

AIDE #1: [*Calmly, no doubt about it.*] King will precipitate bloody riots in Washington ...

AIDE #2: He always does ...

AIDE #3: Going to be a dark Messiah ...

AIDE #4: Electrify and unify the militants ...

AIDE #1: Mess up the whole country ...

AIDE #2: Turn it over to the Commies...

AIDE #3: If somebody don't stop him ...

ALL: Yehhhhhhhh. [*Becomes guttural growl. Lights off on them. Up on* KING *standing at stage right bottom of ramp, wearing pajama top over pants, house slippers.* RAY *calls for him from off stage, sounding anxious.*]

KING: Here I am, Ray. Out here. On the balcony. [RAY *enters.*]

RAY: Scared the life out of me. Woke up feeling something was wrong. Went in your room and ... Martin, you know what we said about windows and balconies, and stuff. Come on off of here.

KING: No hiding place, Ray. What will happen will happen.

RAY: But you don't have to help it. Come on.

KING: See that big rock down there? On the right there? On the beach?

RAY: Yeh?

KING: What does it make you think of?

RAY: Ummm. Strength?

KING: Umm hmm. The Rock Of Ages. How long you think it's been there, Ray?

RAY: [*Irritated.*] I don't know, Martin. For centuries, I guess. Come on, it's cold out here. Let's ...

KING: Tarry with me awhile, Ray. Do you think that that rock has anything to do with the fact that it is standing in that spot at this time?

RAY: Well, naw ... God, and the elements, the conditions, put it there.

KING: God and the conditions, the circumstances. Ray, you and I are just like that rock. I had no choice. I had to find something. I mean I hated 'em so, Ray. The white folks. That little black boy down there in Atlanta, oh my God, he hated 'em. You know how it is when you grow up in the South. I *know you* know.

RAY: Oh, yeh. Don't have to tell me a thing.

KING: All you have to do is look around at things. Hear your relatives, your parents, talking about the things they've suffered at their hands. And before you know it, you're just all filled up with this fear and hate. Hate and fear. Fear and hate ...

RAY: Let it out! Let it out!

KING: [*It becomes an affirming preachment.*] Oh, yes. Let it out. Got to. Because it's diseasing my mind, my spirit, my life. This hate, this fear. Got to find some way to free myself!

RAY: Got to. Got to.

KING: Yes. And then there they were: Like two twin lights at the end of a tunnel—Jesus and Gandhi. Two of God's many gifts.

RAY: Well ...

KING: Holding in their hands this shining tool. This flaming sword. This Universal Love, they talked about. This, Agape! This Satyagraha, Gandhi called it.

RAY: Satyagraha. Even *sounds* right.

KING: Oh, yes. Jesus gave me the key and Gandhi showed me how to use it, beyond personal liberation. You know what I"m talking about, Ray.

RAY: [*Helping the ritual, catharsis, affirmation.*] You know I do.

KING: Talking about seeing every man as "neighbor," as Jesus put it. As "brother." As extension of the body of you, to the body of community, the body of man.

RAY: Speak!

KING: Com-mun-ity! Where communion with the few becomes communion with the many, make community.

RAY: Well, all right. Teach on it, now.

KING: One extending to two, extending to many. Yes, that's

what we're doing, Ray. What Gandhi did. What we're going to do down there in Washington! Forgive seventy times seven. To make the community, Jesus said.

RAY: Turn that cheek!

KING: And that's what we're gonna do. Gonna march in there and grab that Congress with powerful arms of redeeming love!

RAY: Yes sir!

KING: [*Preaching it, acting it.*] And just hold 'em there. No matter how many arrests. Hold 'em. Saying to 'em: Look at me! I'm your brother. Body of your body! Breath of your breath!

RAY: Speak.

KING: Yes, and those diseases of yours are destroying me, destroying us—that greed, that hate, that indifference to life! You are infected, and you are of my body. And my hunger, and my despair, my desperation, is weakening you—because I am of your community! Your body ...

RAY: Talk to 'em.

KING: I ain't no good at fist-fighting, bottle throwing—none of that. But I've got the strong arms of love. And I'm gonna hold on here until you look at me. Recognize me. Hold you here until the world village comes to see this struggle between correctness and incorrectness. Between sickness and health. Between Good and Evil.

RAY: Uh-huh.

KING: Hold on until the pressure of the truth gets you!

RAY: Yes sir!

KING: And you cry out: Enough! You are my brother! My body! Yes! And with that recognition, the chain of hate is cut, and the community of brotherhood begins.

RAY: And exploitation and war are on the way out! Talk about it, Martin.

KING: Yes, that's what we're going to do in Washington, Ray.

That's what we're going to do. Come on. See, you should've had your recorder out here.

RAY: [*Following.*] Now how was I supposed to know you was gon' be preaching at four o'clock in the morning? On a balcony—to me and a rock!

[*Lights out on them as they exit.* AIDES *as sentries in silhouette come up on the ramp; one moving to spot they have vacated, watching in the direction they went. They turn and begin careful pacing again.*]

AIDES: [*Strong stage whispers.*] We know where he is. We always know where he is. [*Repeats. They go down behind ramps, still whispering eerily, as lights come up on hotel suite set.* KING *angrily coming in before* RAY.]

KING: I don't lead no violent demonstrations! How could you let me walk into this!

RAY: Me!

KING: Get on that phone, Ray! Get me out of Memphis! It's just like my dream! They're gonna blame me!

RAY: [*Picking up phone.*] All right. But don't jump on *me*. You the one said everything was arranged down here. [*Into phone.*] Airport ... You said you and Lawson ...

KING: Lawson. How could he do this to me. A riot! You know they'll try to use this to discredit the Washington campaign. How could he not tell me about that violent young gang of what's their names?

RAY: [*Talking on phone.*] Huh ... what? The Invaders ...

KING: They've got the right name all right. A riot. I can't believe, Lawson. We're up-front leading a non-violent protest and these—Invaders—are in the back breaking windows and looting.

RAY: Now we don't know if that was them or not. Yes, a flight tonight.

KING: You know what they're going to say about this, don't you? [*He crosses to television in other room. The T.V. set faces away from audience. Turns it on, stands in doorway, listening.*

On ramp AIDE *as commentator reads from newspaper.*]

TV COMMENTATOR: This evening in Memphis, Tennessee, another so-called peaceful demonstration led by the redoubtable Dr. Martin Luther King became the scene of bloody rioting and looting. Leading many to now wonder if his scheduled Poor People's Campaign in April in the nation's capital will indeed be peaceful and non-violent, or a repeat of the uncontrollable violence seen today in Memphis, and witnessed so often in the wake of Dr. King.

AIDE #1: [*On ramp.*] Dr. King's pose as leader of a *non-violent* movement has been shattered.

AIDE #2: [*On ramp.*] Memphis is merely the prelude to civil strife in our nation's capital.

AIDE #4: King hides behind a facade of non-violence as he provokes violence.

AIDE #1: Furthermore he took off at high speed when violence occurred instead of trying to use his persuasive prestige to stop it. [*They go off ramp.*]

KING: You hear what they're saying! Cancel that flight. I ran away? That's what they're trying to say? Cancel the flight, Ray. They're not running me nowhere.

RAY: Huh? [*At gesture from* KING, *he hangs up.*] What?

KING: Call Lawson, tell him to get all these Memphis folks tomorrow. Including those Invaders, we'll make them marshalls of the march.

RAY: Marshalls?

KING: Yes. They're not running me nowhere. And they are not going to use this incident here to keep me out of Washington, either. Call them for a meeting tomorrow. Tell them I will be back to personally lead this march. We'll do it on the third or fourth of April. We will personally organize and supervise it. We'll show the world how we can have peaceful demonstrations. [RAY *goes off.* KING *begins to mount the ramp, speaking as he ascends.*]

KING: When we were getting ready to take off to come to Memphis, the pilot announced that there were reports of a bomb being on the plane because I was on it. They had checked and everything was all right. And some voiced concern about all that might happen to me if I came on here to Memphis. But that's not the question. The question is, if I do not stop to help these men, then what would happen to *them*? That's the question. Trouble is in the land; confusion all around. But only when it is dark enough, can you see the stars. As for me, it really doesn't matter now. Because I've been to the mountaintop. Like anybody, I would like to live a long life. Longevity has its place. But I'm not concerned about that now. I just want to do God's will. He's allowed me to go up on the mountain. And I've looked over. And I've seen the Promised Land. I may not get there with you. But I want you to know tonight that we as a people will get to the Promised Land. Mine eyes have seen the glory of the coming of the Lord. [KING *is at the top of ramp. Lights diminish slowly on his face. A slide photograph of Dr. Martin Luther King appears overhead at back of ramp as* AIDES *come in to line up along ramp. They are wearing the white gloves and armbands of pallbeareres and are led by* MRS. KING *in the traditional black dress and veil. During this procession, part of a pre-recorded speech by Dr. Martin Luther King is played over the loudspeakers, preferably from his eulogy speech "Drum Major for the Lord." At end of this recording the actor playing* DR. KING *reappears in a robe at the top of the ramp and the following pre-recorded speech by the actor is played.*]

KING: [*On recording.*] ... But I want you to know tonight that we as a people will get to the Promised Land. Sharing this faith, we will be able to achieve a new day when all of God's children—Black and White, Jews and Gentiles, Protestants and Catholics—will be able to join hands and sing in the words of the old Negro Spiritual: Free at last! Free at last! Great God Almighty we are free at last!

[*The actors turn upstage and bow to Dr. Martin Luther King's photograph, then they turn to the audience and bow.*]

END OF PLAY

RONALD (RON) MILNER
(1938 -)

Ron Milner made his commitment to writing while he was still a high school student in Detroit, Michigan, where he was born. After graduating from high school, Milner attended Highland Park Junior College and the Detroit Institute of Technology. In 1962 he won a John Hay Whitney Foundation fellowship to enable him to complete a novel which is unpublished. In 1965 he attended a writing workshop at Columbia University and the following year he was writer-in-residence at Lincoln University, Pennsylvania.

Milner teamed up with Woodie King Jr. and David Rambeau in 1962 to establish the Concept East Theatre (CET) in Detroit. He also founded in the 1970s the Spirit of Shango Theatre Company which became part of CET, and the Langston Hughes Theatre, Detroit. His first production took place at the Concept East Theatre in Detroit in the early 1960s. It was a one-act piece titled *Life Agony* which was later expanded into his three-act play *Who's Got His Own* (1965).

By this time Milner had moved to New York City with King in a touring production and he stayed in the city when King joined the newly formed American Place Theatre (APT). At APT King staged an early draft of Milner's *Who's Got His Own*; in 1966 a final version was directed by Lloyd Richards in a production that toured New York state colleges under State Council of the Arts sponsorship. The play, a family drama focusing on black manhood in a racist society, was also chosen by the New Lafayette Theatre of Harlem for its inaugural production in 1967.

Most of Milner's other plays: *The Monster* (1968), *The Warning: A Theme for Linda* (1969), *What the Winesellers Buy* (1973), the *a cappella* operetta *Season's Reasons* (1976) and the musical

Crack Steppin' (1981) with *Jazz Set* (1980), continue to explore from a moral standpoint relationships among black individuals who find themselves placed in different circumstances within the larger society. Productions of these plays have occurred initially in Detroit, at the Mark Taper Forum in Los Angeles, California, and at Woodie King's New Federal Theatre in New York City. Milner collaborated with King on editing *Black Drama Anthology* (1972) and has also published important essays on black theatre and audiences. His *Roads of the Mountaintop* was commissioned by the Crossroads Theatre Company of New Brunswick, New Jersey, and premiered by the Company in an impressive production in February 1986.

Source: Bernard L. Peterson Jr., *Contemporary Black American Playwrights and Their Plays: A Biographical Directory and Dramatic Index*. New York: Greenwood Press, 1988.

THE THEATRE OF BLACK AMERICANS

Edited by Errol Hill

From the origins of the Negro spiritual and the birth of the Harlem Renaissance to the emergence of a national black theater movement, THE THEATRE OF BLACK AMERICANS offers a penetrating look at the black art form that has exploded into an American cultural institution. Among the essays:

Some African Influences on the Afro-American Theatre
James Hatch

Notes on Ritual in the New Black Theatre
Shelby Steele

The Lafayette Players
Sister M. Francesca Thompson, O.S.F.

The Role of Blacks in the Federal Theatre, 1935-1939
Ronald Ross

paper • ISBN: 0-936839-27-9

WOMENSWORK

FIVE PLAYS FROM THE WOMEN'S PROJECT

Edited by Julia Miles

The voices of five major playwrights converge here, offering a vibrant range of styles and themes.

ABINGDON SQUARE, Maria Irene Fornes
"*What Fornes does is force us to see it (the story) new, with the uniqueness and emotional weight it would have if it happened to our own relatives.*" —VILLAGE VOICE

MA ROSE, Cassandra Medley
"*a warmly funny play.*" —NEW YORK POST

ETTA JENKS, Marlane Meyer
"*the ancient story turned into a sardonic, eye-opening plunge into a contemporary netherworld.*"
—NEW YORK TIMES

FIVE IN THE KILLING ZONE, Lavonne Mueller
(Mueller has) "*a sensibility to be cherished ... with an arresting scabrous vision of the American way of death.*"
—NEW YORK TIMES

MILL FIRE, Sally Nemeth
"*a searing consideration of the cruelty of accidental death.*" —VARIETY

paper • ISBN: 1-55783-029-0

WOMEN HEROES

SIX SHORT PLAYS FROM THE WOMEN'S PROJECT

Edited by Julia Miles

The English Channel, the United States Government, Hitler, cancer—these are a few of the obstacles which these extraordinary women hurdle on their way to tickertape parades, prison cells and anonymous fates.

COLETTE IN LOVE
Lavonne Mueller

PERSONALITY
Gina Wendkos & Ellen Ratner

MILLY
Susan Kander

EMMA GOLDMAN
Jessica Litwak

PARALLAX
Denise Hamilton

HOW SHE PLAYED THE GAME
Cynthia L. Cooper

paper • ISBN: 0-936839-22-8

PLAYS BY AMERICAN WOMEN: 1900-1930

Edited by Judith E. Barlow

These important dramatists did more than write significant new plays; they introduced to the American stage a new and vital character—the modern American woman in her quest for a forceful role in a changing American scene. It will be hard to remember that these women playwrights were ever forgotten.

A MAN'S WORLD
Rachel Crothers

TRIFLES
Susan Glaspell

PLUMES
Georgia Douglas Johnson

MACHINAL
Sophie Treadwell

MISS LULU BETT
Zona Gale

paper • ISBN: 1-55783-008-8 cloth • ISBN: 1-55783-007-X

paper • ISBN: 1-55783-049-5

SPEAK WITH DISTINCTION

by Edith Skinner

Revised with New Material Compiled by Timothy Monich and Lilene Mansell

"Edith Skinner's book is the BEST BOOK ON SPEECH THAT I HAVE EVER ENCOUNTERED. *It was my primer in school and is my reference book now. To the classical actor, or for that matter any actor who wishes to be understood, this method is a sure guide."*

KEVIN KLINE

At last, the "Bible" is back. New chapters and expanded verses join the classic Skinner text to create the authoritative work on American speech for the stage. The long-awaited revised edition of *Speak With Distinction* makes the Skinner Method accessible to all speakers who want to improve their diction. The details of spoken English are examined in a workbook environment, fostering useful voice habits and promoting speech which is efficient, clearly and effortlessly free of regionalisms, appropriate to the dramatic situation, easily articulated, heard and immediately understood in the back rows of a theater.

An optional 90-minute practice tape demonstrates the highlights of the Skinner method and is accompanied by a 36-page guide to Good Speech.

"Edith Skinner CHANGED THE SOUND OF THE AMERICAN THEATRE *and as a director in the classical repertory, I am deeply grateful to her."*

MICHAEL KAHN, Artistic director
The Shakespeare Theatre at the Folger

paper • ISBN: 1-55783-047-9

A FLEA IN HER REAR
(OR ANTS IN HER PANTS)
AND OTHER VINTAGE FRENCH FARCES

English Versions By

Norman R. Shapiro

While the ghosts of Racine and Corneille may fruitlessly wander the globe in search of their spiritual descendants, the spectral authors in this volume need only turn on the television or stumble into the nearest comedy club to locate their teeming brood.

A Flea in Her Rear and Other Vintage French Farces should be the chief operating manual for any writer, actor, director and/or producer whose chief aim, like the farceurs in this volume, is to produce robust laughter, never to be confused with profound philosophy.

In this collection of comedies from farce's half-century heyday, eminent translator Norman Shapiro offers the reader a sampling of farces in brilliantly actable versions. Among the plays:

Allais: ***The Poor Beggar and The Fairy Godmother***
Courteline: ***Boubouroche, or She Dupes to Conquer***
Feydeau: ***A Fitting Confusion; A flea in Her Rear, or Ants in Her Pants; Going to Pot.***
Labiche: ***It's All Relative***
Meilhac and Halévy: ***Mardi Gras; Segnor Nicodemo***
Sardou: ***For Love or Monkey***

ISBN: 1-55783-165-3

VOICES OF COLOR:

50 SCENES AND MONOLOGUES BY AFRICAN AMERICAN PLAYWRIGHTS

Edited and with an introduction by

Woodie King, Jr.

Voices of Color is the first collection of scenes and monologues by African American playwrights. While scene and monologue books proliferate by and for the dominant culture, there has rarely been significant representation of the vibrant literary contributions of African American theatre artists. Until now.

This major omnibus of contemporary American writing will serve as a primary resource for African American artists in search of their own voice for the stage. Actors and directors will now have access to a much larger spectrum of work in which to shine. Readers will be introduced to a rich medley of work of the human spirit. And schools, colleges and libraries will, at last, have the book we all need to fully explore America's potential for drama.

ISBN: 1-55783-174-2